ANTI-BRIBERY AND CORRUPTION LAW AND COMPLIANCE

IN A NUTSHELL®

ELLEN LAFFERTY
Adjunct Professor of Law
Program on Corporate Ethics and Compliance
Fordham University School of Law

WEST ACADEMIC

860 Blue Gentian Road, Suite 350
Eagan, MN 55121
1-877-888-1330

Published in the United States of America

ISBN: 978-1-63659-583-2

Dedicated to my family and friends for their enthusiastic support of this book, especially my mom Ellen, husband Joe, and sons Ryan, Joseph, and Brendan. And in loving memory of Bill Lafferty.

With grateful acknowledgement of the contributions of Jonathan Rusch, Justin Holloway, Toni Jaeger-Fine, and Fordham University School of Law.

PREFACE

This book is a practical guide for legal and compliance students and practitioners. It begins by addressing the underlying reason that its subject is important—the almost incalculable human, monetary, and business costs of bribery and corruption. National governments and international bodies have enacted various laws, regulations, and instruments to combat this scourge. This book addresses four key laws and international instruments—the U.S. Foreign Corrupt Practices Act (the "FCPA"), the Organization for Economic Cooperation and Development Convention on Combating Bribery of Foreign Public Officials in International Business Transactions (the "OECD Convention" or the "Convention"), the United Nations Convention Against Corruption (the "UNCAC") and the U.K. Bribery Act 2010 (the "UK Bribery Act" or the "UKBA"). Each of these instruments could easily be the subject of its own treatise. However, because of its broad extraterritorial application and robust enforcement record, this book focuses largely on the FCPA. The other instruments are discussed from the general perspective of how international anti-bribery and corruption standards have developed, how they have informed the FCPA's development, and how their concepts and provisions compare with those of the FCPA.

After addressing the FCPA, the OECD Convention, the UNCAC, and the UKBA, the book moves on to explain how to design and implement effective anti-bribery and corruption compliance programs. This explanation includes a walk-through of the seven components of effective compliance programs (e.g., policies and procedures) as well as the substantive areas that are generally included in anti-bribery and corruption compliance programs (e.g., gifts and entertainment). Finally, the book closes with a forward look at emerging developments.

Anti-bribery and corruption ("AB&C") Compliance programs are relatively newer and less mature than compliance programs relating to other areas of financial crime such as sanctions and anti-money laundering. Historically there has been a limited amount of information to draw from regarding interpreting the FCPA and understanding how effective AB&C Compliance programs should be structured. For example, FCPA cases involving corporate defendants have rarely been litigated so there is no swath of judicial opinions to review and analyze. The available authority and guidance are diverse in source and scope—e.g., some is specific to the FCPA or UKBA, some relates to compliance programs generally, some is civil in nature, some is criminal, some is from government regulators and law enforcement, some is from international bodies, and some is from industry thought leaders. It comes in the form of case law, speeches, memoranda, guidance documents, government committee meeting reports, and more. It's a patchwork of information that I have reviewed, interpreted, synthesized, and distilled. Over that distillation I've layered my personal experience as an attorney and head of AB&C Compliance groups to explain the FCPA's requirements and how to design and implement effective AB&C Compliance programs. In short, this is the book that would have helped me as an attorney and then as a compliance officer practicing in this space. I hope it's useful to you as well.

ELLEN LAFFERTY

March 1, 2024

AN EXPLANATORY NOTE: THE USE OF "PUBLIC OFFICIALS" AND "ORGANIZATIONS"

This book addresses the FCPA, UKBA, OECD Convention, and the UNCAC. Each of these instruments categorizes and defines different types of public officials. The FCPA uses the term "foreign official," the UKBA and OECD Convention use the term "foreign public official," and the UNCAC defines the terms "public official," "foreign public official," and "official of a public international organization." There is of course overlap between these terms as they are defined in their respective instruments. We provide the specific definition(s) from each instrument, consider their common core, and then use that understanding to create our own definitions that could potentially be used in an AB&C Compliance program. When not referring to a specific instrument, we use "public official" as a generic term to refer to both domestic and foreign government officials, including those who work for or on behalf of state-owned or controlled entities and public international organizations.

This book uses the term "organization" to inclusively refer to all types of entities. In some sections, we also use other terms such as "company" or "corporation" to reflect the language of the specific instrument or document that is being referenced.

OUTLINE

TABLE OF CASES

References are to Pages

TABLE OF STATUTES

References are to Pages

TABLE OF AUTHORITIES

References are to Pages

Release No. 2020–285, Fed. Sec. L. Rep. (CCH) (Nov. 17, 2020), 24

Omnibus Trade and Competitiveness Act of 1988, Conference Report, 100th Congress, 2d Session, Report 100–576 (Apr. 20, 1988), 59

Policy Statement Concerning Cooperation by Individuals in its Investigations and Related Enforcement Actions, Release No. 34-61340, Fed. Sec. L. Rep. (CCH) (Jan. 19, 2010), 211

Policy Statement on Bribery in International Business Transactions, Working Group on Bribery in International Business Transactions, OECD (June 19, 2009), 14

Polite, Kenneth A., Jr. *Assistant Attorney General, Criminal Division, Revised Memorandum on Selection of Monitors in Criminal Division Matters*, U.S. DOJ, CRIM. DIV. (Mar. 1, 2023), 137

Recommendation of the Council for Further Combating Bribery of Foreign Public Officials in International Business Transactions, OECD (Nov. 26, 2021), 18

Recommendation of the Council for Further Combatting Bribery of Foreign Public Officials in International Business Transactions, OECD WORKING GRP. ON INT'L BUS. TRANSACTIONS (2009), 16

Remarks of FTC Director of Enforcement James M. McDonald at the American Bar Association's National Institute on White Collar Crime, COMMODITY FUTURES TRADING COMM'N (Mar. 6, 2019), 102

Report of Investigation Pursuant to Section 21(a) of the Securities Exchange Act of 1934 and Commission Statement on the Relationship of Cooperation to Agency Enforcement Decisions, U.S. SEC (Oct. 23, 2001), 199

Rosenstein, Rod J., Deputy Attorney General, *Letter to Heads of Department Components on Policy on Coordination of Corporate Resolution Penalties*, U.S. DOJ, OFF. OF THE DEPUTY ATT'Y GEN. (May 9, 2018), 131

Rusch, Jonathan J., *Section 7 of the United Kingdom Bribery Act of 2010: A "Fair Warning" Perlustration*, Yale J. of Int'l Law Online, Vol. 43:1, 233

S. REP. NO. 105–277 (1998), 6, 7, 17

S. REP. NO. 95–114 (1977), 3, 46

ANTI-BRIBERY AND CORRUPTION LAW AND COMPLIANCE

IN A NUTSHELL®

CHAPTER 1

WHY WE HAVE ANTI-BRIBERY AND CORRUPTION LAWS: THE MONETARY, HUMAN, AND BUSINESS COSTS OF BRIBERY AND CORRUPTION

It's difficult to over-state the harm that bribery and corruption cause on a daily basis. In the words of the U.S. Securities and Exchange Commission (the "SEC") and the U.S. Department of Justice (the "DOJ"), bribery "undermines the rule of law, empowers authoritarian rulers, distorts free and fair markets, disadvantages honest and ethical companies, and threatens national security and sustainable development."[1] In the words of former U.K. Secretary of State for Justice Kenneth Clarke, "Bribery blights lives. Its immediate victims include firms that lose out unfairly. The wider victims are government and society, undermined by a weakened rule of law and damaged social and economic development. At stake is the principle of free and fair competition, which stands diminished by each bribe offered or accepted."[2]

---

1 *A Resource Guide to the U.S. Foreign Corruption Practices*, CRIM. DIV. OF THE U.S. DOJ AND THE ENF'T DIV. OF THE U.S. SEC, foreword (2d ed. 2020) [hereinafter FCPA Resource Guide], https://www.justice.gov/criminal-fraud/file/1292051/download.

2 *The Bribery Act 2010: Guidance about procedures which relevant organisations can put into place to prevent persons associated with them from bribing (section 9 of the Bribery Act 2010)*, MINISTRY OF JUST., at 2 (2d Ed. 2020) [hereinafter UKBA

Arguably, from purely a moral and ethical viewpoint, we as a society should work to eradicate bribery and corruption. As the U.S. Financial Crimes Enforcement Network ("FinCEN") has observed, corruption "underpins many of the global challenges of our time, to include serious human rights abuse, and has a disproportionate impact on the poor and most vulnerable."[3] The White House has also referred to corruption as "a cancer within the body of societies" that "exacerbates social, political and economic inequality and polarization [and] impedes the ability of states to respond to public health crises or to deliver quality education. . ."[4] Bribery and corruption are, in a very real way, a threat to the well-being of individuals and to society as a whole.

We should also have the same goal of eradicating bribery and corruption from a purely economic and business perspective. Both the U.S. House of Representatives and the Senate recognized this in enacting the FCPA. As the House of Representatives stated in Report No. 95–640, "not only is [bribery] unethical, *it is bad business as well*. It erodes public confidence in the integrity of the free market system.

Guidance], https://assets.publishing.service.gov.uk/media/5d80cfc3ed915d51e9aff85a/bribery-act-2010-guidance.pdf.

[3] U.S. DEPARTMENT OF THE TREASURY, ANTI-MONEY LAUNDERING AND COUNTERING THE FINANCING OF TERRORISM NATIONAL PRIORITIES at 3 (June 30, 2021) [hereinafter FinCEN 2021 Priorities], https://www.fincen.gov/sites/default/files/shared/AML_CFT%20Priorities%20(June%2030%2C%202021).pdf.

[4] *Fact Sheet: U.S. Strategy on Countering Corruption*, THE WHITE HOUSE (Dec. 2021) [hereinafter U.S. 2021 Fact Sheet], https://www.whitehouse.gov/briefing-room/statements-releases/2021/12/06/fact-sheet-u-s-strategy-on-countering-corruption.

It short-circuits the marketplace by directing business to those companies too inefficient to compete in terms of price, quality or service, or too lazy to engage in honest salesmanship, or too intent upon unloading marginal products. In short, it rewards corruption instead of efficiency and puts pressure on ethical enterprises to lower their standards or risk losing business."[5]

The Senate similarly declared that "[c]orporate bribery is bad business. In our free market system it is basic that the sale of products should take place on the basis of price, quality and service. Corporate bribery is fundamentally destructive of this basic tenet. Corporate bribery of foreign officials takes place primarily to assist corporations in gaining business. Thus, foreign corporate bribery affects the very stability of overseas business. Foreign corporate bribes also affect our domestic competitive climate when domestic firms engage in such practices as a substitute for healthy competition for foreign business."[6]

It logically follows, then, that preventing bribery and corruption can and should be helpful to business.

---

[5] UNLAWFUL CORPORATE PAYMENTS ACT OF 1977, H.R. REP. NO. 95–640, at 4–5 (1977) [hereinafter H.R. REP. NO. 95–640] (emphasis added), https://www.justice.gov/sites/default/files/criminal-fraud/legacy/2010/04/11/houseprt-95-640.pdf.

[6] FOREIGN CORRUPT PRACTICES AND DOMESTIC AND FOREIGN INVESTMENT IMPROVED DISCLOSURE ACTS OF 1977, S. REP. NO. 95–114, at 4 (1977) [hereinafter S. REP. NO. 95–114], https://www.justice.gov/sites/default/files/criminal-fraud/legacy/2010/04/11/senaterpt-95-114.pdf.

As then-UK Secretary Clarke argued in his Foreword to the Bribery Act 2010 Guidance,[7]

> the [UKBA] is directly beneficial for business. That's because it creates clarity and a level playing field, helping to align trading nations around decent standards. . . Some have asked whether business can afford this legislation—especially at a time of economic recovery. But the choice is a false one. We don't have to decide between tackling corruption and supporting growth. Addressing bribery is good for business because it creates the conditions for free markets to flourish.

As we'll address in later chapters, preventing, detecting, and deterring bribery and corruption is an area in which compliance and business can work toward shared goals. Fighting bribery and corruption can be both a humanitarian and a commercial cause and doing so is in both the public and private interests. This is part of what makes the topic so fascinating.

---

[7] UKBA Guidance, *supra* n.2, at 3.

CHAPTER 2

A BRIEF HISTORY: THE FCPA, THE OECD CONVENTION, AND THE UNCAC

In the next sections we'll look at the FCPA, the OECD Convention, and the UNCAC at a high level to understand how and when each came into existence, how they may have affected each other, and the general scope of their requirements. This book isn't a history book, and its purpose is not to dissect each paragraph of international conventions. However, the three instruments' chronology, main provisions, and the overlap between them informs our understanding of the concepts of bribery and corruption and their impact on society and tells the story of how our collective thoughts on bribery and corruption have led us to this place and this time.

A. THE U.S. FOREIGN CORRUPT PRACTICES ACT AND THE OECD CONVENTION

The FCPA was enacted in 1977 in the aftermath of the Watergate scandal. It was borne of Congress' realization that well-known U.S. companies had paid hundreds of millions of dollars in bribes to foreign government officials to obtain business and that they were falsifying their corporate financial records to conceal those payments.[1] As House Report No. 95–

---

[1] FCPA Resource Guide, *supra* Chapter 1, n.1, at 2; *see generally* STAFF OF S. COMM. ON BANKING, HOUS., AND URB. AFFS., 94TH CONG., REP. OF THE SECURITIES AND EXCHANGE COMMISSION

640 stated, "[m]ore than 400 corporations have admitted making questionable or illegal payments. The companies, most of them voluntarily, have reported paying out well in excess of $300 million in corporate funds to foreign government officials, politicians, and political parties. These corporations have included some of the largest and most widely held public companies in the United States; over 117 of them rank in the top Fortune 500 industries."[2] Scandals involving payments by such U.S. companies to foreign officials in Japan, Italy and Mexico "led to political repercussions within those countries and severely sullied the reputation of American companies throughout the world."[3] Congress viewed passage of the FCPA, which contains both anti-bribery and accounting provisions, as a critical step to prevent corporate bribery and to prevent the negative consequences of bribery and corruption.[4]

In the late 1980s, the FCPA and the international movement against bribery and corruption received further attention. In 1988, Congress amended the FCPA to add two affirmative defenses—the so-called "local law" defense and the "reasonable and bona fide

---

ON QUESTIONABLE AND ILLEGAL CORPORATE PAYMENTS AND PRACTICES (Comm. Print. 1976) [hereinafter SEC REPORT ON QUESTIONABLE PAYMENTS], https://www.sec.gov/spotlight/fcpa/sec-report-questionable-illegal-corporate-payments-practices-1976.pdf.

[2] H.R. REP. NO. 95–640, *supra* Chapter 1, n.5, at 4.

[3] THE INTERNATIONAL ANTI-BRIBERY ACT OF 1998, S. REP. NO. 105–277, at 1 (1998) [hereinafter S. REP. NO. 105–277], https://www.congress.gov/105/crpt/srpt277/CRPT-105srpt277.pdf.

[4] FCPA Resource Guide, *supra* Chapter 1, n.1, at 2.

business expenditure" defense.[5] *See* Chapter 3 for a full discussion of these affirmative defenses.

During this time there was a rising sentiment that American businesses had operated at a disadvantage since the FCPA was passed because American businesses' foreign competitors had continued to pay bribes without fear of suffering any negative consequences. Even worse, Congress believed that some other nations actually encouraged bribes by permitting businesses to claim them as tax-deductible business expenses.[6] While impossible to calculate the specific losses that American businesses may have suffered, the Commerce Department once noted that it had learned of significant allegations of bribery by foreign companies in approximately 180 international contracts from mid-1994 through mid-1998 that were valued at a total of nearly $80 billion.[7]

As a result, in 1988 Congress asked the Executive branch to actively encourage U.S. trading partners to enact legislation like the FCPA—essentially to attempt to level the playing field in international business.[8] Following this request, the U.S. worked to negotiate an international treaty with OECD member states to prohibit bribery in international business transactions by many of the United States' significant trading partners. Those negotiations

---

[5] *Id.* at 3, 24–25.

[6] S. REP. NO. 105–277, *supra* n.3, at 2.

[7] *Id.*

[8] FCPA Resource Guide, *supra* Chapter 1, n.1, at 3, 102 n.19.

culminated in the OECD Convention, which was signed on December 17, 1997. At that time, thirty-three countries, many of which were heavily engaged in international trade, signed the instrument. The OECD Convention became effective on February 15, 1999, with the U.S. as a founding party.[9] It currently has forty-four signatories—all thirty-eight OECD countries and six non-OECD countries.[10]

The OECD Convention was drafted in shared recognition that "bribery is a widespread phenomenon in international business transactions, including trade and investment, which raises serious moral and political concerns, undermines good governance and economic development, and distorts international competitive conditions[.]"[11]

---

[9] *Convention on Combating Bribery of Foreign Public Officials in International Business Transactions*, OECD (Nov. 21, 1997) [hereinafter The OECD Convention], https://www.oecd.org/daf/anti-bribery/ConvCombatBribery_ENG.pdf.

[10] *Convention on Combating Bribery of Foreign Public Officials in International Business Transactions*, OECD, https://www.oecd.org/corruption/oecdantibriberyconvention.htm.

[11] The OECD Convention, *supra* n.9, at 3; *see also Fighting the Crime of Foreign Bribery,* THE ANTI-BRIBERY CONVENTION AND THE OECD WORKING GROUP ON BRIBERY, (2018) [hereinafter Fighting the Crime of Foreign Bribery], https://www.oecd.org/daf/anti-bribery/Fighting-the-crime-of-foreign-bribery.pdf.

> The Parties' commitment to this fight is grounded in the recognition that no government or market economy can function effectively if it is riddled by bribery. Corruption entails costs that no country can afford. Serious harm results when public officials take bribes, for example, when awarding contracts to foreign businesses in such areas as road construction, water infrastructure, medicines or electricity. In addition to the human suffering caused by inferior products and services, bribery derails the

Importantly, it was based on the understanding that all countries share the responsibility to fight bribery and corruption in international business transactions. Pursuant to the Convention, the signatory nations agreed to do so through enacting and enforcing domestic laws and other obligations. They also agreed to a peer monitoring process to ensure the Convention's effective implementation. The Convention provides a legal baseline from which countries can build or enhance their existing legislation and enforcement capabilities to fight bribery and corruption.

The OECD Convention, like the FCPA, is focused on the "supply-side" of bribery—i.e., on the conduct of the person or entity offering, promising, or giving the bribe. Pursuant to its terms, the signatory nations agreed to establish the bribery of foreign public officials as a criminal offense under their laws and to investigate, prosecute and punish that offense. The OECD Convention required signatory nations to enact laws prohibiting the bribery of foreign public officials that were crafted more broadly than those of the FCPA. As a result, in 1998, Congress amended the FCPA to conform with and to implement the OECD Convention's more expansive requirements. Specifically, the following five changes/updates to the FCPA were made[12]:

---

functioning of markets and undermines economic development.

[12] *See* FCPA Resource Guide, *supra* Chapter 1, n.1, at 3, 10–11 (internal citations omitted).

(1) The existing FCPA prohibited the offer or provision of payments to influence the decision of a foreign official or to induce a foreign official to take or refrain from taking any action. The amendment, tracking the OECD Convention's language, expanded the FCPA to also prohibit the offer or provision of any payments to obtain "any improper advantage."

(2) The existing FCPA covered issuers with securities registered under the Securities Exchange Act of 1934 and domestic concerns. However, the OECD Convention required parties to implement laws against the bribery of foreign public officials that covered "any person." As a result, the FCPA's anti-bribery provisions' coverage was expanded to include *all* foreign persons who commit an act in furtherance of a foreign bribe while in the United States.

(3) The existing FCPA defined "foreign official[s]" as direct government employees and employees of state owned or controlled entities. To mirror the OECD Convention definition of "foreign public official", the amendment expanded the FCPA's definition of "foreign official" to include those who work for and on behalf of public international organizations.

(4) The existing FCPA required territorial jurisdiction for issuers and domestic concerns. However, the OECD Convention

called on parties to assert nationality jurisdiction in cases of bribery of foreign public officials when such jurisdiction would be consistent with each nation's legal and constitutional principles. In line with this requirement, Congress amended the FCPA to include extra-territorial jurisdiction for U.S. issuers, domestic concerns, and U.S. nationals whose actions in furtherance of unlawful payments take place *wholly* outside the United States.[13]

(5) Finally, the existing FCPA subjected foreign nationals who were employed by or acting as agents of U.S. companies only to civil penalties. The 1998 amendments removed this limitation and revised the FCPA to subject all employees or agents of U.S. businesses to potential civil *and* criminal penalties.

The OECD Convention also requires signatory nations to enact laws that hold both individuals and organizations accountable, include liability for offering a bribe even if the bribe is not accepted, and include liability for bribes that are made through intermediaries. In addition to enacting and enforcing laws against bribery of foreign public officials, signatory nations also agree to provide prompt legal

---

[13] *Id.* at 11 (internal citations omitted) ("In particular, the 1998 amendments removed the requirement that there be a use of interstate commerce (e.g., wire, email, telephone call) for acts in furtherance of a corrupt payment to a foreign official by U.S. companies and persons occurring wholly outside the United States.")

assistance to other Convention parties who are investigating potential foreign bribery, to refuse to provide tax deductibility for bribe payments, to prohibit the use of false accounting to hide bribes, to prohibit the laundering of the proceeds of foreign bribery, and to impose penalties for foreign bribery acts. Signatory nations also specifically undertake to ensure that projects that they finance, including those through development aid and export credits, include adequate controls to prevent and detect bribery.

In 2007, senior officials of the OECD Convention's signatory nations gathered in Rome, Italy to celebrate the Convention's tenth anniversary. They issued a Statement reaffirming their Shared Commitment to Fight Against Foreign Bribery.[14] While noting that progress had been made, the parties acknowledged their awareness that "combating this crime has to remain one of our most important tasks to promote sustainable development and ensure a level playing field in worldwide business."[15] The parties pledged to intensify their individual and collective efforts to fight foreign bribery and committed to[16]:

---

[14] *Statement, Shared Commitment to Fight Against Foreign Bribery, Tenth Anniversary of the OECD Convention on Combating Bribery of Foreign Public Officials in International Business Transactions*, OECD (Nov. 21, 2007), https://web-archive.oecd.org/2012-06-15/132217-39656560.pdf.

[15] *Id.*

[16] *Id.*

- Vigorously and comprehensively implement [their] obligations under the [OECD] Convention;
- Ensure that the standards of the [OECD] Convention remain at the forefront of the global fight against foreign bribery and that their enforcement continues to be monitored by a systematic, effective and adequate review mechanism;
- Ensure the enforcement of the [OECD] Convention's standards throughout Parties' governments;
- Use all means and take all necessary actions to effectively investigate and prosecute those who bribe foreign public officials, notably by facilitating international cooperation and mutual legal assistance;
- Continue to raise public awareness of the [OECD] Convention in collaboration with civil society and the private sector;
- Continue to support and encourage initiatives by the business sector to prevent and detect foreign bribery, through, for instance corporate compliance programmes;
- Encourage major emerging economic players not parties to adhere to the [OECD] Convention's standards and further develop partnerships with countries not parties to the [OECD] Convention;

- Deepen collaboration with international and regional organisations fighting bribery and corruption, in particular multilateral development banks[;][17]
- Actively support the ratification and implementation of the [UNCAC] by all countries.

The OECD Working Group on Bribery in International Business Transactions (the "Working Group"), established in 1994, is responsible for monitoring the implementation and enforcement of the OECD Convention as well as related instruments.[18] The Working Group is comprised of members from the signatory nations and has specific procedures for evaluating countries' compliance with the OECD Convention.[19]

On June 19, 2009, the Working Group issued the Policy Statement on Bribery in International Business Transactions (the "Working Group Policy Statement").[20] The Working Group Policy Statement

---

[17] A multi-lateral development bank is an international financial institution that provides loans and grants to member nations to fund social and economic development projects.

[18] *OECD Working Group on Bribery in International Business Transactions*, OECD, https://www.oecd.org/corruption/anti-bribery/anti-briberyconvention/oecdworkinggrouponbribery ininternationalbusinesstransactions.htm.

[19] *Id.*

[20] *Policy Statement on Bribery in International Business Transactions, Working Group on Bribery in International Business Transactions*, OECD (June 19, 2009), [hereinafter The Working Group Policy Statement], https://web-archive.oecd.org/2012-06-14/116908-43117861.pdf.

acknowledged that the global economic crisis could lead to increased pressure on companies to engage in corruption, particularly with respect to public procurement.[21]

The Working Group Policy Statement affirmed that the fight against foreign bribery remained "a high priority and a shared responsibility" and reaffirmed the signatory nations' determination to implement the Convention's obligations, particularly with respect to enforcement. It emphasized that the signatory nations would "be vigilant in ensuring that investigations and prosecutions of the bribery of foreign public officials are not influenced by considerations of national economic interest, the potential effect upon relations with another State or the identity of the natural or legal persons involved . . ."[22] The Working Group Policy Statement also reaffirmed the parties' intention to maintain a rigorous monitoring system to promote the Convention's full implementation.[23]

Finally, the Working Group Policy Statement issued two calls to action. First, it requested that major exporting countries that were not yet Convention parties criminalize the bribery of foreign public officials and join the Convention parties in their fight against transnational bribery as soon as possible. Second, the Working Group Policy Statement called on "all companies operating

[21] *Id.*

[22] *Id.*

[23] *Id.*

internationally to implement or maintain and reinforce compliance and ethics measures for the purpose of preventing and detecting bribery of foreign public officials in their international business transactions."[24]

On November 26, 2009, the OECD Convention's signatory nations agreed to implement additional measures to fortify their efforts to prevent foreign bribery by adopting the OECD Recommendation for Further Combating Bribery of Foreign Public Officials in International Business Transactions (the "2009 OECD Recommendation").[25] The 2009 OECD Recommendation reflected the Working Group Policy Statement's principles and drew from multiple sources, including work from the OECD, the private sector, and civil society, to make a number of recommendations. These recommendations included, for example, urging OECD member countries to completely and timely implement the 2009 Council Recommendation on Tax Measures for Further Combating Bribery of Foreign Public Officials in International Business Transactions (the "2009 OECD Tax Recommendation"). The 2009 OECD Tax Recommendation recommended "in particular 'that Member countries and other Parties to the [OECD] Convention explicitly disallow the tax deductibility of

---

24 *Id.*

25 *Recommendation of the Council for Further Combatting Bribery of Foreign Public Officials in International Business Transactions*, OECD WORKING GRP. ON INT'L BUS. TRANSACTIONS (2009) [hereinafter 2009 OECD Recommendation], https://web-archive.oecd.org/2019-05-10/111174-OECD-Anti-Bribery-Recommendation-ENG.pdf.

bribes to foreign public officials, for all tax purposes in an effective manner'. . ." to establish a legal and administrative framework consistent with this goal.[26] Recall Congress' earlier concern, as expressed in Senate Report No. 105–277, that some nationals were allowing businesses to claim bribes to foreign officials as tax deductible business expenses.

Notably, the 2009 OECD Recommendation recognized the "corrosive effect of small facilitation payments," and called upon member countries to review their approaches to such payments and encourage companies to prohibit them.[27] In addition, the 2009 OECD Recommendation included a separate document entitled Good Practice Guidance on Internal Controls, Ethics and Compliance (the "OECD Good Practice Guidance"). The OECD Good Practice Guidance advised organizations with respect to "establishing effective internal controls, ethics, and compliance programmes or measures for preventing and detecting foreign bribery."[28] Its factors were specific to preventing bribery but otherwise similar in nature to the compliance program elements provided in the U.S. Sentencing Commission Guidelines. We'll address the elements of effective anti-bribery and corruption compliance programs in Chapter 5.

---

[26] 2009 OECD Recommendation, *supra* n.25, at 5.

[27] *Id.*

[28] *Good Practice Guidance on Internal Controls, Ethics, and Compliance*, OECD (Feb. 18, 2010) [hereinafter OECD Good Practice Guidance], https://www.oecd.org/investment/anti-bribery/anti-briberyconvention/44884389.pdf.

In 2018, the OECD Working Group began a review of the 2009 OECD Recommendation to determine whether it adequately reflected the trends, challenges and best practices that had emerged in the fight against bribery and corruption over the past decade. Three years later, the review concluded with the OECD's adoption of the Recommendation of the Council for Further Combating Bribery of Foreign Public Officials in International Business Transactions (the "2021 OECD Recommendation").[29]

The 2021 OECD Recommendation expanded on its 2009 predecessor. Its Preamble referenced emerging topics such as the potential connections between gender and corruption[30] and the use of innovative technology in anti-bribery efforts. Reflecting challenges of the Covid-19 pandemic, it also stressed the importance of Implementing the OECD Convention during times of crisis.

The 2021 OECD Recommendation also added new sections on topics that had emerged or significantly evolved since 2009, including: addressing the

---

[29] *Recommendation of the Council for Further Combating Bribery of Foreign Public Officials in International Business Transactions*, OECD (Nov. 26, 2021) [hereinafter 2021 OECD Recommendation], https://legalinstruments.oecd.org/en/instruments/OECD-LEGAL-0378.

[30] The 2021 OECD Recommendation recognized the need to improve our understanding of the relationship between gender and corruption, including how corruption can affect genders differently, and the importance of promoting gender equality and women's empowerment. However, only limited detail was provided. It would not be surprising if this topic, after further analysis and reflection, became the subject of a future statement or recommendation.

demand side of foreign bribery cases, sanctions and confiscation, non-trial resolutions, international cooperation, protection of reporting persons, compliance incentives, and data protection. It also updated the provisions of existing topics such as enforcement, awareness raising, training and guidance.

With respect to the demand side of bribery, a component notably absent from the FCPA and OECD Convention, the 2021 OECD Recommendation asked that member countries[31]:

i. raise awareness of bribe solicitation risks among relevant public officials, particularly those posted abroad, and the private sector, with particular attention to high-risk geographical and industrial sectors of operation;

ii. provide training to their public officials posted abroad on information and steps to be taken to assist enterprises confronted with bribe solicitation, where appropriate, and provide clear instructions on the authorities to whom allegations of solicitation and foreign bribery should be reported;

iii. where appropriate, undertake coordinated actions with other member and non-member countries, with a view to engaging

---

31 2021 OECD Recommendation, *supra* n.29, at 8.

with the host country on addressing the solicitation and acceptance of bribes;

iv. consider fostering, facilitating, engaging or participating in anti-bribery collective action initiatives with private and public sector representatives, as well as civil society organisations, aiming to address foreign bribery and bribe solicitation.

The 2021 OECD Recommendation also encouraged *all* countries to raise their own public officials' awareness of their domestic anti-bribery and solicitation laws and to publish on a publicly available web site their rules governing gifts, entertainment, hospitality for domestic public officials so that individuals and companies would be aware of those rules and could comply with them.[32]

Monitoring, conducted by the Working Group, is mandatory for all signatory nations. The nation being evaluated has no right to veto the final report or recommendations and all recommendations are published online for transparency and accountability. The process is a peer-review system,

---

[32] This is a fine idea in theory and transparency is a positive concept. However, this could raise difficulties from an organization's internal compliance perspective. It could effectively make the knowledge of the specific rules governing a public official's conduct a shared burden between that public official and any third party with whom they have contact. In other words, how much due diligence should an organization have to do regarding what a particular public official with whom it is dealing can accept? Does the organization need to independently confirm any limitations that apply to the public official? These are just two of the questions that could arise in practice.

in which each country is evaluated by examiners from other countries that are party to the Convention. Country monitoring takes place in four successive phases. The OECD touts this process as rigorous and systematic and Transparency International has referred to it as the "gold standard" of monitoring.[33]

In the first phase, the Working Group evaluates whether a country's legal framework is adequate to implement the recommendations of the Convention and related instruments.[34] The second phase examines whether a country is applying its legislation in practice.[35] The third phase looks at any unimplemented recommendations from the second phase and considers cross-cutting issues and the extent to which the legislation is being enforced. It's generally a shorter and more focused evaluation than that of phase 2 and focuses on the following three priorities: (1) progress made on any weaknesses that were identified in phase 2; (2) issues raised by changes in a nation's domestic legislation or institutional framework; and (3) enforcement efforts and results and "other key group-wide cross-cutting issues".[36]

---

[33] 2021 OECD Recommendation, *supra* n.29, at 4.

[34] *Country Monitoring of the OECD Anti-Bribery Convention*, OECD [hereinafter OECD Country Monitoring], https://www.oecd.org/corruption/countrymonitoringoftheoecdanti-briberyconvention.htm.

[35] *Id.*

[36] *Id.*

Finally, the fourth phase also focuses on enforcement, cross-cutting issues (with respect to specific country needs) and unimplemented recommendations (this time from the third phase).[37] There's a significant amount of overlap between the second, third and fourth phases of the review. Presumably this overlap builds in time for the subject country to fully implement recommendations where it has not yet done so. It also allows for countries to learn from each other about problems, successes, and different implementation approaches. The nature of the Working Group's "peer review" model has both an educational aspect to it, in terms of sharing best practices, as well as a peer pressure aspect in terms of pushing countries into line with the expectations of the other signatory nations.

If the Working Group finds that a country has inadequately implemented or continues to fail to implement the Convention, then it has a number of tools at its disposal, including[38]:

- Conducting a repeat evaluation.
- Requiring the evaluated country to provide regular reports on its progress on implementing the recommendations with the expectation that the country would come into substantial compliance within a set timeframe.

---

37 *Id.*

38 *Id.*

- Forming a monitoring sub-group that would, in conjunction with the OECD Secretariat, focus on the evaluated country and its implementation progress, and make recommendations to the Working Group on next steps.
- Sending a letter to the relevant public official in the evaluated country to draw their attention to the country's failure to fully comply with the recommendations.
- Conducting a mission to the evaluated country. Such a mission could be technical in nature to discuss granular issues regarding implementation and enforcement. Alternatively, it could be a high-level mission where senior members of the Working Group would visit the evaluated country and meet with senior public officials of that country.
- Publishing a formal statement on the OECD web site stating, in essence, that a signatory country is not in sufficient compliance with the Convention and related instruments and requesting prompt implementation.
- Requiring an evaluated country to develop and submit an action plan with proposed steps to address specific deficiencies that were identified by the Working Group.
- Issuing a public statement that an evaluated country's inadequate implementation of the Convention may warrant potential

counterparties to conduct enhanced due diligence on companies from that country.

- Requesting that an evaluated country's ambassador or other senior diplomat participate in a plenary session to address the Working Group's observations and potential solutions.
- Publishing any long-standing unimplemented recommendation as a "high priority unimplemented recommendation" on the OECD web site.
- Suspending the evaluated country's advancement to the next phase of monitoring and thus identifying it as a "non-complying" member of the Working Group. Such decisions can be reviewed every two years or upon a request from any Working Group member.

In November 2020, the OECD issued its Phase 4 Report on the United States, and recognized the United States' sustained and outstanding commitment to enforcing the FCPA.[39]

---

[39] *OECD Working Group on Bribery Issues Report Commending United States for Maintaining Leading Role in the Fight Against Transnational Corruption*, Release No. 2020–285, Fed. Sec. L. Rep. (CCH) (Nov. 17, 2020), https://www.sec.gov/news/press-release/2020-285.

> [B]etween September 2010 and July 2019, through the SEC and Justice Department's efforts, the United States convicted or sanctioned 174 companies and 115 individuals for foreign bribery and related offences under the FCPA. The report indicates that this achievement resulted from a combination of enhanced expertise and resources to investigate and prosecute foreign bribery, the enforcement

B. THE UNITED NATIONS CONVENTION AGAINST CORRUPTION

The UNCAC is an international treaty that was adopted by the United Nations General Assembly in October 2003 and which came into force in December 2005. It has approximately 189 nations as parties. In the words of the 2021 OECD Recommendation, "the OECD [ ] Convention and the [UNCAC] are mutually supporting and complementary, and [ ] ratification and implementation of the UNCAC supports a comprehensive approach to combating the bribery of foreign public officials in international business transactions."[40]

The UNCAC is an extensive document, with eight chapters and seventy-one articles.[41] It contains a mix of mandatory provisions, provisions that signatory nations must consider implementing, and optional provisions. Many provisions also have a conflict of law qualification that defers to a signatory nation's own legislation, signaled by the phrase "where

---

of a broad range of offences in foreign bribery cases, the effective use of non-trial resolution mechanisms, and the development of published policies to incentivize companies' cooperation with law enforcement agencies.

[40] 2021 OECD Recommendation, *supra* n.29, at 5; 2009 OECD Recommendation, *supra* n.25, at 3.

[41] The UNCAC Coalition provides a helpful breakdown of the UNCAC's chapters as well as more in-depth information about the UNCAC on its web site. The UNCAC Coalition describes itself as "a global network of over 350 civil society organizations (CSOs) in over 100 countries, committed to promoting the ratification, implementation and monitoring of the [UNCAC]." *The UN Convention against Corruption (UNCAC) in brief*, UNCAC COAL., https://uncaccoalition.org/the-uncac/about-the-uncac.

appropriate and consistent with their domestic legal system."

Chapter I of the UNCAC, entitled General Provisions, explains its three stated purposes: (1) "[t]o promote and strengthen measures to prevent and combat corruption more efficiently and effectively; (2) "[t]o promote, facilitate and support international cooperation and technical assistance in the prevention of and fight against corruption, including in asset recovery;" and (3) "[t]o promote integrity, accountability and proper management of public affairs and public property."[42] It further states that the UNCAC applies to the "prevention, investigation, and prosecution of corruption and to the freezing, seizure, confiscation and return of the proceeds of offenses established in connection with [the UNCAC].[43] Chapter I also explains that nations should carry out their obligations under the UNCAC consistent with the principles of sovereign equality, national territorial integrity and non-interference in the domestic affairs of other nations.[44]

Chapter II of the UNCAC, entitled Preventative Measures, discusses mandatory and non-mandatory preventative measures that signatory states may or must take. These include developing, implementing and maintaining effective, coordinated, preventative anti-corruption policies that encourage societal

---

[42] *United Nations Convention Against Corruption*, Chapter I, Art. 1 (a)–(c), [hereinafter UNCAC], https://uncaccoalition.org/the-uncac/united-nations-convention-against-corruption.

[43] *Id.* at Chapter I, Art. 3, ¶ 1.

[44] *Id.* at Chapter I, Art. 4, ¶ 1.

participation and reflect the principles of "the rule of law, proper management of public affairs and public property, integrity, transparency and accountability."[45] Among other things, this means periodically reviewing and evaluating existing laws and administrative measures for adequacy and collaborating with international and regional organizations to develop and promote effective anti-corruption preventative measures.[46] Chapter II also focuses on developing and strengthening the ethical culture of a nation's domestic public sector, including through education, training, and possible creation of a code of conduct for domestic public officials.[47]

Chapter III of the UNCAC, entitled Criminalisation and Law Enforcement, contains several different articles that basically break down into two broad categories: (1) bribery and corruption-related offenses that signatory countries should, at a minimum, consider criminalizing; and (2) sections listing framework elements that would be needed to support the criminalization of these offenses. Presumably part of the reason for the framework section is that not every country has the requisite governmental and law enforcement infrastructure to support criminalization of these offenses.

First, Chapter III requires signatory nations to criminalize, or in some situations consider

45 *Id.* at Chapter II, Art. 5, ¶ 1.

46 *Id.* at Chapter II, Art. 5, ¶¶ 2–4.

47 *Id.* at Chapter II, Arts. 7, 8.

criminalizing, various intentional bribery and corruption-related offenses, including[48]:

- Bribery of national public officials (Article 15)
- Bribery of foreign public officials and officials of public international organizations (Article 16)
- Embezzlement, misappropriation, or other diversion of property by a public official (Article 17)
- Trading in influence (Article 18)
- Abuse of functions (Article 19)
- Illicit enrichment (Article 20)
- Bribery in the private sector (Article 21)
- Embezzlement of property in the private sector (Article 22)
- Laundering of proceeds of crime (Article 23)

This list of offenses illustrates the breadth of conduct that may fall under the umbrella of bribery and corruption. Organizations should consider whether and how their new and existing compliance programs address these areas. Particularly note the inclusion of money laundering. As we'll further address in later chapters, governments, regulators, and law enforcement are increasingly recognizing the connections between money laundering and bribery

---

48 UNCAC, *supra* n.42, Chapter III.

and corruption. These connections are often reflected in how compliance functions are organized.

Chapter III also sets out several elements that would necessarily be part of a framework for criminalizing the previously listed offenses and related conduct. Those elements are[49]:

- Concealment (Article 24)
- Obstruction of Justice (Article 25)
- Liability of legal persons (Article 26)
- Knowledge, intent, and purpose as elements of an offense (Article 28)
- Statute of limitations (Article 29)
- Prosecution, adjudication, and sanctions (Article 30)
- Freezing, seizure and confiscation (Article 31)
- Protection of witnesses, experts, and victims (Article 32)
- Protection of reporting persons (Article 33)
- Consequences of acts of corruption (Article 34)
- Compensation for damage (Article 35)
- Specialized authorities (Article 36)
- Cooperation with law enforcement authorities (Article 37)

---

49 *Id.*

- Cooperation between national authorities (Article 38)
- Cooperation between national authorities and the private sector (Article 39)
- Bank secrecy (Article 40)
- Criminal record (Article 41)
- Jurisdiction (Article 42)

Chapter IV of the UNCAC, entitled International Cooperation, addresses international cooperation in investigations, prosecutions and proceedings involving bribery and corruption. Article 43 states that signatory nations "*shall* cooperate in criminal matters in accordance with articles 44 to 50 of [the UNCAC]."[50] Article 43 also addresses, less forcefully, civil bribery and corruption matters, stating that signatory nations "[w]here appropriate and consistent with their domestic legal system[s] . . . shall consider assisting each other in investigations of and proceedings in civil and administrative matters relating to corruption."[51] Chapter IV's subsequent articles support the goal of cross-border cooperation by addressing topics including extradition (Article 44), the transfer of sentenced persons (Article 45), mutual legal assistance (Article 46), the transfer of criminal proceedings (Article 47), law enforcement cooperation (Article 48), joint

---

50 *Id.* at Chapter IV, Art. 43, ¶ 1 (emphasis added).

51 *Id.* at Chapter IV, Art. 43, ¶ 1.

investigations (Article 49), and special investigative techniques (Article 50).[52]

Chapter V of the UNCAC is entitled Asset Recovery, with Article 51 noting that "[t]he return of assets pursuant to his chapter is a fundamental principle of [the UNCAC], and States Parties shall afford one another the widest measure of cooperation and assistance in this regard."[53] To that end, Chapter V addresses the prevention and detection of transfers of proceeds of crime (Article 52), measures for direct recovery of property (Article 53), mechanisms for recovery of property through international cooperation in confiscation (Article 54), international cooperation for purposes of confiscation (Article 55), special cooperation (Article 56), return and disposal of assets (Article 57), establishment of a financial intelligence unit (Article 58), and bilateral and multilateral agreements and arrangements (Article 59).[54]

Chapter V's reference to the "transfers of proceeds of crime" is a reminder of the previously referenced and unsurprising overlap between money laundering and bribery and corruption. Article 58, addressing financial intelligence units ("FIUs"), is particularly noteworthy in this regard. FIUs are country-level centers for the receipt, investigation and analysis of suspicious activity reports relating to financial crime. Article 58 decrees that "States Parties shall

---

52 *Id.* at Chapter IV, Arts. 44–50.

53 *Id.* at Chapter V, Art. 51.

54 UNCAC, *supra* n.42, Chapter V, Arts. 52–59.

cooperate with one another for the purpose of preventing and combating the transfer of proceeds of offences established in accordance with [the UNCAC] and of promoting ways and means of recovering such proceeds and, to that end shall consider establishing a financial intelligence unit to be responsible for receiving, analysing and disseminating to the competent authorities reports of suspicious financial transactions."[55]

Chapter VI of the UNCAC is entitled Technical Assistance and Information Exchange. As with many UNCAC chapters, Chapter VI sets out its concepts both in terms of what individual signatory nations themselves must do, as well as assistance that they should consider providing to other nations. This is certainly logical because joint action is needed to eradicate both the demand for bribes and the willingness to pay them.

Article 60 of Chapter VI requires each signatory nation to "to the extent necessary, initiate, develop or improve specific training programmes for its personnel responsible for preventing and combating corruption."[56] Elements of these training programs include the following (many of which touch on money laundering)[57]:

a. Effective measures to prevent, detect, investigate, punish and control corruption,

---

55 *Id.* at Chapter V, Art. 58.

56 *Id.* at Chapter VI, Art. 60.

57 *Id.* at Chapter VI, Art. 60, ¶ 1, (a)–(j).

including the use of evidence-gathering and investigative methods;

b. Building capacity in the development and planning of strategic anti-corruption policy;

c. Training competent authorities in the preparation of requests for mutual legal assistance that meet the requirements of [the UNCAC];

d. Evaluation and strengthening of institutions, public service management and the management of public finances, including public procurement, and the private sector;

e. Preventing and combating the transfer of proceeds of offenses established in accordance with [the UNCAC] and recovering such proceeds;

f. Detecting and freezing the transfer of proceeds of offenses established in accordance with [the UNCAC];

g. Surveillance of the movement of proceeds of offenses established in accordance with [the UNCAC] and of the methods used to transfer, conceal or disguise such proceeds;

h. Appropriate and efficient legal and administrative mechanisms and methods for facilitating the return of proceeds of offenses established in accordance with [the UNCAC];

i. Methods used in protecting victims and witnesses who cooperate with judicial authorities; and

j. Training in national and international regulations and in languages.

There is an emphasis on the sharing of information, research and expertise between signatory nations. This emphasis also extends to the request for signatory nations to consider providing financial and technical assistance regarding these matters to "developing countries and countries with economies in transition."[58]

Chapter VII, entitled Mechanisms for Implementation, and Chapter VIII of the UNCAC entitled Final Provisions, address the mechanisms for the UNCAC's implementation, such as signature, ratification, acceptance, approval, accession, and settlement of disputes. Chapter VII includes setting up a "Conference of the States Parties to the Convention" to achieve the UNCAC's objectives and to promote and review and its implementation.[59] Article 65 succinctly explains each signatory nation's obligations to implement the UNCAC, stating that "[e]ach State Party shall take the necessary measures, including legislative and administrative measures, in accordance with fundamental principles of its domestic law, to ensure the implementation of its obligations under the

---

[58] *Id.* at Chapter VI, Art. 60, ¶ 7; *id.* at Art. 62.

[59] UNCAC, *supra* n.42, Chapter VII, Art. 63.

[UNCAC]."[60] Article 65 notes that signatory nations may of course also adopt stricter measures to prevent and fight corruption than those required by the UNCAC.[61]

---

60 *Id.* at Chapter VIII, Art. 65, ¶ 1.

61 *Id.* at Chapter VIII, Art. 65, ¶ 2.

CHAPTER 3

THE U.S. FOREIGN CORRUPT PRACTICES ACT

We now turn in more detail to the FCPA. We'll address its anti-bribery provisions, including dissecting the meaning of the provisions' key terms, its facilitation payments exception and its two affirmative defenses. We'll then address the FCPA's accounting provisions, including the books and records and internal controls provisions. Finally, we'll explain the roles of the SEC and the DOJ in FCPA enforcement and address the frameworks pursuant to which organizations may reach FCPA-related enforcement resolutions with those agencies.

A. THE ANTI-BRIBERY PROVISIONS

The FCPA contains three separate anti-bribery provisions, memorialized in Section 30A of the Securities Exchange Act of 1934 (the "SEA"), located at 15 U.S.C. §§ 78dd–1–3. These provisions are organized based on the category of person or entity to which they apply: issuers, domestic concerns, and persons other than issuers or domestic concerns. The core prohibited conduct is the same, but the jurisdictional predicates are different for each. Below is a summary of the jurisdictional requirements necessary for the anti-bribery provisions to apply to different categories of persons and entities:

Person/Entity Type	Jurisdictional Basis
U.S. Issuer	nationality jurisdiction (general principle that a country can exercise jurisdiction over its nationals)
Foreign Issuer	territorial jurisdiction (use of the mails or any instrumentality of interstate commerce in furtherance of an improper payment scheme)
Domestic Concern	nationality jurisdiction (general principle that a country can exercise jurisdiction over its nationals)
Persons Other than Issuers or Domestic Concerns	territorial jurisdiction (use of the mails or any instrumentality of interstate commerce in furtherance of an improper payment scheme *while within the territory of the United States*)

We'll explain each of these categories in more detail in the proceeding sections. As noted above, although the core of the prohibited conduct is the same, jurisdiction under the FCPA's anti-bribery provisions depends on the type of entity or person.[1]

1. ISSUERS

An issuer is an entity that has a class of securities that is registered under SEA Section 12 or that is otherwise required to file reports with the SEC under SEA Section 15(d).[2] This means that any company that has a class of securities listed on a U.S. national securities exchange is an issuer.[3] In addition, any company with a class of securities that is quoted in an over-the-counter market in the U.S. and required to file periodic reports with the SEC is an issuer.[4] Finally, foreign companies with American Depository Receipts that are listed on a U.S. exchange are also issuers.[5]

Jurisdiction for the FCPA's anti-bribery provisions applies differently to U.S. issuers than to foreign issuers, and it is the most expansive for U.S. issuers. Originally, U.S. issuers were subject to territorial jurisdiction, meaning that the anti-bribery provisions would only apply if the issuer used the mail or any means or instrumentality of interstate commerce in furtherance of a corrupt payment to a

---

1 When referring to an entity (like an issuer or domestic concern) we're also referring to "any officer, director, employee, or agent" or "any stockholder thereof acting on behalf of such" entity. 15 U.S.C. § 78dd–1–3.

2 FCPA Resource Guide, *supra* Chapter 1, n.1, at 9 (internal citations omitted).

3 *Id.*

4 *Id.* at 9–10, 104 n.47.

5 *Id.*

foreign official. However, in 1998 the FCPA was amended to remove this requirement for U.S. companies (including issuers and domestic concerns) and U.S. persons. The amendments added alternative jurisdiction provisions, based on nationality jurisdiction, that allow the anti-bribery provisions to apply even if the wrongful conduct occurred wholly outside the United States.[6] This means that the FCPA's anti-bribery provision has extra-territorial jurisdiction for U.S. issuers—*i.e., U.S. issuers (and domestic concerns) can violate the FCPA's anti-bribery provisions even if the prohibited conduct takes place entirely outside of the United States.*

Conversely, territorial jurisdiction is required for foreign issuers. That means that the foreign issuer must use the mail or another instrumentality of interstate commerce to further an improper payment scheme. The SEA defines "interstate commerce" as "trade, commerce, transportation, or communication among the several States, or between any foreign country and any State or between any State and any place or ship outside thereof . . ."[7] As the FCPA Resource Guide explains, "[t]he term also includes the intrastate use of any interstate means of communication, or any other interstate instrumentality. Thus, placing a telephone call or sending an e-mail, text message, or fax from, to, or

---

6 15 U.S.C. §§ 78dd–1(g), 78dd–2(B)(i); FCPA Resource Guide, *supra* Chapter 1, n.1, at 11, 105 n.62.

7 15 U.S.C. §§ 78dd–2(h)(5) (defining "interstate commerce"), 78dd–3(f)(5) (same).

through the United States involves interstate commerce—as does sending a wire transfer from or to a U.S. bank or otherwise using the U.S. banking system, or traveling across state borders or internationally to or from the United States."[8]

2. DOMESTIC CONCERNS

A "domestic concern" [9] is defined as:

(A) any individual who is a citizen, national or resident of the United States; or

(B) any corporation, partnership, association, joint-stock company, business trust, unincorporated organization, or sole proprietorship (other than an issuer) which has its principal place of business in the United States, or which is organized under the laws of a State of the United States or a territory, possession, or commonwealth of the United States.

As with U.S. issuers, jurisdiction of the anti-bribery provision for domestic concerns is extra-territorial, meaning that domestic concerns can violate the FCPA's applicable anti-bribery provision even if the prohibited conduct takes place entirely outside of the United States.[10]

---

[8] FCPA Resource Guide, *supra* Chapter 1, n.1, at 10 (internal citations omitted).

[9] 15 U.S.C. § 78dd–2(h).

[10] 15 U.S.C. § 78dd–2; *see also* FCPA Resource Guide, *supra* Chapter 1, n.1, at 10–11 (internal citations omitted).

3. PERSONS OTHER THAN ISSUERS OR DOMESTIC CONCERNS

For persons other than issuers or domestic concerns, the anti-bribery provision only applies if, *while in the territory of the United States*, they used the mail or any means or instrumentality of interstate commerce in furtherance of a corrupt payment to a foreign official. Contrast this with the jurisdictional requirement for foreign issuers, for which jurisdiction requires the use of use of interstate commerce but such use does *not* have to occur while being within the territory of the United States. This is logical because issuers (whether foreign or domestic) and domestic concerns already have specific U.S. connections. For individuals and entities outside those categories, there needs to be that additional plus factor to trigger jurisdiction.

4. THE ANTI-BRIBERY PROVISIONS AND THE MEANING OF THEIR KEY TERMS

The FCPA's anti-bribery provisions are the statute's most talked-about and most well-known provisions. They prohibit the[11]:

> use of the mails, or any means or instrumentality of interstate commerce corruptly in furtherance of an offer, payment, promise to pay, or authorization of the payment of any money, or offer, gift, promise to give, or

---

[11] 15 U.S.C. § 78dd–1, 2; *see also* 15 U.S.C. § 78dd–1 (containing the same core prohibition but including additional language relating to jurisdiction).

authorization of the giving of anything of value to—

(1) any foreign official for purposes of—

(A) (i) influencing any act or decision of such foreign official in his official capacity, (ii) inducing such foreign official to do or omit to do any act in violation of the lawful duty of such official, or (iii) securing any improper advantage; or

(B) inducing such foreign official to use his influence with a foreign government or instrumentality thereof to affect or influence any act or decision of such government or instrumentality,

in order to assist such [issuer, domestic concern or other person or entity] in obtaining or retaining business for or with, or directing business to, any person;

(2) any foreign political party or official thereof or any candidate for foreign political office for purposes of—

(A) (i) influencing any act or decision of such party, official, or candidate in its or his official capacity, (ii) inducing such party, official, or candidate to do or omit to do an act in violation of the lawful duty of such party, official, or candidate, or (iii) securing any improper advantage; or

(B) inducing such party, official, or candidate to use its or his influence with a foreign government or instrumentality thereof to affect or influence any act or decision of such government or instrumentality,

in order to assist such [issuer, domestic concern or other person or entity] in obtaining or retaining business for or with, or directing business to, any person; or

(3) any person, while knowing that all or a portion of such money or thing of value will be offered, given, or promised, directly or indirectly, to any foreign official, to any foreign political party or official thereof, or to any candidate for foreign political office, for purposes of—

(A) (i) influencing any act or decision of such foreign official, political party, party official, or candidate in his or its official capacity, (ii) inducing such foreign official, political party, party official, or candidate to do or to omit to do any act in violation of the lawful duty of such foreign official, political party, party official, or candidate, or (iii) securing any improper advantage; or

(B) inducing such foreign official, political party, party official, or candidate to use his or its influence with a foreign government or instrumentality thereof to affect or influence any act or decision of such government or instrumentality, in order to assist such [issuer, domestic concern or other person or entity] in obtaining or retaining business for or with, or directing business to, any person.

We'll explore the meaning of the provisions' key terms in the proceeding sections. The beginning of each section includes a summary of the anti-bribery provisions, with the topic term(s) in bold.

a. "Corrupt" Intent (and a Note on "Willful" Intent)

Anti-Bribery Provisions Summary: *The anti-bribery provisions prohibit the* ***corrupt*** *offer, payment, promise to pay, or authorization of the payment of anything of value to any person, while knowing that all or a portion of such money or thing of value will be offered, given, or promised, directly or indirectly, to any foreign official, for the purpose of obtaining or retaining business.*

To run afoul of the anti-bribery provisions, an offer, payment, promise to pay or authorization of payment must be made with a corrupt intent. The FCPA does not define the term "corrupt". However, the SEC and the DOJ have clarified that it has the same meaning in the FCPA as in the domestic bribery statute, which is embodied at 18 U.S.C. § 201.[12] In support of their interpretation, the SEC and DOJ have referenced House of Representatives and Senate Reports dating from the FCPA's enactment.[13] In sum, the person offering a benefit has a corrupt intent *if* they are offering that benefit

---

[12] FCPA Resource Guide, *supra* Chapter 1, n.1, at 13, 106 nn.74–75.

[13] *Id.*

with the intent to improperly or wrongly influence the recipient.

House Report No. 95–640 states that, in order to be corrupt, the offer must be made with the intent to induce the recipient to misuse his or her official position—"for example, wrongfully to direct business to the payor or his client, or obtain preferential legislation or regulations, or to induce a foreign official to fail to perform an official function."[14] Senate Report No. 95–114 echoes this language and adds that the term corruptly "connotes an evil motive or purpose."[15] As the Second Circuit phrased it in *U.S. v. Kozeny*, "[a] person acts corruptly if he acts voluntarily and intentionally, with an improper motive of accomplishing either an unlawful result or a lawful result by some unlawful method or means. The term 'corruptly' is intended to connote that the offer, payment, and promise was intended to influence an official to misuse his official position."[16]

The House and Senate Reports also clarify a further important point relating to the requisite corrupt intent—if the intent is corrupt, then the offer, promise of payment, or authorization of payment is enough for potential liability *even if* the attempted bribe fails. House Report 95–640 states that, "[a]s in 18 U.S.C. 201(b), the word 'corruptly indicates an

---

[14] H.R. REP. NO. 95–640, *supra* Chapter 1, n.5, at 6.

[15] S. REP. NO. 95–114, *supra* Chapter 1, n.6, at 10.

[16] *United States v. Kozeny*, 667 F.3d 122, 135 (2d Cir. 2011). The DOJ has approvingly quoted this definition. *DOJ Opinion Procedure Release No. 22-1* (Jan. 21, 2022), https://www.justice.gov/criminal-fraud/page/file/1466596/download.

intent or desire to wrongfully influence the recipient. It does *not* require that the act [be] fully consummated or succeed in producing the desired outcome."[17] The FCPA Resource Guide similarly explains that "[b]y focusing on intent, the FCPA does not require that a corrupt act succeed in its purpose. Nor must the foreign official actually solicit, accept, or receive the corrupt payment for the bribe payor to be liable."[18] As we'll address in Chapter 5 on AB&C Compliance programs, the fact that *potential liability can arise at the time an offer is made* is the main reason that AB&C Compliance programs require certain conduct and transactions to be "pre-approved"—meaning reviewed and approved prior to an offer being extended.

As explained, corrupt intent is required for liability under the anti-bribery provisions of the FCPA. Assuming the other required elements are present, that corrupt intent is sufficient for both civil and criminal liability for corporate defendants and for civil liability for individual defendants. However, for an individual defendant to be held criminally liable under the FCPA, he or she must act "willfully."[19] The FCPA does not define the term "willfully". However, the SEC and DOJ have explained that to act willfully means to act voluntarily and with a bad purpose.[20]

---

[17] H.R. REP. NO. 95–640, *supra* Chapter 1, n.5, at 7.

[18] FCPA Resource Guide, *supra* Chapter 1, n.1, at 13 (internal citations omitted).

[19] *Id. citing* 15 U.S.C. §§ 78dd–2(g)(2)(A), 78dd–3(e)(2)(A), 78ff(c)(2)(A).

[20] FCPA Resource Guide, *supra* Chapter 1, n.1, at 13, *citing Bryan v. United States*, 524 U.S. 184, 191–92; *see also United*

The individual must act with the knowledge that their conduct is unlawful. General knowledge that the conduct is unlawful is sufficient—the individual does not need to be specifically aware of the FCPA or that their conduct is violating the FCPA.[21]

In the previous sections, we explained the FCPA's requisite intent for an offer, payment, promise to pay or authorization of payment and that the requisite intent is enough for liability even if the offered benefit is not actually accepted. The FCPA is what is sometimes referred to as a "supply-side" statute because the anti-bribery provisions only address the conduct of the person offering the bribe rather than also addressing the conduct of the person who receives it. But then what of foreign official bribe recipients and their ill-gotten gains? So far there is no comprehensive solution to this problem. Foreign official bribe recipients are sometimes charged with other crimes such as money laundering in connection with their receipt of the bribes. In 2022, the United States also created the Kleptocracy Asset Recovery Rewards Program, which was designed to target and recover the proceeds of foreign official corruption that had been laundered through the United States. However, that program lapsed in January 2024.[22]

States v. Kay, 513 F.3d 432, 446–51 (5th Cir. 2007) (discussing *Bryan* and the use of the term "willfully" in the FCPA).

[21] *Id.* at 13–14; *United States v. Kay*, 513 F.3d at 447–48.

[22] *Kleptocracy Asset Recovery Rewards Program*, U.S. DEP'T OF THE TREASURY, https://home.treasury.gov/about/offices/terrorism-and-financial-intelligence/terrorist-financing-and-financial-crimes/kleptocracy-asset-recovery-rewards-program#:~:

b. "Anything of Value"

Anti-Bribery Provisions Summary: *The anti-bribery provisions prohibit the corrupt offer, payment, promise to pay, or authorization of the payment of* ***anything of value*** *to any person, while knowing that all or a portion of such money or thing of value will be offered, given, or promised, directly or indirectly, to any foreign official, for the purpose of obtaining or retaining business.*

The term "anything of value" is not defined in the FCPA. However, that term has been part of a number of U.S. federal criminal statutes over the years, including—as with the term "corrupt"—the domestic bribery statute. The SEC and DOJ have noted with approval that the term, as interpreted in the domestic bribery statute, "has been broadly construed to include tangible and intangible benefits."[23]

From a practice perspective, the term "anything of value" is understood to have its apparent meaning—i.e., literally anything that is of value to the person to whom it is offered. When considering the topic of bribes, people often visualize the proverbial bag of cash. While cash is of course sometimes used as a bribe, bribery schemes are often much more nuanced. As we'll explore in Chapter 6 on AB&C Compliance programs, bribes can take the form of offers of travel

text=Congressëstablished%20the%20KleptocracyÄsset,and%20 feasible'%20return%20those%20stolen.

[23] FCPA Resource Guide, *supra* Chapter 1, n.1, at 106 n.86 (internal citations omitted).

and accommodation, employment opportunities, meals, tickets to sporting or entertainment events, charitable donations, and more.

c. "Foreign Official"

Anti-Bribery Provisions Summary: *The anti-bribery provisions prohibit the corrupt offer, payment, promise to pay, or authorization of the payment of anything of value to any person, while knowing that all or a portion of such money or thing of value will be offered, given, or promised, directly or indirectly, to any* ***foreign official****, for the purpose of obtaining or retaining business.*

In so many ways, understanding the meaning of the term "foreign official" is the key to understanding the FCPA's anti-bribery provisions. If there's no offer of a benefit, whether directly or indirectly, to a foreign official then there's no violation of the anti-bribery provisions. The FCPA defines "foreign official" as[24]:

> any officer or employee of a foreign government or any department, agency, or instrumentality thereof, or of a public international organization, or any person acting in an official capacity for or on behalf of any such government or department, agency, or instrumentality, or for or on behalf of any such public international organization.

[24] 15 U.S.C. §§ 78dd–1(f)(1)(A), 78dd–2(h)(2)(A), 78dd–3(f)(2)(A).

The FCPA's definition of foreign official basically breaks down into three categories:

(1) Direct government employees

(2) Employees of public international organizations

(3) Employees of a department, agency, or instrumentality of a foreign government

and any persons acting for or on behalf of any of the above. Note the use of the term "employees". The anti-bribery provisions address payments to individual foreign officials—not to foreign governments or foreign agencies. For example, later in this book we'll look at the *AGCO* enforcement action, which involved improper payments to a government rather than a foreign official and, as a such, involved violations of the FCPA's accounting provisions but not its applicable anti-bribery provision.

Let's consider each of the three foreign official categories.

(1) Direct Government Employees

It is generally clear whether a person is a direct government employee. For example, a direct government employee might work for a country's Ministry of Finance, Department of Labor, etc.

(2) Employees of Public International Organizations

A "public international organization" is "(i) an organization that has been so designated by

Executive order pursuant to section 288 of title 22; or (ii) any other international organization that is designated by the President by Executive order for the purposes of [the FCPA's anti-bribery provisions]. . ."[25] Examples of public international organizations include the United Nations, the World Bank, the OECD, the International Monetary Fund, the Organization of American States, and others.

(3) Employees of a Department, Agency, or Instrumentality of a Foreign Government

The FCPA does not define department, agency, or instrumentality. It is generally clear whether an entity is government department or agency (e.g., Ministry of the Environment, Department of Defense, Social Services Agency, etc.) However, it is less apparent whether an entity constitutes an instrumentality of a foreign government. When the term "instrumentality" is mentioned in this context, we should be thinking of what are often referred to as "SOEs"—state owned (or controlled) entities. Many foreign governments operate in part through SOEs, particularly in areas like aerospace and defense, manufacturing, banking and finance, healthcare and life sciences, energy and extractive industries, telecommunications, and transportation. By including employees of agencies and instrumentalities within the definition of foreign official, the FCPA accounts for this reality. Indeed, in a significant number of FCPA actions, the foreign

---

[25] 15 U.S.C. §§ 78dd–1(f)(1)(B), 78dd–2(h)(2)(B), 78dd–3(f)(2)(A)(i), (ii).

official at issue is an employee of an SOE.[26] However, if the FCPA does not define "instrumentality," then how do we know what a state-owned or controlled entity is, such that its officers, employees, and representatives are "foreign officials" for FCPA purposes? In 2014, the 11th Circuit considered this question in *United States v. Esquenazi* and specific guidance from its opinion was later incorporated in the FCPA Resource Guide.[27] As the SEC and DOJ have noted, "[w]hether a particular entity constitutes an 'instrumentality' under the FCPA requires a fact-specific analysis of an entity's ownership, control, status and function."[28]

Based on *Esquenazi* and SEC and DOJ advice as expressed in the FCPA Resource Guide, many organizations bifurcate the analysis of whether an entity should be considered state-owned or controlled (and therefore whether individuals who work for or on behalf of that entity should be considered foreign officials). As a practical matter, organizations may divide the analysis into two prongs—(1) ownership; and (2) control.

Ownership

First, consider an entity's ownership. If an entity is owned by a foreign government, then anyone who

---

26 FCPA Resource Guide, *supra* Chapter 1, n.1, at 20.

27 *United States v. Esquenazi*, 752 F.3d 912 (11th Cir. 2014); FCPA Resource Guide, *supra* Chapter 1, n.1 at 20–21.

28 FCPA Resource Guide, *supra* Chapter 1, n.1, at 20, 108 n.119 ("To date, consistent with the approach taken by the DOJ and SEC, all district courts that have considered this issue have concluded that it is an issue of fact for a jury to decide.")

works for or on behalf of that entity, regardless of their seniority level, should be considered a foreign official for purposes of the FCPA's anti-bribery provisions. However, what does it mean for an entity to be owned by a foreign government? Does it mean *any* percentage of foreign government ownership, a majority ownership, 100 percent ownership?

The SEC and the DOJ have not prescribed a specific percentage of government ownership at which an entity should be presumptively considered a government instrumentality. Deciding that percentage is a risk-based decision that falls to an organization's legal and compliance functions. For example, an organization may define "ownership" in the instrumentality context as follows:

- Ownership: any entity in which a foreign government owns a [35%] or greater interest should presumptively be treated as government-owned and therefore an instrumentality of the government. Consequently, anyone who works for or on behalf of that entity, regardless of their seniority level, should be considered a foreign official for purposes of the FCPA's anti-bribery provisions.

In our sample definition, the organization has chosen to use a 35% threshold for government ownership. So, if the organization is dealing with an entity that is 40% government owned then it knows that anyone who works for or on behalf of that entity should be considered a foreign official pursuant to that organization's policy. However, what happens if an organization is dealing with an entity that is 32% owned by a foreign government? Then the organization should look at the second prong of the analysis—control.

Control

If the level of foreign government ownership is below the organization's specified percentage, then the organization should look at whether the foreign government is in a position to exert influence over that entity such that it is effectively state-controlled. For example, an organization may define "control" in the instrumentality context as follows:

- Control: if an entity has foreign government ownership of less than [35%] then thought should be given to whether there are nevertheless indicia of government control such that the entity should be considered an instrumentality of the government. Consider the following non-exhaustive list of factors:
  - Whether the government can hire and fire the entity's principals
  - The extent to which the entity's profits (if any) go directly to the government
  - The extent to which the government subsidizes the costs associated with the entity providing services
  - Whether the entity has a monopoly over the function it exists to carry out

- Whether the entity provides services to the public at large
- Whether the government and the public of the foreign country generally perceive the entity to be performing a public function
- Whether the entity performs a function that the government treats as its own.
- How long any of the above factors have existed

In this type of situation there is often no clear-cut answer as to whether an entity is an instrumentality of a foreign government. There is no set government ownership percentage threshold that must be used and the "control" analysis leaves room for interpretation. Reasonable minds could differ on the ultimate decision of whether the control factors are such that, when combined with the ownership information, the entity should be considered an instrumentality of a foreign government. The important thing is that the analysis is conducted according to the organization's written policies and procedures and that the analysis and conclusion is documented. Even if the organization decides that an individual is not a foreign official and the DOJ or SEC ultimately disagrees, the process that the organization carried out to reach its conclusion can provide significant protection from any potential enforcement consequences.

It's important to remember that once an entity is considered state-owned or controlled, then any person who works for or on behalf of that entity, regardless of their seniority level, must be considered a foreign official for purposes of the FCPA's anti-bribery provisions. Recall the "any officer or employee" language in the FCPA's foreign official definition. "[T]he FCPA broadly applies to corrupt payments to 'any' officer or employee of a foreign government and to those acting on the foreign government's behalf. The FCPA thus covers corrupt payments to low-ranking employees and high-level officials alike."[29] This should be emphasized in AB&C policies and training. Employees may not consider an individual at an SOE to be a foreign official if the individual is not very senior. That inclination, while perhaps natural, is incorrect.

The SEC and the DOJ themselves essentially used this two-prong ownership/control approach even before the *Esquenazi* case.[30] In the FCPA Resource Guide, the SEC and the DOJ noted that "as a practical matter, an entity is unlikely to qualify as an instrumentality if a government does not own or control a majority of its shares."[31] However, the agencies noted that that there are circumstances in which an entity would qualify as an instrumentality even without majority government ownership.[32]

---

29 *Id.* at 19 (internal citations omitted).

30 *Id.* at 20 ("DOJ and SEC have pursued cases involving instrumentalities since the time of the FCPA's enactment and have long used an analysis of ownership, control, status, and function to determine whether a particular entity is an agency or instrumentality of a foreign government.")

31 *Id.* at 21.

32 *Id.*

As an enforcement example, the agencies referred to a case where a French issuer's three subsidiaries were convicted of paying bribes to employees of a Malaysian telecom company that was 43% owned by Malaysia's Ministry of Finance.[33] The agencies noted that, notwithstanding the government's minority ownership of the company, there were factors that weighed in favor of considering the telecom company to be an instrumentality of the Malaysian government. Namely, Malaysia's Ministry of Finance was a " 'special shareholder', had veto power over all major expenditures, and controlled important operational decisions."[34] In addition, most senior officers of the telecom were political appointees.[35] As a result of combination of these control factors with the government's minority ownership, the agencies concluded that "the company was an instrumentality of the Malaysian government as the government [ ] had substantial control over the company."[36] In Chapter 6 we'll further explore how organizations define and identify foreign officials in practice.

d. "Directly or Indirectly" and "Knowing"

Anti-Bribery Provisions Summary: *The anti-bribery provisions prohibit the corrupt offer, payment, promise to pay, or authorization of the payment of anything of value to any person, while* ***knowing*** *that all or a portion of such money or thing of value will be*

---

[33] *Id.*

[34] FCPA Resource Guide, *supra* Chapter 1, n.1, at 21.

[35] *Id.*

[36] *Id.*

*offered, given, or promised, **directly or indirectly**, to any foreign official, for the purpose of obtaining or retaining business.*

As reflected above, the FCPA's anti-bribery provisions prohibit not only direct payments to a foreign official to obtain or retain business but also payments to "any person" (such as a third party) "while knowing that all or a portion of such money or thing of value" will be provided to a foreign official.[37] This language is intended to catch bribes that are paid to foreign officials through third-party intermediaries. It's common for organizations that are operating in a foreign country to retain local individuals or entities to assist with services in that country. However, this comes with the risk that these third parties may, with or without the organization's knowledge, bribe a foreign official on the organization's behalf.

In drafting the FCPA, Congress anticipated this risk and defined "knowing" to prevent companies from avoiding liability by paying bribes through a third party. Congress made it clear that the FCPA is intended to impose liability not just on those with actual knowledge of wrongdoing, but on those who purposely avoid having actual knowledge.[38] In

---

[37] 15 U.S.C. §§ 78dd–1(a)(3), 78dd–2(a)(3), 78dd–3(a)(3).

[38] FCPA Resource Guide, *supra* Chapter 1, n.1, at 23; *Omnibus Trade and Competitiveness Act of 1988*, Conference Report, 100th Congress, 2d Session, Report 100–576 at 920 (Apr. 20, 1988) [hereinafter H.R. REP. NO. 100–576], https://www.finance.senate.gov/imo/media/doc/crpt100-576.pdf.

keeping with that intention, the FCPA states that a person's state of mind is "knowing" with respect to conduct, a circumstance, or a result if that person "is aware that [they are] engaging in such conduct, that such circumstance exists, or that such result is substantially certain to occur; or has a firm belief that such circumstance exists or that such result is substantially certain to occur."[39] "When knowledge of the existence of a particular circumstance is required for an offense, such knowledge is established if a person is aware of a high probability of the existence of such circumstance, unless the person actually believes that such circumstance does not exist."[40]

A significant portion of FCPA enforcement actions involve bribes that are paid through third-party intermediaries. As a result, many organizations now have extensive third-party due diligence and vetting programs to ensure that they have a thorough knowledge of the third parties with whom they are dealing and that they properly manage those relationships. We'll address the bribery and

---

> [T]he so-called 'head-in-the-sand' problem—variously described in the pertinent authorities as 'conscious disregard,' 'willful blindness' or 'deliberate ignorance'—should be covered so that management officials could not take refuge from the Act's prohibitions by their unwarranted obliviousness to any action (or inaction), language or other 'signaling device' that should reasonably alert them of the 'high probability' of an FCPA violation.

[39] 15 U.S.C. §§ 78dd–1(f)(2)(A), 78dd–2(h)(3)(A), 78dd–3(f)(3)(A).

[40] 15 U.S.C. §§ 78dd–1(f)(2)(B), 78dd–2(h)(3)(B), 78dd–3(f)(3)(B).

corruption-related risks of third-party relationships and how to mitigate those risks in Chapter 6.

e. "Obtaining or Retaining Business"

Anti-Bribery Provisions Summary: *The anti-bribery provisions prohibit the corrupt offer, payment, promise to pay, or authorization of the payment of anything of value to any person, while knowing that all or a portion of such money or thing of value will be offered, given, or promised, directly or indirectly, to any foreign official, for the purpose of* ***obtaining or retaining business****.*

What does it mean to obtain or retain business? It certainly includes the classic example of a payment to a foreign official to secure a foreign government contract. Indeed, case law and the FCPA Resource Guide have clarified that its meaning is much broader than that classic example. In fact, obtaining or retaining business should also be understood to include obtaining an *advantage* in business.

To provide some history on this, the U.S. Court of Appeals for the Fifth Circuit in *U.S. v. Kay* considered the issue of whether payments to foreign officials to avoid paying customs duties and to lower sales taxes could satisfy the "obtaining or retaining business" element of the anti-bribery provisions.[41] The Fifth Circuit determined that the "obtaining or retaining business" language was ambiguous and analyzed the legislative history.

---

41 *United States v. Kay*, 359 F.3d 738 (5th Cir. 2004).

The Fifth Circuit's view was that Congress intended to prohibit a much broader range of payments than only those directly linked with obtaining or retaining a contract and that conduct that provided an advantage or assisted in obtaining or retaining business could satisfy that element. The Fifth Circuit held "that Congress intended for the FCPA to apply broadly to payments intended to assist the payor, either directly or indirectly, in obtaining or retaining business for some person, and that bribes paid to foreign tax officials to secure illegally reduced customs and tax liability constitute a type of payment that can fall within this broad coverage."[42] In the FCPA Resource Guide, the DOJ and SEC confirmed their agreement with the Fifth Circuit that the phrase "obtaining or retaining business" also includes gaining a business advantage.

With that clarification in mind, some examples of conduct that could fall within the meaning of "obtaining or retaining business" are[43]:

- Winning a contract
- Influencing the procurement process
- Evading taxes or penalties
- Obtaining exceptions to regulations
- Avoiding contract termination

---

[42] FCPA Resource Guide, *supra* Chapter 1, n.1, at 12 *quoting United States v. Kay*, 359 F.3d at 749–55 (5th Cir. 2004).

[43] *Id.*

- Influencing the adjudication of lawsuits or enforcement penalties

5. SECONDARY LIABILITY THEORIES FOR VIOLATIONS OF THE ANTI-BRIBERY PROVISIONS

In addition to primary liability for violating the anti-bribery provisions, organizations and individuals can also be held secondarily liable for aiding a direct violation of those provisions. This is true in both the criminal and civil contexts.

a. Criminal: Aiding and Abetting and Conspiracy

Under the federal aiding and abetting statute, individuals or companies that aid or abet a crime, including a violation of the FCPA's anti-bribery provisions, are guilty as if they had directly committed the crime themselves.[44] However, aiding and abetting is not an independent crime—there must be an underlying FCPA violation.[45]

---

[44] 18 U.S.C. § 2(a) states that "[w]hoever commits an offense against the United States or aids, abets, counsels, commands, induces or procures its commission, is punishable as a principal." 18 U.S.C. § 2(b) states that "[w]hoever willfully causes an act to be done which if directly performed by him or another would be an offense against the United States, is punishable as a principal."

[45] FCPA Resource Guide, *supra* Chapter 1, n.1, at 35, 113 n.204 *citing* H.R. REP. NO. 95–640 at 8 ("The concepts of aiding and abetting and joint participation would apply to a violation under [the FCPA] in the same manner in which those concepts have always applied in both SEC civil actions and in implied private actions brought under the securities laws generally.")

With respect to conspiracy to violate the FCPA's anti-bribery provisions, it's instructive to read an actual plea agreement to understand the elements of that offense. It's rare for a corporation to plead guilty in a FCPA matter—it's much more common for corporate FCPA matters to be resolved via consensual resolutions. However, in 2022, the commodity trading and producing company Glencore International AG ("Glencore") pled guilty to conspiracy to violate the FCPA.[46] The "essential elements" of the offense of conspiracy to violate the FCPA as laid out in the *Glencore* Plea Agreement are as follows[47]:

a. An unlawful agreement between two or more individuals to violate the FCPA existed; specifically, as a person or entity, while in the territory of the United States, to make use of the mails and means and instrumentalities of interstate commerce corruptly in furtherance of an offer, payment, promise to pay, and authorization of the payment of any money, offer, gift, promise to give, and authorization of the giving of anything of value, to a foreign official, and to a person, while knowing that

---

[46] *Glencore Entered Guilty Pleas to Foreign Bribery and Market Manipulation Conspiracies*, U.S. ATT'Y OFF., S.D.N.Y. (May 24, 2022), https://www.justice.gov/usao-sdny/pr/glencore-entered-guilty-pleas-foreign-bribery-and-market-manipulation-conspiracies.

[47] *United States v. Glencore International A.G., Plea Agreement*, U.S. DOJ, S.D.N.Y., at 3–4, (May 24, 2022), https://www.justice.gov/d9/press-releases/attachments/2022/05/24/u.s._v._glencore_international_a.g._plea_agreement.pdf.

all or a portion of such money and thing of value would be and had been offered, given, and promised to a foreign official, for purposes of: (i) influencing acts and decisions of such foreign official in his or her official capacity; (ii) inducing such foreign official to do and omit to do acts in violation of the lawful duty of such official; (iii) securing an improper advantage; and (iv) inducing such foreign official to use his or her influence with a foreign government and agencies and instrumentalities thereof to affect and influence acts and decisions of such government and agencies and instrumentalities, in order to assist the Defendant and its co-conspirators in obtaining and retaining business for and with, and directing business to, any person;

b. The Defendant knowingly and willfully joined that conspiracy;

c. One of the members of the conspiracy knowingly committed or caused to be committed, in the Southern District of New York or elsewhere in the United States, at least one of the overt acts charged in the Information; and

d. The overt acts were committed to further some objective of the conspiracy.

i. Practice Question

What if the individual or organization that conspired to violate the FCPA or aided and abetted the FCPA violation does not fall within a category that is capable of committing a substantive FCPA violation (i.e., is not a person or entity within the scope of the anti-bribery provisions)? Can such an individual or organization still be held liable for conspiracy or aiding and abetting?

The FCPA Resource Guide states that, pursuant to principles of conspiracy liability, individuals and entities may be liable for conspiracy to violate the FCPA, even if they are not (or could not) be independently charged with a substantive FCPA violation.[48] However, the FCPA Resource Guide also references contrary authority. For now, the answer may depend in part on where a case is brought. In *United States v. Hoskins*, the Second Circuit specifically considered the question of whether individuals not directly covered by the FCPA's anti-bribery provisions could still be found guilty of aiding and abetting a violation of the anti-bribery provisions or conspiring to violate the anti-bribery provisions and determined that they could not.[49] However, other courts may disagree. The FCPA Resource Guide cites

---

[48] FCPA Resource Guide, *supra* Chapter 1, n.1, at 35.

[49] *United States v. Hoskins*, 902 F.3d 69, 76–97 (2d Cir. 2018). However, even if the individual, as in the *Hoskins* case, does not himself or herself fall within the three categories of persons and entities covered by the anti-bribery provisions, there is also the possibility that such person could be found culpable because they were acting as an agent of a person or entity in one of the three covered categories.

United States v. Firtash for the proposition, contrary to the *Hoskins* holding, that defendants *can* be held criminally liable for conspiracy to violate the FCPA even if they do not "belong to the class of individuals capable of committing a substantive FCPA violation."[50]

b. Civil: Aiding and Abetting and Causing

In the civil context, individuals and organizations can be held liable for aiding and abetting violations of the anti-bribery provisions if they "knowingly or recklessly provide[ ] substantial assistance to [the primary violator]".[51] In the administrative proceeding context, individuals and organizations may also be held liable for causing FCPA violations. Pursuant to Section 21C(a) of the Exchange Act, the SEC may impose a cease-and-desist order through the SEC's administrative proceedings upon any person that is, was, or would be a cause of the primary violation due to an act or omission that the person knew or should have known would contribute to the primary violation.[52]

---

50 FCPA Resource Guide, *supra* Chapter 1, n.1, at 36, 113 n.209 *quoting United States v. Firtash*, 392 F.Supp. 3d 872, 889 (N.D. Ill. 2019) ("defendants could be criminally liable for conspiracy to violate the FCPA anti-bribery provisions, and aiding and abetting a violation, even though they do not 'belong to the class of individuals capable of committing a substantive FCPA violation.").

51 *Id.* at 36, 113 n.210 *quoting* 15 U.S.C. § 78t(e).

52 *Id.* at 36, 113 n.211 *citing* 15 U.S.C. § 78u–3(a).

6. STATUTES OF LIMITATION

The FCPA does not specify a statute of limitations, so the general statutes of limitation periods apply.[53] These periods differ between criminal and civil cases and we'll address each in turn.

a. Criminal Cases

The five-year statute of limitations set out in 18 U.S.C. § 3282 applies to substantive violations of the anti-bribery provisions.[54] Violations of the accounting provisions are defined as "securities fraud offense[s]" under 18 U.S.C. § 3301 and have a six-year statute of limitations period.[55]

As a practical matter, there is some flexibility on these statutes of limitation in cases involving conspiracy. In such cases, the government generally only needs to prove that one act in furtherance of the conspiracy occurred during the limitations period.[56] This has the effect of enabling the government to prosecute bribes that were paid or accounting violations that occurred more than five or six years, respectively, before charges were filed.[57]

The applicable limitations period may also be extended. There are at least a couple of ways that this could happen. First, organizations or individuals may enter into a tolling agreement that voluntarily

---

53 *Id.* at 36.

54 *Id.* at 36, 113 n.213 *citing* 18 U.S.C. § 3282(a).

55 *Id. quoting* 18 U.S.C. § 3301(a), (b).

56 FCPA Resource Guide, *supra* Chapter 1, n.1, at 37.

57 *Id.*

extends the statute of limitations period. This commonly happens when an organization is in cooperating with the DOJ, and is in the process of conducting an investigation and producing responsive information. Second, the DOJ may request a court order suspending the statute of limitations period in a criminal case for up to three years in order to obtain evidence from foreign countries.[58]

b. Civil Cases

There is a five-year statute of limitations for civil FCPA cases brought by the SEC where the SEC is seeking civil penalties.[59] That statute of limitations is set by 28 U.S.C. § 2462, which provides for the five-year limitation on any "suit or proceeding for the enforcement of any civil fine, penalty or forfeiture."[60] However, that five-year statute of limitations does not prevent the SEC from seeking equitable remedies for conduct that occurred before the five-year period.

As with criminal cases, the statute of limitations may also be voluntarily extended in civil cases pursuant to a tolling agreement. In addition, in cases against individuals who are not U.S. residents, the statute of limitations is tolled for any period when the defendants are not "found within the United States in order that proper service may be made thereon."[61]

---

58 *Id. citing* 18 U.S.C. § 3292.

59 *Id. citing* 28 U.S.C. § 2462.

60 *Id. quoting* 28 U.S.C. § 2462.

61 *Id. quoting* 28 U.S.C. § 2462.

7. THE FACILITATION PAYMENTS EXCEPTION

The anti-bribery provisions contain only one exception for facilitation payments. The exception, officially titled "[e]xception for routine governmental action," states that the anti-bribery prohibitions do not apply to "any facilitating or expediting payment to a foreign official, political party, or party official the purpose of which is to expedite or to secure the performance of a routine governmental action by a foreign official, political party, or party official."[62]

The definition of "routine governmental action" is key to understanding and applying this exception. "Routine governmental action" means "*only* an action which is ordinarily and commonly performed by a foreign official in"[63]—

(i) obtaining permits, licenses, or other official documents to qualify a person to do business in a foreign country;

(ii) processing governmental papers, such as visas and work orders;

(iii) providing police protection, mail pick-up and delivery, or scheduling inspections associated with contract performance or inspections related to transit of good across country;

---

[62] 15 U.S.C. §§ 78dd–1(b), 78dd–2(b), 78dd–3(b).

[63] 15 U.S.C. §§ 78dd–1(f)(3)(A), 78dd–2(h)(4)(A), 78dd–3(f)(4)(A) (emphasis added).

(iv) providing phone service, power and water supply, loading and unloading cargo, or protecting perishable products or commodities from deterioration; or

(v) actions of a similar nature.

"Routine governmental actions" do not include any acts by a foreign official that are discretionary. Specifically, they do not include "any decision by a foreign official whether, or on what terms, to award new business to or to continue business with a particular party, or any action taken by a foreign official involved in the decision-making process to encourage a decision to award new business or to continue business with a particular party.[64]

There is no monetary threshold above which a payment will be considered a bribe rather than a facilitation payment. The definition focuses on the reason for the payment rather than its amount. However, as a practical matter, the higher the payment is, the less likely it is to be considered a facilitation payment.

a. Hypothetical

A cargo ship owned by a U.S. issuer pulls into a foreign port. The captain disembarks with all of the required paperwork for unloading the cargo. A local government official who is charged with administration of the port is standing on the dock. He takes the paperwork and notes that it is complete but

[64] 15 U.S.C. §§ 78dd–1(f)(3)(A), 78dd–2(h)(4)(B), 78dd–3(f)(4)(B).

refuses to allow the ship to unload unless the Captain "pays him for his trouble." If the Captain pays the official, would that payment fall within the facilitation payments exception?

Yes, it likely would. The official was performing a routine, non-discretionary governmental action within the scope of his role. In that case, absent other facts, the Captain would not have any corrupt intent in making the requested payment. He would merely be paying the foreign official to carry out the duty that the foreign official was required to undertake as part of his job.

However, what if the cargo ship's required paperwork isn't complete and the Captain offers a payment to "push this through" or "move things along"? Would this payment still be considered a facilitation payment? No, the Captain's payment is now more likely to be considered a bribe than a facilitation payment. Why—what has changed? The Captain's intent may have changed. The vessel's paperwork is incomplete and the Captain may essentially be offering to pay the foreign official to look the other way and allow the vessel to unload anyway. If that is the case, then the Captain would be paying the foreign official to violate the duties of that official's role, moving the offer squarely into bribery territory.

b. Justification and Rationale for the Facilitation Payments Exception

It's often questioned why the FCPA even includes an exception for facilitation payments. A justification for excluding facilitation payments from the anti-bribery provisions lies in the absence of corrupt intent. Recall the crux of the anti-bribery prohibitions—the corrupt offer or payment of money or anything of value to a foreign official to obtain or retain business. In the case of true facilitation payments, there will be no corrupt intent on the part of the offeror or payor. The offeror is simply making a payment to get a foreign official to undertake a routine, non-discretionary action that is part of the official's legitimate role. The foreign official almost certainly has corrupt intent in requesting and accepting the payment. However, as previously explained, the FCPA is not focused on the foreign official's intent or conduct. The FCPA is focused solely on the intent and conduct of the person offering or paying the bribe.

This is not to say that the United States supports the making of facilitation payments. Rather, from the time that the FCPA was enacted, Congress has consistently taken the position that such payments are disfavored but that it would not be a practical or efficient use of resources to enforce a prohibition against them. Facilitation payments have historically been viewed as a necessary evil rather than a desirable option.

c. The Trend Against Allowing Facilitation Payments

Although it's a statutory exception to the FCPA's anti-bribery provisions, many organizations prohibit facilitation payments as a matter of policy. There are a number of reasons for this. First, the facilitation payments exception is quite narrow.[65] Only very specific and limited conduct will properly fall within this exception. This makes it riskier for organizations to permit facilitation payments because it's likely that some payments will fall outside that limited exception and instead may constitute bribes.

Second, many companies that operate internationally are also subject to other anti-bribery and corruption laws, such as the UKBA, that do not allow facilitation payments. *See* Chapter 4 for an explanation of how the UKBA treats facilitation payments.

Third, from a practical perspective, allowing facilitation payments can muddle an organization's messaging to its employees that the organization has a zero-tolerance approach to bribery and corruption. As the UKBA Guidance notes, creating exceptions for such payments "create[s] artificial distinctions that are difficult to enforce, undermine corporate anti-bribery procedures, confuse anti-bribery communication with employees and other associated persons, perpetuate an existing 'culture' of bribery and have the potential to be abused."[66]

Fourth, even with training, the facilitation payments exception is often misunderstood. One reason for this is that the colloquial understanding of the term "facilitation payment" can be very different than the FCPA meaning of it. Consider this potential

---

65 FCPA Resource Guide, *supra* Chapter 1, n.1, at 25.

66 UKBA Guidance, *supra* Chapter 1, n.2, at 18.

employee statement, "I paid that government official to get it done—I facilitated it. It was a facilitation payment." This of course may or may not be an accurate characterization depending on the facts and circumstances. *Whether a payment is a facilitation payment is a legal conclusion and it is not a determination that should be made independently by employees.*

Finally, facilitation payments are disfavored from compliance and ethical perspectives. Facilitation payments are an exception to the FCPA as a matter of enforcement practicality—not because of a view that they are ethically acceptable. In recent years, industry groups and thought leaders in the ethics and compliance space have taken a strong position opposing facilitation payments. For example, the OECD Working Group on Bribery recommends that all countries encourage companies to prohibit or discourage facilitation payments. Referring to their "corrosive effect .... particularly on sustainable economic development and the rule of law," the Working Group asked in its 2021 OECD Recommendation that member countries[67]:

i. [U]ndertake to periodically review their policies and approach on small facilitation payments in order to effectively combat the phenomenon;

ii. [E]ncourage companies to prohibit or discourage the use of small facilitation payments in internal controls, ethics, and

[67] 2021 OECD Recommendation, *supra* Chapter 2, n.29, at 8.

> compliance programmes or measures, recognising that such payments are generally illegal in the countries where they are made and must in all cases be accurately accounted for in such companies' books and financial records.

Transparency International has stated that "[a]ll companies must cease making facilitation payments immediately. Companies must recognise these as bribes and prohibit them."[68] Finally, the Society of Corporate Compliance and Ethics has the following advice for compliance officers who are confronted with the issue of facilitation payments: "Lead, follow or get out of the way does not accurately portray the options available to a compliance professional. It is our job to lead and the handwriting is on the wall. Regardless of the FCPA's tolerance, the only tenable option for a U.S. compliance officer is to advise your company that facilitation payments need to be prohibited."[69]

So, what is the result of this groundswell against facilitation payments? Elimination? Possibly, but not today. As the UKBA Guidance recognizes, effectively confirming the reality that the exception was created

---

[68] *Facilitation Payments*, TRANSPARENCY INT'L, https://www.transparency.org/en/corruptionary/facilitation-payments#:~:text=All%20companies%20must%20cease%20making,on%20their%20anti%2Dcorruption%20programmes.

[69] Ernesto Grijalva, *FCPA Compliance: Don't misread the debate on facilitation payments*, THE COMPLIANCE & ETHICS BLOG, SCCE AND HCCA (Sept. 21, 2020), https://www.complianceandethics.org/fcpa-compliance-dont-misread-the-debate-on-facilitating-payments.

to address, not being able to make facilitation payments may cause practical difficulties for organizations who function in certain areas of the world and certain sectors where these payments are more common. The UKBA Guidance realistically acknowledges that eliminating facilitation payments is a long-term objective that will involve collaboration at various international governmental, private sector, and industry levels[70]:

> The eradication of facilitation payments is recognised at the national and international level as a long term objective that will require economic and social progress and sustained commitment to the rule of law in those parts of the world where the problem is most prevalent. It will also require collaboration between international bodies, governments, the anti-bribery lobby, business representative bodies and sectoral organisations. Businesses themselves also have a role to play . . . through the selection of bribery prevention procedures . . .

Facilitation payments will not be eliminated without collective action. As long as some organizations are willing to make facilitation payments, then the demand for those payments will still exist.

---

[70] UKBA Guidance, *supra* Chapter 1, n.2, at 18.

d. Best Practices for Facilitation Payments

As a best practice, organizations should prohibit facilitation payments. At a minimum, organizations should require that any potential facilitation payments are pre-approved in writing by the General Counsel or a designated member of the Legal department. Where pre-approval is not possible because of the time frame of the request, the AB&C policy should state that the person who paid the facilitation payment should promptly contact Legal with the details of the payment. If Legal determines that the payment does not meet the criteria for a facilitation payment (and therefore was likely a bribe) then Legal can work with AB&C Compliance and senior management to determine the next appropriate steps.

i. A Note on the Proper Recording of Facilitation Payments

There may be times where a payment is a facilitation payment under the FCPA but constitutes a bribe under local law. Nevertheless, if an organization makes the payment (which violates local law) that payment still needs to be properly recorded in the organization's books and records. Organizations may be reluctant to properly record a facilitation payment if that payment was not legal under local law in the jurisdiction in which it was made. However, a facilitation payment must be properly recorded to avoid a violation of violation of the FCPA's books and records and internal controls provisions.

The SEC's enforcement action against Triton Energy Corp. focused on the mis-recording of facilitation payments. An Indonesian Triton subsidiary had been making monthly payments of approximately $1,000 to low-level employees of a state-owned oil company in order to ensure the timely processing of monthly crude oil invoices.[71] Seemingly acknowledging that they were facilitation payments, the SEC did not allege that these payments violated the FCPA's anti-bribery provisions.[72] However, the SEC did allege that these payments were falsely documented and recorded and therefore violated the FCPA's books and records and internal controls provisions.[73] Triton consented to an injunction against future violations of the FCPA and was fined $300,000.[74]

e. Common Questions Regarding Facilitation Payments

As referenced in the previous sections, the meaning and application of the facilitation payments exception often causes confusion. Two common topics of consternation are (1) whether the facilitation payments exception applies to cases of extortion or duress; and (2) whether expediting payments to a

---

[71] *Securities and Exchange Commission v. Triton Energy Corp., et al.*, Civil Action No. 1:97 CV 00401 (D.D.C.), Litigation Release No. 15266 (Feb. 27, 1997), https://www.sec.gov/litigation/litreleases/lr15266.txt.

[72] *Id.*

[73] *Id.*

[74] *Id.*

government agency fall within the facilitation payments exception. The answer to both is "NO."

i. Extortion and Duress

Payments made to a foreign official under circumstances of extortion or duress are outside the scope of the FCPA's anti-bribery provisions. The facilitation payments exception would therefore not apply.

When in doubt over whether conduct falls within the scope of any legal provision, always return to the text of the provision itself. In sum, the anti-bribery provisions prohibit the corrupt offer, payment, promise to pay, or authorization of the payment of anything of value (whether directly or indirectly) to a foreign official for the purpose of obtaining or retaining business. The SEC and the DOJ have clarified that situations involving extortion or duress *cannot* give rise to FCPA liability because a payment made in response to a demand for money under the threat of imminent physical harm is, by definition, not being made with the requisite corrupt intent to obtain or retain business.[75] Since the anti-bribery provisions themselves do not apply in situations of extortion or duress, there can be no need for an exception.

Notwithstanding the above, some organizations' AB&C policies incorrectly lump payments that are made under circumstances of extortion or duress together with a potential facilitation payment

---

75 FCPA Resource Guide, *supra* Chapter 1, n.1, at 27–28.

exception. Again, always return to the legal language at issue. The facilitation payment exception de-scopes payments to foreign officials for routine governmental action from the FCPA's anti-bribery provisions. Unless threatening someone with imminent physical harm is somehow a "routine governmental action" that is within the scope of a foreign official's duties, then a payment to avoid such harm is *not* a facilitation payment.[76]

Similarly, the UKBA implicitly recognizes that facilitation payments ("[s]mall bribes paid to facilitate routine [g]overnment action") and payments made under duress fall into two separate categories.[77] Although the UKBA does not permit facilitation payments, the UKBA Guidance recognizes that "there are circumstances in which individuals are left with no alternative but to make payments in order to protect against loss of life, limb or liberty" and that "the common law defence of duress is very likely to be available in such circumstances."[78]

(a) The Distinction Between Extortion and Economic Coercion

Note that there is a distinction between extortion and economic coercion. Simply put, in the case of extortion the potential payor does not have a meaningful opportunity to walk away—rather, they have no choice but to make the payment in exchange

---

[76] *Id.*

[77] UKBA Guidance, *supra* Chapter 1, n.2, at 18–19.

[78] *Id.* at 19.

for their physical safety.[79] However, this is not the case with economic coercion, where the potential payor *does* have a choice whether to make the payment—i.e., the payment is being made to obtain an advantage rather than to avoid the risk of physical harm. The FCPA Resource Guide cites *United States v. Kozeny* for the proposition that, contrary to a defendant who makes a payment under duress, a defendant who claims that a payment was demanded as a price to gain market entry or to obtain a contract "cannot argue that he lacked the intent to bribe the official because he made the conscious decision to pay the official" and "could have turned his back and walked away."[80]

The DOJ confirmed this distinction in its FCPA Opinion Release (the "FCPA Opinion") No. 22–1.[81] In that instance, a domestic concern (the "Requestor") sought an opinion (the "Opinion Request") as to

---

79 FCPA Resource Guide, *supra* Chapter 1, n.1, at 27, 111 n.174 (internal citations omitted).

> In order to establish duress or coercion, a defendant must demonstrate that the defendant was under unlawful, present, immediate, and impending threat of death or serious bodily injury; that the defendant did not negligently or recklessly create a situation where he would be forced to engage in criminal conduct (*e.g.*, had been making payments as part of an ongoing bribery scheme); that the defendant had no reasonable legal alternative to violating the law; and that there was a direct causal relationship between the criminal action and the avoidance of the threatened harm.

80 *Id.* at 28, 112 n.179 *citing United States v. Kozeny*, 582 F.Supp.2d at 540 (internal citations omitted).

81 FCPA Opinion Procedure Release No. 22–1, at 2 (Jan. 21, 2022) [hereinafter FCPA Opinion No. 22–1], https://www.justice.gov/criminal-fraud/page/file/1466596/download.

whether a potential $175,000 payment in connection with getting its vessel and crew released from detention would violate the FCPA's anti-bribery provisions. The basic facts were as follows: The Requestor vessel sought to anchor in international waters while waiting to enter Country B's port for required maintenance and to renew technical maritime certificates. One of the Requestor's shipping agents advised the vessel captain that Country B's ports were full and that the vessel should anchor outside of Country B for two weeks. The shipping agent provided incorrect anchoring coordinates to the vessel captain, which led the vessel to unintentionally anchor in Country A's waters. The Country A Navy intercepted the vessel, confiscated its logbook and certain documents, ordered the crew members and officers to remain onboard, and brought the captain ashore and detained him for questioning. The captain was detained in jail, was not questioned, and was not provided any documentation authorizing his arrest or detention.

Country A Navy's incident report stated that the vessel was in Country A waters in violation of various laws and treaties. In support of its Opinion Request, the Requestor provided documentation and information demonstrating that the captain was suffering at that time from serious medical conditions that would be significantly exacerbated by his detention and that created a significant risk to his life and well-being.

Shortly after the captain and crew were separately detained, a third party purporting to act on behalf of the Country A Navy (the "Third-Party Intermediary") contacted the Requestor and demanded a financial payment to release the captain and to permit the crew and vessel to leave Country A waters. It's unclear from the FCPA Opinion whether the Third-Party Intermediary in fact represented Country A, represented one or more government officials of Country A, or neither of those. The FCPA Opinion states that "[a]lthough the Third-Party Intermediary represented the payment to be an official payment to the government of Country A, the nature of the demand and the manner of payment raised concerns for Requestor that the payment was intended for one or more Country A government officials."[82] The FCPA Opinion does not provide any details as to the nature of the demand or the manner of the requested payment (other than that it was in cash, which of courses raises a red flag) that led the Requestor to harbor these concerns.[83]

After the Third-Party Intermediary's demand, the Requestor then retained an agent (the "Requestor Agent"), with whom the Requestor was previously familiar and on which it had recently conducted due diligence. Together the Requestor and the Requestor Agent took several steps to attempt to resolve the situation, including:

- making multiple requests to the Third-Party Intermediary for documentation stating the charges or fine amount (to ensure that the

---

82 *Id.*

83 *Id.*

requested payment would be made pursuant to a fine or other penalty for a purported legal or regulatory violation);

- seeking assistance from U.S. government agencies to end the captain's detention and to help the vessel and its crew to quickly leave Country A; and
- requesting that the U.S. government agencies from which it sought assistance notify relevant Country A authorities about the detention of the captain, crew, and vessel.

These steps did not resolve the situation. The Third-Party Intermediary then told the Requestor and the Requestor Agent that the Requestor needed to make a cash payment.

The FCPA Opinion concluded that, based on the specific facts provided by the Requestor, the proposed payment would not trigger an enforcement action under the FCPA's anti-bribery provisions because the Requestor would not be making the payment "corruptly" or to "obtain or retain business." Instead, the FCPA Opinion concluded that "the primary reason for the payment was to avoid imminent and potentially serious harm to the captain and the crew of the Requestor vessel."[84] It stated that the Requestor had no ongoing or anticipated business with Country A, that the situation appeared to result from an error based on incorrect advice about where to anchor, and that the Requestor may have

[84] *Id.* at 3.

inadvertently violated Country A (and perhaps other) laws and regulations regarding shipping routes and anchoring locations.[85] The FCPA Opinion concluded that it was this error that resulted in the Third-Party Intermediary's payment demand.[86]

In delivering its conclusion[87], the FCPA Opinion also emphasized transparency. It noted that, rather than attempting to hide the situation, the Requestor communicated with various U.S. government agencies to request assistance. The FCPA Opinion recognized that these actions were in line with the FCPA Resource Guide's recommendation that "[i]f such a situation [of imminent threats to health or safety of its employees] arises, and to ensure the safety of its employees, companies should immediately contact the appropriate U.S. embassy for assistance."[88] It was only after the Requestor's

---

85 *Id.*

86 *Id.*

87 Note that as with all FCPA opinions, FCPA Opinion No. 22–1's analysis and conclusion was limited. *See* FCPA Opinion No. 22–1, *supra* n.81, at 4 (containing the following specific limiting language):

> [T]his Opinion is limited to an analysis of whether the payment at issue would trigger an enforcement action under the FCPA's anti-bribery provisions. Beyond this narrow analysis, the Department offers no view on the permissibility or legality of the payment under any laws, including the laws of Country A. This FCPA Opinion Release has no binding application to any party other than Requestor and can be relied on by Requestor only to the extent that the disclosure of facts and circumstances in its Request and supplemental information is accurate and complete.

88 *Id.* at 3 *quoting* FCPA Resource Guide, *supra* Chapter 1, n.1, at 28.

transparent efforts to resolve the situation failed, that the Requestor considered making the payment and submitted the Opinion Request to do so.[89]

ii. *Expediting Payments to a Foreign Government Agency*

The FCPA's anti-bribery provisions apply to offers and payments to foreign officials themselves—not to foreign government agencies. Payments that are made directly to a foreign government agency itself, rather than to an individual foreign official, are outside the scope of the anti-bribery provisions and therefore the facilitation payment exception is neither necessary nor relevant.

8. AFFIRMATIVE DEFENSES

The FCPA's anti-bribery provisions have two affirmative defenses, both of which were added in 1988—one based on the premise that the offer or payment at issue was legal under local law and the other based on the premise that the offer or payment was a reasonable and bona fide promotional expense. As affirmative defenses, both would be the defendant's burden to prove. We'll explore each of these in turn.

a. The Local Law Defense

The local law defense states that "the payment, gift, offer, or promise of anything of value that was made, was lawful under the written laws and

---

[89] *Id.* at 3.

regulations of the foreign official's, political party's, party official's, or candidate's country[.]"[90] The phrase "written laws and regulations" is very important. This defense is not referring to customs or traditions. The fact that providing something of value may be customary for a certain holiday in a certain jurisdiction would not be sufficient to successfully invoke this defense.

This defense's requirements will also not be satisfied if the relevant local law either (1) does not expressly prohibit the payment (i.e., is silent with respect to such payments); or (2) decriminalizes the payment. Rather, this affirmative defense contemplates that the written local law will *specifically* legalize the payment. There is limited but very clear case law on this point.

In *United States v. Kozeny*, the District Court for the Southern District of New York found that a provision under Azeri law that relieved bribe payors of criminal liability if they were extorted was insufficient to successfully assert this defense. Although the local law precluded prosecution of the bribe payor, it did not *specifically* make the payments legal.[91]

The local law defense was also addressed in *United States v. Ng Lap Seng*.[92] The defendant in this case

---

[90] 15 U.S.C. §§ 78dd–1(c)(1), 78dd–2(c)(1), 78dd–3(c)(1).

[91] *United States v. Kozeny*, 582 F.Supp.2d at 535, 537–41.

[92] FCPA Resource Guide, *supra* Chapter 1, n.1, at 24 *citing United States v. Ng Lap Seng*, No. 15-cr-706, 2017 WL 2693625 (S.D.N.Y. July 26, 2017).

requested a jury instruction that his payments to Antiguan and Dominican government officials did not violate the FCPA as long as those payments were not expressly prohibited by local laws or regulations. The DOJ argued the opposite, requesting a jury instruction that the local law defense only applied if there was proof that the defendant's conduct was expressly lawful under the written laws of Antigua and the Dominican Republic.[93] The District Court for the Southern District of New York agreed with the DOJ, finding that the defendant's proposed instruction was inconsistent with the FCPA's statutory language and would lead to impractical results.[94]

In practice, the local law defense is largely hypothetical. It is difficult to imagine a situation where a foreign country's written law would specifically legalize bribery of its own government officials.

b. The Reasonable and Bona Fide Promotional Expense Defense

The second affirmative defense to the anti-bribery provisions is that "the payment, gift, offer, or promise of anything of value that was made, was a reasonable and bona fide expenditure, such as travel and lodging expenses, incurred by or on behalf of a foreign official, party, party official, or candidate and was directly related to—(A) the promotion, demonstration, or explanation of products or services; or (B) the

93 *Id.*

94 *Id.*

execution or performance of a contract with a foreign government or agency thereof."[95]

As a practical matter, this defense provides some level of comfort to organizations that their good faith provision of hospitality in connection with potential or ongoing business will not snare them in the FCPA enforcement net. However, whether a particular offer or provision of hospitality falls within this affirmative defense is of course a fact-specific matter. For this reason, many organizations have detailed policies on the types of gifts and entertainment that are permissible, often including AB&C Compliance pre-approval requirements. Where the provision of hospitality may be viewed as higher risk from an FCPA perspective, then the company's legal and/or compliance officers may be required to review the proposed hospitality before it is offered. In Chapter 6 we'll explain how AB&C Compliance programs around hospitality are often structured as well as address some of the questions that commonly arise in this area.

c. Is Having an Effective AB&C Compliance Program Actually a Third Affirmative Defense?

Having an effective AB&C Compliance program is not a statutory affirmative defense for a violation of the FCPA's anti-bribery provisions. However, is it actually a defense as a matter of practice? Or should

---

95 15 U.S.C. §§ 78dd–1(c)(2), 78dd–2(c)(2), 78dd–3(c)(2).

it be? These questions bear consideration, and the DOJ has offered some recent thoughts.

To begin with some contemporary history, on October 28, 2021, the DOJ published a memorandum announcing steps to strengthen its corporate criminal enforcement policies and practices with respect to individual accountability, the treatment of a corporation's prior misconduct, and the use of corporate monitors (the "2021 DOJ Memo").[96] On September 21, 2022, the DOJ published a follow-up memorandum announcing additional revisions to its existing criminal enforcement policies and practices (the "2022 DOJ Memo"). It "provides guidance on how prosecutors should ensure individual and corporate accountability, including through evaluation of: a corporation's history of misconduct; self-disclosure and cooperation provided by a corporation; the strength of a corporation's existing compliance program; and the use of monitors, including their selection and the appropriate scope of a monitor's work."[97]

These memoranda help us explore the question of whether having an effective AB&C Compliance

---

[96] Deputy Attorney General Lisa O. Monaco, *Corporate Crime Advisory Group and Initial Revisions to Corporate Criminal Enforcement Policies*, U.S. DOJ, OFF. OF THE DEPUTY ATT'Y GEN. (Oct. 28, 2021) [hereinafter 2021 DOJ Memo], https://www.justice.gov/dag/page/file/1445106/download.

[97] Deputy Attorney General Lisa O. Monaco, *Further Revisions to Corporate Criminal Enforcement Policies Following Discussions with Corporate Crime Advisory Group*, U.S. DOJ, OFF. OF THE DEPUTY ATT'Y GEN., at 2 (Sept. 15, 2022) [hereinafter 2022 DOJ Memo], https://www.justice.gov/d9/pages/attachments/2022/09/15/2022.09.15_ccag_memo.pdf.

program is a de facto affirmative defense to violations of the FCPA's anti-bribery provisions. For example, the 2022 DOJ Memo states that "[a]lthough an effective compliance program and ethical corporate culture do not constitute a defense to prosecution of corporate misconduct, they can have a direct and significant impact on the terms of a corporation's potential resolution with the [DOJ]."[98] Indeed, prosecutors are directed to "assess the adequacy and effectiveness of a corporation's compliance program at two points in time: (1) the time of the offense; and (2) the time of the charging decision" and "[t]he same criteria should be used in each instance."[99] The hope/expectation is that sufficient compliance program improvements will have been made between the time of the offense and the time of the resolution.

The Justice Manual ("JM")[100] also provides some guidance relating this question, explaining that "the existence of a compliance program is not sufficient, in

---

[98] *Id.* at 9.

[99] *Id.*

[100] The JM, previously known as the United States Attorneys' Manual, provides internal DOJ guidance. "It is not intended to, does not, and may not be relied upon to create any rights, substantive or procedural, enforceable at law by any party in any matter, civil or criminal." *The Justice Manual,* U.S. DOJ, § 1–1.200 [hereinafter JM], https://www.justice.gov/jm/justice-manual. That caveat notwithstanding, the JM is a very helpful resource for practitioners. For example, it provides guidance for how prosecutors should evaluate corporate compliance programs in the context of determining how to resolve potential enforcement matters. *Id.* § 9–28.800. That guidance is certainly useful information for AB&C Compliance and Legal officers as they seek to evaluate and continuously improve AB&C Compliance programs at their own organizations.

and of itself, to justify not charging a corporation for criminal misconduct undertaken by its officers, directors, employees or agents.[101] In addition, the nature of some crimes may be such that national law enforcement policies mandate prosecutions of corporations notwithstanding the existence of a compliance program."[102] So, unsurprisingly, the fact that an organization has a compliance program is not (by itself) a blanket protection from criminal FCPA charges. However, in this context, the JM refers to the mere existence of a compliance program—not an organization having an *effective* compliance program. It's not clear whether this distinction was intentional. However, there is certainly a difference between the two and the JM effectively acknowledges this distinction later in the same comment. Specifically, the JM notes that "[p]rosecutors should therefore attempt to determine whether a corporation's compliance program is merely a 'paper program'; or whether it was designed, implemented, resourced, reviewed, and revised, as appropriate, in an effective manner."[103]

It's no doubt true that the mere existence of a compliance program is not a blanket protection against FCPA prosecution. But what about an *effective* AB&C Compliance program? The answer to that question is less stark. However, at a minimum, having an effective AB&C Compliance program is certainly an organization's best protection against

---

[101] *Id.* § 9–28.800.

[102] *Id.*

[103] *Id.*

employees and related third parties who engage in bribery or corruption and it can have a significant and positive effect on how a potential FCPA enforcement matter is resolved.

B. THE ACCOUNTING PROVISIONS

It's important to understand that the FCPA contains more than just the anti-bribery provisions. The FCPA also contains accounting provisions. These provisions are applicable to issuers, as that term is defined in the FCPA. As a practical matter, there is an increased risk of bribery in companies that have poor internal control environments. The accounting provisions implicitly acknowledge that fact by requiring that issuers implement and maintain a reasonable set of controls regarding their financial transactions.

The accounting provisions are extremely broad and can be violated *even if there is no violation of the anti-bribery provisions*. The accounting provisions break down into two components—(1) the books and records provision; and (2) the internal controls provision.

1. THE BOOKS AND RECORDS PROVISION

What has become known as the books and records provision requires issuers to "make and keep books, records, and accounts, which, in reasonable detail, accurately and fairly reflect the transactions and dispositions of the assets of the issuer."[104] In this context, "reasonable detail" means the level of detail

[104] 15 U.S.C. § 78m(b)(2)(A).

that would "satisfy prudent officials in the conduct of their own affairs."[105]

On its face, this is a very common-sense provision. It seeks to prevent bribery by clarifying that issuers cannot mischaracterize payments in their books and records—e.g., cannot hide bribes under the names of legitimate payments such as consulting fees. With its use of the "reasonable detail" language, the books and records provision also goes one step further. It seeks to prevent issuers from hiding bribes by using vague language and descriptions such that it is difficult to discern the purpose of a payment.

Thus, there are two potential enforcement theories for breach of the books and records provision—(1) that a payment was mischaracterized; and (2) that a payment lacked sufficient detail to determine its true nature.

2. THE INTERNAL CONTROLS PROVISION

The internal controls provision requires that issuers[106]

> (B) devise and maintain a system of internal accounting controls sufficient to provide reasonable assurances that—
>
> > (i) transactions are executed in accordance with management's general or specific authorization;

---

105 15 U.S.C. § 78m(b)(7).

106 15 U.S.C. § 78m(b)(2)(B).

> (ii) transactions are recorded as necessary (I) to permit preparation of financial statements in conformity with generally accepted accounting principles or any other criteria applicable to such statements, and (II) to maintain accountability for assets;
>
> (iii) access to assets is permitted only in accordance with management's general or specific authorization; and
>
> (iv) the recorded accountability for assets is compared with the existing assets at reasonable intervals and appropriate action is taken with respect to any differences[.]

Like the "reasonable detail" requirement in the books and records provision, "reasonable assurances" is defined to mean such "degree of assurance as would satisfy prudent officials in the conduct of their own affairs."[107] In some enforcement actions, the SEC has alleged a breach of the books and records and internal controls provisions where there is a perceived insufficiency in a company's internal control environment such that it creates an increased opportunity for bribery to occur.[108]

---

[107] 15 U.S.C. § 78m(b)(7).

[108] The Oracle, Las Vegas Sands, and Mondelez actions illustrate this enforcement theory. *See SEC Charges Oracle Corporation with FCPA Violations Related to Secret Side Funds in India*, U.S. SEC (Aug. 16, 2012), https://www.sec.gov/news/press-release/2012-2012-158htm; *Securities and Exchange Commission v. Oracle Corp.*, Civil Action No. CV-12-4310 CRB (N.D.Cal. August 16, 2012), https://www.sec.gov/files/litigation/complaints/2012/comp-pr2012-158.pdf; *In the Matter of Las Vegas Sands Corp.*, File No. 3-17204 (Apr. 7, 2016), https://www.sec.gov/files/

3. COMPLIANCE WITH THE ACCOUNTING PROVISIONS

Neither the FCPA nor available law enforcement and regulatory guidance provide a specific set of the internal accounting controls that issuers must implement. Issuers must use their own judgment coupled with an understanding of the circumstances and risks of their own organizations to design an effective set of controls. Some guiding principles regarding the books and records and internal controls provisions that may be used in AB&C policies include the following statements:

- All records must accurately reflect the transactions that they record.
- All assets and liabilities must be recorded in the regular accounting system. There must be no "off book" or "off-the-record" payments.
- No undisclosed or unrecorded funds, vehicles or assets should be created for any reason.
- No person should make false, inaccurate or artificial entries in the books and records for any reason.
- No payment should be proposed, approved, or made with the intention or understanding that all or part of such payment will be used

---

litigation/admin/2016/34-77555.pdf; *In the Matter of Cadbury Limited and Mondelez International, Inc.*, File No. 3-17759 (Jan. 6, 2017), https://www.sec.gov/files/litigation/admin/2017/34-79753.pdf.

for any purpose other than the purpose described by the supporting documentation.

a. Liability for Breach of the Accounting Provisions

Primary and secondary civil and criminal liability are possible for breach of the accounting provisions. The proceeding sections address these possibilities as well as potential parent company liability for a subsidiary or affiliate's breach of the accounting provisions.

i. Parent Company Liability Generally

An issuer's books and records also include those of its consolidated subsidiaries and affiliates.[109] This means that "[a]n issuer's responsibility [ ] extends to ensuring that subsidiaries or affiliates under its control, including foreign subsidiaries and joint ventures, comply with the accounting provisions.[110] However, if a parent company owns 50% or less of a subsidiary or affiliate, the parent is only required to undertake good faith efforts to "cause the minority-owned subsidiary or affiliate to devise and maintain a system of internal accounting controls consistent with the issuer's own obligations under the FCPA."[111] Whether an issuer has in fact engaged in such good faith efforts is of course a fact-specific matter.

---

109 FCPA Resource Guide, *supra* Chapter 1, n.1, at 43.

110 *Id.*

111 *Id.* at 44, 115 n.256 (internal citations omitted).

ii. Civil Liability

There are several possibilities for primary and secondary civil liability under the accounting provisions:

- Individuals and entities may be held directly civilly liable for falsifying an issuer's books and records or for circumventing an issuer's internal controls.[112]
- Individuals and entities may be held civilly liable for aiding and abetting or causing an issuer's violation of the accounting provisions.[113]
- An issuer's officers and directors may be held civilly liable for making false statements to a company's auditor.[114] SEA Rule 13b2–2 "prohibits officers and directors from making (or causing to be made) materially false or misleading statements, including an omission of material facts, to an accountant."[115] This potential liability can arise in connection with any audit, review, or examination of a company's financial statements or in connection with the filing of any document with the SEC.[116]

---

[112] *Id.* at 44, 116 n.264 (internal citations omitted).

[113] *Id.* at 44, 115 n.258 (internal citations omitted).

[114] *Id.* at 45.

[115] FCPA Resource Guide, *supra* Chapter 1, n.1, at 45.

[116] *Id.* at 45, 116 n.267 *citing* SEA Rule 13b2–2, 17 C.F.R. § 240.13b2–2.

- Section 302 of the Sarbanes-Oxley Act[117] requires a company's principal officers to certify the integrity of their company's financial reports on a quarterly basis. Pursuant to SEA 13a–14, each periodic report that an issuer files must include a certification, sometimes referred to as the "SOX certification," signed by the issuer's principal executive officer and principal financial officer.[118] These principal officers can be held liable for violating SEA Rule 13a–14 if they sign false personal certifications.[119]

iii. Criminal Liability

Individuals and entities can be held criminally liable for knowingly and willfully failing to comply with the accounting provisions.[120] They also may be held criminally liable for conspiring to commit or for aiding and abetting violations of the accounting provisions. The accounting provisions apply to "any person" so this is true even if the individual or entity who conspired or aided and abetted is not itself subject to the FCPA's accounting provisions. Contrast this with aiding and abetting liability for breach of the anti-bribery provisions, which may be

---

117 The Sarbanes Oxley Act, enacted in 2002, strengthened the accounting requirements for issuers. *See, e.g., id.* at 42 ("All issuers must comply with Sarbanes-Oxley's requirements, several of which have FCPA implications.")

118 *Id.*

119 *Id.* at 45.

120 *Id. citing* 15 U.S.C. § 78ff(a).

limited to those persons and entities who are themselves subject to the anti-bribery provisions.

C. FCPA ENFORCEMENT AUTHORITY AND POTENTIAL ENFORCEMENT CONSEQUENCES

The SEC and the DOJ share enforcement authority for the FCPA. There is no private right of action to enforce the FCPA itself. Only the SEC and DOJ can bring actions for FCPA violations. However, some shareholder actions have resulted from underlying FCPA enforcement actions. For example, shareholders have brought securities fraud actions alleging that a company's securities lost value upon disclosure of an FCPA issue. Shareholders of affected companies have also brought derivative claims against officers and directors for breach of fiduciary duty for allowing the underlying wrongful conduct to occur and/or for failing to effectively monitor the company's operations.

In addition to the SEC and the DOJ, other agencies sometimes also bring actions relating to foreign corrupt practices—specifically with respect to financial institutions. For example, in March 2019, the U.S. Commodity Futures Trading Commission ("CFTC")[121] announced that the agency would more closely partner with law enforcement and start to bring its own actions relating to foreign corrupt

---

[121] The CFTC's mission is "to promote the integrity, resilience, and vibrancy of the U.S. derivatives markets through sound regulation." *Mission Statement,* COMMODITY FUTURES TRADING COMM'N, https://www.cftc.gov/About/AboutTheCommission.

practices.[122] The nexus here is that violations of the Commodities Exchange Act may be carried out through foreign corrupt practices. James McDonald, a former CFTC Director of Enforcement, provided the following illustrations of how this might occur[123]:

> Bribes might be employed, for example, to secure business in connection with regulated activities like trading, advising, or dealing in swaps or derivatives. Corrupt practices might be used to manipulate benchmarks that serve as the basis for related derivatives contracts. Prices that are the product of corruption might be falsely reported to benchmarks. Or corrupt practices in any number of forms might alter the prices in commodity markets that drive U.S. derivatives prices.

The CFTC would not be enforcing the FCPA itself. However, Director McDonald's comment describes a situation in which the CFTC could potentially take enforcement action in situations connected to or arising from FCPA matters. This very situation occurred in the CFTC's 2022 charges against Glencore International AG, Glencore Ltd., and Chemoil Corp. With respect to these charges, CFTC

---

122 *Remarks of FTC Director of Enforcement James M. McDonald at the American Bar Association's National Institute on White Collar Crime,* COMMODITY FUTURES TRADING COMM'N (Mar. 6, 2019), https://www.cftc.gov/PressRoom/SpeechesTestimony/opamcdonald2.

123 *Id.*

Commissioner Christy Goldsmith Romero announced[124]:

> Today, the CFTC charged Glencore, one of the largest oil traders in the world, with a wide-ranging scheme to manipulate oil markets to increase their profits. The CFTC also charged Glencore with defrauding market participants through corruption (kickbacks and bribes) and misappropriation of material non-public information. This impactful case, for which Glencore will pay more than $1.1 billion, exemplifies the capabilities and impact of the CFTC's Division of Enforcement, and our strong partnership with the Department of Justice.

1. THE ROLES OF THE DOJ AND SEC

The SEC and the DOJ share enforcement authority for the FCPA's anti-bribery and accounting provisions. The DOJ has criminal enforcement authority over issuers, their officers, directors, employees, agents, and those acting on the issuer's behalf. The DOJ also has both criminal and civil enforcement authority for the FCPA's anti-bribery provisions over domestic concerns, including U.S. citizens, nationals, residents, U.S. businesses (including their officers, directors, employees, agents and those acting on their behalf), and certain foreign

---

[124] *Statement of Commissioner Christy Goldsmith Romero Regarding Charges Against Glencore International AG, Glencore Ltd., and Chemoil Corporation*, COMMODITY FUTURES TRADING COMM'N (May 24, 2022), https://www.cftc.gov/PressRoom/SpeechesTestimony/romerostatement052422.

persons and businesses that take actions in furtherance of an FCPA violation while in the territory of the United States.[125] The SEC has civil enforcement authority over issuers, including their officers, directors, employees, agents, stockholders, and any person acting on an issuer's behalf. The DOJ and SEC collaborate often and extensively on FCPA investigations and enforcement matters.

The proceeding sections provide additional detail on how the DOJ and SEC each manage their FCPA enforcement responsibilities. We'll focus largely on the DOJ's activity as the DOJ has provided significant recent guidance regarding both FCPA enforcement and compliance programs generally.

a. The DOJ

The Fraud Section of the DOJ's Criminal Division has primary responsibility for all of the DOJ's FCPA matters.[126] The Fraud Section itself has three subject matter litigating units—the Healthcare Fraud Unit

---

[125] FCPA Resource Guide, *supra* Chapter 1, n.1, at 3.

[126] JM, *supra* n.100, § 9–47.110.

The investigation and prosecution of particular allegations of violations of the FCPA or FEPA will raise complex enforcement problems abroad as well as difficult issues of jurisdiction and statutory construction. For example, part of the investigation may involve interviewing witnesses in foreign countries concerning their activities with high-level foreign government officials. In addition, relevant accounts maintained in United States banks and subject to subpoena may be directly or beneficially owned by senior foreign government officials. For these reasons, the need for centralized supervision of investigations and prosecutions under the FCPA and FEPA is compelling.

("HCF Unit"), the Market Integrity and Major Frauds Unit ("MIMF Unit"), and the Foreign Corrupt Practices Act Unit ("FCPA Unit").[127]

The FCPA Unit fights bribery and corruption several ways. First, the FCPA Unit of course investigates and prosecutes cases under the FCPA and related statutes, "focus[ing] its enforcement efforts on both the supply side and demand side of corrupt transactions."[128] Increasingly, this has meant collaborating with international law enforcement partners to investigate and prosecute foreign bribery offenses committed by both U.S. and foreign individuals and companies. Second, the FCPA Unit provides training to foreign law enforcement agencies to help them fight international bribery and corruption more effectively.[129]

Third, the FCPA Unit works with other U.S. agencies to ensure that the U.S. is complying with its anti-corruption treaty obligations, including but not limited to those under the OECD Convention.[130] Finally, the FCPA Unit plays a strategic role in setting both domestic and international priorities for the fight against bribery and corruption. For example, in recent years, FCPA Unit attorneys participated in meetings with various anti-

---

[127] *Year in Review*, U.S. DOJ, CRIM. DIV., FRAUD SECTION, at 2 (2021) [hereinafter 2021 Year in Review], https://www.justice.gov/criminal-fraud/file/1472076/download.

[128] *Id.* at 3.

[129] *Id.*

[130] *Id.* at 10.

corruption global bodies and took an active role in drafting the 2021 OECD Anti-Bribery Recommendation and the United States Strategy on Countering Corruption.[131]

The three subject matter litigating units—the FCPA Unit, the MIMF Unit and the HCF Unit—are then supported by four units that work to enhance their respective missions—the Litigation Unit, the Special Matters Unit, the Administration & Management Unit and, of particular relevance here, the Corporate Enforcement, Compliance, and Policy ("CECP") Unit. CECP was previously known as the Strategy, Policy and Training Unit. However, the DOJ renamed it CECP in November 2021 to more accurately describe its focus and mandate.[132] CECP plays a key role in how DOJ resolves FCPA investigations, particularly with respect to evaluating corporate compliance programs, determining whether a monitor should be imposed, and handling matters post-resolution.

As the DOJ describes it, CECP "has responsibility for all aspects of the Fraud Section's corporate criminal enforcement practice, including working with and advising prosecution teams on the structural, monetary, and compliance components of corporate resolutions; evaluating corporate compliance programs and determining whether an independent compliance monitor should be imposed as part of a corporate resolution. The CECP Unit also

---

131 *Id.*

132 *Id.* at 3, 4 n.2.

oversees post-resolution matters, including oversight of monitors and compliance and reporting obligations and handling the Section's policy matters[.]"[133]

Further supporting the DOJ's FCPA enforcement efforts, in October 2021 it announced the formation of the Corporate Crime Advisory Group ("CCAG"), which is made up of representatives from every part of the DOJ that is involved in corporate criminal enforcement.[134] CCAG has a broad mandate and considers issues such as monitor selection, recidivism, NPA/DPA non-compliance, and appropriate benchmarks to measure a company's cooperation.[135] It also makes recommendations on topics such as the types of resources that could assist more rigorous enforcement, how the DOJ can ensure that it prioritizes individual accountability, and possible revisions to the DOJ's policies on corporate criminal enforcement.[136]

In September 2022, citing the benefit of CCAG's input, the DOJ announced further revisions to its existing corporate criminal enforcement policies and practices.[137] The DOJ focused on three areas: individual accountability, corporate accountability, and independent compliance monitorships. In

---

[133] 2021 Year in Review, *supra* n.127, at 3.

[134] *Deputy Attorney General Lisa O. Monaco Gives Keynote Address at ABA's 36th National Institute on White Collar Crime*, U.S. DOJ, OFF. OF PUB. AFFAIRS (Oct. 28, 2021), https://www.justice.gov/opa/speech/deputy-attorney-general-lisa-o-monaco-gives-keynote-address-abas-36th-national-institute.

[135] *Id.*

[136] *Id.*

[137] 2022 DOJ Memo, *supra* n.97, at 1–2.

January 2023, the DOJ issued the Corporate Enforcement and Voluntary Self-Disclosure Policy (the "CEVS Policy"), which expanded and re-named what was formerly known as the FCPA Corporate Enforcement Policy.[138]

i. Advisory Opinions

If an issuer or domestic concern wishes to do so, it may request a written opinion (an "Opinion Request") from the Attorney General regarding whether contemplated conduct conforms with the DOJ's current enforcement policy with respect to the FCPA's anti-bribery provisions (an "FCPA Opinion").[139] On its web site the DOJ publishes the up-to-date version of its Foreign Corrupt Practices Act Opinion Procedure, which can also be found at 28 C.F.R. part 80. The SEC does not have an analogous process. There are several requirements for requesting an FCPA Opinion.

First, the party requesting the opinion must be an issuer or domestic concern, as those terms are defined in the FCPA, that is a party to the transaction which is the subject of the request.[140] Any

---

[138] JM, *supra* n.100, § 9–47.120. The CEVS Policy is available as a stand-alone document at https://www.justice.gov/criminal/criminal-fraud/file/1562831/dl.

[139] *Foreign Corrupt Practices Act Opinion Procedure*. 28 C.F.R. part 80, § 80.1, https://www.justice.gov/sites/default/files/criminal-fraud/legacy/2012/11/14/frgncrpt.pdf.

[140] *Id.* § 80.4.

FCPA Opinion that may be issued will not apply to any party which does not join the Opinion Request.[141]

Second, the Opinion Request must be made in writing and must be specific.[142] It should include all material information, including background information, concerning the conduct for which an opinion is being sought and include copies of all relevant documents. The requesting issuer or domestic concern has an affirmative obligation to make full and accurate disclosures regarding the conduct for which an opinion is requested.[143]

Third, the Opinion Request must be signed by "an appropriate senior officer with operational responsibility for the conduct that is the subject of the request and who has been designated by the requestor's chief executive officer. . ."[144] In some cases, the DOJ may require each requestor's CEO themselves to sign the Opinion Request.[145] The individual signing the Opinion Request "must certify that it contains a true, correct and complete disclosure with respect to the proposed conduct and the circumstances of the conduct."[146]

Finally, the Opinion Request must concern an actual transaction—not a hypothetical one—and the

---

[141] *Id.* § 80.5.

[142] *Id.* §§ 80.2, 80.6.

[143] *Id.* § 80.6.

[144] *Id.* § 80.6.

[145] *Foreign Corrupt Practices Act Opinion Procedure*, 28 C.F.R. part 80, § 80.6.

[146] *Id.*

opinion being sought must be with respect to *prospective* conduct.[147] FCPA Opinions will not be provided with respect to conduct that has already taken place.

The Opinion Procedure process presents an appealing proposition—i.e., to potentially get what might be considered a non-objection from the DOJ regarding potential conduct. However, in practice, this process is of relatively limited use. There are several reasons for this.

First, even if desired, there simply may not be enough time for an organization to prepare and submit an Opinion Request and then wait for a response before having to decide whether to take the contemplated action. Once an Opinion Request is submitted, the Attorney General or their designee has up to thirty days to respond.[148] At that time, the Attorney General may provide an opinion or may request additional information. If the Attorney General requests additional information, then that of course adds additional time into the process, as the organization collects and submits the requested information.[149] Then, once received by the Attorney General, the 30-day clock re-sets.[150] Therefore, an

---

[147] *Id.* § 80.3. The transaction that is the subject of the request does not need to *solely* involve prospective conduct. "However, [an Opinion Request] will not be considered unless that portion of the transaction for which an opinion is sought involves only prospective conduct." *Id.*

[148] *Id.* § 80.8.

[149] *Id.* § 80.7.

[150] *Id.*

Opinion Request could easily take sixty days to be resolved.

Second, FCPA Opinions are self-limited in a number of ways. As previously explained, an FCPA Opinion will only opine as to whether potential conduct, relating to an actual transaction, conforms with the DOJ's current enforcement policy regarding the FCPA's anti-bribery provisions.[151] An FCPA Opinion will not opine as to past conduct or conduct involving books and records or internal controls, such as how transactions or payments were or should be recorded.

Third, the written FCPA Opinion is the only opinion that may be relied upon. To the extent that an organization had helpful discussions with the Attorney General's Office or the Department of Justice as part of the Opinion Procedure process, any such discussions or statements are not binding.[152]

Fourth, to the extent an FCPA Opinion *is* binding, it's only binding on the DOJ and not on other agencies. As noted in the Opinion Procedure, an

---

[151] *Foreign Corrupt Practices Act Opinion Procedure*. 28 C.F.R. part 80, §§ 80.1, 80.13. As a compliance or legal practitioner who may be reading FCPA Opinions for general guidance, particularly consider, among the Opinion Procedure's other limitations, the reference to the DOJ's "current enforcement policy." This means that the FCPA Opinion will be based on the DOJ's understanding of the anti-bribery provisions and its own enforcement priorities at the actual point in time that an opinion is requested. By extension, older FCPA opinions, while an interesting read, have limited direct relevance to any given situation.

[152] *Id.* § 80.9.

FCPA Opinion "will not affect the requesting issuer's or domestic concern's obligations to any other agency or under any statutory or regulatory provision other than those specifically cited in the particular FCPA Opinion."[153] Furthermore, an FCPA Opinion cannot even be taken to indicate the DOJ's views on legal or factual matters in the FCPA Opinion itself if the conduct at issue is being reviewed or is subject to approval by another agency. As stated in 28 C.F.R. § 80.13, "[i]f the conduct for which an FCPA Opinion is requested is subject to approval by any other agency, such FCPA Opinion shall in no way be taken to indicate the Department of Justice's views on the legal or factual issues that may be raised before that agency or in an appeal from that agency's decision."[154]

Finally, should there ever be a later DOJ enforcement action with respect to the requesting organization pursuant to the anti-bribery provisions, even the written FCPA Opinion that the conduct at issue was in conformity with the DOJ's enforcement policy at the time does not resolve the matter. It does create a rebuttable presumption that the conduct at issue was lawful. However, this presumption can of course be overcome by a preponderance of the evidence otherwise. In considering the validity of the presumption a court will "weigh all relevant factors, including but not limited to whether the information submitted to the Attorney General was accurate and complete and whether the activity was within the

---

[153] *Id.* § 80.11.

[154] *Id.*

scope of the conduct specified in any request received by the Attorney General."[155]

With these limitations in mind, it is perhaps not surprising that there are a relatively small number of FCPA Opinions. As a practical matter, it may be best to conduct robust due diligence on a proposed action, run the question of its advisability up the proverbial internal flagpole, and have the organization's senior Legal and AB&C Compliance personnel "take a view" as to whether the proposed action may violate the FCPA.

b. The SEC

The SEC has civil FCPA enforcement authority over issuers and their officers, directors, employees, agents, or stockholders acting on the issuer's behalf.[156] The SEC's Enforcement Division includes a specialized FCPA Unit which is responsible for investigating and prosecuting FCPA violations.[157] The SEC and the DOJ coordinate with each other as well as other domestic and international law enforcement agencies to enforce the FCPA.

c. How FCPA Matters Come to the Attention of the DOJ and SEC

There are a number of ways that potential FCPA violations can come to the attention of the SEC and the DOJ. These include voluntary disclosure,

---

155 *Id.* § 80.10.

156 FCPA Resource Guide, *supra* Chapter 1, n.1, at 4.

157 *Id.*; *SEC Enforcement Actions: FCPA Cases*, U.S. SEC, https://www.sec.gov/enforce/sec-enforcement-actions-fcpa-cases.

whistleblower reports, international law enforcement cooperation and of course the agencies' own independent investigations. Cooperation in international anti-corruption matters has been a strong trend in recent years. This may be because of an increasing awareness of the prevalence of bribery and corruption and the damage that they inflict on society. Alternatively, international cooperation may be driven (at least in part) by the huge fines that governments have been able to collect after sharing informational resources to unearth broader webs of problematic conduct. For example, in the 2020 Airbus matter, Airbus SE agreed to pay combined penalties of approximately $4 billion to authorities in the U.S., U.K. and France to resolve its conspiracy to violate the FCPA's applicable anti-bribery provision as well as its conspiracy to violate the Arms Export Control Act and its implementing regulations, the International Traffic in Arms Regulations.[158]

d. The DOJ: Bringing Charges and Resolving Enforcement Actions

Pursuant to the Federal Rules of Criminal Procedure, the DOJ can bring charges against organizations and individuals in three different ways: criminal complaints, criminal informations, and indictments.[159] The DOJ's decision to bring or to

---

158 *Airbus Agrees to Pay Over $3.9 Billion in Global Penalties to Resolve Foreign Bribery and ITAR Case*, U.S. DOJ, OFF. OF PUBLIC AFFAIRS (Jan. 31, 2020), https://www.justice.gov/opa/pr/airbus-agrees-pay-over-39-billion-global-penalties-resolve-foreign-bribery-and-itar-case.

159 FCPA Resource Guide, *supra* Chapter 1, n.1, at 75.

decline to bring an FCPA enforcement action is made pursuant to the Principles of Federal Prosecution[160] in the case of individuals and the Principles of Federal Prosecution of Business Organizations[161] and the Corporate Enforcement and Voluntary Self-Disclosure Policy in the case of companies.[162]

With respect to individuals, the Principles of Federal Prosecution require the DOJ to determine whether a prosecution would serve a substantial federal interest. To make this determination, the DOJ must weigh all relevant considerations, including but not limited to[163]:

1. Federal law enforcement priorities, including any federal law enforcement initiatives or operations aimed at accomplishing those priorities;
2. The nature and seriousness of the offense;
3. The deterrent effect of prosecution;
4. The person's culpability in connection with the offense;
5. The person's history with respect to criminal activity;
6. The person's willingness to cooperate in the investigation or prosecution of others;

---

160 JM, *supra* n.100, § 9–27.00.

161 *Id.* § 9–28.00.

162 *Id.* § 9–47.120.

163 *Id.* § 9–27.230.

7. The person's personal circumstances;
8. The interests of any victims; and
9. The probable sentence or other consequences if the person is convicted.

The Principles of Federal Prosecution provide significant additional commentary on each of these factors. In most cases, no single factor will be dispositive. Not all of these factors will be applicable to every case and sometimes one or more factors could weigh more heavily than the others depending on the case facts.[164] Conversely, some considerations should not be given *any* weight in the determination of whether or not to bring charges, such as the time and resources that have already been expended in conducting the federal investigation of the case. In the words of the Principles of Federal Prosecution, "[n]o amount of investigative effort warrants commencing a federal prosecution that is not fully justified on other grounds."[165]

With respect to organizations, the DOJ uses the Principles of Federal Prosecution of Business Organizations (the "Principles") and the Corporate Enforcement and Voluntary Self-Disclosure Policy to determine whether to prosecute an organization for an FCPA violation. The factors are similar to those that the DOJ considers with respect to individuals.

---

[164] *Id.*

[165] *Id.*

Pursuant to the Principles, the DOJ considers the following factors in making its decision[166]:

1. "the nature and seriousness of the offense, including the risk of harm to the public, and applicable policies and priorities, if any, governing the prosecution of corporations for particular categories of crime"[167];
2. "the pervasiveness of wrongdoing within the corporation, including the complicity in, or the condoning of, the wrongdoing by individuals in corporate management"[168];

In its commentary to the Principles, the DOJ emphasizes that the role and conduct of management is key to this consideration. The DOJ explains that "[a]lthough acts of even low-level employees may result in criminal liability, a corporation is directed by its management, and management is responsible for a corporate culture in which criminal conduct is either discouraged or tacitly encouraged."[169] In support of this point, the DOJ refers to the following commentary in the U.S. Federal Sentencing Guidelines (the "Sentencing Guidelines"): "Pervasiveness [is] case specific and [will] depend on the number, and degree of responsibility, of

---

166 JM, *supra* n.100, § 9–28.300; *see also id.* § 9–28.200 n.1 (noting that "[w]hile these guidelines refer to corporations, they apply to the consideration of the prosecution of all types of business organizations, including partnerships, sole proprietorships, government entities, and unincorporated associations.")

167 *Id.* § 9–28.300 *citing id.* § 9–28.400.

168 *Id.* § 9–28.300 *citing id.* § 9–28.500.

169 JM, *supra* n.100, § 9–28.500.

individuals [with] substantial authority ... who participated in, condoned, or were willfully ignorant of the offense. Fewer individuals need to be involved for a finding of pervasiveness if those individuals exercised a relatively high degree of authority. Pervasiveness can occur either within an organization as a whole or within a unit of an organization."[170]

3. "the corporation's history of similar misconduct, including prior criminal, civil, and regulatory enforcement actions against it, both domestically and internationally;"[171]
4. "the corporation's willingness to cooperate, including as to potential wrongdoing by its current and former employees, directors, officers, and agents, as well as other individuals and entities that engaged in the misconduct under investigation;"[172]
5. "the adequacy and effectiveness of the corporation's compliance program at the time of the offense, as well as at the time of a charging decision;"[173]
6. "the corporation's timely and voluntary self-disclosure of wrongdoing;"[174]

---

170 *Id. quoting* U.S.S.G. § 8C2.5, cmt. (n.4).

171 *Id.* § 9–28.300 *citing id.* § 9–28.600.

172 *Id.* § 9–28.300 *citing* § 9–28.700.

173 JM, *supra* n.100, § 9–28.300 *citing* § 9–28.800.

174 *Id.* § 9–28.300 *citing* § 9–28.900.

7. "the corporation's remedial actions, including, but not limited to, any efforts to implement an adequate and effective corporate compliance program or to improve an existing one, to replace responsible management, to discipline or terminate wrongdoers, to execute financial compensation measures that punish wrongdoing, or to pay restitution;"[175]
8. "collateral consequences, including whether there is disproportionate harm to shareholders, pension holders, employees, and others not proven personally culpable, as well as impact on the public arising from the prosecution;"[176]
9. "the adequacy of remedies such as civil or regulatory enforcement actions, domestically or internationally, including remedies resulting from the corporation's cooperation with relevant government agencies;"[177]
10. "the adequacy of the prosecution of individuals responsible for the corporation's misconduct;"[178] and
11. "the interests of any victims (*see* JM 9–28.1400), including what steps the corporation has taken to identify potential victims, or other persons or entities who

---

[175] *Id.* § 9–28.300 *citing* § 9–28.1000.

[176] *Id.* § 9–28.300 *citing* § 9–28.1100.

[177] *Id.* § 9–28.300 *citing* § 9–28.1200.

[178] *Id.* § 9–28.300 *citing* § 9–28.1300.

were significantly, even if indirectly, harmed by the criminal conduct, and what steps the corporation has taken to mitigate such harm."[179]

i. Resolutions

The DOJ may of course prosecute an FCPA matter. However, FCPA prosecutions of companies are extremely rare. Instead, it's more likely that the DOJ will decline to prosecute the company or reach a consensual resolution with the company that results in a plea agreement, deferred prosecution agreement, or non-prosecution agreement. Let's take each of these in turn.

(a) Declination to Prosecute

With respect to companies, a declination to prosecute has sometimes been the result of application of the FCPA Corporate Enforcement Policy, the updated and expanded version of which is now the CEVS Policy. In cases where a declination is granted, it's likely that the organization has voluntarily self-disclosed the misconduct, fully cooperated with the DOJ in investigating the matter, and timely and appropriately remediated the misconduct. The meaning of each of these components is explored in detail later in this chapter.

The DOJ generally does not provide non-public information on matters that it has declined to

---

179 JM, *supra* n.100, § 9–28.300.

prosecute unless it has the parties' consent.[180] However, declinations that are made pursuant to the CEVS Policy are made public on the DOJ's web site on the theory that such cases would have been prosecuted *but for* the company's voluntary-self-disclosure, full cooperation, and timely and appropriate remediation.[181]

(b) Plea Agreement

Rule 11 of the Federal Rules of Criminal Procedure governs plea agreements for both organizations and individuals. Pursuant to a plea agreement, the defendant generally admits the facts supporting the charges and admits guilt. The defendant is then convicted of the charged crime(s) when the plea agreement is presented to and accepted by the relevant court.[182] The plea agreement may or may not deal with the potential sentence or a fine. It may set out a jointly recommended sentence or fine, jointly recommend an analysis under the Sentencing Guidelines, or leave those items open for argument at the time of sentencing.[183]

(c) Deferred Prosecution Agreement

A deferred prosecution agreement ("DPA") is a consensual arrangement between the defendant(s) and the DOJ. The DOJ files a charging document with the relevant court but simultaneously requests

---

[180] FCPA Resource Guide, *supra* Chapter 1, n.1, at 77.

[181] *Id.*

[182] *Id.* at 7 *citing* Fed. R. Civ. P. 11.

[183] *Id.* at 75.

that the prosecution be deferred to allow the defendant to satisfy certain agreed-upon conditions. "DPAs generally require a defendant to agree to pay a monetary penalty, waive the statute of limitations, cooperate with the government, admit the relevant facts, and enter into certain compliance and remediation commitments, potentially including a corporate compliance monitor."[184]

(d) *Non-Prosecution Agreement*

A non-prosecution agreement ("NPA") is a consensual agreement between the DOJ and the defendant(s). It is not filed with the court and is generally maintained privately by the parties. However, in cases involving FCPA-related offenses, NPAs are made public via the DOJ's web site.

Pursuant to an NPA, the DOJ maintains the right to file charges but refrains from doing so to allow the company to comply with the NPA's conditions during its term. NPAs have similar requirements to those of DPAs. They "generally require a waiver of the statute of limitations, ongoing cooperation, admission of the material facts, and compliance and remediation commitments, in addition to payment of a monetary penalty."[185] If the relevant company (or individual) complies with the NPA during its term, then the DOJ will not file charges.[186]

---

184 *Id.*

185 *Id.* at 76.

186 FCPA Resource Guide, *supra* Chapter 1, n.1, at 76.

(e) Criticisms of Consensual Resolutions

Criticisms of the declination, NPA, and DPA methods of case resolution come from both sides of the aisle. On one hand, critics argue that these resolutions are not strict enough because guilty organizations are not being "prosecuted." Conversely, others argue that organizations are entering into significant monetary settlements even though the DOJ and/or SEC may not actually be able to prove their cases. Organizations often choose to enter into such consensual resolutions to obtain certainty in the outcome and to hedge against risk. As a practical matter, FCPA cases against companies are rarely litigated.

(f) Non-Compliance with NPAs and DPAs

What if companies do not comply with the terms of their NPAs and DPAs? NPAs and DPAs should be thought of like any other contracts—if their terms are breached then there are potential consequences. In 2021, the DOJ reiterated its existing commitment to hold companies accountable to the terms of their NPAs and DPAs. As Deputy Attorney General (D.A.G.) Monaco stated, "[W]e will hold accountable any company that breaches the terms of its DPA or NPA. DPAs and NPAs are not a free pass, and there will be serious consequences for violating their terms."[187]

---

[187] *Deputy Attorney General Lisa O. Monaco Gives Keynote Address at ABA's 36th National Institute on White Collar Crime*, U.S. DOJ, OFF. OF PUB. AFFAIRS (Oct. 28, 2021), https://www.

The *Telefonaktiebolaget LM Ericsson* ("*Ericsson*") matter illustrates what can happen when an organization does not satisfy its DPA conditions. Ericsson is a multinational telecommunications company headquartered in Sweden. In 2019, Ericsson entered into a DPA to resolve FCPA violations relating to its conduct in several countries over a multi-year period.[188] Ericsson paid over $1 billion to resolve the FCPA case, which included a criminal penalty of over $520 million as well as $540 million to the SEC in a related case.[189]

However, in the DOJ's view, Ericsson breached the DPA by violating its cooperation and disclosure provisions. As Assistant Attorney General Polite explained[190]:

> When the department afforded Ericsson the opportunity to enter into a DPA to resolve an investigation into serious FCPA violations, the company agreed to comply with all provisions of that agreement. Instead of honoring that commitment, Ericsson repeatedly failed to fully

---

justice.gov/opa/speech/deputy-attorney-general-lisa-o-monaco-gives-keynote-address-abas-36th-national-institute.

188 *Ericsson Agrees to Pay Over $1 Billion to Resolve FCPA Case*, U.S. DOJ, OFF. OF PUB. AFFAIRS (Dec. 16, 2019), https://www.justice.gov/opa/pr/ericsson-agrees-pay-over-1-billion-resolve-fcpa-case.

189 *Id.*

190 *Ericsson to Plead Guilty and Pay Over $206M Following Breach of 2019 FCPA Deferred Prosecution Agreement*, U.S. DOJ, OFF. OF PUB. AFFAIRS (Mar. 2, 2023) [hereinafter *Ericsson* Settlement], https://www.justice.gov/opa/pr/ericsson-plead-guilty-and-pay-over-206m-following-breach-2019-fcpa-deferred-prosecution.

> cooperate and failed to disclose evidence and allegations of misconduct in breach of the agreement. As a result of these broken promises, Ericsson must plead guilty to two criminal offenses and pay an additional fine. Companies should be on notice that we will closely scrutinize their compliance with all terms of corporate resolution agreements and that there will be serious consequences for those that fail to honor their commitments.

As a result of its failure to comply with the DPA, Ericsson agreed to plead guilty to the original charges that had been deferred in the 2019 DPA—one count of conspiracy to violate the FCPA's anti-bribery provisions and one count of conspiracy to violate the FCPA's books and records and internal controls provisions.[191] Ericsson was also required to serve a probation term through June 2024 and extend its independent compliance monitor's term by one year.[192] Finally, Ericsson also agreed to pay an additional criminal penalty of $206,728,848, which reflects elimination of the cooperation credit that it was originally awarded pursuant to the 2019 DPA.[193]

The *Ericsson* matter signals the seriousness with which the DOJ is willing to treat organizations' failures to fully comply with FCPA-related DPAs. Ericsson's DPA included partial cooperation credit, the benefits of which were subsequently wiped out.

---

[191] *Id.*

[192] *Id.*

[193] *Id.*

Ericsson had to plead guilty to the very charges that had been deferred, pay an additional fine, accept probation and extend its monitorship. Organizations entering into DPAs should heed this cautionary tale: "The company's breach of its obligations under the DPA indicate that Ericsson did not learn its lesson, and it is now facing a steep price for its continued missteps. As Ericsson's anticipated guilty plea makes abundantly clear, the Southern District of New York will hold to account companies that fail to live up to obligations to root out and voluntarily report their misconduct to the Department of Justice."[194]

2. POTENTIAL CONSEQUENCES OF FCPA VIOLATIONS

There are a number of serious potential consequences for organizations that violate the FCPA. These include forfeiture and disgorgement, fines and penalties (civil and criminal), private litigation, legal and investigative costs, monitor fees, reputational damage and sector-specific consequences (e.g., World Bank de-barment).

a. Forfeiture and Disgorgement

As an initial matter, organizations will be required to forfeit or disgorge the profits generated from their FCPA violations. Indeed, such forfeiture/ disgorgement is a pre-requisite for cooperation credit under the DOJ's CEVS Policy. While fines are meant to punish an organization and to deter it from similar future misconduct, forfeiture and disgorgement are

---

[194] *Id.*

meant to return the organization to the position it was in before the FCPA violation so that it does not profit from its misconduct.[195] In other words, even if an organization is not levied with fines or penalties, it will not be permitted to keep its ill-gotten gains!

b. Fines

Civil and criminal monetary penalties are another potentially significant consequence of FCPA violations. The sections below separately explain the potential civil and criminal penalties.

i. Criminal

For each violation of the anti-bribery provisions, the FCPA provides that organizations are subject to a fine of up to $2 million.[196] Individuals, including officers, directors, stockholders, and agents of companies are subject to a fine of up to $250,000 and imprisonment of up to five years.[197]

For each violation of the accounting provisions, the FCPA provides that organizations are subject to a fine of up to $25 million.[198] Individuals face a fine of

---

[195] FCPA Resource Guide, *supra* Chapter 1, n.1, at 71 (internal citations omitted). Note that the remedy of civil disgorgement is subject to the same five-year statute of limitations as a penalty under 28 U.S.C. § 2462.

[196] *Id.* at 69 *citing* 15 U.S.C. §§ 78dd–2(g)(1)(A), 78dd–3(e)(1)(A), 78ff(c)(1)(A).

[197] *Id. citing* 15 U.S.C. §§ 78dd–2(g)(2)(A), 78dd–3(e)(2)(A), 78ff(c)(2)(A); 18 U.S.C. § 3571(b)(3), (e) (fine provision that supersedes FCPA-specific fine provisions).

[198] *Id. citing* 15 U.S.C. § 78ff(a).

up to $5 million and imprisonment for up to twenty years.[199]

Courts may also use the Alternative Fines Act to impose higher fines than those provided under the FCPA. Courts may impose up to twice the benefit that the defendant obtained by making the corrupt payment, provided that the facts supporting those increased fines are included in the indictment and either proved to a jury beyond a reasonable doubt or admitted in a guilty plea proceeding.[200]

The DOJ uses the U.S. Sentencing Guidelines to calculate a potential penalty range in all of its FCPA resolutions, including guilty pleas, DPAs, and NPAs.[201] The Sentencing Guidelines provide a broad structure for calculating the penalties for all federal crimes. The first step, after identifying the applicable offense guideline section from Chapter 2 (Offense Conduct), is to determine the "base offense level." That offense level can then be adjusted up or down based on aggravating or mitigating circumstances.

Section 2C1.1 is used to determine the base offense level for violation of the anti-bribery provisions. Additional levels may then be added on to that base level depending on specific characteristics of unlawful activity, such as the number of bribes, the value of the bribe, and the level of the foreign official. That level is then adjusted using Sections 3.B1.1 and 3B1.2 based on the defendant's aggravating or

---

[199] *Id.*

[200] *Id.* at 69 *citing* 18 U.S.C. § 3571(d).

[201] FCPA Resource Guide, *supra* Chapter 1, n.1, at 69.

mitigating role in the offense. Whether an adjustment is applied depends on both the size and scope of the criminal activity and on the defendant's particular role in that activity.[202]

Section 3B1.1 increases the defendant's base offense if the defendant was an organizer, leader or supervisor of the criminal activity, while Section 3B2.2 decreases the defendant's base offense level if the defendant was only a minimal participant in the criminal activity.[203] In the words of the Sentencing Commission, "[t]ogether, §§ 3B1.1 and 3B1.2 serve the guidelines' objective of ensuring that sentences appropriately reflect the defendant's culpability and specific offense conduct."[204]

Section 2B1.1 is used to calculate the base offense level for violations of the accounting provisions.[205] That base level is then adjusted using a similar process, but different factors, to that used with violation of the anti-bribery provisions. For example, with respect to a violation of the accounting provisions, the offense level may be increased if a substantial part of the criminal scheme occurred outside the United States or if the defendant was an

---

[202] *Aggravating and Mitigating Role Adjustments, Primer*, THE OFF. OF GEN. COUNS., at 1 (2023 ed.), https://www.ussc.gov/sites/default/files/pdf/training/primers/2023_Primer_Role.pdf.

[203] *Id.*

[204] *Aggravating and Mitigating Adjustments Primer §§ 3B1.1 & 3B1.2*, THE OFF. OF GEN. COUNS., at 1 (2013 ed.).

[205] FCPA Resource Guide, *supra* Chapter 1, n.1, at 70.

officer or director of a publicly traded company at the time of the offense.[206]

This process of calculating the offense level is the same for both organizational and individual defendants. However, with respect to organizational defendants, Chapter 8 of the Sentencing Guidelines provides a framework for determining the "final advisory guideline fine range" for organizations.[207] As this quoted phrase suggests, there is (despite the Sentencing Guidelines' framework) a vast amount of discretion and flexibility regarding where a fine may ultimately land.

Pursuant to the Sentencing Guidelines, the base fine amount will be the greater of: (a) the amount corresponding to the total offense level as calculated by the Guidelines or (b) the monetary gain or loss from the offense.[208] This base fine will then be multiplied by a culpability score.

The culpability score is calculated by taking into account factors such as:

- size of the organization and number of employees
- whether high-level personnel were directly involved in the conduct or condoned the conduct

206 *Id. citing* U.S.S.G. § 2B1.1(b)(10)(B), 2B1.1(b)(18)(A).

207 *Id.*

208 *Id. citing* U.S.S.G. § 8C2.4(a).

- whether the organization has a prior criminal history or prior obstructive behavior
- whether the issue was voluntarily disclosed
- whether the organization cooperated in the investigation
- the strength of the company's existing compliance program

The result of multiplying the base fine and the culpability score may either reduce the fine to as little as five percent of the base fine or increase the recommended fine to as much as four times the amount of the base fine.[209]

Finally, the DOJ will also take into account amounts that the organizational defendant may have paid to other federal, state, local or foreign enforcement authorities to resolve a case involving the same misconduct. In determining whether and how much credit to allow to a defendant for amounts paid to another authority, the DOJ will consider factors such as[210]:

- the egregiousness of the organization's misconduct
- statutory mandates regarding penalties, fines, and/or forfeitures

---

[209] *Id.* at 70 *citing* U.S.S.G. § 8C2.5.

[210] *Id.* at 71 *quoting* Rod J. Rosenstein, Deputy Attorney General, *Letter to Heads of Department Components on Policy on Coordination of Corporate Resolution Penalties*, U.S. DOJ, OFF. OF THE DEPUTY ATT'Y GEN. (May 9, 2018), https://www.justice.gov/opa/speech/file/1061186/download.

- the risk of unwarranted delay in achieving a final resolution
- the adequacy and timeliness of an organization's disclosures and its cooperation with the DOJ

ii. Civil

The FCPA provides that, for violations of the anti-bribery provisions, organizations are subject to a civil penalty of up to $21,410 per violation.[211] Individuals are subject to that same civil penalty and such penalty may not be paid by their organization or employer.

For violations of the accounting provisions in district court actions, the SEC may obtain a civil penalty up to the greater of the following: (a) the gross amount of the monetary gain to the defendant as a result of the violations; or (b) a specified dollar limitation.[212] The specified dollar limitations are based on the nature of the violation and the potential risk to investors.[213] They range from $96,384 to $963,837 for an organization and from $9,639 to $192,768 for an organization.[214]

---

[211] FCPA Resource Guide, *supra* Chapter 1, n.1, at 71 *citing* 15 U.S.C. §§ 78dd–2(g)(1)(B), 78dd–3(e)(1)(B), 78ff(c)(1)(B) and 17 C.F.R. § 201.1004 (providing adjustments for inflation).

[212] *Id.* at 71.

[213] *Id.* at 71, 121 n.378 (internal citations omitted).

[214] *Id.*

c. Legal and Investigative Costs

An organization will likely have significant legal and investigative costs as a result of an FCPA-related investigation and resolution. Such costs are often a multiple of the actual fine. These include costs of law firms and/or consultants to investigate the potential violation(s) and begin to remediate them prior to the resolution, as well as outside legal counsel to represent the company in discussions with regulators and law enforcement. In many cases, this significant work (and its significant cost) will also continue after the resolution has been negotiated and documented. For example, if the matter is resolved via a DPA, there will likely be compliance program-related conditions in the DPA that will have to be satisfied in order for the organization to avoid further enforcement action. Most DPAs are for a term of at least two years. This means significant and costly ongoing work, especially if a monitor is imposed.

d. Imposition of Independent Compliance Monitors

A monitor is an independent third party, generally a law firm or a consultant, that assesses and monitors an organization's adherence to the compliance-related requirements of the organization's consensual agreement with an agency. The DOJ has noted that requiring independent compliance monitorships can "be an effective means of reducing the risk of a recurrence of the misconduct and compliance lapses that gave rise to the underlying corporate criminal resolution."[215]

The imposition of independent monitors has been the subject of several DOJ memoranda from 2008 through 2023 and it's helpful to briefly walk through their chronology. On March 7, 2008, the DOJ published a memorandum, authored by Acting Deputy Attorney General Craig Morford, entitled Selection and Use of Monitors in Deferred Prosecution Agreements and Non-Prosecution Agreements with Corporations (the "Morford Memo").[216] The Morford Memo explained that the Principles of Federal Prosecution of Business Organizations provides "guidance to federal prosecutors regarding charges against corporations."[217] Consideration of those Principles and the facts of a particular case could result in a decision to negotiate an agreement to resolve a criminal case against a corporation without an actual

---

[215] Brian A. Benczkowski, *Selection of Monitors in Criminal Division Matters*, U.S. DOJ, CRIM. DIV., at 1 (Oct. 11, 2018) [hereinafter Benczkowski Memo] https://www.justice.gov/opa/speech/file/1100531/download.

[216] Craig S. Morford, Acting Deputy Attorney General, *Selection and Use of Monitors in Deferred Prosecution Agreements and Non-Prosecution Agreements with Corporations*, U.S. DOJ, OFF. OF THE DEPUTY ATT'Y GEN. (Mar. 7, 2008) [hereinafter Morford Memo], https://www.justice.gov/sites/default/files/dag/legacy/2008/03/20/morford-useofmonitorsmemo-03072008.pdf. Note that the Morford Memo uses the "corporation" to "refer to all types of business organizations, including partnerships, sole proprietorships, government entities, and unincorporated associations." *Id.* at 1 n.1.

[217] *Id.* at 1.

conviction—i.e., through an NPA or a DPA.[218] In such cases, the corporation might benefit from the compliance expertise of a third party.[219] By extension, the corporation's "shareholders, employees and the public at large [would] then benefit from reduced recidivism of corporate crime and the protection of the integrity of the marketplace."[220] With those potential benefits in mind, the Morford Memo provided "a series of principles for drafting provisions pertaining to the use of monitors in connection with [DPAs and NPAs] with corporations."[221] These principles addressed monitor selection, the scope of monitor duties (including independence, monitoring compliance with the DPA or NPA, communications and recommendations by the monitor, and reporting of previously undisclosed or new misconduct), monitorship duration, and extension or early termination of the monitorship.[222]

On October 11, 2018, the DOJ published a memorandum entitled Selection of Monitors in Criminal Division Matters (the "Benczkowski Memo") to supplement the Morford Memo's guidance.[223] The Benczkowski Memo provided a set of principles to help prosecutors determine whether a monitor would be needed in a particular case,

---

218 *Id.*

219 *Id.* at 1–2.

220 *Id.*

221 Morford Memo, *supra* n.216, at 2–8.

222 *Id.*

223 Benczkowski Memo, *supra* n.215.

elaborating on the considerations set out in the Morford Memo. The Benczkowski Memo also provided details on the monitor selection process and information regarding monitor agreements.

On October 28, 2021, The DOJ's Office of the Deputy Attorney General published a memorandum entitled Corporate Crime Advisory Group and Initial Revisions to Corporate Criminal Enforcement Policies (the "October 2021 Memo").[224] The October 2021 Memo outlined a number of revisions to the DOJ's existing criminal enforcement policies and practices, including with respect to monitorships. It updated the guidance provided in the previously referenced memoranda, in some areas supplementing that guidance and, in some areas, providing superseding guidance.

On September 15, 2022, the DOJ's Office of the Deputy Attorney General published a memorandum, entitled Further Revisions to Corporate Criminal Enforcement Policies Following Discussions with the Corporate Crime Advisory Group (the "September 2022 Memo").[225] Building on the October 2021 Memo, the September 2022 Memo announced additional

---

[224] Deputy Attorney General Lisa Monaco, *Corporate Crime Advisory Group and Initial Revisions to Corporate Criminal Enforcement Policies*, U.S. DOJ, OFF. OF THE DEPUTY ATT'Y GEN. (Oct. 28, 2021) [hereinafter October 2021 Memo], https://www.justice.gov/dag/page/file/1445106/download.

[225] Deputy Attorney General Lisa Monaco, *Further Revisions to Corporate Criminal Enforcement Policies Following Discussions with Corporate Crime Advisory Group*, U.S. DOJ, OFF. OF THE DEPUTY ATT'Y GEN. (Sept. 15, 2022) [hereinafter September 2022 Memo], https://www.justice.gov/d9/pages/attachments/2022/09/15/2022.09.15_ccag_memo.pdf.

revisions to the DOJ's corporate criminal enforcement policies and procedures, including with respect to monitor selection and the appropriate scope of a monitor's work.

Finally, on March 1, 2023, the DOJ's Criminal Division published a memorandum entitled Revised Memorandum on Selection of Monitors in Criminal Division Matters (the "Polite Memo").[226] We'll draw from the referenced memoranda to address whether a monitorship will likely be imposed, monitor selection, the scope of a monitorship, an organization's obligation to cooperate with its monitor, continued review of a monitorship, and certifications.

i. Whether a Monitor Will Be Required

Monitorships are not imposed in connection with all consensual resolutions and there is no general presumption for or against imposing one.[227] Whether a monitor is required will depend on the facts and circumstances of each case.[228] However, monitorships are often imposed where an organization's compliance program is deemed

---

[226] Kenneth A. Polite, Jr. Assistant Attorney General, Criminal Division, *Revised Memorandum on Selection of Monitors in Criminal Division Matters*, U.S. DOJ, CRIM. DIV. (Mar. 1, 2023) [hereinafter Polite Memo], https://www.justice.gov/criminal-fraud/file/1100366/download.

[227] *Id.* at 2 *citing* October 2021 Memo, *supra* n.224, September 2022 Memo, *supra* n.225.

[228] *Id.*

ineffective or inadequately resourced at the time of the resolution.

The DOJ has explained that, when "assessing the need and propriety of a monitor," it is guided by two broad considerations: "(1) the potential benefits that employing a monitor may have for the corporation and the public, and (2) the cost of a monitor and its impact on the operations of a corporation."[229]

The Polite Memo states that "prosecutors should consider the following ten non-exhaustive factors when assessing the necessity and potential benefits of a monitor"[230]:

1. Whether the corporation voluntarily self-disclosed the underlying misconduct in a manner that satisfies the particular DOJ component's voluntary self-disclosure policy;
2. Whether, at the time of the resolution and after a thorough risk assessment, the corporation has implemented an effective compliance program and sufficient internal controls to detect and prevent similar misconduct in the future;
3. Whether, at the time of the resolution, the corporation has adequately tested its compliance program and internal controls to demonstrate that they would likely

---

[229] *Id.* at 2 *quoting* Morford Memo, *supra* n.216.

[230] *Id.* at 2.

detect and prevent similar misconduct in the future;

4. Whether the underlying criminal conduct was long-lasting or pervasive across the business organization or was approved, facilitated, or ignored by senior management, executives, or directors (including by means of a corporate culture that tolerated risky behavior or misconduct, or did not encourage open discussion and reporting of possible risks and concerns);
5. Whether the underlying criminal conduct involved the exploitation of an inadequate compliance program or system of internal controls;
6. Whether the underlying criminal conduct involved active participation of compliance personnel or the failure of compliance personnel to appropriately escalate or respond to red flags;
7. Whether the corporation took adequate investigative or remedial measures to address the underlying criminal conduct, including, where appropriate, the termination of business relationships and practices that contributed to the criminal conduct, and discipline or termination of personnel involved, including with respect to those with supervisory, management, or oversight responsibilities for the misconduct;

8. Whether, at the time of the resolution, the corporation's risk profile has substantially changed, such that the risk of recurrence of the misconduct is minimal or nonexistent;
9. Whether the corporation faces any unique risks or compliance challenges, including with respect to the particular region or business sector in which the corporation operates or the nature of the corporation's customers; and
10. Whether and the extent to which the corporation is subject to oversight from industry regulators or is receiving a monitor from another domestic or foreign enforcement authority or regulator.

Remember, one of the purposes of a consensual resolution is to make sure the appropriate groundwork is in place so that the misconduct won't happen again. The ten factors listed above help assess that. In practical terms, the basic question is whether, as of the day of the resolution, circumstances still exist in the organization such that similar misconduct could potentially occur again. If the answer to that question is yes, then a monitorship is more likely to be imposed. However, if the answer is no, possibly due to new corporate leadership and/or an enhanced compliance program, then a monitorship is much less likely to be imposed. As the DOJ has noted, "Criminal Division attorneys should consider whether the changes in corporate culture and/or leadership are adequate to safeguard against a recurrence of misconduct."[231]

In deciding whether to require a monitorship, the DOJ takes into account the monetary cost to the organization for the monitor as well as whether the proposed scope of a monitor's role is appropriately tailored to avoid unnecessarily burdening the organization's operations.[232] The DOJ has been clear that a monitor should never be imposed for punitive purposes and that "the scope of any monitorship should be appropriately tailored to address the specific issues and concerns that created the need for the monitor" in the first place.[233]

ii. Monitor Selection

The Polite Memo sets out the detailed process for nominating, interviewing and approving a potential monitor.[234] The selection process should "(i) instill public confidence in the process; and (ii) result in the selection of a highly qualified person or entity, free of any actual or potential conflict of interest or appearance of a potential or actual conflict of interest, and suitable for the assignment at hand."[235] The monitor will generally be a candidate that has been agreed upon by the subject organization and the DOJ.

---

231 Polite Memo, *supra* n.226, at 3.

232 Benczkowski Memo, *supra* n.215, at 2.

233 *Id.*

234 Polite Memo, *supra* n.226, at 5–10.

235 *Id.* at 5.

iii. The Scope of a Monitorship

The subject company should (to the extent possible) review and negotiate the scope of a monitorship prior to its commencement. A monitorship should be tailored to focus on specific areas of identified compliance program gaps or necessary enhancements. As the September 2022 Memo explains, "[i]n matters where an independent corporate monitor is imposed pursuant to a resolution with the Department, prosecutors should ensure that the monitor's responsibilities and scope of authority are well-defined and recorded in writing, and that a clear workplan is agreed upon between the monitor and the corporation—all to ensure agreement among the corporation, monitor, and Department as to the proper scope of review."[236] A monitorship will generally be for a set period of time but that period of time could be shortened or lengthened depending on the organization's progress with its compliance program improvements.

Taking a real-world example, the "Monitor's Mandate" in the *Glencore* resolution was stated as follows[237]:

> The Monitor's primary responsibility is to assess and monitor the Company's compliance with the terms of the Agreement, including the Corporate Compliance Program in Attachment C, to

---

[236] September 2022 Memo, *supra* n.225, at 14.

[237] *U.S. v. Glencore Int'l A.G.*, S.D.N.Y. Plea Agreement (May 24, 2022) [hereinafter Glencore Plea Agreement] at D-1, https://www.justice.gov/criminal/file/1508266/download.

> specifically address and reduce the risk of any recurrence of the Company's misconduct. During the Term of the Monitorship, the Monitor will evaluate, in the manner set forth below, the effectiveness of the internal accounting controls, record-keeping, and financial reporting policies and procedures of the Company as they relate to the Company's current and ongoing compliance with the FCPA and other applicable anti-corruption laws (collectively, the "anti-corruption laws") and take such reasonable steps as, in his or her view, may be necessary to fulfill the foregoing mandate (the "Mandate"). This Mandate shall include an assessment of the Board of Directors' and senior management's commitment to, and effective implementation of, the corporate compliance program described in Attachment C of the Agreement.

While this mandate is certainly broad, it shouldn't be taken as a license to boil the ocean. As stated in the Glencore Plea Agreement, "[t]he Monitor's reviews should use a risk-based approach, and thus, the Monitor is not expected to conduct a comprehensive review of all business lines, all business activities, or all markets."[238]

---

[238] *Id.* at D-3.

iv. A Company's Obligation to Cooperate with Its Monitor

A company is expected to cooperate with the monitor and to provide access to the systems, information, and personnel that monitor requires to execute its mandate. For example, in the *Glencore* resolution, the "Company's Obligations" were set out as follows[239]:

> The Company shall cooperate fully with the Monitor, and the Monitor shall have the authority to take such reasonable steps as, in his or her view, may be necessary to be fully informed about the Company's compliance program in accordance with the principles set forth herein and subject to applicable law, including applicable data protection and labor laws and regulations. To that end, the Company shall: facilitate the Monitor's access to the Company's documents and resources; not limit such access, except as provided in Paragraphs 5–6 [governing privileged materials]; and provide guidance on applicable local law (such as relevant data protection and labor laws). The Company shall provide the Monitor with access to all information, documents, records, facilities, and employees, as reasonably requested by the Monitor, that fall within the scope of the Mandate of the Monitor under the Agreement. The Company shall use its best efforts to provide the Monitor with access to the Company's

---

[239] *Id.* at D-2.

former employees and its third-party vendors, agents, and consultants.

A company's level of expected cooperation is certainly full and extensive, but it is not unlimited. For example, note the use of the qualifier "reasonably requested by the Monitor" in the *Glencore* example. If a company believes that its monitor's requests are unduly burdensome or outside the scope of the mandate, the company should first try to resolve the matter with the monitor and then contact the DOJ if necessary. However, a company should make any arguments regarding monitorship scope and burden with the necessary care and reflection because it of course does not want to be perceived by the DOJ as uncooperative.

Though responding to a monitor's requests for information, system and control demonstrations, etc. may at times seem onerous for legal and compliance officers, a monitor can and should have an overall positive effect on the company's compliance program. Monitors' recommendations come with a heavy weight to them, as well as specific time frames, that drive their implementation. Compliance and legal officers should strive to develop a positive and constructive relationship with the monitor's staff so that they can develop and achieve shared program goals.

v. Continued Review of Monitorships

After a monitor is in place, both the company and the monitor are expected to keep the DOJ updated regarding progress as well as any challenges. These updates help to ensure that the monitor's work remains within the agreed-upon scope, that the company is giving the monitor the information that it needs, and that the company and is proceeding as expected with compliance program improvements and enhancements.[240] Depending on the nature of the updates, the term of the monitorship may be shortened or extended. The DOJ can also consider cost to the company when reviewing the monitor's continued engagement.[241]

e. Certifications

On March 25, 2022, Assistant Attorney General Kenneth Polite announced that, for all Criminal Division corporate resolutions, the DOJ would consider requiring both the CEO and the CCO to sign a certification at the end of the agreement's term.[242] Such a document would state that "the company's compliance program is reasonably designed [and] implemented to detect and prevent violations of the law, and is functioning effectively."[243]

---

[240] September 2022 Memo, *supra* n.225, at 14.

[241] *Id.*

[242] *Assistant Attorney General Kenneth A. Polite Jr. Delivers Remarks at NYU Law's Program on Corporate Compliance and Enforcement (PCCE)*, U.S. DOJ, OFF. OF PUB. AFFAIRS (Mar. 25, 2022), https://www.justice.gov/opa/speech/assistant-attorney-general-kenneth-polite-jr-delivers-remarks-nyu-law-s-program-corporate.

[243] *Assistant Attorney General Kenneth A. Polite Delivers Remarks at the University of Texas Law School*, U.S. DOJ, OFF. OF PUB. AFFAIRS (Sept. 16, 2022), https://www.justice.gov/opa/speech/assistant-attorney-general-kenneth-polite-delivers-remarks-university-texas-law-school.

At least part of the reason for this potential requirement is driven by the DOJ's goal of supporting and empowering compliance officers. Requiring such a certification could help ensure that an organization's Chief Compliance Officer receives all relevant information and can raise any questions or concerns. It would also underscore the point that compliance officers must have appropriate independence, seniority, and decision-making power within an organization. In short, "[t]his certification is meant to guarantee a seat at the table that all compliance officers should have in an organization with a functioning compliance program."[244] However, consistent with the DOJ's focus on individual accountability and increasing interest in gatekeepers, the potential certification requirement also raises the specter of individual criminal liability for compliance officers.

The *Glencore* Plea Agreement Attachment H[245] is the first example of a "Plea Agreement Compliance Certification". Pursuant its terms, the CEO and CCO would certify, under penalty of perjury, that they:

> are aware of the Company's compliance obligations under Paragraphs 9 and 10 and attachment C of the Agreement [the portions relating to compliance], and that, based on the undersigned's review and understanding of the Company's anti-corruption compliance program, the Company has implemented an anti-

---

[244] *Id.*

[245] Glencore Plea Agreement, *supra* n.237, at H-1 (emphasis in original).

corruption compliance program that meets the requirements set forth in Attachment C to the Agreement. The undersigned certifies that such compliance program is reasonably designed to detect and prevent violations of the Foreign Corrupt Practices Act and other applicable anti-corruption laws throughout the Company's operations. [*If applicable*: The undersigned further certifies that based on a review of the Company's reports submitted to the Department of Justice, Criminal Division, Fraud Section and Money Laundering and Asset Recovery Section and the U.S. Attorney's Office for the Southern District of New York pursuant to Paragraph 30 of the Agreement, the reports were true, accurate, and complete as of the date they were submitted.]

The undersigned hereby certify that they are respectively the Chief Executive Officer ("CEO") and the Head of Compliance of the Glencore Group and that each has been duly authorized by the Company to sign this Certification on behalf of the Company.

This Certification shall constitute a material statement and representation by the undersigned and by, on behalf of, and for the benefit of, the Company to the executive branch of the United States for purposes of 18 U.S.C. § 1001, and such material statement and representation shall be deemed to have been made in the Southern District of New York. This Certification shall also constitute a record, document, or tangible object in connection with a matter within the jurisdiction of a department and agency of the United States for purposes of 18 U.S.C. § 1519, and such record, document, or tangible object shall be deemed to have been made in the Southern District of New York.

Such certifications are likely to become increasingly more commonplace in corporate criminal resolutions.

f. Reputational Damage

Finally, reputational damage is another type of harm suffered by organizations that violate the FCPA. Reputational damage manifests itself in many different ways, some of which are difficult to quantify in dollar amounts—although a drop in stock price after the announcement of an FCPA investigation or resolution is certainly one way! There may also be loss of employee confidence, some of which may be evidenced by attrition. There may also be a reduction of the customer base and its corresponding revenue, and loss of or damage to relationships with third parties.

g. Fines and Imprisonment for Individuals

For each criminal violation of the anti-bribery provisions, individuals are subject to a fine of up to $250,000 and imprisonment of up to five years.[246] For

---

[246] FCPA Resource Guide, *supra* Chapter 1, n.1, at 69, 120 n.359 *citing* 15 U.S.C. §§ 78dd–2(g)(2)(A), 78dd–3(e)(2)(A), 78ff(c)(2)(A); 18 U.S.C. § 3571(b)(3), (e) ("fine provision that supersedes FCPA-specific fine provisions").

each criminal violation of the accounting provisions, individuals are subject to a fine of up to $5 million and imprisonment for up to twenty years.[247] Note that fines imposed on individuals are the sole responsibility of those individuals. Those fines cannot be paid by their employers.[248]

D. DOJ ENFORCEMENT: THE CORPORATE ENFORCEMENT AND VOLUNTARY SELF-DISCLOSURE POLICY

When an organization learns that it may have a potential FCPA violation it faces the decision of whether to voluntarily self-disclose the circumstances of that potential violation to the SEC and/or DOJ. This can be a complex decision and it ultimately needs to be made by a organization's senior management with the aid of legal advice.

Organizations have sometimes shied away from voluntary self-disclosure because of uncertainty about the consequences of such disclosure—e.g., prolonged investigations, large fines, drop in stock price upon disclosure of an FCPA investigation, loss of investor confidence, and huge legal and investigative fees, to name a few. Recognizing this hesitancy, the DOJ in particular has taken steps over the past several years to make the process of voluntary disclosure and cooperation more

---

[247] *Id.* at 69, 120 n.361 *citing* 15 U.S.C. § 78ff(a).

[248] *Id.* at 69, 120 n.363 *citing* 15 U.S.C. §§ 78dd–2(g)(3), 78dd–3(e)(3), 78ff(c)(3).

transparent and to encourage companies to come forward. As the DOJ has stated[249]:

> Transparency regarding the Department's corporate criminal enforcement priorities and processes—including its expectations as to corporate cooperation and compliance, and the consequences of meeting or failing to meet those expectations—can encourage companies to adopt robust compliance programs, voluntarily disclose misconduct, and cooperate fully with the Department's investigations. Transparency can also instill public confidence in the Department's work.

It's helpful to briefly walk through DOJ guidance history on the topics of voluntary self-disclosure, cooperation, and remediation.

In 2016, the DOJ's Fraud Section created the FCPA Enforcement Pilot Program (the "Pilot Program") to encourage companies to voluntarily self-disclose potential FCPA violations and to remediate those violations. Its goals included providing greater transparency to companies regarding potential consequences as they decided whether to self-disclosure and to provide additional benefits to companies who modeled appropriate behavior once they learned of potential misconduct. The Pilot Program's incentives seemingly resulted in an uptick in voluntary disclosures. "In the first year of the Pilot Program, the FCPA Unit received 22 voluntary disclosures, compared to 13 during the

---

[249] September 2022 Memo, *supra* n.225, at 15.

previous year. In total, during the year and a half that the Pilot Program was in effect, the FCPA Unit received 30 voluntary disclosures, compared to 18 during the previous 18-month period."[250]

In November 2017, elements of the Pilot Program were made permanent through issuance of an updated FCPA Corporate Enforcement Policy ("CEP"). As explained by Deputy Attorney General Rosenstein, "[t]he new policy enables the Department to efficiently identify and punish criminal conduct, and it provides guidance and greater certainty for companies struggling with the question of whether to make voluntary disclosures of wrongdoing."[251]

On January 17, 2023, the DOJ published a revised version of the CEP and re-named it the Corporate Enforcement and Voluntary Self-Disclosure Policy (the "CEVS Policy"). The CEVS Policy broadens the reach of what was formerly the CEP to include *all* corporate criminal matters. As the CEVS Policy explained regarding the rationale for its genesis[252]:

> In the years since the creation of the [CEP], the Criminal Division has observed that transparency concerning benefits that a company may obtain as a result of voluntary

---

[250] *Deputy Attorney General Rosenstein Delivers Remarks at the 34th International Conference on the Foreign Corrupt Practices Act*, U.S. DOJ, OFF. OF PUB. AFFAIRS (Nov. 29, 2017), https://www.justice.gov/opa/speech/deputy-attorney-general-rosenstein-delivers-remarks-34th-international-conference-foreign.

[251] *Id.*

[252] JM, *supra* n.100, § 9–47.120.

self-disclosure of misconduct can create important incentives for corporate behavior.

The CEVS Policy became effective on a prospective basis as of January 2023 and was updated in March 2024.[253] It includes some updates to and clarifications of the CEP's basic framework. To accomplish its goal of greater transparency, the CEVS Policy, like its CEP predecessor, offers a significant carrot: "[A]bsent aggravating circumstances involving the seriousness of the offense or the nature of the offender"[254], it will be presumed that a company will receive a declination[255] to prosecute *if* the company does each of the following three things[256]:

(1) Voluntarily self-discloses the potential misconduct; and

(2) Fully cooperates with the DOJ; and

(3) Timely and appropriately remediates the misconduct.

In addition, to qualify for the declination[257], a company is required "to pay all disgorgement/

---

[253] *Id.*

[254] *Id.*

[255] *Id.* ("A declination pursuant to this Policy is a case that would have been prosecuted or criminally resolved except for the company's voluntary disclosure, full cooperation, remediation, and payment of disgorgement/forfeiture, and/or restitution/victim compensation. If a case would have been declined in the absence of such circumstances, it [would not be] a declination pursuant to this Policy. Declinations under this Policy will be made public.")

[256] *Id.*

[257] *Id.*

forfeiture, and/or restitution/victim compensation payments resulting from the misconduct at issue."[258] This is separate and apart from any fines that may be levied. If such disgorgement, forfeiture, or restitution has already been collected by another agency from the same company for the same conduct, the DOJ may apply the Policy on Coordination of Corporate Resolution Penalties in Parallel and/or Joint Investigations and Proceedings Arising from the Same Misconduct, sometimes colloquially referred to as the Policy Against Piling On, to avoid imposing duplicative penalties.[259]

Receiving a declination from the DOJ can be a powerful incentive for companies to come forward and report misconduct. If, however, a declination is not available due to the circumstances of the case, other possible incentives include as much as a 75% reduction in fines from the low end of the Sentencing Guidelines.[260]

While these incentives are potentially powerful, there's also a lot baked into their three requirements of voluntary self-disclosure, full cooperation, and timely and appropriate remediation. We'll draw from the CEP, the CEVS Policy's predecessor, as well as the Principles of Federal Prosecution of Business Organizations, DOJ memoranda, and government

---

[258] JM, *supra* n.100, § 9–47.120.

[259] *Id.* § 1–12.100. Although it has not issued a formal policy to this effect, the SEC similarly seeks to avoid imposing duplicative penalties. FCPA Resource Guide, *supra* Chapter 1, n.1, at 71.

[260] JM, *supra* n.100, § 9–47.120.

officials' speeches to understand the meaning of each of the three requirements.

1. VOLUNTARY SELF-DISCLOSURE

What does it mean for a company to voluntarily self-disclose potential misconduct? There are volitional, timing, and substantive components built into the meaning of "voluntarily." There is also some overlap between the "voluntary self-disclosure" and "cooperation" requirements.

a. Volition

Several factors may affect whether a company's self-disclosure will be considered voluntary. Specifically:

- The potential misconduct must qualify under the Sentencing Guidelines as being made "prior to an imminent threat of disclosure or government investigation".[261] Put bluntly, the company must not disclose an issue simply because it believes it has a proverbial gun to its head and that the information will be revealed shortly anyway.
- The company must not be subject to any pre-existing obligation to disclose the misconduct.[262]

---

[261] *Id. quoting* U.S.S.G. § 8C2.5(g)(1).

[262] *Id.* § 9–47.120.

- The voluntary self-disclosure must be made to the DOJ's Criminal Division.[263] There is a small degree of flexibility with respect to this requirement. As stated in the CEVS Policy Comment, "the Criminal Division will also apply the provisions of [the CEVS] Policy where a company made a good faith disclosure to another office or component of the Department of Justice and the matter is partnered with or transferred to, and resolved with, the Criminal Division."[264]

b. Timing

With respect to timeliness, the company must make its disclosure "within a reasonably prompt time after [the company becomes] aware of the misconduct."[265] The DOJ encourages organizations to disclose criminal conduct early—even before all of the facts are known to the company—and does not expect such early disclosures to be complete.[266] However, in such circumstances, the DOJ does expect that the company will move expeditiously to conduct an appropriate investigation and provide the DOJ with timely updates.[267] *See* Chapter 5 for a discussion of internal investigations, addressing the importance of having an established investigation process in place so that an company will be able to comply with

---

263 *Id.*

264 JM, *supra* n.100, § 9–47.120.

265 *Id.*

266 *Id.* § 9–28.700 n.1.

267 *Id.*

the voluntary self-disclosure element of the CEVS Policy in the event that the company discovers a potential FCPA violation.

It is the company's burden to demonstrate timeliness.[268] There's no specified period that will be considered "reasonably prompt." However, the more time that elapses between the discovery of the misconduct and its disclosure, the less likely it is that the disclosure will be considered "reasonably prompt" and therefore voluntary.

c. Completeness

Finally, over-lapping with the cooperation element, in order for its self-disclosure to be considered voluntary, a company must disclose *all* of the relevant, non-privileged facts that it knows. This particularly includes "all relevant facts and evidence about all individuals involved in or responsible for the misconduct at issue, including individuals inside and outside of the company regardless of their position, status, or seniority."[269] The DOJ previously emphasized the disclosure of facts concerning individual misconduct in both its October 2021 Memo and its September 2022 Memo and linked this disclosure with a timing aspect. In its September 2022 Memo, the DOJ stated that[270]:

> Going forward, in connection with every corporate resolution, Department prosecutors

---

[268] *Id.* § 9–47.120.

[269] *Id.*

[270] September 2022 Memo, *supra* n.225, at 3.

must specifically assess whether the corporation provided cooperation in a timely fashion. Prosecutors will consider, for example, whether a company promptly notified prosecutors of particularly relevant information once it was discovered, or if the company instead delayed disclosure in a manner that inhibited the government's investigation. Where prosecutors identify undue or intentional delay in the production of information or documents—particularly with respect to documents that impact the government's ability to assess individual culpability—cooperation credit will be reduced or eliminated.

d. The Importance of Voluntary Self-Disclosure

The DOJ places a premium on voluntary self-disclosure in determining how to resolve FCPA matters. As explained by Assistant Attorney General Polite, [w]hen a company has uncovered criminal misconduct in its operations, the clearest path to avoiding a guilty plea or an indictment is voluntary self-disclosure. It is also the clearest path to the greatest incentives that [the DOJ offers], such as a declination with disgorgement of profits."[271] There are a couple potential reasons for this. First, there's

---

[271] *Assistant Attorney General Kenneth A. Polite, Jr. Delivers Remarks on Revisions to the Criminal Division's Corporate Enforcement Policy*, U.S. DOJ, OFF. OF PUB. AFFAIRS (Jan. 17, 2023), https://www.justice.gov/opa/speech/assistant-attorney-general-kenneth-polite-jr-delivers-remarks-georgetown-university-law.

always the possibility that the DOJ would not have learned of the misconduct without the voluntary self-disclosure. Second, it's a sign of an effective compliance program when a company identifies a problem, self-discloses it and (presumably) begins remediating it.

i. What Happens if a Company Does Not Voluntarily Self-Disclose Misconduct but Does Fully Cooperate and Remediate?

What if a company *does not* voluntarily self-disclose the misconduct, but *does* fully cooperate and timely and appropriately remediate the misconduct? In this scenario, there will still be a benefit to the company, but it may be significantly less than if the company had also voluntarily self-disclosed the misconduct. This underscores how important the DOJ considers the voluntary disclosure element. In this scenario, the DOJ will effectuate *up to a 50% reduction* from the low end of the U.S. Sentencing Guidelines fine range in cases where there are no aggravating circumstances.[272] This is of course still significant but it's much less than *the potential 75% discount* that was possible if the company had voluntarily self-disclosed.

If there are aggravating circumstances, then the "up to 50% reduction" will be taken from a different point in the Sentencing Guidelines' fine range—generally not from the low end.[273] The DOJ always has discretion in how it resolves matters and

---

[272] JM, *supra* n.100, § 9–47.120.

[273] *Id.*

negotiates and imposes fines. However, we see that discretion being underlined here with the use of *up to* a 50% reduction. In theory then, although perhaps unlikely, there could be no reduction at all or even just a single digit percentage reduction. The company would, of course, also still be responsible to pay all disgorgement, forfeiture, and/or restitution resulting from the misconduct.

(a) Voluntary Self-Disclosure and the Curious Example of ABB

The DOJ will exercise its discretion, based on the facts of the case, in determining the appropriate resolution. Some amount of credit may be given for full cooperation and timely and appropriate remediation even in cases where the company has not voluntarily self-disclosed the misconduct. The DOJ's resolutions with the ABB entities in December 2022 has been referenced by the DOJ as an example of how this scenario could play out[274]:

> ABB had entered into FCPA resolutions with the Department back in 2004 and in 2010. In the wake of its prior misconduct, ABB implemented a compliance program that detected the FCPA misconduct in South Africa, and the company planned to promptly self-disclose it—it had even

---

[274] *Assistant Attorney General Kenneth A. Polite, Jr. Delivers Remarks on Revisions to the Criminal Division's Corporate Enforcement Policy*, U.S. DOJ, OFF. OF PUB. AFFAIRS (Jan. 17, 2023), https://www.justice.gov/opa/speech/assistant-attorney-general-kenneth-polite-jr-delivers-remarks-georgetown-university-law.

scheduled a meeting with the government to do so.

Before the meeting, however, a media report drew public attention to the wrongdoing. But because the company could demonstrate intent and efforts to self-disclose prior to, and without any knowledge of, the media report, the Department weighed both the early detection of the misconduct and the intent to disclose it significantly in ABB's favor. ABB also demonstrated its extensive remediation and cooperation. Despite ABB's recidivist history and the Department's policy disfavoring successive deferred prosecution agreements, parent company ABB Ltd. was still able to avoid a guilty plea, entering into a deferred prosecution agreement with the Department, with two subsidiaries pleading guilty. That said, because ABB was a recidivist, we did not give the company the benefit of a reduction from the low-end of the Guidelines range. Instead, to account for the recidivism, the reduction was from the mid-point between the middle and high-end of the Guidelines.

It's interesting that the DOJ has specifically referred to this case for the proposition that partial credit can be given in cases where the company cooperated and remediated but did not voluntarily self-disclose.[275] The fact that ABB didn't voluntarily

---

[275] *U.S. v. ABB Ltd.*, Case No. 1:22-CR-220 (Ed. Va. 2022), Deferred Prosecution Agreement, at 3, https://www.justice.gov/opa/press-release/file/1556131/download.

disclose was really a technicality. For all intents and purposes it did so—even having scheduled the requisite meeting.[276]

e. Practice Note: Presenting to the DOJ

When preparing a presentation to the DOJ, an organization should carefully consider who is best suited to deliver the presentation. Selection of the presenter(s) can convey nearly as much information as the presentation's content. While outside counsel

---

> The Company did not receive voluntary disclosure credit pursuant to the FCPA Corporate Enforcement Policy in the Department of Justice Manual § 9–47.120, or pursuant to the United States Sentencing Guidelines . . . because it did not voluntarily and timely disclose to the Offices the conduct described in the Statement of Facts; although the Company did not receive voluntary disclosure credit, the Offices, in evaluating the appropriate disposition of this matter—including the appropriate form of the resolution—considered evidence that, within a very short time of learning of the misconduct, the Company contacted the Fraud Section and scheduled a meeting to discuss matters under investigation by the Fraud Section and the Company.

See also Assistant Attorney General Kenneth A. Polite, Jr. Delivers Remarks on Revisions to the Criminal Division's Corporate Enforcement Policy, U.S. DOJ, OFF. OF PUB. AFFAIRS (Jan. 17, 2023) (The DOJ's "corporate resolutions with ABB entities in December 2022 illustrate how the CEP applies to companies that fully cooperate and remediate, even if they did not voluntarily disclose the misconduct."), https://www.justice.gov/opa/speech/assistant-attorney-general-kenneth-polite-jr-delivers-remarks-georgetown-university-law.

[276] In this vein, Deputy Attorney General Monaco referred to ABB's efforts as an attempt to voluntarily self-disclose. *Deputy Attorney General Lisa Monaco Delivers Remarks at American Bar Association National Institute on White Collar Crime*, U.S. DOJ, OFF. OF PUB. AFFAIRS (Mar. 2, 2023), https://www.justice.gov/opa/speech/deputy-attorney-general-lisa-monaco-delivers-remarks-american-bar-association-national.

may be the reflexive choice to deliver a presentation, someone from either the organization's senior business management and/or Chief Compliance Officer may be a better choice for at least certain portions of the presentation—e.g., the portions on the compliance program and any remediation efforts. This demonstrates responsibility, knowledge, and ownership of the situation. As Assistant Attorney General Polite once stated: "We prefer not to hear a 'check-the box' presentation from outside counsel. We like to see the Chief Compliance Officer leading the compliance presentation and demonstrating knowledge and ownership of the compliance program. Not for show, but because we want to empower these teams. Other senior management should also participate, taking ownership of their role in the compliance program and demonstrating commitment to compliance."[277]

2. FULL COOPERATION

The DOJ has repeatedly emphasized that it both encourages and rewards cooperation. "Full" cooperation, along with satisfaction of the other requirements, can result in a declination. Where declination is not an option, and a criminal resolution is warranted, the DOJ has stated that "the extent and quality of a company's cooperation will be an

---

[277] *Assistant Attorney General Kenneth A. Polite, Jr. Delivers Remarks at NYU Law's Program on Corporate Compliance and Enforcement (PCCE)*, U.S. DOJ, OFF. OF PUB. AFFAIRS (Mar. 25, 2022), https://www.justice.gov/opa/speech/assistant-attorney-general-kenneth-polite-jr-delivers-remarks-nyu-law-s-program-corporate.

important part of the Criminal Division's overall analysis of the case and may impact the proposed form of the resolution, as well as the fine range and fine amount."[278]

What does it mean for a company to *fully* cooperate with the DOJ in the context of an FCPA investigation? In short, it means the most proactive, whole-hearted cooperation that one can imagine, short of all waiving attorney-client and work product privileges.[279] To enumerate, it means satisfying all of the threshold conditions for cooperation credit that are contained in the Principles of Federal Prosecution of Business Organizations as well as "timely disclosure of all non-privileged facts relevant to the wrongdoing at issue, including[280]:

1) facts gathered during a company's independent internal investigation, if the company chooses to conduct one;

2) attribution of facts to specific sources where such attribution does not violate the attorney-client privilege, rather than a general narrative of the facts;

3) timely updates on a company's internal investigation, if the company chooses to conduct

---

[278] JM, *supra* n.100, § 9–47.120.

[279] *Id.* § 9–28.720; September 2022 Memo, *supra* n.225, at 8, *citing* JM, *supra* n.100, § 9–28.720 ("Eligibility for cooperation credit is not predicated upon the waiver of attorney-client privilege or work product protection.")

[280] JM, *supra* n.100, § 9–47.120.

> one, including but not limited to rolling disclosures of information;
>
> 4) identification of all individuals involved in or responsible for the misconduct at issue, regardless of their position, status, or seniority, including the company's officers, employees, customers, competitors, or agents and third-parties, and all non-privileged information relating to the misconduct and involvement by those individuals[.]

a. Proactive Cooperation

The DOJ expects genuinely proactive cooperation. This means that the company is expected to provide information, on a continuing basis, even when it is not asked to do so. The DOJ distinguishes between proactive and reactive cooperation, explaining that[281]:

> the company must timely disclose all facts that are relevant to the investigation, even when not specifically asked to do so, and, where the company is or should be aware of opportunities for the Criminal Division to obtain relevant evidence not in the company's possession and not otherwise known to the Criminal Division, it must identify those opportunities to the Criminal Division[.]

The DOJ will make specific information requests during its investigation and the company must of

281 *Id.*

course comply with those requests. However, proactive cooperation means going further than just responding to the DOJ's specific requests. It includes, as addressed above, disclosing facts that the company obtains through its own independent investigation. It could include, for example, information about potential instances of bribery about which the DOJ is not otherwise aware.

b. Disclosing Facts on a Timely Basis: "Rolling Disclosure"

The DOJ expects that documents and information will be produced promptly and on a rolling basis. Doing so is a sign of cooperation and good faith on the company's part. It also helps make the investigation go more smoothly for the DOJ. FCPA investigations may (and often do) last for several years and involve huge volumes of information. Producing information to the DOJ on a regular or staggered basis—rather than in one deluge at the end of the company's investigation and review—is more helpful and efficient.

c. Disclosing Information Discovered Through the Company's Independent Investigation

When a company becomes aware of a potential bribery or corruption issue, it should begin an investigation to determine the events that have occurred and if there may be a breach of applicable law. Depending on the company's size and resources, it may employ outside consultants and/or attorneys to lead or assist in such an investigation. The DOJ expects that the company will disclose facts that it discovers through its independent investigation.

d. Disclosing Information About Individuals

The DOJ has repeatedly emphasized in various policies, memoranda, and speeches that a cooperating company must provide all relevant facts about potentially culpable individuals. "[A company] may be eligible for cooperation credit . . . if it timely provides all relevant facts about the individuals who were involved in the misconduct. But if the [company] does not disclose such facts, it will not be entitled to receive *any* credit for cooperation."[282] Note that not even partial cooperation credit will be available if the company does not provide the required information about individuals.[283] The importance is such that disclosure regarding individuals' conduct may even need to continue post-resolution. In such cases, the DOJ's 2015 Yates

---

[282] *Id.* § 9–28.720 (emphasis added).

[283] Deputy Attorney General Sally Quillian Yates, *Individual Accountability for Corporate Wrongdoing*, U.S. DOJ, OFF. OF THE DEPUTY ATT'Y GEN. (Sept. 9, 2015) [hereinafter Yates Memo], https://www.justice.gov/archives/dag/file/769036/download. Also, although disclosing information relating to individuals' misconduct is key to obtaining cooperation credit, such disclosure will not per se immunize an organization from prosecution of guarantee a favorable resolution for the organization. *See* JM, *supra* n.100, § 9–28.740 ("A corporation's offer of cooperation or cooperation itself does not automatically entitle it to immunity from prosecution or a favorable resolution of its case. A corporation should not be able to escape liability merely by offering up its directors, officers, employees, or agents."). In other words, there is no magic bullet by which companies can avoid potential FCPA liability.

Memo[284] instructed that "the plea or settlement agreement should include a provision that requires the company to provide information about all culpable individuals and that is explicit enough so that a failure to provide the information results in specific consequences, such as stipulated penalties and/or a material breach."[285] In addition, the DOJ's position is that corporate resolutions should not provide the associated individuals with protection from criminal liability.[286]

e. Helping to Make Witnesses Available

The DOJ expects that companies will assist in making witnesses available.[287] For example, the company should provide access to overseas employees and also aid in producing third-party witnesses.[288] When deciding whether or when to suspend or terminate employees or sever relationships with third parties, companies should consider how such decisions could affect those individuals' availability for purposes of the DOJ's

---

284 The Yates Memo, *supra* n.283, was issued in 2015 and explained the DOJ's approach for holding individuals accountable for corporate wrongdoing.

285 Yates Memo, *supra* n.283, at 4.

286 JM, *supra* n.100, § 9–28.210 ("Absent extraordinary circumstances. . .no corporate resolution should provide protection from criminal liability for any individuals.")

287 *Id.* § 9–47.120(3)(b) ("[T]his includes, where appropriate and possible, officers, employees, and agents located overseas as well as former officers and employees (subject to the individuals' Fifth Amendment rights), and, where possible, the facilitation of third-party production of witnesses.")

288 *Id.*

investigation.[289] For example, an employee who has been terminated is much less likely to participate in interviews or willingly provide information in an investigation.

f. Preserving, Collecting, and Producing Relevant Documents Despite Potential Legal Impediments

The DOJ expects companies to preserve, collect and produce relevant documents, including those that are maintained in the United States and abroad. Full cooperation specifically includes[290]:

> Timely voluntary preservation, collection, and disclosure of relevant documents and information relating to their provenance, including (a) disclosure of overseas documents, the locations in which such documents were found, their custodians, and individuals who authored and/or located the documents; (b) facilitation of third-party production of documents; and (c) where requested, provision of translations of relevant documents in foreign languages[.]

If a company cannot disclose documents that are maintained abroad due to legal reasons (e.g., data privacy, blocking statutes, other reasons relating to foreign law, etc.), the burden is on the company to

---

[289] Full cooperation specifically includes "[d]e-confliction of witness interviews and other investigative steps that a company intends to take as part of its internal investigation with steps that the Department intends to take as part of its investigation." *Id.*

[290] *Id.*

demonstrate the prohibition(s). And the company cannot even stop there. The company then must go one step further to identify "reasonable and legal alternatives to help the Criminal Division preserve and obtain the necessary facts, documents, and evidence for its investigations and prosecutions."[291]

g. Having Effective Policies Governing the Use of Personal Devices and Third-Party Applications

Although not specific to the FCPA and AB&C Compliance programs, it's important to highlight that a company's compliance program should have effective policies governing the use of personal devices and third-party messaging platforms. The DOJ has emphasized this program element's importance as part of the DOJ's consideration of whether a company will receive cooperation credit. This is certainly logical as having such a policy shows that a company's compliance program is keeping pace with technology. From a practical perspective, it also directly affects a company's ability to produce responsive documents and information in an investigation.

The September 2022 Memo makes clear that whether a company has such a policy will be considered with respect to whether that company will be granted cooperation credit in a criminal investigation. Specifically, the September 2022 Memo states that "[p]rosecutors should [ ] consider

---

[291] *Id.*

whether a corporation seeking cooperation credit in connection with an investigation has instituted policies to ensure that it will be able to collect and provide to the government all non-privileged responsive documents relevant to the investigation, including work-related communications (*e.g.*, texts, e-messages, or chats), and data contained on phones, tablets, or other devices that are used by its employees for business purposes."[292] The CEVS Policy only addresses this topic within the context of the remediation requirement. However, the DOJ's Evaluation of Corporate Compliance Programs guidance describes factors that prosecutors should consider in evaluating whether a company has effective electronic communications policies in place.[293]

h. Questions and Clarifications Regarding "Full Cooperation"

We've addressed the expansive meaning of "full cooperation". A couple of common questions regarding its interpretation and import are (1) whether less than full cooperation can still result in some cooperation credit (Yes) and (2) whether a company must waive to attorney-client and/or work product privileges to "fully" cooperate (Generally,

---

[292] September 2022 Memo, *supra* n.225, at 11.

[293] *Evaluation of Corporate Compliance Programs*, U.S. DOJ, CRIM. DIV. at 17 (updated Mar. 2023) [hereinafter Corporate Compliance Programs], https://www.justice.gov/criminal-fraud/page/file/937501/download.

no). We'll address these two questions in some detail in the proceeding sections.

i. Can a Company Receive Partial Cooperation Credit?

If the DOJ determines that a company has not "fully" cooperated, can the company still receive partial cooperation credit? Yes—it's not a zero-sum game. The DOJ recognizes that not all companies will satisfy all of the pre-requisites for full cooperation, either because they did not meet all of the full cooperation criteria previously explained or because they started cooperating at a later point in the DOJ's investigation.[294] Such companies would still be eligible for some cooperation credit if they met the criteria of JM 9.28–700 but that credit would generally "be markedly less than for full cooperation, depending on the extent to which the cooperation was lacking."[295]

The CEVS Policy provides the following explanation of how the Criminal Division has discretion to address varying levels of cooperation through reductions from the U.S. Sentencing Guidelines' fine ranges[296]:

> To fairly and meaningfully distinguish between companies that provide differing levels and qualities of cooperation, prosecutors should consider, *inter alia*, (i) varying starting points

---

294 JM, *supra* n.100, § 9–47.120.

295 *Id.*

296 *Id.*

> for calculating a fine within the U.S. Sentencing Guidelines range and (ii) varying percentage reductions from the Guidelines range as set forth herein. For example, where a company has demonstrated extraordinary cooperation that exceeds the factors listed herein, the Criminal Division will generally afford a substantial reduction available under this Policy from the bottom of the applicable U.S.S.G. fine range, absent a history of serious prior misconduct. By contrast, a lack of genuine cooperation will result in a company receiving no or minimal credit, and there will be no general presumption to recommend a sentence at or below the low-end of the U.S.S.G. fine range. Prosecutors are encouraged to use the full spectrum of credit reductions available under this Policy and the starting point in the guidelines to appropriately distinguish between companies, with the most substantial reductions being reserved for only the most extraordinary levels of cooperation and remediation. Moreover, a corporation that fails to demonstrate full cooperation at the earliest opportunity might reduce its ability to earn full cooperation credit.

So what does partial cooperation (and therefore partial credit under the CEVS Policy) look like in practice? In short, we don't have a definitive answer yet because the CEVS Policy only became prospectively effective in late January 2023. In addition, these determinations are always fact-specific. However, the concepts of full and partial cooperation are not new and presumably future resolutions will bear significant similarity to past resolutions at least in this limited regard. With that in mind, we can consider the *Glencore* resolution for illustrative purposes. In the *Glencore* resolution, the DOJ awarded Glencore only partial cooperation credit. The DOJ noted that Glencore had cooperated by[297]:

> among other things, providing information obtained through its internal investigation, which allowed the government to preserve and obtain evidence as part of its own independent investigation, making regular and detailed factual presentations to the Offices, producing a significant amount of documents located outside the United States to the Offices in ways that did not implicate foreign data privacy laws, collecting and producing voluminous evidence and information to the Offices, accompanied by translations of documents, and producing an analysis of complex trading activity conducted by the company's outside forensic accounting firm; in addition, the Defendant also provided to the Offices all relevant facts known to it, including information about the individuals involved in the conduct described in the [ ] Statement of Facts and conduct disclosed to the Offices prior to the Agreement[.]

On its face, this description reads as quite extensive cooperation. For example, in addition to providing the information itself, Glencore also

---

[297] Glencore Plea Agreement, *supra* n.237, at 5–6.

provided work relating to that information such as document translations and a trading activity analysis. So, what was the problem? What *didn't* Glencore do? According to the plea agreement, Glencore did not receive full cooperation credit under the FCPA Corporate Enforcement Policy, the CEVS Policy's predecessor, because it "did not at all times demonstrate a commitment to full cooperation and was delayed in producing some relevant evidence . . ."[298] The plea agreement does not expand on this. It does not provide any examples of how Glencore's conduct may have demonstrated that it was not committed to full cooperation. It also does not provide any detail about the information that was delayed in production, the nature, relative importance, or volume of that information, or the reason(s) for the production delay (i.e., avoidable versus unavoidable). The list of the ways in which Glencore cooperated was long and detailed and the explanation of how it did not cooperate was short and vague.

Glencore also did not receive full credit for its remediation which, for practical purposes, gets folded into the overall consideration of "cooperation". The explanation of the remedial actions that Glencore took and the explanation of why those actions were not sufficient for full cooperation credit is also somewhat lopsided. The Plea Agreement lists Glencore's remedial measures as including[299]:

---

[298] *Id.* at 6.

[299] *Id.*

> (i) terminating and separating certain employees who were involved in the conduct; (ii) establishing a centralized compliance function, hiring a Head of Compliance, and significantly increasing the number of employees in compliance functions; (iii) enhancing its business partner management, including reducing the number of third-party business partners engaged and implementing due diligence procedures, payment controls, and post-engagement monitoring measures (iv) investing in increased head count and data analytics to support real time compliance monitoring and risk assessment and continuous improvement, and (v) requiring global anti-corruption compliance and business ethics training as well as additional risk-based training for high-risk and control employees, directors and business partners[.]

So where did Glencore fall short with remediation? The plea agreement states that Glencore did not receive full credit for its remediation "because it did not timely and appropriately remediate with respect to disciplining certain employees involved in the misconduct".[300] There are no additional details provided on this point—e.g., number of employees, their seniority, the size of their role in the conspiracy to violate the FCPA, etc. Apparently, Glencore did appropriately terminate other employees, as stated in the plea agreement's very first point regarding its remediation steps, but this was not sufficient. The

---

300 *Id.*

fine details of what was done and not done and why Glencore did not receive full credit were likely the subject of conversations between Glencore, its counsel and the DOJ and didn't make it into the formal written documentation.

ii. Does a Company Need to Waive Attorney-Client and/or Work Product Privileges to Receive Full Cooperation Credit?

A company generally does not need to waive the attorney-client or work product privileges to "fully" cooperate with the DOJ, with the following two exceptions: (1) if the company is using an advice-of-counsel defense based on communications with counsel that occurred prior to or contemporaneously with the conduct at issue; or (2) the communications with counsel were made in furtherance of a crime or fraud. These two categories are exceptions to the rule that companies do not need to disclose, and prosecutors may not request, attorney-client communications or non-factual or core attorney work product as a condition for the company's eligibility to receive cooperation credit.[301]

The DOJ has stated that "eligibility for cooperation or voluntary self-disclosure credit is not in any way predicated upon waiver of the attorney-client privilege or work product protection . . ."[302] To the

---

301 JM, *supra* n.100, § 9–28.720(b).

302 *Id.* § 9–47.120(4); *id.* § 9–28.720; *id.* § 9–28.710 ("[W]aiving the attorney-client and work product protections has never been a pre-requisite under the Department's prosecution guidelines for a corporation to be viewed as cooperative.")

contrary, the DOJ views such protections (when properly invoked) as promoting good corporate governance and compliance with the law. As the JM notes, "[t]he value of promoting a corporation's ability to seek frank and comprehensive legal advice is particularly important in the contemporary global business environment, where corporations often face complex and dynamic legal and regulatory obligations imposed by the federal government and also by states and foreign governments. The work product doctrine serves similarly important goals."[303]

Rather than seeking materials that may be privileged, the DOJ's stated focus is ensuring that a company provides all of the relevant factual information about the misconduct, including but not limited to relevant information regarding individuals and third parties.[304] JM 9–28.720 explains that "the sort of cooperation that is most valuable to resolving allegations of misconduct by a corporation and its officers, directors, employees, or agents is disclosure of the relevant *facts* concerning such misconduct. In this regard, the analysis parallels that for a non-corporate defendant, where cooperation typically requires disclosure of relevant factual knowledge and not of discussions between an individual and his attorneys."[305] In some cases this may mean that the company will produce documents that are partially

---

303 *Id.* § 9–28.710.

304 *Id.* § 9–28.720.

305 JM, *supra* n.100, § 9–28.720 (emphasis in original).

redacted to protect legal impressions and conclusions but still provide the underlying facts.

However, as previously referenced, there are two potential exceptions to the general premise that waiver of the attorney-client privilege and work product doctrines cannot be requested and is not expected as a pre-requisite for cooperation credit. The first arises with respect to communications with counsel that took place prior to or contemporaneously with the underlying conduct at issue. Presumably the DOJ would be aware of this temporal link based on the factual information provided by the company combined with the company's privilege log through which it might seek to withhold documents reflecting such communications. The DOJ has taken the position that if it is aware of such a temporal link then it would not be discharging its responsibility to the public to investigate corporate crime if it simply accepted a company's declaration of attorney-client privilege at face value.[306] Where an advice-of-counsel defense has been asserted in this context, then the DOJ may request disclosure of the communications that the company claims support that defense.[307]

The second exception arises where the attorney client communications may have been made in furtherance of a crime or a fraud.[308] The DOJ views such communications between a company (through its officers, employees, directors, or agents) and its

---

[306] *Id.* § 9–28.720(b)(i).

[307] *Id.*

[308] *Id.* § 9–28.720(b)(ii).

counsel as squarely outside of the scope and protection of the attorney-client privilege.[309] As a result, the DOJ may request any such communications.[310]

iii. Practice Note: Even Full Cooperation May Not Result in Absolution

This may be obvious from both common sense and the "aggravating circumstances" caveat to the declination presumption, but it's worth noting that even full cooperation can only take a company so far in mitigating the potential for fines and prosecution. As the DOJ has observed, "even the most sincere and thorough effort to cooperate cannot necessarily absolve a corporation that has, for example, engaged in an egregious, orchestrated, and widespread fraud. Cooperation is a potential mitigating factor, but it alone is not dispositive."[311]

3. TIMELY AND APPROPRIATE REMEDIATION

What does it mean for a company to timely and appropriately remediate its misconduct? It means several in-depth and multi-step processes. First, it means that the company demonstrates that it has conducted a thorough root cause analysis and, where

---

[309] *Id.*

[310] *Id.*

[311] JM, *supra* n.100, § 9–28.720.

appropriate, has remediated the root cause(s) of the misconduct.[312]

Second, a company must appropriately discipline its relevant employees.[313] This includes "those identified by the company as responsible for the misconduct, either through direct participation or failure in oversight, as well as those with supervisory authority over the area in which the criminal conduct occurred[.]"[314] Depending on the size and scope of the organization, this is a potentially broad group of people that must be identified based on a combination of direct participation and review of organizational charts. A company is not per se required to conduct an independent internal investigation. However, particularly for large organizations, an independent investigation would seem to be necessary to generate this information.

Third, timely and appropriate remediation means that a company must appropriately retain business records and prohibit the improper destruction of business records. This includes "implementing appropriate guidance and controls on the use of personal communications and messaging applications, including ephemeral messaging platforms that undermine the company's ability to appropriately retain business records or communications or otherwise comply with the company's document retention policies or legal

[312] *Id.* § 9–47.120.

[313] *Id.*

[314] *Id.*

obligations[.]"[315] An organization must, at all times, have a document retention policy in place and employees must comply with that policy. What should be an existing status quo takes on heightened importance with the specter of misconduct or an internal or external investigation. In addition to any existing retention policy, companies will often distribute a specific "hold" notice at the start of an investigation regarding any materials or communications that may be relevant to the investigation to help further ensure that those records are maintained.

Fourth, the company must implement an effective, risk-based compliance and ethics program. *See* Chapter 5 for an exploration of the seven factors that compromise an effective AB&C Compliance program. The CEVS Policy acknowledges that what constitutes an effective program may vary depending on an organization's size, resources, and risk profile. It suggests that an effective program "may" include[316]:

1) The company's commitment to instilling corporate values that promote compliance, including awareness among employees that any criminal conduct, including the conduct underlying the investigation, will not be tolerated;

2) The resources the company has dedicated to compliance;

---

[315] *Id.*

[316] *Id.*

3) The quality and experience of the personnel involved in compliance, such that they can understand and identify the transactions and activities that pose a potential risk;

4) The authority and independence of the compliance function, including the access the compliance function has to senior leadership and governance bodies and the availability of compliance expertise to the board;

5) The effectiveness of the company's compliance risk assessment and the manner in which the company's compliance program has been tailored based on that risk assessment;

6) The reporting structure of any compliance personnel employed or contracted by the company;

7) The compensation and promotion of the personnel involved in compliance, in view of their role, responsibilities, performance, and other appropriate factors; and

8) The testing of the compliance program to assure its effectiveness.

Finally, timely and appropriate remediation also includes what could be thought of as the "kitchen sink"—basically anything that senior management, AB&C Compliance, Legal, and outside counsel can conceive of doing that has not yet been done. As it is more formally described in the CEVS Policy, remediation also includes "*[a]ny* additional steps that demonstrate recognition of the seriousness of the company's misconduct, acceptance of responsibility for it, and the implementation of measures to reduce the risk of repetition of such misconduct, including measures to identify future risks."[317] Note that a company must have effectively remediated *at the time of the resolution* in order to receive full credit for remediation.[318]

4. THE BENEFITS OF VOLUNTARY SELF-DISCLOSURE, FULL COOPERATION, AND TIMELY AND APPROPRIATE REMEDIATION

If there are no aggravating circumstances, *and if* a company has voluntarily self-disclosed, fully cooperated, and timely and appropriately remediated (within the meaning of these terms as explained in the previous sections) *and* the company has paid/committed to pay all disgorgement, forfeiture, and/or restitution *then* the presumption is that the company will receive a declination.[319]

What if a company falls short of this perfect scenario? A company *may* still receive a declination. However, that coveted *presumption of a declination* would not be in place. Let's consider some of the conditions associated with receiving a declination presumption and how those conditions could influence the ultimate resolution.

---

317 *Id.* (emphasis added).

318 JM, *supra* n.100, § 9–47.120.

319 *Id.*

a. What if There Are Aggravating Circumstances?

The first condition for an company to receive a declination presumption is that there are no aggravating circumstances. But what does *aggravating circumstances* really mean? The CEVS Policy defines aggravating circumstances as including but not limited to "involvement by executive management of the company in the misconduct; a significant profit to the company from the misconduct; egregiousness or pervasiveness of the misconduct within the company; or criminal recidivism."[320] The concept of criminal recidivism/ prior misconduct, in particular, bears further exploration.

i. Criminal Recidivism/Prior Misconduct

What happens when there is a history of prior misconduct? What does "prior misconduct" even mean? Does it have to be the same misconduct as in the instant action or just misconduct generally? The CEVS Policy does not address this specific question. However, prior DOJ memoranda and related remarks do provide guidance.

On October 28, 2021, Deputy Attorney General Lisa Monaco clarified that "*all* prior misconduct needs to be evaluated when it comes to decisions about the proper resolution with a company, whether or not that misconduct is similar to the conduct at issue in a particular investigation" and that the

---

[320] *Id.*

Principles of Federal Prosecution of Business Organizations would be amended to reflect this approach.[321] Deputy Attorney General Monaco explained[322]:

> Going forward, prosecutors can and should consider the full range of prior misconduct, not just a narrower subset of similar conduct—for instance, only the past FCPA investigations in an FCPA case, or only the tax offenses in a Tax Division matter. A prosecutor in the FCPA Unit needs to take a department-wide view of misconduct: Has this company run afoul of the Tax Division, the Environment and Natural Resources Division, the money laundering sections, the U.S. Attorney's Offices, and so on? He or she also needs to weigh what has happened outside the department—whether this company was prosecuted by another

---

[321] *Deputy Attorney General Lisa O. Monaco Gives Keynote Address at ABA's 36th National Institute on White Collar Crime*, U.S. DOJ, OFF. OF PUB. AFFAIRS (Oct. 28, 2021), https://www.justice.gov/opa/speech/deputy-attorney-general-lisa-o-monaco-gives-keynote-address-abas-36th-national-institute. (emphasis supplied).

[322] *Id.*; *see also* October 2021 Memo, *supra* n.224, at 3.

> A corporation's record of past misconduct—including violations of criminal laws, civil laws, or regulatory rules—may be indicative of whether the company lacks the appropriate internal controls and corporate culture to disincentivize criminal activity, and whether any proposed remediation or compliance programs, if implemented, will succeed. Prosecutors must therefore take a holistic approach when considering a company's characteristics, including its history of corporate misconduct, without limiting their consideration to whether past misconduct is similar to the instant offense.

> country or state, or whether this company has a history of running afoul of regulators. Some prior instances of misconduct may ultimately prove to have less significance, but prosecutors need to start by assuming all prior misconduct is potentially relevant.

The September 2022 Memo provides guidance to prosecutors regarding how to compare and weigh different instances of prior misconduct. Its guidance runs with common sense in that it generally advises prosecutors to "assign the greatest significance to recent U.S. criminal resolutions, and to prior misconduct involving the same personnel or management."[323] Conversely, "[d]ated conduct addressed by prior criminal resolutions entered into more than 10 years before the conduct currently under investigation, and civil or regulatory resolutions that were finalized more than five years before the conduct currently under investigation, should generally be accorded less weight as such conduct may be generally less reflective of the corporation's current compliance culture, program, and risk tolerance."[324] However, this is a general proposition and decisions must be made based on the facts of the specific case. Conduct falling outside of these ranges may still be problematic because it may signal that a corporation does not have a sufficiently

---

[323] September 2022 Memo, *supra* n.225, at 5.

[324] *Id.*

robust culture of compliance and ethics and/or that it has insufficient internal controls.[325]

When evaluating prior misconduct, the September 2022 Memo indicates that prosecutors should take into account:

- Each of a corporation's prior resolutions[326] (focusing on the most potentially significant as discussed above)
    - The underlying facts and circumstances
    - Any factual admissions by the corporation
    - The "seriousness and pervasiveness of the misconduct"[327]
    - Whether the prior misconduct was "similar in nature to the instant misconduct under investigation, even if it was prosecuted under different statutes."[328]
- Whether, at the time of the instant misconduct, "the corporation was serving a term of probation or was subject to

[325] *Id.*

[326] *Id.* at 5 n.4. In this context, the DOJ intends the term "resolution" to include "both post-trial adjudications and stipulated non-trial resolutions, such as plea agreements, non-prosecution agreements, deferred prosecution agreements, civil consent decrees, and stipulated orders, and pre-trial regulatory enforcement actions." *Id.*

[327] *Id.* at 5.

[328] *Id.*

supervision, monitorship, or other obligation imposed by the prior resolution."[329]

- "[W]hether the conduct at issue in the prior and current matters reflects broader weaknesses in a corporation's compliance culture or practices."[330]
- Whether the prior and current misconduct occurred under the same senior leadership.[331]
- Whether the prior and current misconduct share the same root cause(s).[332]
- What types of remediation the corporation undertook to remediate the prior misconduct—e.g., "employee discipline, compensation clawbacks, restitution, management restructuring, and compliance program upgrades."[333]

As Deputy Attorney General Monaco explained, taking this broader view of a corporation's historical misconduct will help ensure that the DOJ doesn't unnecessarily disregard important history in determining the appropriate type of resolution.[334]

---

[329] September 2022 Memo, *supra* n.225, at 5.

[330] *Id.* at 6.

[331] *Id.* at 6.

[332] *Id.* at 6.

[333] *Id.* at 6.

[334] *Deputy Attorney General Lisa O. Monaco Gives Keynote Address at ABA's 36th National Institute on White Collar Crime*, U.S. DOJ, OFF. OF PUB. AFFAIRS (Oct. 28, 2021), https://www.justice.gov/opa/speech/deputy-attorney-general-lisa-o-monaco-gives-keynote-address-abas-36th-national-institute.

Interestingly, Monaco observed that between 10% and 20% of recent significant corporate criminal resolutions involved companies which had previously entered into resolutions with the DOJ.[335] This of course, as also noted by Monaco, raises the question of whether companies who are already under or were recently under consensual resolutions take their compliance obligations seriously enough. This then leads to the further question of whether NPAs or DPAs should even be on the table for such companies. As Deputy Attorney General Monaco acknowledged[336]:

> Corporate recidivism undermines the purpose of pretrial diversion, which is after all to give a break to corporations in exchange for their promise to fix what ails them, as well as to recognize a company's cooperation. Some have questioned whether pretrial diversion is appropriate for any company who has benefited previously from such an arrangement. Does the opportunity to receive multiple NPAs and DPAs instill a sense among corporations that these resolutions and the attendant fines are just the cost of doing business? Are there other approaches that can promote cultural and institutional changes that will have a greater impact on deterring misconduct?

We'll likely hear more from the DOJ on these questions.

---

[335] *Id.*

[336] *Id.*

ii. The Analysis and Possible Outcome

As previously explained, the *presumption* of a declination is not available if the company has aggravating circumstances. However, according to the CEVS Policy, the company *may* still receive a declination when it has aggravating circumstances *if* it can demonstrate that it has satisfied *all* of the following criteria[337]:

- The voluntary self-disclosure was made immediately upon the company becoming aware of the allegation of misconduct;
- At the time of the misconduct and disclosure, the company had an effective compliance program and system of internal accounting controls, which enabled the identification of the misconduct and led to the company's voluntary self-disclosure; and
- The company provided extraordinary cooperation with the Department's investigation and undertook extraordinary remediation that exceeds the respective factors listed herein.

At a cursory glance, these factors appear similar to those generally required for a declination. However, these factors include terminology that reflects an increased burden—a higher standard that presumably helps compensate for the presence of the aggravating factor(s). First, with respect to voluntary

---

[337] JM, *supra* n.100, § 9–47.120.

self-disclosure, the requirement changes from "within a reasonably prompt time" to "immediately".

Second, the temporal expectation for the existence of an effective compliance program shifts. Rather than being an element of remediation that is judged at that the time of the resolution, the expectation is that such an effective program (including a system of accounting controls) has already been implemented at the time of the voluntary self-disclosure. Even more, the expectation is that it was pursuant to such effective program that the issue was identified and voluntarily self-disclosed.

Finally, there are references not just to cooperation and remediation, but to "extraordinary cooperation" and "extraordinary remediation". What do those concepts look like in practice, given the already-expansive definitions of full cooperation and timely and appropriate remediation that we previously addressed? Time will tell. Perhaps there will be very specific situations in which the DOJ will deem that the terms "extraordinary cooperation" and "extraordinary remediation" really do apply to a company's efforts. Assistant Attorney General Polite acknowledged that practitioners may wonder how prosecutors might distinguish between "full" and "extraordinary' and cooperation under the CEVS Policy and offered the following comments[338]:

---

[338] *Assistant Attorney General Kenneth A. Polite, Jr. Delivers Remarks on Revisions to the Criminal Division's Corporate Enforcement Policy*, U.S. DOJ, OFF. OF PUB. AFFAIRS (Jan. 17, 2023), https://www.justice.gov/opa/speech/assistant-attorney-

> In many ways, we know 'extraordinary cooperation' when we see it, and the differences between 'full' and 'extraordinary' cooperation are perhaps more in degree than kind. To receive credit for extraordinary cooperation, companies must go above and beyond the criteria for full cooperation set in [the DOJ's] policies—not just run of the mill, or even gold-standard cooperation, but truly extraordinary.

If a company with aggravating circumstances does not satisfy the heightened requirements (but does satisfy the standard requirements of voluntarily self-disclosing, fully cooperating and timely and appropriately remediating) then a criminal resolution will be warranted. Such a criminal resolution could take the form of a conviction, guilty plea, DPA, or NPA.[339]

In this scenario, the DOJ will generally require the company to pay a criminal penalty/fine in addition to the always-required disgorgement, forfeiture and/or restitution.[340] The company will still receive a reduction from the potential maximum fine or penalty. For a company that is *not* a criminal recidivist, the DOJ's Criminal Division will recommend between a 50% and 75% reduction from the low end of the Sentencing Guidelines' fine range.[341] For a company that *is* a criminal recidivist,

---

general-kenneth-polite-jr-delivers-remarks-georgetown-university-law.

[339] JM, *supra* n.100, § 9–47.120.

[340] *Id.*

[341] *Id.*

the Criminal Division will recommend between a 50% and 75% reduction from another point in the fine range, though generally not from the low end.[342] As the CEVS Policy notes, "prosecutors will have discretion to determine the starting point for the reduction based on the particular facts and circumstances of the case[.]"[343]

If there are parallel resolutions with other authorities where fines/penalties, disgorgement, forfeiture and/or restitution are collected, then the DOJ may take that into account by applying its Policy on Coordination of Corporate Resolution Penalties in Parallel and/or Joint Investigations and Proceedings Arising from the Same Misconduct.[344] Finally, a monitor will generally not be required "*if* a company has, at the time of resolution, demonstrated that it has implemented and tested an effective compliance program and remediated the root cause of the misconduct."[345]

b. A Note on the DOJ's Transparency Efforts

In its September 2022 Memo, the DOJ once again emphasized its goal of providing greater transparency in connection with resolving corporate criminal matters. To that end, the September 2022

---

342 *Id.*

343 *Id.*

344 *Id.*

345 JM, *supra* n.100, § 9–47.120.

Memo directs that, wherever possible, agreements to resolve corporate criminal liability should include[346]:

(1) an agreed-upon statement of facts outlining the criminal conduct that forms the basis for the agreement; and

(2) a statement of relevant considerations that explains the Department's reasons for entering into the agreement.

The September 2022 Memo expands on the second point, noting that such considerations may include, for example[347]:

- the corporation's voluntary self-disclosure, cooperation, and remedial efforts (or lack thereof);
- the cooperation credit, if any, that the corporation is receiving;
- the seriousness and pervasiveness of the criminal conduct;
- the corporation's history of misconduct;
- the state of the corporation's compliance program at the time of the underlying criminal conduct and the time of the resolution;

---

[346] September 2022 Memo, *supra* n.225, at 15.

[347] *Id.*

- the reasons for imposing an independent compliance monitor or any other compliance undertaking, if applicable;
- other applicable factors from JM § 9–28.300[348]; and
- any other key considerations related to the Department's decision regarding the resolution.

The September 2022 Memo also states that, absent exceptional circumstances, corporate criminal resolution agreements should be published on the DOJ's web site.[349] We know this to be the case as several such examples are in this book!

E. SEC ENFORCEMENT

As discussed in the previous sections, the DOJ has been quite vocal in recent years regarding its FCPA corporate enforcement policies and the meaning of key provisions of those policies. The SEC has arguably assumed a relatively lower profile with respect to such communications. However, since 2001 the SEC has used what have become known as the Seaboard Factors to determine whether and what type of enforcement action it will take with respect to companies. Although the Seaboard Factors' organization and terminology is not identical to the CEVS Policy and the DOJ's approach, many of the

---

[348] *See* JM, *supra* n.100, § 9–28.300 (addressing the factors that prosecutors should consider when deciding whether to charge a company).

[349] September 2022 Memo, *supra* n.225, at 15.

underlying principles are the same. In the next sections we'll explain the Seaboard Factors and the SEC's general approach to enforcement.

1. SEC ENFORCEMENT DIVISION COOPERATION PROGRAM

The SEC's Enforcement Division has had an Enforcement Cooperation Program in place since 2010. Like the DOJ's CEVS Policy, the SEC's approach is geared toward incentivizing greater self-disclosure and cooperation in investigations and enforcement actions. The SEC, through its creation of the Enforcement Cooperation Program, made three updates to the functioning of the Enforcement Division. First, the SEC added three new resolution mechanisms that had not previously been available in SEC enforcement matters—cooperation agreements[350], deferred prosecution agreements[351],

---

[350] *SEC Announces Initiative to Encourage Individuals and Companies to Cooperate and Assist in Investigations*, U.S. SEC. AND EXCH. COMM'N (Jan. 13, 2010), https://www.sec.gov/news/press/2010/2010-6.htm. In this context, the term "cooperation agreements" is defined as "[f]ormal written agreements in which the Enforcement Division agrees to recommend to the Commission that a cooperator receive credit for cooperating in investigations or related enforcement actions if the cooperator provides substantial assistance such as full and truthful information and testimony." *Id.*

[351] *Id.* In this context, the term "deferred prosecution agreements" is defined as "[f]ormal written agreements in which the Commission agrees to forego an enforcement action against a cooperator if the individual or company agrees, among other things, to cooperate fully and truthfully and to comply with express prohibitions and undertakings during a period of deferred prosecution." *Id.*

and non-prosecution agreements.[352] When making this addition, the SEC explained that, "[f]or many years, similar cooperation tools have been regularly and successfully used by the Justice Department in its criminal investigations and prosecutions."[353] Second, the SEC also "streamlined the process for submitting witness immunity requests to the Justice Department for witnesses who have the capacity to assist in its investigations and related enforcement actions."[354] Third, the SEC issued a policy statement regarding how it would evaluate the cooperation of individuals (as opposed to companies) and credit that cooperation.[355]

The SEC, like the DOJ, values voluntary self-disclosure, cooperation, and remediation. However, as initially noted, there is less detail available about how the SEC defines and measures corporate adherence with these concepts. We'll look at SEC releases, SEC memoranda, speeches of SEC officials, SEC resolutions, and the SEC Enforcement Manual to reach our own functional understanding.

---

[352] *Id.* In this context, the term "non-prosecution agreements" is defined as "[f]ormal written agreements, entered into under limited and appropriate circumstances, in which the Commission agrees not to pursue an enforcement action against a cooperator if the individual or company agrees, among other things, to cooperate fully and truthfully and comply with express undertakings." *Id.*

[353] *Id.*

[354] *Id.*

[355] *Id.*

2. SEC ENFORCEMENT WITH RESPECT TO COMPANIES

In October 2001, the SEC "issued a Report of Investigation and Statement explaining its decision not to take enforcement action against a public company it had investigated for financial statement irregularities."[356] Often referred to as the Seaboard Report,[357] it "articulated an analytical framework for evaluating cooperation by companies. The report detailed the many factors the Commission considered in determining whether, and to what extent, it grants leniency to investigated companies for cooperating in its investigations and for related good corporate citizenship."[358] The Seaboard Report lists four categories of a company's potential cooperation, and the SEC Enforcement Manual defines those categories, as follows[359]:

- <u>Self-policing</u> prior to the discovery of the misconduct, including establishing effective compliance procedures and an appropriate tone at the top;

---

[356] *Enforcement Manual*, SEC. AND EXCH. COMM'N, DIV. OF ENF'T, OFF. OF CHIEF COUNS., (Nov. 28, 2017) [hereinafter SEC Enforcement Manual], https://www.sec.gov/divisions/enforce/enforcementmanual.pdf, at 98.

[357] *Report of Investigation Pursuant to Section 21(a) of the Securities Exchange Act of 1934 and Commission Statement on the Relationship of Cooperation to Agency Enforcement Decisions*, U.S. SEC (Oct. 23, 2001) [hereinafter Seaboard Report], https://www.sec.gov/litigation/investreport/34-44969.htm.

[358] SEC Enforcement Manual, *supra* n.356, at 98.

[359] *Id.*

- Self-reporting of misconduct when it is discovered, including conducting a thorough review of the nature, extent, origins and consequences of the misconduct, and promptly, completely and effectively disclosing the misconduct to the public, to regulatory agencies, and to self-regulatory organizations;

- Remediation, including dismissing or appropriately disciplining wrongdoers, modifying and improving internal controls and procedures to prevent recurrence of the misconduct, and appropriately compensating those adversely affected; and

- Cooperation with law enforcement authorities, including providing the Commission staff with all information relevant to the underlying violations and the company's remedial efforts.

The Seaboard Report lists thirteen non-exclusive criteria (the "Seaboard Factors") that the SEC will consider "in determining whether, and how much, to credit self-policing, self-reporting, remediation and cooperation—from the extraordinary step of taking no enforcement action to bringing reduced charges, seeking lighter sanctions, or including mitigating language in documents that [the SEC] use[s] to announce and resolve enforcement actions"[360]. The SEC hasn't specifically clarified which of the numbered factors fit into which theme. There's

[360] Seaboard Report, *supra* n.357.

substantial overlap between many of the thirteen factors and their supporting questions. While certainly interesting, the Seaboard Factors do not provide a formal structure by which to determine whether cooperation credit will be granted and, if so, the potential value of being granted that credit.[361]

The thirteen Seaboard Factors are:

1. Nature of the Misconduct

The question of the nature of the misconduct involves looking at the state of mind/intent that led to the misconduct. "Did it result from inadvertence, honest mistake, simple negligence, reckless or deliberate indifference to indicia of wrongful conduct, willful misconduct or unadorned venality?"[362] It also raises the question of whether the company's auditors were misled.[363]

2. How the Misconduct Arose

The question of how the misconduct arose looks at the nature of the company's ethical culture as well as the effectiveness of the company's compliance program. Was the misconduct "the result of pressure placed on employees to achieve specific results, or a

---

[361] Although the SEC Enforcement Manual refers to the Seaboard Report as an "analytical framework," it also seemingly acknowledges the Seaboard Report's limitations by stating that it sets forth "*general principles* but does not limit the Commission's broad discretion to evaluate every case individually, on its own unique facts and circumstances." SEC Enforcement Manual, *supra* n.356, at 98 (emphasis added).

[362] Seaboard Report, *supra* n.357.

[363] *Id.*

tone of lawlessness set by those in control of the company? What compliance procedures were in place to prevent the misconduct now uncovered? Why did those procedures fail to stop or inhibit the wrongful conduct?"[364]

3. Where in the Company the Misconduct Occurred[365]

The question of where in the company the misconduct occurred includes the consideration of whether there was senior executive involvement in misconduct. "Involvement" should be understood broadly to mean direct involvement in the misconduct itself, as well as failure to supervise, willful blindness, etc. This factor also takes into account the extent to which the misconduct was systemic within the organization—i.e., whether it was an isolated incident or more widespread (in terms of both personnel and location).

4. How Long the Misconduct Lasted

The question of how long the misconduct lasted of course plays into the calculus of its seriousness. The longer the misconduct continued, then the worse the situation. This is both because of the continued misconduct itself and the presumed ongoing weakness in the organization's internal controls that enabled the misconduct to continue. When applying this factor to public companies, the SEC also asks whether the misconduct occurred before the company

---

364 *Id.*

365 *Id.*

went public and, if so, if it facilitated the company's ability to go public.[366]

5. How Much Harm the Misconduct Caused Investors

In keeping with its priority of investor protection, the SEC seeks to determine how much harm the misconduct inflicted upon investors "and other corporate constituencies."[367] It also asks whether the company's share price dropped significantly upon the discovery and disclosure of the misconduct.[368]

6. How and By Whom the Misconduct Was Detected[369]

It's important to know how and by whom the misconduct was detected. Even companies with effective compliance programs can have employees who engage in misconduct. If a company discovers this misconduct in the ordinary course and self-reports and remediates it, that's a sign that the compliance program is working. Or, alternatively, if the SEC becomes aware of the misconduct through a whistleblower report or another source, then the company's compliance program may not be effective.

---

366 *Id.*

367 *Id.*

368 Seaboard Report, *supra* n.357.

369 *Id.*

7. How Long It Took the Company to Implement an Effective Response After the Misconduct Was Discovered[370]

Companies should assume that a proverbial clock starts running as soon as they learn of misconduct. As we address in Chapter 5, companies must have a process in place to promptly and effectively investigate potential misconduct as soon as it's reported/discovered. This is of course also a theme in the CEVS Policy and the DOJ's statements on voluntary self-disclosure. How long it takes a company to implement an effective response upon learning of misconduct speaks to the strength of a company's compliance program and its internal controls.

8. Steps the Company Took Upon Learning of the Misconduct

The eighth factor, referring to the steps that the company took upon learning of the misconduct, is basically a holistic review of how the company dealt with the misconduct upon learning of it. The Seaboard Report includes the following questions in connection with this inquiry, some which overlap with other Seaboard Factors[371]:

> Did the company immediately stop the misconduct? Are persons responsible for any misconduct still with the company? If so, are they still in the same positions? Did the

---

[370] *Id.*

[371] *Id.*

company promptly, completely and effectively disclose the existence of the misconduct to the public, to regulators and to self-regulators? Did the company cooperate completely with appropriate regulatory and law enforcement bodies? Did the company identify what additional related misconduct is likely to have occurred? Did the company take steps to identify the extent of damage to investors and other corporate constituencies? Did the company appropriately recompense those adversely affected by the conduct?

9. Processes the Company Followed to Resolve the Issues and Discover Necessary Information

A company must have a documented process for investigating and remediating potential misconduct, including procedures for obtaining the necessary information. In connection with this factor, the SEC also asks whether and when the Audit Committee and the Board of Directors were fully informed about the potential misconduct.[372]

10. Whether the Company Conducted a Good Faith Root Cause Analysis

The Seaboard Report does not actually use the term "root cause" analysis but that's essentially what is described in its 10th factor. As with the 9th factor, the SEC also asks for details about the process that

[372] *Id.*

the company has undertaken to investigate, disclose and remediate the conduct[373]:

> Did the company commit to learn the truth, fully and expeditiously? Did it do a thorough review of the nature, extent, origins and consequences of the conduct and related behavior? Did management, the Board or committees consisting solely of outside directors oversee the review? If outside persons, had they done other work for the company? Where the review was conducted by outside counsel, had management previously engaged such counsel? Were scope limitations placed on the review? If so, what were they?

As with the other Seaboard Factors, these questions are (at a minimum) questions that Legal and AB&C Compliance should be asking themselves in connection with any instance of potential misconduct.

11. Whether the Company Promptly Made Its Investigation Results Available to the SEC

Like the DOJ's concept of full cooperation, the 11th Seaboard Factor poses questions regarding when, how, and in what level of detail the company provided information about the misconduct to the SEC[374]:

> Did the company promptly make available to our staff the results of its review and provide sufficient documentation reflecting its response

[373] *Id.*

[374] Seaboard Report, *supra* n.357.

> to the situation? Did the company identify possible violative conduct and evidence with sufficient precision to facilitate prompt enforcement actions against those who violated the law? Did the company produce a thorough and probing written report detailing the findings of its review? Did the company voluntarily disclose information our staff did not directly request and otherwise might not have uncovered? Did the company ask its employees to cooperate with our staff and make all reasonable efforts to secure such cooperation?

Here, as with the DOJ's approach, we see the themes of proactive and thorough cooperation—e.g., offering information that has not been specifically requested and which the agency may not have known of otherwise. As SEC Commissioner Crenshaw stated, "[C]ooperation credit is not afforded to companies that merely respond to [SEC] Enforcement Division requests, or to those that offer to conduct a not-so-independent investigation led by corporate counsel. Meaningful cooperation requires a commitment to proactively identifying and remediating wrongdoing, as well as holding accountable those individuals responsible for misconduct. It's about substantially shortening the staff's investigation and working with the staff toward an efficient resolution."[375]

---

[375] Commissioner Caroline A. Crenshaw, *Speech, Moving Forward Together*, U.S. SEC (Mar. 8, 2021), https://www.sec.gov/news/speech/crenshaw-moving-forward-together.

12. Assurances That the Misconduct Would Be Unlikely to Recur

Relating back to the 10th factor, the company must be able to explain the steps that it has taken to ensure that the misconduct under consideration would be unlikely to occur again. Essentially, it must be able to explain in detail how it has remediated the root cause of the misconduct. For example, "[d]id the company adopt and ensure enforcement of new and more effective internal controls and procedures designed to prevent a recurrence of the misconduct?"[376]

13. Whether the Company is the Same Company in Which the Misconduct Occurred or Has Changed Through a Merger, Etc.

In its thirteenth and final Seaboard Factor, the SEC asks whether the company is the same company in which the misconduct occurred or whether it has changed through a merger or other reorganization.[377] The underlying thrust of this question goes to the company's compliance program and any remediation steps that the company may have taken. For example, as we explain in Chapter 6 with respect to mergers and acquisitions, an important part of post-acquisition due diligence is implementing an effective AB&C Compliance program in a new or merged entity.

---

376 Seaboard Report, *supra* n.357.

377 *Id.*

These thirteen Seaboard Factors are largely common-sense and should be questions that an organization considers as part of its own investigation, analysis, and response to any potential misconduct. As with the DOJ's CEVS Policy, there's the strong assumption that, although not technically required, a company will conduct its own thorough and detailed investigation of the misconduct. As the SEC's Division of Enforcement Director David Ceresney reflected in 2015, "the bar has been raised for what counts as good corporate citizenship in the last 15 years or so. For example, internal investigations have now become common, a clear best practice for any company that discovers significant potential misconduct. And sharing the results of those internal investigations with the government has become commonplace, as companies recognize the immense benefits that can accrue to them from doing so."[378]

When considering the Seaboard Factors, it's helpful to keep in mind the DOJ's CEVS Policy and other guidance. As SEC Chair Gary Gensler commented with respect to the October 2021 Memo, "[w]hile our organizations are independent, and our enforcement tools, authorities, and missions are

---

[378] Andrew Ceresney, Director, Division of Enforcement, *The SEC's Cooperation Program: Reflections on Five Years of Experience, Remarks at University of Texas School of Law's Government Enforcement Institute in Dallas, Texas,* U.S. SEC (May 13, 2015) [hereinafter SEC's Cooperation Program], https://www.sec.gov/news/speech/sec-cooperation-program.

distinct, these changes are broadly consistent with my view of how to handle corporate offenders."[379]

a. The Seaboard Factors and the FCPA

Discussing how the Seaboard Factors "play[ ] out in practice," Director Ceresney cited highlighted two FCPA resolutions in connection with the self-reporting and cooperation factors—*FLIR Systems, Inc.* and *Goodyear Tire and Rubber Co.*[380] With respect to the *FLIR* matter, Director Ceresney emphasized that the company self-reported, cooperated, and undertook significant remedial efforts. He recited that the settlement required FLIR to disgorge about $7.5 million, plus pre-judgment interest, but included a penalty of only $1 million, observing that SEC penalties in FCPA cases are often set at an amount equal to the disgorgement amount.[381] With respect to the *Goodyear* settlement, Director Ceresney referred to "the company's prompt self-reporting, remedial acts, cooperation, and disciplinary actions against employees" when explaining that the disgorgement and pre-judgment interest came to over $16 million but that there was no actual penalty.[382]

---

[379] Chair Gary Gensler, *Speech, Prepared Remarks at the Securities Enforcement Forum*, U.S. SEC (Nov. 4, 2021), https://www.sec.gov/news/speech/gensler-securities-enforcement-forum-20211104.

[380] SEC's Cooperation Program, *supra* n.378.

[381] *Id.*

[382] *Id.*

3. SEC ENFORCEMENT WITH RESPECT TO INDIVIDUALS

The SEC has stated that the standards and expectations for individual cooperation are similar to those in the Seaboard Report and identified four general considerations[383]:

- The assistance provided by the cooperating individual.
- The importance of the underlying matter in which the individual cooperated.
- The societal interest in ensuring the individual is held accountable for his or her misconduct.
- The appropriateness of cooperation credit based upon the risk profile of the cooperating individual.

The SEC places a similar emphasis on voluntary disclosure for individuals as it does for organizations[384]:

---

[383] *SEC Announces Initiative to Encourage Individuals and Companies to Cooperate and Assist in Investigations*, Release No. 2010–6, Fed. Sec. L. Rep. (CCH) (Jan. 13, 2010), https://www.sec.gov/news/press/2010/2010-6.htm; *see also Policy Statement Concerning Cooperation by Individuals in its Investigations and Related Enforcement Actions*, Release No. 34-61340, Fed. Sec. L. Rep. (CCH) (Jan. 19, 2010), https://www.sec.gov/rules/policy/2010/34-61340.pdf.

[384] Andrew Ceresney, Director, Division of Enforcement, *Speech, The SEC's Cooperation Program: Reflections on Five Years of Experience*, U.S. SEC (May 13, 2015), https://www.sec.gov/news/speech/sec-cooperation-program.

> [C]ounsel should keep in mind that, just as corporate cooperation credit is greatly enhanced by early self-reporting, the same is true with individuals. The earlier that someone comes in to start a conversation about cooperation, the better it will be for the client, because early action allows us to achieve the efficiency, speed, and effectiveness that result in the highest amount of cooperation credit being given. So, just as we have seen the bar raised in terms of corporate cooperation, I think we are seeing a similar evolution when it comes to individuals.

F. A SHARED DOJ AND SEC OBJECTIVE: INDIVIDUAL ACCOUNTABILITY FOR CORPORATE WRONGDOING

The SEC and the DOJ have different roles and mandates. However, they share enforcement authority for the FCPA and have several compatible, if not overlapping, priorities. One such priority is holding individuals accountable for their misconduct. It has long been recognized that, because a business organization can only act through individuals, it's not enough just to prosecute and punish the organization itself for misconduct. It's a "general principle" in the Principles of Prosecution of Business Organizations that "[p]rosecution of a corporation is not a substitute for the prosecution of criminally culpable individuals within or outside the corporation.[385] There is often a natural overlap between how corporate investigations/resolutions and individual

[385] JM, *supra* n.100, § 9–28.210.

investigations/resolutions are handled because of a common nexus of facts. However, the DOJ has been clear that the management of corporate investigations and resolutions should in no way hamper the DOJ's ability to pursue individual accountability.

The DOJ has been stating for more than a decade that holding individuals accountable for their role in corporate misconduct is a key DOJ enforcement priority. Over time, the DOJ's approach with respect to the information it requires organizations to disclose about potentially culpable individuals (in order to receive cooperation credit) has varied. A brief recitation of recent history is helpful. In 2015, the DOJ underlined that individual accountability was a priority in what thereafter became known as the Yates memo. The Yates Memo laid out the following six steps meant to strengthen the DOJ's "pursuit of individual wrongdoing"[386]:

(1) in order to qualify for any cooperation credit, corporations must provide to the Department all relevant facts relating to the individuals responsible for the misconduct;

(2) criminal and civil corporate investigations should focus on individuals from the inception of the investigation;

---

[386] Yates Memo, *supra* n.283, at 2–3; *see also* JM 9–28.000, *supra* n.100, which includes the principles of the Yates Memo.

(3) criminal and civil attorneys handling corporate investigations should be in routine communication with one another;

(4) absent extraordinary circumstances or approved departmental policy, the Department will not release culpable individuals from civil or criminal liability when resolving a matter with a corporation;

(5) Department attorneys should not resolve matters with a corporation without a clear plan to resolve related individual cases, and should memorialize any declinations as to individuals in such cases; and

(6) civil attorneys should consistently focus on individuals as well as the company and evaluate whether to bring suit against an individual based on considerations beyond that that individual's ability to pay.

The first point is perhaps the most significant and the starkest: "To be eligible for <u>any</u> cooperation credit, corporations must provide to the Department all relevant facts about the individuals involved in the corporate misconduct."[387] As explained in the Yates Memo, and as understood by practitioners, this was a very broad requirement and potentially quite burdensome[388]:

> Companies cannot pick and choose what facts to disclose. That is, to be eligible for any credit

[387] *Id.* at 3 (emphasis in original).

[388] *Id.*

> for cooperation, the company must identify all individuals involved in or responsible for the misconduct at issue, regardless of their position, status or seniority, and provide the Department with all facts relating to that misconduct.

In 2018, Deputy Attorney General Rosenstein reiterated the DOJ's commitment to holding individuals accountable.[389] However, he acknowledged that while the Yates Memo's requirement of identifying *all* involved individuals was a great idea in theory, it was not practical in the civil or criminal contexts.[390] Rosenstein summarized the DOJ's revised approach on this point as follows[391]:

> The most important aspect of our policy is that a company must identify all wrongdoing by senior officials, including members of senior management or the board of directors, if it wants to earn any credit for cooperating in a civil case. If a corporation wants to earn maximum credit, *it must identify every individual person who was*

[389] *Deputy Attorney General Rod J. Rosenstein Delivers Remarks at the American Conference Institute's 35th International Conference on the Foreign Corrupt Practices Act*, U.S. DOJ, OFF. OF PUB. AFFAIRS (Nov. 29, 2018), https://www.justice.gov/opa/speech/deputy-attorney-general-rod-j-rosenstein-delivers-remarks-american-conference-institute-0.

[390] *Id.* ("In response to concerns raised about the inefficiency of requiring companies to identify every employee involved regardless of relative culpability, however, we now make clear that investigations should not be delayed merely to collect information about individuals whose involvement was not substantial, and who are not likely to be prosecuted.")

[391] *Id.* (emphasis added).

substantially involved in or responsible for the misconduct.

In October 2021, Deputy Attorney General Monaco announced a shift *back* to the Yates Memo's requirement that a company identify *all* individuals who may be involved in the misconduct at issue[392]:

> It will no longer be sufficient for companies to limit disclosures to those they assess to be 'substantially involved' in the misconduct. Such distinctions are confusing in practice and afford companies too much discretion in deciding who should and should not be disclosed to government. Such a limitation also ignores the fact that individuals with a peripheral involvement in misconduct may nonetheless have important information to provide to agents and prosecutors. The department's investigative team is often better situated than company counsel to determine the relevance and culpability of individuals involved in misconduct, even for individuals who may be deemed by a corporation to be less than substantially involved in the misconduct. To aid this assessment, cooperating companies will now be required to provide the government with all non-privileged information about individual wrongdoing.

---

[392] *Deputy Attorney General Lisa O. Monaco Gives Keynote Address at ABA's 36th National Institute on White Collar Crime*, U.S. DOJ, OFF. OF PUB. AFFAIRS (Oct. 28, 2021), https://www.justice.gov/opa/speech/deputy-attorney-general-lisa-o-monaco-gives-keynote-address-abas-36th-national-institute.

In September 2022, the DOJ stated that its "first priority in corporate criminal matters is to hold accountable the individuals who commit and profit from corporate crime."[393] It explained that "[s]uch accountability deters future illegal activity, incentivizes changes in individual and corporate behavior, ensures that the proper parties are held responsible for their actions, and promotes the public's confidence in our justice system."[394] The DOJ's view is that focusing on individuals from the beginning of an investigation, and endeavoring to hold individuals accountable, accomplishes a number of goals:

1. It increases the DOJ's "ability to identify the full extent of corporate misconduct"[395];

2. It "increases the likelihood that those with knowledge of the corporate misconduct will be identified and provide information about the individuals involved, at any level of the organization"[396]; and

3. It "maximizes the likelihood that the criminal investigation appropriately identifies and holds accountable culpable individuals and not just the corporation."[397]

We see evidence of the DOJ's focus on individual accountability in the Sentencing Guidelines, the

---

393 September 2022 Memo, *supra* n.225, at 2.

394 *Id.*

395 JM, *supra* n.100, § 9–28.010.

396 *Id.*

397 *Id.*

Principles of Federal Prosecution of Business Organizations, Yates Memo, the CEVS Policy, the October 2021 Memo, and the September 2022 Memo. All are clear that an organization must provide information regarding the conduct of involved individuals (as each document interprets this concept) in order to receive cooperation credit. Moreover, absent extraordinary circumstances, the presumption is that corporate resolutions will *not* protect individuals from criminal or civil liability.[398]

The SEC has similarly taken the position that evaluating an organization's cooperation will in part depend on the extent to which an organization provides detailed information about the identity and conduct of individuals who were involved in the

---

398 Yates Memo, *supra* n.283, at 5.

> There may be instances where the Department reaches a resolution with the company before resolving matters with responsible individuals. In these circumstances, Department attorneys should take care to preserve the ability to pursue these individuals. Because of the importance of holding responsible individuals to account, absent extraordinary circumstances or approved departmental policy . . . Department lawyers should not agree to a corporate resolution that includes an agreement to dismiss charges against, or provide immunity for, individual officers or employees. The same principle holds true in civil corporate matters; absent extraordinary circumstances, the United States should not release claims related to the liability of individuals based on corporate settlement releases. Any such release of criminal or civil liability due to extraordinary circumstances must be personally approved in writing by the relevant Assistant Attorney General or United States Attorney.

potential FCPA violations. As Director Ceresney remarked[399]:

> Some government officials have reemphasized recently the need for companies to share information on individual wrongdoers in order to receive credit for their cooperation. I wholeheartedly agree, and this has long been a central tenet of cooperation with the SEC. When a company commits to cooperation and expects credit for that assistance, the Enforcement staff expects them to provide us with all relevant facts, including facts implicating senior officials and other individuals. In short, when something goes wrong, we want to know who is responsible so that we can hold them accountable. If a company helps us do that, they will benefit.

---

399 SEC's Cooperation Program, *supra* n.378.

CHAPTER 4
THE UK BRIBERY ACT

The UKBA received Royal Assent on April 8, 2010 and became effective on July 1, 2011. It replaced existing legislation that was viewed as splintered and outdated.[1] Its purpose was "to reform the criminal law of bribery to provide for a new consolidated scheme of bribery offenses to cover bribery both in the United Kingdom (UK) and abroad."[2] On March 30, 2011, the Ministry of Justice published The Bribery Act 2010 Guidance, subsequently updated in October 2012 (the "UKBA Guidance"), which discusses procedures that companies can implement to prevent their employees from engaging in bribery. It's basically the UKBA equivalent of the DOJ and SEC's Resource Guide. On that same day, the Director of Public Prosecutions and the Director of the Serious Fraud Office issued joint guidance for prosecutors setting out the Directors' approach to determining whether to bring a prosecution under the UKBA.[3]

Understanding the UKBA is important for a number of reasons related to designing and

---

1 The UKBA replaced existing common law offenses as well as offenses under the Public Bodies Corrupt Practices Act 1889, the Prevention of Corruption Act 1906, and the Prevention of Corruption Act 1916. *Bribery Act 2010* [hereinafter UKBA], Explanatory Notes, ¶ 4, https://www.legislation.gov.uk/ukpga/2010/23/notes/division/2.

2 *Id.*, Explanatory Notes, ¶ 3.

3 Bribery Act: Joint Prosecution Guidance of the Director of the Serious Fraud Office and the Director of Public Prosecutions (Mar. 30, 2011), https://www.sfo.gov.uk/publications/guidance-policy-and-protocols/bribery-act-guidance/.

implementing effective AB&C Compliance programs. For example:

- Many organizations that operate internationally may be subject to the UKBA. Even if an organization is not, best practice is still to construct an AB&C Compliance program that would effectively comply with the UKBA.

- The UKBA is broader than the FCPA in some respects and narrower in others. Understanding the similarities and contrasts between the two is a prerequisite for mapping out an effective AB&C Compliance program, as we'll explain in Chapter 5.

- The UKBA contains the unique element of a corporate offense for failing to prevent bribery. It also provides an organizational defense to that offense if an organization can prove that it had adequate procedures in place to prevent bribery. This offense and corresponding defense send a number of signals, including that AB&C Compliance programs are of great importance. The UKBA Guidance provides advice and recommendations regarding what constitutes "adequate procedures" or, as we might say in the U.S., an effective AB&C Compliance program.

The next sections explain the UKBA's Section 1 offense of bribing another person, its Section 2 offenses relating to being bribed, its Section 6 offense of bribing a foreign public official, and its Section 7 offense of a commercial organization's failure to prevent bribery. As we did with the FCPA, we'll break down the meaning of the key terms in each of these offenses. We'll also compare these offenses to the FCPA's anti-bribery provisions. Unlike the FCPA, the UKBA does not contain accounting provisions.

A. SECTION 1: OFFENSES OF BRIBING ANOTHER PERSON

The first section of the UKBA concerns active bribery—the concept of improperly offering a "financial or other advantage"[4] to any person, whether in the public or private sectors, and whether directly or indirectly (i.e., through a third party). This language is far broader than that of the FCPA's anti-bribery provisions, which focus solely on the bribery of foreign officials and do not include commercial bribery. As explained below, the UKBA also contains an offense prohibiting the bribery of foreign public officials.

UKBA Section 1 specifies that a person ("P") will be guilty of an offense if *either* of the following cases applies:

---

[4] The UKBA's reference to "a financial or other advantage" is effectively equivalent to the FCPA anti-bribery provisions' use of the term "anything of value". UKBA, *supra* n.1, § 1. *See also id.*, Explanatory Notes, ¶ 15 ("The meaning of 'financial or other advantage' is left to be determined as a matter of common sense by the tribunal of fact.").

Case 1[5]: "P offers, promises or gives a financial or other advantage to another person," *and* "P intends the advantage":

(i) "to induce a person to perform improperly a relevant function or activity, or"

(ii) "to reward a person for the improper performance of such a function or activity."

Case 2[6]: "P offers, promises or gives a financial or other advantage to another person" while "P knows or believes that the acceptance of the advantage would itself constitute the improper performance of a relevant function or activity."

The UKBA defines "improper performance" in Sections 3, 4, and 5. The UKBA Guidance summarizes that definition to mean "performance which amounts to a breach of an expectation that a person will act in good faith, impartially, or in accordance with a position of trust."[7] A reasonable person test is used to determine whether a function or activity has been performed improperly. It's generally a test of what a reasonable person in the UK would expect regarding how a function or activity is performed. However, if the performance of the function or activity is *not* subject to UK law (e.g., the activity takes place in a country outside UK jurisdiction) *and* there is a local custom or practice that is permitted or required by that country's

5 *Id.* § 1, ¶ 2.

6 *Id.* § 1, ¶ 3.

7 UKBA Guidance, *supra* Chapter 1, n.2, at 10.

written law, then expectations relating to that local custom or practice will be considered.[8]

Although there are many differences between the UKBA and the FCPA, there is also quite a bit of common ground between the two. This common ground is important to understand when designing and implementing AB&C Compliance programs. As we'll address in Chapter 5, one of the first steps in designing an AB&C Compliance program is mapping out the laws that are appliable to the organization. When thinking about applicable AB&C laws (and particularly considering the FCPA versus the UKBA) visualize a Venn diagram with a large overlapping center. A few of examples of what comprise the center overlap:

Liability/Culpability at the time of an offer: Cases 1 and 2 both refer not only to the giving of an advantage but, consistent with the FCPA's anti-bribery provisions, to the offer or promise to give something with the requisite (improper) intent. So, as it is with the FCPA, an offer itself is potentially enough for liability under the UKBA. This understanding has very practical ramifications for compliance program concepts like required pre-approval of higher risk gifts or entertainment. Pre-approval—meaning AB&C Compliance approval of a request to offer a contemplated thing of value *before* it is offered—is important because liability/ culpability is possible *at the time of the offer* even if

---

8 *Id.*

the benefit or thing of value is ultimately not given or accepted.

Concept of a benefit or advantage: Section 1 refers to "a financial or other advantage," which basically equates to the FCPA's term "anything of value". As we explained in Chapter 3, the Fifth Circuit in *U.S. v. Kay* opined that the FCPA meaning of "anything of value" includes an advantage in business and the SEC and DOJ confirmed this understanding in their FCPA Resource Guide.

Directly or indirectly: Both the FCPA's anti-bribery provisions and the UKBA's Section 1 include payments (or provision of anything of value) directly or indirectly (i.e., through a third party) to the recipient.

B. SECTION 2: OFFENSES RELATING TO BEING BRIBED

The UKBA's Section 2 describes four separate offenses relating to being bribed. This is what we might refer to as passive bribery—the act of improperly *agreeing to accept or accepting* a benefit or advantage. The FCPA, as we know, is a supply-side statute that focuses only on the *offering* of benefits or advantages, and it does not include this concept of passive bribery.

Section 2 specifies that a person ("R") is guilty of an offense if *any* of the following cases (referred to as cases 3–6 in the UKBA) apply:

Case 3: "R requests, agrees to receive or accepts a financial or other advantage intending that, in consequence, a relevant function or activity should be performed improperly (whether by R or another person)."[9]

Case 4: "where

(a) R requests, agrees to receive or accepts a financial or other advantage, and

(b) the request, agreement or acceptance itself constitutes the improper performance by R of a relevant function or activity."[10]

Case 5: "where R requests, agrees to receive or accepts a financial or other advantage as a reward for the improper performance (whether by R or another person) of a relevant function or activity."[11]

Case 6: "where, in anticipation of or in consequence of R requesting, agreeing to receive or accepting a financial or other advantage, a relevant function or activity is performed improperly—

(a) by R, or

(b) by another person at R's request or with R's assent or acquiescence."[12]

Cases 3 through 6 apply whether R themselves directly requests, agrees to receive, or accepts the advantage, or whether R does so through a third party.[13] Cases 3 through 6 also apply regardless of

---

9 UKBA, *supra* n.1, § 2, ¶ 2.

10 *Id.* § 2, ¶ 3.

11 *Id.* § 2, ¶ 4.

12 *Id.* § 2, ¶ 5.

13 *Id.* § 2, ¶ 6(a).

whether the advantage is or will be for R's benefit or that of a third party.[14]

Interestingly, in Cases 4 through 6 "it does not matter whether R knows or believes that the performance of the function or activity is improper."[15] Correspondingly, in Case 6, if a person other than R is performing the function or activity, "it also does not matter whether that person knows or believes that the performance of the function or activity is improper."[16] Basically this eliminates what we might think of as an "intent" requirement and essentially imposes a strict liability standard for passive bribery.

Note that with each offense scenario, there is a link between the request or agreement to accept a benefit or advantage and the improper performance. The UKBA's Explanatory Notes highlight that this linkage may take any of three different forms:

- "R may intend improper performance to follow as a consequence of the request, agreement to receive or acceptance of the advantage"[17] (referring to Case 3).
- "requesting, agreeing to receive or accepting the advantage may itself amount to improper

---

14 *Id.* § 2, ¶ 6(b).

15 UKBA, *supra* n.1, § 2, ¶ 7; *see also id.*, Explanatory Notes, ¶ 26 ("Subsection (7) makes it clear that in cases 4 to 6, it is immaterial whether R knows or believes that the performance of the function is improper.")

16 *Id.* § 2, ¶ 8; *see also id.*, Explanatory Notes, ¶ 26.

17 *Id.*, Explanatory Notes, § 2, ¶ 22.

performance of the relevant function or activity"[18] (referring to Case 4).

- "the advantage may be a reward for performing the function or activity improperly."[19] (referring to Case 5).

Like Section 1, Section 2 uses the term "relevant function or activity" to define the fields in which bribery can occur. Section 3, entitled the "Function or activity to which bribe relates," addresses the definition of this phrase. This section's purpose is "to ensure that the law of bribery applies equally to public and to selected private functions without discriminating between the two."[20] In terms of relative importance, this seemingly places offering a bribe on a par with accepting a bribe.

C. SECTION 6: BRIBERY OF A FOREIGN PUBLIC OFFICIAL

The UKBA's Section 6 sets out the offense of bribery of a foreign public official—the UKBA corollary to the FCPA's anti-bribery provisions. This offense was intentionally drafted to reflect the requirements of the OECD's Convention on Combating Bribery of Foreign Public Officials in International Business Transactions.[21] Section 6 defines a "foreign public official" as a person who[22]

---

18 *Id.*

19 UKBA, *supra* n.1, Explanatory Notes, § 2, ¶ 22.

20 *Id.*, Explanatory Notes, § 3, ¶ 28.

21 *Id.*, Explanatory Notes, § 6, ¶ 34.

22 *Id.* § 6, ¶ 5.

(a) holds a legislative, administrative or judicial position of any kind, whether appointed or elected, of a country or territory outside the United Kingdom (or any subdivision of such a country or territory),

(b) exercises a public function—

(i) for or on behalf of a country or territory outside the United Kingdom (or any subdivision of such a country or territory), or

(ii) for any public agency or public enterprise of that country or territory (or subdivision), or

(c) is an official or agent of a public international organisation.

A public international organisation is defined as "an organisation whose members are any of the following—

(a) countries or territories,

(b) governments of countries or territories,

(c) other public international organisations,

(d) a mixture of any of the above."[23]

For a person ("P") to be guilty of an offence under Section 6, P must intend to influence a foreign public official ("F") "in F's capacity as a foreign public

---

[23] *Id.* § 6, ¶ 6.

official"[24] for the purpose of obtaining or retaining business or "an advantage in the conduct of business."[25] Influencing a foreign public official in their capacity as a foreign public official means "influencing [the foreign public official] in the performance of [their] functions as such an official, which includes—(a) any omission to exercise those functions, and (b) any use of [the foreign public official's] position as such an official, even if not within [that foreign public official's] authority."[26]

Unlike UKBA Section 2's provision on passive bribery, note that Section 6's prohibition on the bribery of foreign public officials includes an intent requirement. Also note its similarity to the FCPA's language on obtaining or retaining business and the specific inclusion of an advantage in business. As previously explained, the "advantage" in business language isn't stated in the FCPA's anti-bribery provisions but it is understood to be within the meaning of their "obtaining or retaining business" language. We also see similarities between the FCPA's definition of "foreign official" and the UKBA's definition of "foreign public official," including but not limited to the inclusion of individuals who work for or on behalf of public international organizations.

As with the FCPA's anti-bribery provisions, bribery can occur when offered or provided to a foreign public official through a third party. Also, the

---

24 *Id.* § 6, ¶ 1.

25 UKBA, *supra* n.1, § 6, ¶ 2.

26 *Id.* § 6, ¶ 4.

benefit or advantage can go to someone other than the foreign public official themselves so long as it was at the request or agreement of the foreign public official. A common example where this can occur is in the hiring space. For example, a foreign public official in country A might suggest their niece for a position at a company in country B when the company is pitching business to that foreign public official's government. The company then hires the niece. Assuming other criteria are met, this could then be a bribery offense under UKBA Section 6 and a violation of the FCPA's anti-bribery provisions even though one might consider that all or most of the benefit is being provided to the niece rather than to the foreign public official.

Section 6 clarifies that P *only* bribes F *if* the following occurs: P (whether directly or through a third party) "offers, promises, or gives any financial or other advantage—

(i) to F, or

(ii) to another person at F's request or with F's assent or acquiescence,"[27] *and*

"F is neither permitted nor required by the written law[28] applicable to F to be influenced in F's capacity

---

[27] *Id.* § 6, ¶ 3(a)(ii).

[28] *Id.* § 6, ¶ 7. The "written law applicable to F" is:

(a) where the performance of the functions of F which P intends to influence would be subject to the law of any part of the United Kingdom, the law of that part of the United Kingdom, as a foreign public official by the offer, promise or gift."[29]

This second piece is hardly surprising. If in fact a public official were allowed by their country's written law to accept and be influenced within the scope of their official duties by a benefit provided by a third party, then there could be no bribery. The public official would not be violating a duty. The FCPA essentially recognizes this point with its local law affirmative defense. *See* Chapter 3 for an explanation of this statutory, though largely hypothetical, defense.

D. SECTION 7: FAILURE OF COMMERCIAL ORGANISATIONS TO PREVENT BRIBERY

Section 7 contains the corporate offense of *failing to prevent* bribery.[30] In this context, bribery only

---

(b) where paragraph (a) does not apply and F is an official or agent of a public international organisation, the applicable written rules of that organization,

(c) where paragraphs (a) and (b) do not apply, the law of the country or territory in relation to which F is a foreign public official so far as that law is contained in—

(i) any written constitution, or provision made by or under legislation, applicable to the country or territory concerned, or

(ii) any judicial decision which is so applicable and is evidenced in published written sources.

[29] *Id.* § 6, ¶ 3(b).

[30] *See generally* Jonathan J. Rusch, *Section 7 of the United Kingdom Bribery Act of 2010: A "Fair Warning" Perlustration*, Yale J. of Int'l Law Online, Vol. 43:1, https://bpb-us-w2.wpmucdn.com/campuspress.yale.edu/dist/8/1581/files/2017/10/Rusch_Section-7-of-the-United-Kingdom-Bribery-Act-2010-A-%E2%80%9CFair-Warning%E2%80%9D-Perlustration-238o4jw.pdf.

means active bribery—offenses under UKBA Sections 1 or 6.[31] There is no corresponding offense for a commercial organization's failure to prevent the solicitation or acceptance of a bribe.

Pursuant to Section 7, a commercial organization faces potential prosecution if a person associated with that commercial organization bribes another person while intending to obtain or retain business or an advantage in business for that organization. Section 7 provides that[32]:

> (1) A relevant commercial organisation ("C") is guilty of an offense under this section if a person ("A") associated with C bribes another person intending—
>
> (a) to obtain or retain business for C, or
>
> (b) to obtain or retain an advantage in the conduct of business for C.

When the UKBA first came into being, there was much anxious discussion about the seemingly unique offense of *failing to prevent bribery*. This was likely due more due to the unique name of the offense than its actual substance. The essence of Section 7 is that an organization may be held liable if someone who works for or on its behalf bribes another person while trying to obtain or retain business for the organization. Put that way, it's not exactly shocking. Rather, it's an expression of the U.S. law doctrine of

---

31 UKBA, *supra* n.1, § 7; *see also id.*, Explanatory Notes, ¶ 51.

32 *Id.* § 7, ¶ 1.

respondeat superior.[33] "Under the doctrine of *respondeat superior,* a corporation may be held criminally liable for the illegal acts of its directors, officers, employees, and agents. To hold a corporation liable for these actions, the government must establish that the corporate agent's actions (i) were within the scope of their duties and (ii) were intended, at least in part, to benefit the corporation."[34] Emphasizing the expansiveness of *respondeat superior,* the Comment to JM 9–28.210 further states that "[a] corporate prosecution may be viable even where a corporation has a policy against the particular activity [and] [m]oreover, the corporation need not even necessarily profit from its agent's actions for it to be held liable."[35]

We'll unpack some of Section 7's key terms and phrases—specifically "relevant commercial organization" and "associated person"—and explore its "adequate procedures" defense to understand Section 7's meaning.

---

[33] *See, e.g.,* JM, *supra* Chapter 3, n.100, § 9–28.500 ("A corporation can only act through natural persons, and it is therefore held responsible for the acts of such persons fairly attributable to it.")

[34] *Id.* § 9–28.210 (internal citations omitted).

[35] *Id.*

1. THE MEANING OF "RELEVANT COMMERCIAL ORGANISATION"

A "relevant commercial organisation" means[36]:

(a) a body which is incorporated under the law of any part of the United Kingdom and which carries on a business (whether there or elsewhere),

(b) any other body corporate (wherever incorporated) which carries on a business, or part of a business, in any part of the United Kingdom,

(c) a partnership which is formed under the law of any part of the United Kingdom and which carries on a business[37] (whether there or elsewhere), or

(d) any other partnership (wherever formed) which carries on a business, or part of a business, in any part of the United Kingdom,

and . . . . a trade or profession is a business.

The term "relevant commercial organisation" is fairly broad in scope. It's generally any organization that (1) carries on *any part* of its business[38] in the UK; and/or (2) was formed under the laws of the UK. Whether an organization that was formed or

---

36 UKBA, *supra* n.1, § 7; *see also id.*, Explanatory Notes at ¶ 48.

37 *See* UKBA Guidance, *supra* Chapter 1, n.2, at 15.

38 Note that a trade or a profession is considered a business for the purposes of Section 7. UKBA, *supra* n.1, § 7, ¶ 5.

incorporated in the UK carries on a business within the UKBA's meaning of that phrase will be determined by a common-sense approach. The courts will be the final arbiter of this determination and will consider the facts and circumstances of the specific case.[39]

Whether an organization formed or incorporated *outside* of the UK will be deemed to be carrying on business in the UK will also be an issue of fact to be determined by the courts using a common-sense approach.[40] The UKBA Guidance implies that there will be more flexibility with respect to non-UK formed entities and that a token connection or presence will not generally amount to carrying on business in the UK within the meaning of Section 7. As the UKBA Guidance explains[41]:

> [T]he Government anticipates that applying a common sense approach would mean that organisations that do not have a demonstrable business presence in the United Kingdom would not be caught. The Government would not expect, for example, the mere fact that a company's securities have been admitted to the UK Listing Authority's Official List and therefore admitted to trading on the London Stock Exchange, in itself, to qualify that company as carrying on a business or part of a business in the UK and therefore falling within

---

39 UKBA Guidance, *supra* Chapter 1, n.2, at 15.

40 *Id.*

41 *Id.* at 15–16.

the definition of a 'relevant commercial organisation' for the purposes of section 7. Likewise, having a UK subsidiary will not, in itself, mean that a parent company is carrying on a business in the UK, since a subsidiary may act independently of its parent or other group companies.

Despite this stated practical approach to dealing with entities formed outside the UK, the statutory definition of "relevant commercial organisation" remains broad and the determination of whether an entity is "carrying on business" is ultimately in the courts' discretion. The resulting uncertainty about whether an organization may ultimately be considered subject to the UKBA is at least part of the reason why many organizations—even those with limited UK connections—design their AB&C Compliance programs to comply with the UKBA.

2. THE MEANING OF "ASSOCIATED PERSON"

An "associated person" within the meaning of UKBA Section 7 is a person ("A") who performs services for or on behalf of ("C"), regardless of the capacity in which A does so.[42] The determination of whether A is an associated person of C is fact specific. As stated in Section 8, paragraph 4, "[w]hether or not A is a person who performs services for or on behalf of C is to be determined by reference to *all the relevant circumstances* and not merely by reference to the nature of the relationship between A and C."[43]

---

42 UKBA, *supra* n.1, § 8, ¶¶ 1–2.

43 *Id.* § 8, ¶ 4 (emphasis added).

To illustrate this point, whether or not a supplier will be considered an organization's associated person will not be determined by the term "supplier" itself but by the specific nature of the services that the supplier actually provides. As the UKBA Guidance recognizes, "where a supplier can properly be said to be performing services for a commercial organisation rather than simply acting as the seller of goods, it may also be an 'associated' person."[44] Looking at the actual nature of a relationship, versus simply what it's labeled, of course makes sense. This is why it is a best practice to review third-party relationships on an engagement-by-engagement basis rather than based simply on generic categorizations like vendor, supplier, or intermediary.

Employees should generally be considered associated persons of their organizations. Returning to the A/C references, if A is an employee of C, then it is a rebuttable presumption that A is an associated person of C.[45] A does not have to have already been successfully prosecuted for the organization to have a Section 7 offense. However, the prosecution would

---

[44] UKBA Guidance, *supra* Chapter 1, n.2, at 16.

[45] UKBA, *supra* n.1, § 8, ¶ 5 ("[I]f A is an employee of C, it is to be presumed unless the contrary is shown that A is a person who performs services for or on behalf of C."). An individual employee's conduct is particularly likely to be attributed to the organization if that employee is of a very senior level. *See e.g.*, *The Bribery Act 2010, Quick start guide*, MINISTRY OF JUST., at 3 ("Your organisation could be liable if a very senior person in the organisation (for example, a managing director) commits a bribery offence. This person's activities would then be attributed to the organisation.") [hereinafter UKBA Quick Start Guide], https://assets.publishing.service.gov.uk/media/5d80cfd5ed915d5257b5b693/bribery-act-2010-quick-start-guide.pdf.

have to show that A would have been guilty of a Section 1 or 6 offense if it had been prosecuted.

The UKBA's definition of "associated person" is intentionally expansive. As the UKBA Guidance explains, this definition "is intended to give section 7 broad scope so as to embrace the whole range of persons connected to an organisation who might be capable of committing bribery on the organisation's behalf."[46]

Jurisdiction for a Section 7 offense goes back to the definition of "relevant commercial organisation." So long as the organization itself fits within that definition, then A does not need to have a close connection to the UK as defined in UKBA Section 12.[47]

3. THE "ADEQUATE PROCEDURES" DEFENSE

UKBA Section 9 directs and empowers the Secretary of State to publish guidance regarding the procedures "that relevant commercial organisations can put in place to prevent persons associated with them from bribing. . ."[48] Pursuant to that directive, the UKBA Guidance states that a "commercial organisation will have a full defence if it can show

---

[46] UKBA Guidance, *supra* Chapter 1, n.2, at 16.

[47] UKBA, *supra* n.1, Explanatory Notes, ¶ 51 ("*[S]ubsection 3(b)* makes clear that there is no need for A to have a close connection to the UK as defined in section 12; rather, so long as C falls within the definition of 'relevant commercial organisation' that should be enough to provide courts in the UK with jurisdiction.") (emphasis in original).

[48] *Id.* § 9(1).

that despite a particular case of bribery it nevertheless has adequate procedures in place to prevent persons associated with it from bribing."[49] The organization would need to demonstrate these adequate procedures by a preponderance of the evidence or, as the UKBA Guidance puts it, "a balance of probabilities."[50]

So, what constitutes "adequate procedures"? In general terms, "adequate procedures" are what we're referring to as an "effective AB&C Compliance program" and consider extensively in Chapter 5. There's no one single answer. As we'll explore, the question of whether an organization's AB&C Compliance program is effective or its procedures adequate will depend on a myriad of factors specific to the organization and its particular bribery and corruption risks. As the UKBA Guidance states, "[t]he question of adequacy of bribery prevention procedures will depend in the final analysis on the facts of each case, including matters such as the level of control over the activities of the associated person and the degree of risk that requires mitigation."[51] The UKBA Guidance also provides a non-prescriptive list of six principles that organizations can apply using a risk-based approach to help them implement adequate procedures. We'll explain these principles in Chapter 5 in connection with the seven elements of effective AB&C Compliance programs.

---

49 UKBA Guidance, *supra* Chapter 1, n.2, at 15.

50 *Id.*

51 *Id.* at 18.

E. QUASI-DEFENSES

The UKBA includes a potential defense to a Section 7 (failure of a commercial organization to prevent bribery) offense but does not include specific defenses for other sections.[52] However, the UKBA Guidance does call out two categories for consideration that reflect the FCPA's two affirmative defenses for bona fide business expenses and conduct that's legal under written local law.[53]

1. HOSPITALITY, PROMOTIONAL, AND BUSINESS EXPENDITURES

The UKBA Guidance, using similar language to that of the DOJ and SEC's FCPA Resource Guide, states that[54]:

---

[52] UKBA Section 13 provides a defense that we do not address in the text because of its specific and limited nature. *See* UKBA, *supra* n.1, Explanatory Notes ¶ 62:

> Section 13 deals with the legitimate functions of the intelligence services or the armed forces which may require the use of a financial or other advantage to accomplish the relevant function. The section provides a defence where a person charged with a relevant bribery offence can prove that it was necessary for:
>
> - the proper exercise of any function of one of the intelligence services; or
> - the proper exercise of any function of the armed forces when engaged on active service.
>
> Although not explicit on the face of the Act, in accordance with established case law, the standard of proof the defendant would need to discharge in order to prove the defence is the balance of probabilities.

[53] 15 U.S.C. § 78dd–1(c)(2); 15 U.S.C. §§ 78dd–2(c)(2), 78dd–3(c)(2).

[54] UKBA Guidance, *supra* Chapter 1, n.2, at 12.

> Bona fide hospitality and promotional, or other business expenditure which seeks to improve the image of a commercial organisation, better to present products and services, or establish cordial relations, is recognised as an established and important part of doing business and it is not the intention of the Act to criminialise such behaviour. The Government does not intend for the Act to prohibit reasonable and proportionate hospitality and promotional or other similar business expenditure intended for these purposes.

Notwithstanding this statement, the UKBA Guidance of course also recognizes that what appear as business or promotional expenses can be used as bribes.[55] For the purposes of Section 6 (bribery of a foreign public official) the UKBA Guidance emphasizes that, in order for there to be a bribe, there has to be (1) the intent for a financial or other advantage to influence the foreign public official in their official role (2) for the purpose of obtaining or retaining business or a business advantage.[56] Keeping this in mind, the UKBA Guidance notes that travel and accommodation costs will sometimes not even amount to a "financial or other advantage" to a foreign public official because that official's government would have paid for that travel or accommodation anyway.[57] *See* Chapter 6 for a discussion of how real-world AB&C Compliance

---

[55] *Id.*

[56] *Id.*

[57] UKBA Guidance, *supra* Chapter 1, n. 2, at 12.

programs address the bribery and corruption risks related to gifts, entertainment and hospitality.

2. LOCAL LAW

The UKBA does not offer a formal "local law" defense to its prohibition against bribery of foreign public officials as the FCPA does. However, that defense is essentially baked into the predicate requirements of the Section 6 offense. There will be no offense if the foreign public official is either permitted or required by the applicable written law to be influenced in their capacity as a public official by the financial or other advantage.[58] The UKBA Guidance describes a somewhat specific context in which written local law may allow an official to request or benefit from a financial or other advantage. That conduct would then be outside the scope of UKBA offenses.

The UKBA Guidance explains that some governments allow or require parties competing for public contracts to include in their proposals offers to invest in the local economy or otherwise assist the local community. In that situation, those offers could "amount to a financial or other 'advantage' to a public official or to another person at the official's request, assent or acquiescence."[59] If the relevant written local law either permits or requires the public official to be influenced by such an offer, then it would be outside the scope of a Section 6 offense.

---

58 UKBA, *supra* n.1, § 6(3)(b).

59 UKBA Guidance, *supra* Chapter 1, n.2, at 12.

Recall that the FCPA's local law affirmative defense requires that the conduct be specifically permissible by *written* local law. Mere local custom or practice, for example, would not be sufficient. It would also not be sufficient if the local law were merely silent regarding the permissibility of influencing a foreign official. With respect to the UKBA, where the written local law is silent regarding whether a foreign public official is permitted to be influenced, prosecutors will consider the public interest in determining whether to pursue a prosecution.[60] As the UKBA Guidance states, "[t]his will provide an appropriate backstop in circumstances where the evidence suggests that the offer of additional investment is a legitimate part of a tender exercise."[61]

F. FACILITATION PAYMENTS

The UK Bribery Act itself does not specifically reference facilitation payments. However, the UKBA Guidance clarifies that the UKBA, like the laws it replaced, does not provide any exemption for such payments.[62] The UKBA Guidance acknowledges that the UKBA differs from the FCPA in this respect. It also notes that the OECD's 2009 Recommendation requests that signatory nations actively discourage companies from making such payments.[63] The UKBA

---

60 *Id.*

61 *Id.*

62 *Id.* at 18.

63 *Id.*

Guidance also unequivocally refers to facilitation payments as bribes.[64]

If the UKBA does not define "facilitation payment", how do we know what that term means in the UKBA context? Does that term, for example, have the same meaning as it does in the FCPA? We can look to the available guidance. The Quick Start Guide to the UKBA, issued by the Ministry of Justice, refers to facilitation payments as "payments to induce officials to perform routine functions they are otherwise obligated to perform. . . ."[65] On its face, that bears a significant resemblance to the FCPA's definition of facilitation payments. Similarly, and again akin to the FCPA's language, the UKBA Guidance refers to facilitation payments as "small bribes paid to facilitate routine Government action."[66]

Since facilitation payments are bribes under the UKBA, how do they fall within the UKBA's various offenses? The UKBA Guidance provides a brief explanation of several possibilities. First, a facilitation payment could constitute the Section 6 offense of bribery of a foreign public official.[67] Recall that Section 6 creates an offense based on the offer or promise of a financial or other advantage to a foreign public official, with the intent to influence that official in the performance of their function, for the purpose of obtaining or retaining business or a

---

64 *Id.*

65 UKBA Quick Start Guide, *supra* n.45, at 7.

66 UKBA Guidance, *supra* Chapter 1, n.2, at 18.

67 *Id.*

business advantage. Notice the absence of the word "improper." Section 6 does not require the official to improperly perform their function, or for the offeror to intend to induce the official to do so, for there to be an offense. A small payment to a foreign public official to encourage that official to perform one of their non-discretionary duties could fall within this section. That payment would likely be considered a facilitation payment under the FCPA and UKBA. As such, it would be *legal* pursuant to the FCPA's facilitation payments exception and *illegal* under the UKBA.

The UKBA Guidance also suggests that where the offeror intends to induce improper conduct, including where the acceptance of the benefit is itself improper, a facilitation payment could also be a Section 1 offence of bribing another person.[68] Then, connecting to that Section 1 offense, there could also be potential liability under Section 7 for the organization's failure to prevent the prohibited conduct.[69]

Although they are illegal under the UKBA, are facilitation payments actually prosecuted? As the SFO has stated[70]:

> A facilitation payment is a type of bribe and should be seen as such. A common example is where a government official is given money or

---

[68] *Id.*

[69] *Id.*

[70] *Bribery Act Guidance,* SERIOUS FRAUD OFF., https://www.sfo.gov.uk/publications/guidance-policy-and-protocols/bribery-act-guidance.

goods to perform (or speed up the performance of) an existing duty. Facilitation payments were illegal before the Bribery Act came into force and they are illegal under the Bribery Act, regardless of their size or frequency.

However, despite the SFO's unequivocal statement that facilitation payments are bribes, there seems to be some flexibility, or at least a perception of flexibility, about whether the SFO will prosecute such bribes. The SFO highlights this point in the "Questions and answers" section on its web site, asking "Is there now no flexibility in relation to facilitation payments?"—thus implying that there has been some flexibility in the past.[71] The SFO provided the following response to its self-reflective question[72]:

> It would be wrong to say there is no flexibility. Facilitation payments were illegal before the Bribery Act 2010 came into force and they remain illegal under the Act. Whether or not the SFO prosecutes in relation to facilitation payments will always depend on (a) whether it is a serious or complex case which falls within the SFO's remit and, if so, (b) whether the SFO concludes, applying the Full Code Test in the Code for Crown Prosecutors, that there is an offender that should be prosecuted. If the requirements of the Full Code Test are not

---

[71] *Id.*

[72] *Id.*

established, the SFO may consider civil recovery as an alternative to prosecution.

In short, are facilitation payments considered bribes under the UKBA? Definitely. Will the SFO prosecute them as such? Maybe, maybe not. It depends. There is apparently some flexibility (a/k/a prosecutorial discretion).[73]

G. CONSEQUENCES

As with the FCPA, violating the UK Bribery Act comes with serious consequences for individuals and organizations. If an individual commits an offense under Sections 1, 2, or 6, that individual can be punished by a fine and/or imprisonment for up to ten years.[74] The fine for individuals and organizations can go up to the statutory maximum (currently £5000 in England, Wales and Northern Ireland, and £10000 in Scotland) if the conviction is summary, and the fine is unlimited if it is on indictment.[75]

---

[73] *See, e.g.*, UKBA Guidance, *supra* Chapter 1, n.2, at 19. ("In cases where hospitality, promotional expenditure or facilitation payments do, on their face, trigger the provisions of the Act prosecutors will consider very carefully what is in the public interest before deciding whether to prosecute. The operation of prosecutorial discretion provides a degree of flexibility which is helpful to ensure the just and fair operation of the Act.")

[74] UKBA, *supra* n.1, Explanatory Notes, ¶ 56.

[75] *Id.*

CHAPTER 5

EFFECTIVE ANTI-BRIBERY AND CORRUPTION COMPLIANCE PROGRAMS

We have addressed the OECD Convention, the UNCAC, the FCPA, and the UKBA. However, how do organizations translate the requirements and principles of these instruments into effective AB&C Compliance programs? The answer to that question is best broken up into three thematic components. First, we'll introduce the purpose and structure of AB&C Compliance programs, including reasons that such programs may be organized in certain ways. Second, we'll identify and explore the seven key structural components of effective AB&C Compliance programs. Third, we'll address specific subject areas that are often included in AB&C Compliance programs, including gifts and entertainment, charitable contributions, public officials, third-party practices, facilitation payments, hiring practices, and business transactions.

A. INTRODUCTION TO ANTI-BRIBERY AND CORRUPTION COMPLIANCE PROGRAMS

The bribery and corruption risks of every organization are different. AB&C Compliance officers need a deep understanding of the industry in which their organization operates, its products and services, and its customers and third-party relationships. They, and senior management, can then decide whether and how to best deploy compliance resources.

Before delving into the nuts and bolts of AB&C Compliance programs and their substantive areas, it's helpful to take a step back and think about the driving forces and theories behind those programs and why they may be structured and in organized in certain ways.

Some considerations include:

- AB&C Compliance's purpose and function;
- AB&C Compliance as an infrastructure function;
- AB&C Compliance's appropriate location within an organization;
- AB&C Compliance's nature as an activist or advisory function;
- An AB&C Compliance officer's role;
- The meaning of a "risk-based" program;
- The relationship between organizational size and regulatory expectations; and
- How to "know" your organization.

1. THE PURPOSE AND FUNCTION OF EFFECTIVE AB&C COMPLIANCE PROGRAMS

The purpose and function of an effective AB&C Compliance program is to prevent, detect and deter bribery and corruption. The DOJ has stated the purpose is to prevent and detect bribery and corruption.[1] From a program perspective, an AB&C Compliance officer also needs to consider how to deter problematic and potentially illegal conduct. This "deterrence" will likely involve both incentive and disciplinary measures, which we'll explore in Chapter 5.

Having an effective AB&C Compliance program is an important end unto itself—the moral good of preventing bribery and corruption and the harms that they inflict upon individuals and society. It's also important for reasons of business efficiency. The goals of compliance and business (i.e., profit) can and should align. Finally, having an effective AB&C Compliance program helps protect an organization when it does have a potential bribery or corruption issue. An effective AB&C Compliance program can be a significant mitigating factor in a bribery and corruption law enforcement investigation.

2. AB&C COMPLIANCE AS AN INFRASTRUCTURE FUNCTION

Many organizations currently have what is referred to as a "three lines of defense" model. The first line might be referred to as the "business". It's the client-facing or outward-facing portion of the organization and generally the portion of the organization that generates revenue. The second line

---

[1] JM, *supra* Chapter 3, n.100, § 9–28.800 ("Compliance programs are established by corporate management to prevent and detect misconduct and to ensure that corporate activities are conducted in accordance with applicable criminal and civil laws, regulations, and rules.")

of defense includes the legal and compliance functions, and the third line of defense is an internal audit function.

As a second-line function, AB&C Compliance is often referred to as an "infrastructure function" or as a "cost center". There can be a subtle (or in some cases not so subtle) bias embedded in these terms. Compliance and legal officers need to be aware of this potential bias and be prepared to manage it.

Generally, the terms "infrastructure function" and "cost center" refer to the fact that a compliance function costs an organization money rather than makes it money. This is true in one sense (that compliance is not itself revenue-producing) but it's also inaccurate in the sense that compliance can save an organization significant sums of money in terms of risk mitigation—i.e., avoiding costly legal issues, settlements, etc. As Deputy Attorney General Monaco once phrased it[2],

> a company can fulfill its fiduciary duty to shareholders and maintain a commitment to compliance and lawfulness. In fact, companies serve their shareholders when they proactively put in place compliance functions and spend resources anticipating problems. They do so both by avoiding regulatory actions in the first place and receiving credit from the government.

---

[2] *Deputy Attorney General Lisa O. Monaco Gives Keynote Address at ABA's 36th National Institute on White Collar Crime*, U.S. DOJ, OFF. OF PUB. AFFAIRS (Oct. 28, 2021), https://www.justice.gov/opa/speech/deputy-attorney-general-lisa-o-monaco-gives-keynote-address-abas-36th-national-institute.

> Conversely . . . the absence of such programs inevitably proves a costly omission for companies who end up the focus of department investigations.

In this vein, compliance is sometimes positively referred to as the "revenue protection unit."

The concepts of compliance and business efficiency do not have to be opposed to one another. When designed and executed correctly, compliance programs promote effective business. Compliance sometimes suffers from the stereotype of being inefficient, not attune to business concerns, and making everything take longer. To the extent this sentiment may exist, there are proactive steps a compliance officer can take to address it. A key step is to get to know people and let them get to know you. For example, go to business committee meetings as a guest speaker to explain what you do and how you and the AB&C Compliance function can help. Meet with people in person where possible. Let them know that you as a compliance officer are there to advise them and to assist them. This helps build trust. If you have a relationship of trust, then people will come to you earlier with questions and information. This will ideally give you the chance to identify issues and provide advice and support before a problem arises. Helping your organization in this way—advising on decisions and helping shape transactions, etc.—can be a very rewarding part of being a compliance officer.

3. AB&C COMPLIANCE'S LOCATION WITHIN AN ORGANIZATION

An initial and strategic decision for each AB&C Compliance program is where it should sit within its organization's structure—e.g., within a business function, within the Legal Department, or as a stand-alone program? The resolution of this question differs widely across organizations. At some organizations AB&C Compliance is a stand-alone function; at some organizations AB&C-relevant components are splintered throughout functions—crossing Legal, Compliance, Human Resources, etc. There's no one right answer (just like there's no "one size fits all program"—an oft-repeated phrase in this book.) However, there are numerous considerations that should inform the decision of where to place an AB&C Compliance program. To name a few:

- <u>Independence</u>: The AB&C Compliance function should have sufficient independence from the organization's business unit(s) so that it can comfortably make impartial decisions and recommendations to the business based on the available facts. This generally means that AB&C Compliance should not have a direct reporting relationship to a business unit and AB&C Compliance officers' compensation should not be determined by business units.

- <u>Privilege</u>: There can sometimes be a very thin line between legal advice and compliance advice. AB&C Compliance may become involved in internal investigations and other matters that are highly confidential and involve legal issues—such as investigating and opining on whether an employee has violated an internal policy and possibly a law or regulation. Though not ideal, as a practical matter AB&C Compliance officers may also review contracts and advise on contract language. AB&C Compliance officers need to be sensitive to privilege issues and make sure that information is properly protected. Because of this—though it's certainly not a blanket protection—organizations sometimes have the AB&C Compliance function either sit within Legal or formally coordinate with Legal.

- Expertise: Is there already a department within the organization that has personnel with the relevant experience and the appropriate skillset to deal with AB&C questions? If so, perhaps the AB&C Compliance function would best reside there.

4. AB&C COMPLIANCE: AN ADVISORY OR ACTIVIST FUNCTION?

If AB&C Compliance is an advisory function, that means that it gives advice regarding the propriety of conduct but does not have the authority to approve or reject a request to engage in specified conduct. If AB&C Compliance is "activist", then it's empowered by the organization to allow or refuse to allow certain conduct. This is a distinction of both philosophy and practicality.

Advice implies optionality rather than mandatory conduct—i.e., "You gave me advice, I considered it, and I made a different decision." *If* an AB&C compliance program is advisory, and therefore its recommendations are not binding, then it must make sure that its advice has the appropriate weight.

Many organizations structure AB&C Compliance (and Compliance generally) as an advisory function as part of the "three lines of defense" model. Referencing that model, the first line of defense (the business) owns the risk and therefore has the ultimate decision-making authority. Within that model, AB&C Compliance would then advise the business regarding how to manage its bribery and corruption risk. While commonly used at large organizations, this model is not without potential pitfalls. For example, its embedded concept that the business "owns the risk" can unintentionally create the impression that first line management has the authority to make business decisions that could expose the organization to unacceptable levels of bribery and corruption risk.

As a practical matter, what could or should happen if, in a three lines of defense model, AB&C Compliance advises an employee against engaging in certain conduct and the employee expresses a preference[3] to do so anyway? This issue can come up

[3] Note the use of "preference". If an employee does not wish to follow AB&C Compliance advice, the employee is *not* free to immediately proceed as desired. Instead, this should open a dialogue between the employee (the first line of defense) and AB&C Compliance (the second line of defense) regarding how to proceed.

in a well-run organization. It's not necessarily a sign that the organization or its employees don't appreciate risk or don't want to comply with the law. There can be a natural push-pull between the compliance side and the business side and reasonable minds can sometimes differ on the way issues should be resolved. There are a few possible ways to deal with this situation, none of which are mutually exclusive.

First, is there a compromise that can be reached—or conditions that could be imposed—where AB&C Compliance would be comfortable with the level of bribery and corruption risk to the organization and the business would largely achieve its objective? For example, if the business wants to retain the services of a third party who is higher risk from a bribery and corruption perspective, AB&C Compliance could potentially become comfortable with this request by requiring enhanced due diligence and monitoring and including robust AB&C representations and warranties in the contract.

A second option is escalation. When AB&C Compliance advises against taking a certain action, and the business still wants to proceed, both sides can escalate the issue to the next level (or levels if necessary) on their respective sides. Minds may meet on either side of the issue at one of those levels. AB&C Compliance may want to include specific language regarding the escalation process in the appropriate policies and procedures.

Third, an AB&C Compliance officer can obtain written confirmation that the business is aware of and has declined AB&C Compliance advice. AB&C Compliance (with the potential assistance of Legal) should document its advice in a communication to the business and have the businessperson who "owns" that decision acknowledge the advice and state that he or she is proceeding contrary to that advice. In practice, this often is a meaningful deterrent. Generally, even if people are certain that they want to take a particular action, people do not like having to state for the record that they are declining AB&C Compliance advice. Note that this approach refers to questions that purely involve matters of compliance with organizational policy and evaluating and accepting risk. If a potential violation of a law or regulation is at issue, then Legal must opine and there's significantly less (if any) room for the business to decide to assume the risk of declining advice.

5. ROLE OF AN AB&C COMPLIANCE OFFICER

Within an AB&C Compliance program, the AB&C Compliance officer's role is to develop, implement, assess, and improve the program on an ongoing basis—i.e., to "own" the program. AB&C Compliance officers provide advice relating to AB&C policy requirements and assist the business and other functions with embedding and operationalizing the policy by providing advice, training, etc.

Understanding who the AB&C Compliance program's stakeholders are, including their key concerns and their relative significance, and defining the AB&C Compliance function's relationship with them, can help avoid pitfalls. It's useful to think of stakeholders broadly, as any person or group that has an interest in or who can affect or be affected by AB&C Compliance's objectives, policies, and decisions.

Of course, not all stakeholders are equal. Some individuals and groups will be more significant stakeholders than others. For example, consider a large financial institution with multiple specialized compliance functions and where some employees are FINRA licensed and therefore subject to specific rules regarding gifting. Then suppose AB&C Compliance publishes a policy addressing certain aspects of employee conduct, such as the giving and receiving of gifts, without first consulting the organization's Regulatory Compliance function that advises the FINRA-licensed employees. Regulatory Compliance would be an AB&C Compliance stakeholder because of the overlap of expertise, interests, and advisory populations between the two functions. If AB&C Compliance does not consult Regulatory Compliance regarding employee gifting requirements, that could create a situation where an AB&C Compliance policy contains the wrong advice or standards.

Being an AB&C Compliance officer is not—and should not—be an easy role. When I think of the challenges of being an AB&C Compliance officer, I recall Assistant Attorney General Polite's apropos remarks when he reflected on his previous role as a Chief Compliance Officer. Assistant Attorney General Polite acknowledged "the resource challenges. The challenges you have accessing data. The relationship challenges. The silo-ing of your function. You are called upon to be a resource for information, an enforcer of law and policy, and somehow the primary architect of your company's ethical culture."[4] He tied this reflection into his role as Head of the Criminal Division, and what the DOJ looks for from compliance officers[5]:

> When you are asked about your compliance program and whether [it is] adequately creating, maintaining, and supporting an ethical culture, the question again goes to individual accountability . . . . I want to know whether you are doing everything you can to ensure that when [an] individual employee is facing a singular ethical challenge, he has been informed, trained, and empowered to choose right over wrong. Or if he makes the wrong choice, you have a system that immediately detects, remediates, disciplines, and then adapts to ensure that others do not follow suit. That is how powerful a role you have in improving our world. Embrace that calling, today and every day.

---

[4] *Assistant Attorney General Kenneth A. Polite, Jr. Delivers Remarks at NYU Law's Program on Corporate Compliance and Enforcement (PCCE)*, U.S. DOJ, Off. Of Pub. Affairs (Mar. 25, 2022), https://www.justice.gov/opa/speech/assistant-attorney-general-kenneth-polite-jr-delivers-remarks-nyu-law-s-program-corporate.

[5] *Id.*

Assistant Attorney General Polite's words are an eloquent reminder of the both the challenges and the importance of a compliance officer's role.

6. THE MEANING OF A "RISK-BASED" AB&C COMPLIANCE PROGRAM

U.S. and international regulators and law enforcement share the expectation that AB&C Compliance programs are risk-based.[6] This means that organizational resources are deployed in proportion to the bribery and corruption risks of the organization. For example, higher-risk areas should be given the commensurate amount of priority for resources like compliance personnel and policies, procedures, and controls. Treating all risks or categories of risk the same is neither effective from a compliance perspective nor efficient from a business perspective. As the UKBA Guidance explains, "[a] risk-based approach will [ ] serve to focus the effort where it is needed and will have the most impact. A risk-based approach recognises that the bribery threat to organisations varies across jurisdictions, business sectors, business partners and transactions."[7]

---

6 *See, e.g.*, FCPA Resource Guide *supra* Chapter 1, n.1, at 68 (providing a Compliance Program Case Study to "illustrate the benefits of implementing and enforcing a comprehensive risk-based compliance program."); UKBA Guidance, *supra* Chapter 1, n.2 at 7, ("As the principles [in this Guidance] make clear commercial organisations should adopt a risk-based approach to managing bribery risks.")

7 UKBA Guidance, *supra* Chapter 1, n.2 at 7.

For example, consider third party risk management. Most organizations have a spectrum of third-party relationships. Does it make sense to have the same level of AB&C Compliance oversight over the paper delivery vendor as over the intermediary who has contact with public officials to obtain or retain business for the organization? In the absence of other facts, probably not. And frankly if the organization did apply the same level of oversight to those very different types of relationships, a regulator's response is unlikely to be applause. Rather, the likely response would be that the organization adopted a standardized approach because it didn't adequately understand its third-party bribery and corruption risk.

AB&C Compliance programs can and should look different from one organization to the next because they should be tailored to the particular organization's business and bribery and corruption risks. Small, medium, and large organizations should have the same rigorous level of commitment to preventing, detecting, and deterring bribery and corruption. However, they may express that commitment in different ways appropriate to their size and available resources. The next section further explains the connection between organizational size and regulatory expectations.

7. ORGANIZATIONAL SIZE AND REGULATORY EXPECTATIONS

Relevant guidance logically acknowledges that the size of an organization is relevant to the formality and scope of the actions that the organization can realistically take to achieve an effective compliance program.[8] For example, the Sentencing Guidelines note that "[i]n appropriate circumstances, reliance on existing resources and simple systems can demonstrate a degree of commitment that, for a large organization, would only be demonstrated through more formally planned and implemented systems."[9] The Sentencing Guidelines also provide the following examples of how a small organization might satisfy the requirements for an effective compliance program[10]:

(I) the governing authority's discharge of its responsibility for oversight of the compliance and ethics program by directly managing the organization's compliance and ethics efforts;

(II) training employees through informal staff meetings, and monitoring through regular 'walk-arounds' or continuous observation while managing the organization;

(III) using available personnel, rather than employing separate staff, to carry out the compliance and ethics program; and

(IV) modeling its own compliance and ethics program on existing, well-regarded

---

8 *Guidelines Manual*, U.S. SENT'G COMM'N, § 8B2.1, Commentary, 2(C)(iii), 520 (2021) [hereinafter Sentencing Guidelines], https://www.ussc.gov/sites/default/files/pdf/guidelines-manual/2021/GLMFull.pdf.

9 *Id.*

10 *Id.*

compliance and ethics programs and best practices of other similar organizations.

Guidance relating to the UKBA similarly conveys this concept of scalability. Prior to the UKBA entering into force, small businesses were encouraged to review the Quick Start Guide published by the UK Ministry of Justice.[11] This Quick Start Guide was prepared with small businesses in mind and with the goal of providing a "concise introduction to how they [could] meet the requirements of the [UKBA]."[12] In addition, the UKBA Guidance provided six guiding principles that organizations could use to develop adequate procedures to prevent bribery. That guidance specifically recognized that small organizations might apply these principles in different ways than large, multi-national organizations.[13]

8. KNOWING YOUR ORGANIZATION

It can't be said enough that there is no such thing as a one-size-fits-all AB&C Compliance program. The program needs to be tailored to its specific organization and that organization's particular bribery and corruption risks. As the JM explains, "[c]ompliance programs should be designed to detect and prevent the particular types of misconduct most

---

11 UKBA Quick Start Guide, *supra* Chapter 4, n.45.

12 UKBA Guidance, *supra* Chapter 1, n.2, at 2.

13 *Id.* at 20 ("Small organisations will, for example, face different challenges to those faced by large multi-national enterprises. Accordingly, the detail of how organisations might apply these principles, taken as a whole, will vary, but the outcome should always be robust and effective anti-bribery procedures.")

likely to occur in a particular corporation's line of business."[14] The bribery and corruption risks of every organization are different. In order to create a risk-based AB&C Compliance program, you first need to know your organization.

Below are some initial questions to ask to help understand an organization. These questions may seem basic but the responses to them will inform various program development and enhancement decisions—e.g., how to allocate AB&C Compliance resources, whether certain areas of the organization need specific bribery and corruption-related policies and procedures, training, etc. These questions are bulleted and explained below.

- In what jurisdictions does the organization do business?

Some jurisdictions are considered higher risk from a bribery and corruption perspective, meaning that bribery and corruption are perceived as more likely to occur in those jurisdictions. There are a number of ways to obtain information about the bribery and corruption risks of various jurisdictions. For example, Transparency International—a global non-profit—provides a publicly-available Corruption Perceptions Index. Some organizations use this index as a shorthand for jurisdictional bribery and corruption risk. Others use it as a starting point or a factor in their own risk methodology. If available, organizations may also utilize data from the their

---

[14] JM, *supra* Chapter 3, n.100, § 9–28.800.

anti-money laundering risk ratings as part of an AB&C country risk rating formula.

- What AB&C laws are applicable to the organization?

The answer to this question grows out of the understanding of the jurisdictions in which the organization conducts business and how it conducts business in each such jurisdiction—i.e., whether its contacts with a particular jurisdiction are sufficient to render the AB&C laws of that jurisdiction applicable to the organization. Depending on the size and business model of the organization, this may be a more or less complicated task. AB&C Compliance and/or Legal need to map the AB&C laws of all the jurisdictions in which the organization does business, compare those laws, and synthesize their requirements into a set of rules for the organization's employees (and possibly its third parties) to follow. AB&C Compliance must then help the rest of the organization to operationalize those rules.

For example, imagine an organization that is subject to both the FCPA and the UKBA. The FCPA's anti-bribery provisions are focused only on the conduct of persons who offer bribes (i.e., "active bribery") to foreign officials. The UKBA of course also prohibits this conduct. However, the UKBA also includes prohibitions on accepting bribes (i.e., "passive bribery") and offering bribes to *any* persons (i.e., "commercial bribery"). If an organization is subject to the both the FCPA and the UKBA, then that organization necessarily must have broader bribery and corruption-related prohibitions than if it were only subject to the FCPA. For example, that organization would need rules governing what its employees (and some or all of its third parties) could offer to and accept from *any* person in connection with the organization's business.

- What is the organization's business from a commercial perspective? What are its products and services?

Once you understand the scope of an organization's products and services, you can consider the bribery and corruption risks that may be attendant to those products and services. For example, cash intensive businesses and transactions are generally higher risk from a bribery and corruption perspective because cash is fungible and can be susceptible to misuse.

- Who are the organization's current and prospective customers?

All customers are not created equal when it comes to bribery and corruption risk. For example, a higher risk customer may be one who is a foreign official or who has contact with foreign officials. Or, it could be a customer about whom there has been negative information in the press relating to bribery and corruption or possibly financial crime in general.

- With what types of third parties does the organization have current and prospective relationships?

As with customers, some third-party relationships will have a higher bribery and corruption risk than others. Third parties who are compensated for acting on behalf of an organization to obtain or retain business for the organization and, while doing so, interact with public officials, generally have a high level of bribery and corruption risk relative to other types of third-party relationships.

- What is the culture like in the organization? Is there a strong ethical backbone to the organization and its actions or does that aspect need to be strengthened?

Ethics and culture should be a cornerstone of any compliance program, but particularly of an AB&C Compliance program where decisions are often not black and white but are values and risk based.

B. THE 7 KEY ELEMENTS OF EFFECTIVE AB&C COMPLIANCE PROGRAMS

You may or may not be in a position where you're building an AB&C Compliance program from scratch. Depending on their particular industry and regulatory environment, many organizations will have a program already in place. But that program will necessarily change over time—whether it's because of changes in the organization's leadership, changes in its products and services and/or geographical footprint, or a myriad of other factors. Therefore, it's important to know the right questions to ask when thinking about whether an organization's AB&C Compliance program is effectively designed. Moreover, an AB&C Compliance officer should always be actively considering ways in which the AB&C Compliance program can be improved. That will often mean re-evaluating initial or previous decisions about how the program has been structured or organized. Ensuring that an AB&C Compliance program is effective is a *continuing* task so it's helpful to walk through program design considerations.

1. INTRODUCTION: SOURCES OF GUIDANCE AND AUTHORITY

When we are considering how to design and implement an effective AB&C Compliance program, it's helpful to look to some of the previously-referenced sources. We'll walk through Chapter 8 of the Sentencing Guidelines, the OECD's Good Practice Guidance, the UKBA Guidance, the SEC and DOJ's FCPA Resource Guide, deferred prosecution agreements with the DOJ, and the DOJ's Evaluation of Corporate Compliance Programs guidance. Each of these sources has its own unique perspective and recites its own set of required compliance program elements. We'll use these a jumping-off point to ultimately identify and define our own seven elements of an effective AB&C Compliance program.

a. Chapter 8 of the Sentencing Guidelines

Historically, Chapter 8 of the Sentencing Guidelines, which deals with the sentencing of organizations, outlined compliance program components that have been the general benchmark for more than twenty-five years. The Sentencing Guidelines state that to have an effective compliance and ethics program, an organization must "(1) exercise due diligence to prevent and detect criminal conduct; and (2) otherwise promote an organizational culture that encourages ethical conduct and a commitment to compliance with the law."[15] In order to do this, the Sentencing Guidelines set out the following requirements[16]:

(1) The organization shall establish standards and procedures to prevent and detect criminal conduct.

(2) (A) The organization's governing authority shall be knowledgeable about the content and operation of the compliance and ethics program and shall exercise reasonable oversight with respect to the implementation and effectiveness of the compliance and ethics program.

(B) High-level personnel of the organization shall ensure that the organization has an effective compliance and ethics program, as described in this guideline. Specific individual(s) within high-level personnel shall be assigned overall responsibility for the compliance and ethics program.

(C) Specific individual(s) within the organization shall be delegated day-to-day operational responsibility for the compliance and ethics program. Individual(s) with operational

---

15 Sentencing Guidelines, *supra* n.8, § 8B2.1(a)(1)–(2).

16 *Id.* § 8B2.1(b).

responsibility shall report periodically to high-level personnel and, as appropriate, to the governing authority, or an appropriate subgroup of the governing authority, on the effectiveness of the compliance and ethics program. To carry out such operational responsibility, such individual(s) shall be given adequate resources, appropriate authority, and direct access to the governing authority or an appropriate subgroup of the governing authority.

(3) The organization shall use reasonable efforts not to include within the substantial authority personnel of the organization any individual whom the organization knew, or should have known through the exercise of due diligence, has engaged in illegal activities or other conduct inconsistent with an effective compliance and ethics program.

(4) (A) The organization shall take reasonable steps to communicate periodically and in a practical manner its standards and procedures, and other aspects of the compliance and ethics program, to the individuals [who are the members of the governing authority, high-level personnel, substantial authority personnel, the organization's employees, and, as appropriate, the organization's agents] by conducting effective training programs and otherwise disseminating information

appropriate to such individuals' respective roles and responsibilities.

(B) [ ]

(5) The organization shall take reasonable steps—

(A) to ensure that the organization's compliance and ethics program is followed, including monitoring and auditing to detect criminal conduct;

(B) to evaluate periodically the effectiveness of the organization's compliance and ethics program; and

(C) to have and publicize a system, which may include mechanisms that allow for anonymity or confidentiality, whereby the organization's employees and agents may report or seek guidance regarding potential or actual criminal conduct without fear of retaliation.

(6) The organization's compliance and ethics program shall be promoted and enforced consistently throughout the organization through (A) appropriate incentives to perform in accordance with the compliance and ethics program; and (B) appropriate disciplinary measures for engaging in criminal conduct and for failing to take reasonable steps to prevent or detect criminal conduct.

(7) After criminal conduct has been detected, the organization shall take reasonable

> steps to respond appropriately to the criminal conduct and to prevent further similar criminal conduct, including making any necessary modifications to the organization's compliance and ethics program.

In implementing the above, "the organization shall periodically assess the risk of criminal conduct and shall take appropriate steps to design, implement, or modify each requirement set forth [above] to reduce the risk of criminal conduct identified through this process."[17]

b. The OECD Good Practice Guidance

The OECD's 2010 Good Practice Guidance on Internal Controls, Ethics, and Compliance (the "OECD Good Practice Guidance") makes the following twelve recommendations regarding the practices of effective compliance programs to prevent and detect foreign bribery[18]:

> 1. strong, explicit and visible support and commitment from senior management to the company's internal controls, ethics and compliance programmes or measures for preventing and detecting foreign bribery;
>
> 2. a clearly articulated and visible corporate policy prohibiting foreign bribery;

---

[17] *Id.*

[18] *Good Practice Guidance on Internal Controls, Ethics, and Compliance*, OECD (adopted Feb. 18, 2020), https://www.oecd.org/investment/anti-bribery/anti-briberyconvention/44884389.pdf.

3. compliance with this prohibition and the related internal controls, ethics, and compliance programmes or measures is the duty of individuals at all levels of the company;

4. oversight of ethics and compliance programmes or measures regarding foreign bribery, including the authority to report matters directly to independent monitoring bodies such as internal audit committees of boards of directors or of supervisory boards, is the duty of one or more senior corporate officers, with an adequate level of autonomy from management, resources, and authority;

5. ethics and compliance programmes or measures designed to prevent and detect foreign bribery, applicable to all directors, officers, and employees, and applicable to all entities over which a company has effective control, including subsidiaries, on, *inter alia*, the following areas:

i) gifts;

ii) hospitality, entertainment and expenses;

iii) customer travel;

iv) political contributions;

v) charitable donations and sponsorships;

vi) facilitation payments; and

vii) solicitation and extortion[.]

6. ethics and compliance programmes or measures designed to prevent and detect foreign

bribery applicable, where appropriate and subject to contractual arrangements, to third parties such as agents and other intermediaries, consultants, representatives, distributors, contractors and suppliers, consortia, and joint venture partners (hereinafter "business partners"), including, *inter alia*, the following essential elements:

i) properly documented risk-based due diligence pertaining to the hiring, as well as the appropriate and regular oversight of business partners;

ii) informing business partners of the company's commitment to abiding by laws on the prohibitions against foreign bribery, and of the company's ethics and compliance programme or measures for preventing and detecting such bribery; and

iii) seeking a reciprocal commitment from business partners.

7. a system of financial and accounting procedures, including a system of internal controls, reasonably designed to ensure the maintenance of fair and accurate books, records, and accounts, to ensure that they cannot be used for the purpose of foreign bribery or hiding such bribery;

8. measures designed to ensure periodic communication, and documented training for all levels of the company, on the company's ethics and compliance programme or measures

regarding foreign bribery, as well as, where appropriate, for subsidiaries;

9. appropriate measures to encourage and provide positive support for the observance of ethics and compliance programmes or measures against foreign bribery, at all levels of the company;

10. appropriate disciplinary procedures to address, among other things, violations, at all levels of the company, of laws against foreign bribery, and the company's ethics and compliance programme or measures regarding foreign bribery;

11. effective measures for:

i) providing guidance and advice to directors, officers, employees, and, where appropriate, business partners, on complying with the company's ethics and compliance programme or measures, including when they need urgent advice on difficult situations in foreign jurisdictions;

ii) internal and where possible confidential reporting by, and protection of, directors, officers, employees, and, where appropriate, business partners, not willing to violate professional standards or ethics under instructions or pressure from hierarchical superiors, as well as for directors, officers, employees, and, where appropriate, business partners, willing to report breaches of the law or professional standards or ethics occurring within the company, in good faith and on reasonable grounds; and

iii) undertaking appropriate action in response to such reports[.]

12. periodic reviews of the ethics and compliance programmes or measures, designed to evaluate and improve their effectiveness in preventing and detecting foreign bribery, taking into account relevant developments in the field, and evolving international and industry standards.

The OECD Good Practice Guidance also highlights the important role that professional associations can play in preventing bribery and corruption. Professional associations can be a valuable resource for subject matter experts within companies. They can provide information and benchmarking opportunities on an array of relevant topics including international developments in the bribery and corruption space, information about effective compliance tools and training materials and methods, and advice on how to handle common advisory questions. As anti-bribery and corruption continues to increase in profile as a compliance and legal priority, compliance benchmarking groups have sprung up in various industries.

c. The UKBA Guidance

The UKBA Guidance provides six "flexible and outcome focussed" principles to help organizations implement "robust and effective anti-bribery procedures".[19] These principles, and their summary concepts, are:

1. Proportionate Procedures

"A commercial organisation's procedures to prevent bribery by persons associated with it are proportionate to the bribery risks it faces and to the nature, scale and complexity of the commercial organisation's activities. They are also clear, practical, accessible, effectively implemented and enforced."[20]

2. Top-level Commitment

"The top-level management of a commercial organisation (be it a board of directors, the owners or any other equivalent body or person) are committed to preventing bribery by persons associated with it. They foster a culture within the organisation in which bribery is never acceptable."[21]

3. Risk Assessment

"The commercial organisation assesses the nature and extent of its exposure to potential external and internal risks of bribery on its behalf by persons associated with it. The assessment is periodic, informed and documented."[22]

---

[19] UKBA Guidance, *supra* Chapter 1, n.2, at 20. These principles are also expressed in the UKBA Quick Start Guide, *supra* Chapter 4, n.45.

[20] *Id.* at 21.

[21] *Id.* at 23.

[22] *Id.* at 25.

4. Due Diligence

"The commercial organisation applies due diligence procedures, taking a proportionate and risk based approach, in respect of persons who perform or will perform services for or on behalf of the organisation, in order to mitigate identified bribery risks."[23]

5. Communication (including training)

"The commercial organisation seeks to ensure that its bribery prevention policies and procedures are embedded and understood throughout the organisation through internal and external communication, including training, that is proportionate to the risks it faces."[24]

6. Monitoring and Review

"The commercial organisation monitors and reviews procedures designed to prevent bribery by persons associated with it and makes improvements where necessary."[25]

These principles can be considered as a high-level, consolidated version of the principles in the Sentencing Guidelines and the OECD Good Practice Guidance. The UKBA Guidance provides helpful commentary on each of these principles.

---

23 *Id.* at 27.

24 *Id.* at 29.

25 UKBA Guidance, *supra* Chapter 1, n.2, at 31.

d. DOJ Deferred Prosecution Agreements, the DOJ's Evaluation of Corporate Compliance Programs Guidance, and the FCPA Resource Guide

Shifting focus back to the U.S., Chapter 8 of the Sentencing Guidelines of course remains, and its requirements have been further amplified by agency guidance, including the DOJ'S Evaluation of Corporate Compliance Programs, the SEC/DOJ FCPA Resource Guide, and Attachment C to various deferred prosecution agreements that specify the minimum standards for an effective corporate compliance program.

Attachments to various FCPA-related DPAs, entitled Corporate Compliance Program, list several elements that the DOJ has prescribed as the minimum standard for an effective AB&C Compliance program. The names and descriptions of each element vary slightly but the overall thrust is the same:

1. Commitment to Compliance/High Level Commitment
2. Policies and Procedures
3. Periodic Risk-Based Review
4. Proper Oversight and Independence
5. Training and Guidance
6. Internal Reporting and Investigation
7. Enforcement and Discipline
8. Third-Party Relationships
9. Mergers and Acquisitions

10. Monitoring, Testing, and Remediation

This list is a mix of what could be considered pure compliance program elements (e.g., policies and procedures) and substantive AB&C Compliance advisory areas (e.g., third-party relationships).

In 2020, the SEC and the DOJ published the second edition of the FCPA Resource Guide, which provided the following "Hallmarks of Effective Compliance Programs"[26]:

- "Commitment from Senior Management and a Clearly Articulated Policy Against Corruption"
- "Code of Conduct and Compliance Policies and Procedures"
- "Oversight, Autonomy, and Resources"
- "Risk Assessment"
- "Training and Continuing Advice"
- "Incentives and Disciplinary Measures"
- "Third-Party Due Diligence and Payments"
- "Confidential Reporting and Internal Investigation"
- "Continuous Improvement: Periodic Testing and Review"

---

[26] FCPA Resource Guide, *supra* Chapter 1, n.1, at 58–68.

- "Mergers and Acquisitions: Pre-Acquisition Due Diligence and Post-Acquisition Integration"
- "Investigation, Analysis, and Remediation of Misconduct"

In addition to providing these hallmarks of effective compliance programs, the FCPA Resource Guide also outlined the SEC and DOJ's general approach to evaluating compliance programs. This approach was further highlighted in 2023 when the DOJ published an updated version of its Evaluation of Corporate Compliance Programs guidance for prosecutors.[27] Like its previous version and the language in the FCPA Resource Guide, this update clarifies that the DOJ doesn't use a rigorous formula to assess program effectiveness. Rather, it considers the specifics of each organization at issue—e.g., size, industry, geographic footprint, regulatory landscape, etc.—and examines the organization's compliance program in that context.

To guide the program evaluation, the Evaluation of Corporate Compliance Programs guidance lays out three "fundamental questions" prosecutors must ask when evaluating a company's compliance program in the wake of misconduct. These are also questions that AB&C Compliance and Legal officers should be regularly asking themselves to reflect on the status of their own programs[28]:

---

[27] Corporate Compliance Programs, *supra* Chapter 3, n.293, at 17.

[28] *Id.* at 1–2.

1) "Is the corporation's compliance program well designed?"

This design aspect includes consideration of the existence and sufficiency of some of the basic compliance program elements that we have previously referenced. For example, are there adequate policies and procedures? Are training and communication efforts tailored to the unique requirements and needs of the company? Why has the company has set up its compliance program the way it has and why and how has its program evolved over time?

As DOJ Criminal Division Assistant Attorney General Kenneth Polite explained in a March 22, 2022 speech at NYU's Program on Corporate Compliance and Ethics[29]:

> First, when we say that we expect a company's compliance program to be well designed, we closely examine the company's process for assessing risk and building a program that is tailored to manage its specific risk profile. We want to see whether the company has implemented policies and procedures that are designed to address the key risk areas identified in its risk assessments, and that those policies and procedures are easily accessible and

---

[29] *Assistant Attorney General Kenneth A. Polite, Jr. Delivers Remarks at NYU Law's Program on Corporate Compliance and Enforcement (PCCE)*, U.S. DOJ, OFF. OF PUB. AFFAIRS (Mar. 25, 2022), https://www.justice.gov/opa/speech/assistant-attorney-general-kenneth-polite-jr-delivers-remarks-nyu-law-s-program-corporate.

understandable to the company's employees and business partners. We want to know how the company is training employees, management, and third-parties on the risk areas and responsibilities applicable to those individuals. Policies, training, and other processes should address relevant high-risk elements of the company's business model, such as third-party relationships or mergers and acquisitions. We want to see that the company has established a process for reporting violations of law or company policy that encourages employees to speak up without fear of retaliation, and that those reports are taken seriously, appropriately documented, investigated and—if substantiated—remediated.

2) **"Is the program being applied earnestly and in good faith? In other words, is the program adequately resourced and empowered to function effectively?"**

Assistant Attorney General Polite expanded on this question of resourcing and empowerment by explaining that[30]:

> [W]hen we are evaluating whether a compliance program is adequately resourced and empowered to function effectively, we want to know more than dollars, headcount, and reporting lines. We will review the qualifications and expertise of key compliance personnel and

[30] *Id.*

> other gatekeeper roles. We want to know if compliance officers have adequate access to and engagement with the business, management, and the board of directors. We seek to understand whether and how a company has taken steps to ensure that compliance has adequate stature within the company and is promoted as a resource. A company's commitment to promoting compliance and ethical values at all levels—from the chief executive on down to middle and lower-level managers—is critical.

For example, has the company's senior leadership set the tone for the rest of the company? To what extent has senior management clearly articulated the company's ethical standards, conveyed and disseminated them in clear and unambiguous terms, and demonstrated rigorous adherence by example? And has that commitment been instilled at all levels? The updated guidance makes clear that the DOJ will evaluate programs at two points—the time of the offense and the time of the charging decision or resolution.

3) "Does the corporation's compliance program work in practice?"

A key consideration here is whether the compliance program has evolved over time to address existing and changing compliance risks. For example, when a company's AB&C Compliance program has identified a problem, how has it dealt with that problem? The DOJ emphasizes the expectation that a company undertake an honest root cause analysis to determine both what contributed to the misconduct and the degree of remediation needed to prevent similar events in the future. As Assistant Attorney General Polite phrased it[31]:

> [W]e want to see evidence that the compliance program is working in practice. We look at whether the company is continuously testing the effectiveness of its compliance program, and improving and updating the program to ensure that it is sustainable and adapting to changing risks. We want to know that a company can identify compliance gaps or violations of policy or law. Equally importantly, we want to see how the company addresses the root causes of these gaps or violations and finds ways to improve its controls and prevent recurrence of issues. We want to see examples of compliance success stories—the discipline of poor behavior, the rewarding of positive behavior, the transactions that were rejected due to compliance risk, positive trends in whistleblower reporting, and the partnerships that have developed between compliance officers and the business. We are also interested in how a company measures and tests its culture—at all levels of seniority and throughout its operations—and how it uses the data from that testing to embed and continuously improve its ethical culture.

---

31 *Id.*

Two points about these questions and related remarks should be noted. First, they take a practical approach—is the program well designed, is it adequately resourced, and does it *actually* work in practice? Second, these questions underscore the concept that AB&C Compliance programs don't have to be bulletproof. There's no such thing as 100% coverage of all risks—it's not necessary, efficient, or expected. The Sentencing Guidelines also support the conclusion that "effective" doesn't equal perfect. The Sentencing Guidelines note that compliance programs should "be reasonably designed, implemented, and enforced so that the program is generally effective in preventing and detecting criminal conduct. The failure to prevent or detect the instant offense does not necessarily mean that the program is not generally effective in preventing and detecting criminal conduct."[32]

Upon reflection, we can distill the available U.S. and international guidance into the following seven components of effective AB&C Compliance programs:

(1) Commitment to Compliance/Conduct from the Top

(2) Policies and Procedures

(3) Communication & Training

(4) Reporting Mechanism

(5) Investigation and Remediation

(6) Enforcement, Discipline & Incentives

(7) Ongoing Program Improvement

---

[32] Sentencing Guidelines, *supra* n.8, § 8B2.1(a).

While all seven elements must be present for there to be an effective AB&C Compliance program, these elements will look different in every organization. They will be implemented on a scalable basis to reflect the organization's size and bribery and corruption risks. As the UKBA Guidance notes with respect to its six principles, "[s]mall organisations will, for example, face different challenges to those faced by large multi-national enterprises. Accordingly, the detail of how organisations might apply these principles, taken as a whole, will vary, but the outcome should always be robust and effective anti-bribery procedures."[33]

2. COMMITMENT TO COMPLIANCE/ CONDUCT FROM THE TOP

When the Commitment to Compliance/Conduct From the Top concept was first introduced, it was referred to as "tone at the top."[34] That gradually evolved into "conduct from the top," as the SEC and DOJ emphasized that they were looking for an active commitment to compliance by an organization's senior management. And we're not talking only about Legal and Compliance here—we're talking about senior management from the first line. In the words

---

33 UKBA Guidance, *supra* Chapter 1, n.2, at 20.

34 *See e.g.*, Stephen M. Cutler, Director, Division of Enforcement, U.S. Securities and Exchange Commission, *Speech by SEC Staff: Second Annual General Counsel Roundtable: Tone at the Top: Getting it Right*, U.S. SEC (Dec. 3, 2004), https://www.sec.gov/news/speech/spch120304smc.htm.

of Stephen Cutler, former Director of the SEC's Division of Enforcement[35]:

> [I]t has to be senior management—not just the legal department, the compliance professionals, or human resource experts—that does the talking. Matters of ethics and culture shouldn't be shunted off to the outer edges (or cost centers) of a corporate organization. In order to convey the importance of integrity and honesty to a corporation's employees, those who run the business, those who are responsible for the bottom line, have to be the ones to tell employees that integrity and honesty matter. For if they don't do it, employees won't believe that those values are core values; they won't believe that integrity and honesty are important to those who really matter; they won't believe that their path to success will require adherence to those values. So when you take your ethics roadshow to your employees, have your most senior managers play an active role.

Commitment to Compliance has been defined as senior management's "strong, explicit, and visible support and commitment to [the] corporate policy against violations of the anti-corruption laws and its compliance codes, and demonstrate[ion] [of] rigorous

---

[35] *Id.*; *see also* UKBA Guidance, *supra* Chapter 1, n.2, at 23 ("The top-level management of a commercial organisation (be it a board of directors, the owners or any other equivalent body or person) are committed to preventing bribery by persons associated with it. They foster a culture within the organisation in which bribery is never acceptable.")

adherence by example."[36] Senior management needs to model—by conduct, not just words—the desired behavior for all employees. How can senior management do so? There's no single answer and it depends on the culture of the organization as well as its size and complexity.

The UKBA Guidance suggests that senior management's communication of a formal statement can be an effective way to establish an anti-bribery and corruption culture. The UKBA Guidance explains that such a statement could include, for example, an expression of the organization's commitment to carry out its business fairly and transparently and with a zero-tolerance approach to bribery and corruption.

Such a statement is of course helpful. However, it should be viewed as a baseline—a starting point rather than an end point. Senior management needs to go further than this. How can senior management go beyond mere words to demonstrate commitment? What are some practical manifestations of Commitment to Compliance/Conduct from the Top?

Resourcing is certainly one concrete way to demonstrate commitment. Senior management can sufficiently fund and staff an AB&C Compliance function with personnel of appropriate seniority and experience. Senior management can also take opportunities to highlight the organization's

---

[36] *U.S. v. Deutsche Bank Aktiengesellschaft*, Cr. No. 20-00584, Attachment C, ¶ 1. (E.D.N.Y. 2021) [hereinafter DB DPA], https://www.justice.gov/d9/press-releases/attachments/2021/01/27/deutsche_bank_dpa_0.pdf.

commitment to anti-bribery and corruption by discussing the program at employee townhall meetings, in email updates, etc.

As the UKBA Guidance explains, regardless of the size, scope, and management structure of the organization, "top-level engagement is likely to reflect the following elements[37]:

- Selection and training of senior managers to lead anti-bribery work where appropriate.
- Leadership on key measures such as a code of conduct.
- Endorsement of all bribery prevention related publications.
- Leadership in awareness raising and encouraging transparent dialogue throughout the organisation so as to seek to ensure effective dissemination of anti-bribery policies and procedures to employees, subsidiaries, and associated persons, etc.
- Engagement with relevant associated persons and external bodies, such as sectoral organisations and the media, to help articulate the organisation's policies.
- Specific involvement in high profile and critical decision making where appropriate.
- Assurance of risk assessment.

---

[37] UKBA Guidance, *supra* Chapter 1, n.2, at 24.

- General oversight of breaches of procedures and the provision of feedback to the board or equivalent, where appropriate, on levels of compliance."

A strong commitment to AB&C Compliance is not just for senior personnel. The commitment starts at the top, but it needs to permeate through all layers of an organization. The DOJ recognized this in the Deutsche Bank DPA when it specifically referred also to middle management and employees at all levels. The DPA stated that "[t]he Company will also ensure that middle management, in turn, require employees and agents to abide by [its corporate policy against violations of the anti-corruption laws and its compliance codes]. The Company will create and foster a culture of ethics and compliance with the law in its day-to-day operations at all levels of the company."[38]

3. POLICIES AND PROCEDURES

Policies and procedures are the foundation of an AB&C Compliance program. We'll address initial and overall AB&C policy framework considerations, the many types of AB&C policies, and provide practical tips for maximizing their utility.

a. Initial and Overall AB&C Policy Framework Considerations

Before delving into the specific types of AB&C-related policies, it's helpful to discuss some

---

[38] DB DPA, *supra* n.36, Attachment C, ¶ 1.

fundamental questions regarding the policy framework and approach:

- Whether the AB&C policies should be principles-based or rules-based;
- Whether and how to define a minimum standard of compliance;
- The population to whom the AB&C policies will apply; and
- The key characteristics that make AB&C policies effective.

i. Whether AB&C Policies Should Be Principles-Based or Rules-Based

As an initial matter, the AB&C policy writers need to determine whether the approach of the policies and procedures will be principles-based or rules-based. Each of these approaches has its own benefits and challenges.

With a principles-based approach, policies will provide guidelines rather than specific rules. For example, a principles-based policy might state that employees should not provide "lavish" gifts or entertainment to current or prospective customers or third parties. The term "lavish" might be left undefined and employees would be expected to use their own judgment to comply with the principle.

One benefit to a principles-based approach is that it empowers employees to make their own decisions. Employees may feel trusted and, in turn, exercise their responsibilities with care and deliberation. A second benefit to a principles-based approach is that it may save time on up-front administrative tasks. For example, employees may not be required to obtain AB&C Compliance pre-approval for all gifts and entertainment.

A downside of a principles-based policy approach is that it can be difficult to confirm that employees are complying with the policy. If, for example, employees are not required to obtain pre-approval for all gifts and entertainment, then there must be back-end testing (e.g., review of credit card bills, etc. to confirm compliance with the policy). However, can such testing necessarily even be done? Consider the prohibition on "lavish" gifts and entertainment as an example. If "lavish" is not defined by a dollar amount, then how can compliance with that prohibition be tested? How can AB&C Compliance officers determine whether or not employees are acting in line with the policy? Reasonable minds (especially across varying geographies and cultures) could easily differ on the question of whether something is or is not lavish. If a standard is not objective, then it can't be tested and therefore the effectiveness of the policy cannot be demonstrated. If an organization is in a highly regulated industry like financial services, it is difficult to have a purely principles-based policy approach. Such an approach works best in a small organization with knowledgeable professionals in a light to moderately regulated industry.

Conversely, if a policy was rules-based, then the policy would provide specific requirements. For example, a rules-based policy might state that employees should not provide gifts or entertainment to current or prospective customers or third parties that cost more than $100 per person.

There are many benefits to a rules-based policy approach. The policy requirements are clear and objective and therefore compliance with the policy is measurable and demonstrable. However, a downside of a rules-based approach is that it may carry a heavier administrative burden than a principles-based approach. To continue with our "lavish" example, a rules-based policy may include a relatively low monetary threshold over which AB&C Compliance pre-approval for a gift or entertainment is required. The intent is of course the same as with the principles-based approach—to prevent employees from offering lavish gifts or entertainment to current or prospective clients or third parties. However, additional time and resources will be required for employees to seek pre-approval for gifts and entertainment and for AB&C Compliance officers to evaluate those requests.

Organizations may use a combination of the principles based and rules-based approaches. This is especially common in large, multi-jurisdictional organizations. In such organizations there will often be a code of conduct/code of ethics and an AB&C policy. Those documents will be high level and largely principles based. Underneath those documents will be additional layers of more specific policies and procedures that may be rules-based.

ii. Whether and How to Define a General Minimum Standard of Compliance

An organization must define minimum standards of behavior that it requires of its employees (and possibly of its third parties). Generally speaking, the strictest requirements among the applicable AB&C laws should be the ones that become the standards embodied in the AB&C policies. However, there are some benefits to this approach and some downsides.

In terms of benefits, it simplest to have a single set of standards to which all employees must adhere. It's simplest for employees because it's consistent across the population. It's also simplest for AB&C Compliance because there's a single set of standards to apply rather than disparate rules. Finally, this approach is the simplest to implement from a systems and technology perspective.

However, conversely, there are also downsides to adopting a single set of standards. For example, jurisdictions or business lines subject to less stringent AB&C laws may have to comply with stricter standards even though the AB&C laws specifically applicable to a particular jurisdiction or business line do not require it.

Given these benefits and downsides, is there is compromise that may be reached on minimum policy standards? Yes, there are a couple of different possibilities. Policies may have a single set of minimum standards that apply across the board. Then those regions or employee populations that are subject to less stringent AB&C laws or requirements may be carved out from that set of minimum standards. Conversely, those regions or employee populations that are subject to more stringent AB&C laws or requirements may be subject to a policy addendum that details those more stringent requirements.

iii. To Whom the AB&C Policies and Procedures Will Apply

At a minimum, an organization's AB&C policies and procedures must apply to its employees, as that term is defined by applicable law and the organization's Human Resources and Legal departments. Beyond that, an organization then needs to consider other categories of persons that it may want to bring within its policy scope. Although these individuals will not technically be employees, they may be people over whom the organization (1) has some degree of control or responsibility; and/or (2) who potentially present a certain degree of bribery and corruption risk. Some possible examples are temporary employees, contractors, and consultants.

It should be noted that there can be some overlap between who may be considered employees and who may be considered third parties. AB&C Compliance officers must watch this potential gap to ensure that all relevant categories of persons are appropriately addressed in policy language. An example of this potential gap, which particularly occurs at large organizations, is senior personnel who retire as employees but are later re-hired as consultants to provide their particular expertise. Often these individuals are outside the technical scope of the organization's definition of "employee" but are not really third parties so they fall in a gap where they may not be governed by AB&C policies. A second example is independent directors on boards of directors. Again, these individuals are not employees, but are also not third parties so by what policies are they governed? Mind the gap!

Finally, a common sense but important point—if an organization's AB&C policies and procedures purport to govern consultants or other quasi-employee groups, then the organization needs to make sure those groups have access to the policy and procedures, have the relevant training, and have access to any systems needed to effectuate the policy—e.g., like systems that record gifts and entertainment.

b. Key Characteristics of Effective AB&C Policies and Procedures

To be effective, AB&C policies and procedures should be accessible, realistic, measurable, and enforceable. Below are brief explanations of these characteristics.

Accessible: Employees need to know that the AB&C policies and procedures exist and how to access them. The policies and procedures must also be available in the appropriate language or languages. Finally, the policies and procedures should be plainly written so that they are easily understood.

Realistic: An organization could have a law firm or consultant write a beautiful policy with all the bells and whistles, requiring extensive due diligence on all third parties, etc. However, a policy can't just be a piece of paper; it must be operationalized. Therefore, it needs to be realistic and not aspirational. An organization needs to have the capability to comply with its AB&C policy *at the time that it goes into effect*. An organization will be judged by its auditors and by its regulators about whether it's complying with its own policies. An organization may of course make its policies more stringent over time. However, an organization should not set itself up for failure by creating a standard that it cannot meet.

Measurable: There must be ways to assess whether employees are complying with the AB&C policy. The policy requirements need to be clear enough so that employee compliance with them can be tested.

Consider the following practice example: An organization is updating its gifts and entertainment policy. The existing policy requires employees to submit final documentation (e.g., receipts, names of attendees, etc.) of an entertainment event no later than 30 calendar days after the event. A proposed policy revision would require employees to submit final documentation of an entertainment event "as soon as is practicable" after an event.

What is the key difference between these two policy requirements? The first is objective and measurable—30 calendar days from the date of the event. The second is not. "As soon as is practicable" is subjective and could be different for different people depending on their individual circumstances. Maybe an employee was out of the office traveling so she would say it wasn't practicable for her to submit the documentation until two weeks after an event. How would an AB&C Compliance officer judge what is or is not practicable for an individual employee? Since the "as soon as is practicable" standard is not objective, it's not measurable. This means that audit and testing functions, not to mention regulators, would not be able to tell if employees were complying with the policy. Also, since the standard not measurable, it's arguably not enforceable—i.e., AB&C Compliance would not be able to issue policy violations based on an employee's failure to submit documentation "as soon as is practicable."

Enforceable: Policies and procedures need to have consequences if they are violated. The potential consequences should be spelled out in the relevant policy or procedure and there must be a person or persons empowered to (1) determine whether a specific instance of conduct violated an AB&C policy or procedure and, (2) if it did violate an AB&C policy or procedure, decision and impose consequences.

c. Types of AB&C Policies and Procedures

Like all elements of an AB&C Compliance program, the scope of the policies and procedures should depend on the size, complexity, and bribery and corruption risks of the organization. For example, a small organization with limited bribery and corruption risks may simply have a code of conduct, which includes anti-bribery and corruption language as well as text on other relevant compliance topics.

Similarly, how an AB&C Compliance function organizes its AB&C policies will depend on the organization's particular structure and on the views of those responsible for the AB&C Compliance program. For example, AB&C policies may be stand-alone policies focusing only on AB&C issues. Alternatively, AB&C topics may be broken up and dispersed among a number of different policies. For example, AB&C-related rules regarding hiring may be contained in a Human Resources policy as opposed to an AB&C-titled policy.

There's no single correct way to organize and structure an AB&C policy framework. It can be done in a number of ways so long as the organization's bribery and corruption risks are appropriately addressed, and the policies and procedures are effective. For illustrative purposes, we'll assume a large, complex organization with a Code of Conduct as well as several layers of AB&C-specific policies, which are described below.

i. Code of Ethics or Code of Conduct

The Code of Ethics or Code of Conduct (the "Code") is generally the basis for all of an organization's other policies and procedures. It states the organization's overarching emphasis ethics and on compliance with all applicable laws and regulations. The Code is meant for all employees and all representatives of the organization, not just those most actively involved in known compliance and ethics issues. An organization may also want its Code of Ethics to apply to some or all of the third parties with whom it deals.

All members of the organization from the most senior to the most junior must receive, read, understand, and agree (often through a written acknowledgement process) to abide by the Code's standards. For this reason, the Code should be written in a simple and concise manner that is reader-friendly and it should be available in multiple language for a diverse workforce.

The Code's contents must be tailored to the organization's culture, industry, and corporate identity. Disciplinary procedures and consequences—up to and including termination for violations of the Code—should be referenced to emphasize the organization's commitment to ethics and compliance and to set reader expectations.

ii. Global AB&C Policy

While the Code provides overarching guidance on the organization's standards for behavior and decision making, the global AB&C Policy is of course specific to bribery and corruption risk.

The UK Bribery Act Guidance provides the following "indicative" and "non-exhaustive" list of the topics that may be included in an AB&C policy[39]:

---

[39] UKBA Guidance, *supra* Chapter 1, n.2, at 22. (Internal references to Principles have been omitted.)

- "its commitment to bribery prevention";
- "its general approach to mitigation of specific bribery risks, such as those arising from the conduct of intermediaries and agents, or those associated with hospitality and promotional expenditure, facilitation payments or political and charitable donations or contributions";
- "an overview of its strategy to implement its bribery prevention policies";
- "[t]he involvement of the organisation's top-level management";
- "[r]isk assessment procedures";
- "[d]ue diligence of existing or prospective associated persons";
- "[t]he provision of gifts, hospitality and promotional expenditure; charitable and political donations; or demands for facilitation payments";
- "[d]irect and indirect employment, including recruitment, terms and conditions, disciplinary action and remuneration";
- "[g]overnance of business relationships with all other associated persons including pre and post contractual agreements";
- "[f]inancial and commercial controls such as adequate bookkeeping, auditing and approval of expenditure";

- "[t]ransparency of transactions and disclosure of information";
- "[d]ecision making, such as delegation of authority procedures, separation of functions and the avoidance of conflicts of interest";
- "[e]nforcement, detailing discipline processes and sanctions for breaches of the organisation's anti-bribery rules";
- "[t]he reporting of bribery including 'speak up' or 'whistle blowing' procedures";
- "[t]he detail of the process by which the organisation plans to implement its bribery prevention procedures, for example, how its policy will be applied to individual projects and to different parts of the organisation";
- "[t]he communication of the organisation's policies and procedures, and training in their application"; and
- "[t]he monitoring, review and evaluation of bribery prevention procedures".

The sections below explain some of the core elements of global AB&C policies, many elements of which should also be included in the downstream AB&C policies.

(a) Reason(s) for the Policy/Policy Statement

The global AB&C policy may contain an introductory section discussing why the policy is in place and why compliance with the policy is important. It should set out the organization's zero tolerance approach to bribery and corruption. This includes the organization's commitment to complying with both the letter and the spirit of the applicable AB&C laws in the jurisdictions in which it operates. AB&C policies often make a general statement to this effect and then name one or more of the AB&C laws to which the organization is subject. For example, a policy may state: "Organization X will comply with all applicable laws in the jurisdictions in which it operates or conducts business, including but not limited to the U.S. Foreign Corrupt Practices Act and the UK Bribery Act 2010. This global AB&C Policy, together with the Code of Conduct and other related policies, procedures, and controls, is designed to help Organization X comply with applicable laws and regulations and to effectively manage bribery and corruption risks."

A policy statement may also include the organization's expectation that there will be transparency and integrity in all facets of its business operation to avoid improper conduct and the appearance of impropriety.

(b) Global Minimum Standard

The global AB&C policy should state that it provides the minimum global standard to be applied across all jurisdictions in which the organization operates and with respect to all persons and entities subject to the policy.

(c) *Definitions*

The global AB&C policy should include a definitional section. Throughout the text of the policy, defined terms should be capitalized or bolded to alert the reader that these terms are fully explained in the definitional section. The policy should explain this by stating, for example: "Definitions of bolded terms and phrases used in this policy are contained in Appendix 1." For illustrative purposes, we will give thought to potential policy definitions of "bribery," "corruption," and "anything of value."

Effective AB&C Compliance programs (even those for purely domestic U.S. companies) should be designed more broadly than simply to comply with the FCPA. For this reason, it's helpful to use a basic definition of bribery from a melding of different sources. For example, "bribery" may be defined as:

> Any action involving the offer, promise, authorization, giving, solicitation, request, receipt, or acceptance of Anything of Value to or from any person (whether directly or indirectly) to improperly: obtain or retain business, obtain or retain an advantage in business, influence the performance of a public or private function, or to induce or reward someone to act contrary to applicable laws, regulations, rules or policies, or to act in contravention of a duty or without honesty and integrity. There is no minimum value amount for a bribe.

You will notice that this sample definition of bribery is very broad. It includes what is sometimes referred to as "active bribery"—meaning the offering or giving of a bribe. It also includes what can be referred to as "passive bribery"—meaning the request, receipt, or acceptance of a bribe. This working definition also references "any person" so it is not limited to the bribery of foreign officials but rather also includes "commercial bribery," which is the bribery of private individuals.

As previously explained in Chapter 3, "anything of value" should be understood to have its literal meaning. Policies may include a definition of "anything of value" to illustrate this point to employees. For example, a policy could provide the following explanation:

> Anything of Value should be interpreted broadly to literally include anything (whether monetary or non-monetary, and whether offered or provided directly or indirectly) that provides a benefit to any person. It includes Gifts, Entertainment, Charitable Contributions, Political Contributions, discounts, favors, rewards, contract awards, loans or loan guarantees, fees, inside information, commissions, refunds, rebates, the payment of expenses or debts, the use of property or equipment, employment or work experience of any type (whether paid or unpaid, temporary or permanent), rewards, gift cards, commissions, preferential access to business or other

opportunities, goods or services, or other things of value.

Note that this sample definition of "anything of value" itself includes several other capitalized terms that would also need to be independently defined.

Many policies will simply and effectively define "corruption" as "the abuse of an entrusted power for personal gain." Colloquially, the term corruption is sometimes used interchangeably with bribery. It is also sometimes (and more correctly) used as a blanket term for various types of abuse of entrusted power—not just bribery. Corruption can take many different forms and can be used to further various kinds of illegal behavior. It is often associated with organized crime, money laundering, and even terrorist financing. Corruption may be private (e.g., insider trading, embezzlement, etc.) or public. Some examples of public corruption typologies, as recognized by the U.S. government, are[40]:

Grand corruption: when senior government officials steal large sums of public funds or otherwise abuse their power for personal or political advantage.

Administrative corruption: when low to mid-level government officials abuse their entrusted power for their own gain in their interactions with private citizens and businesses. This can include

---

40 *United States Strategy on Countering Corruption, Pursuant to the National Security Study Memorandum on Establishing the Fight Against Corruption as a Core United States National Security Interest*, THE WHITE HOUSE, at 6 (Dec. 2021), https://www.whitehouse.gov/wp-content/uploads/2021/12/United-States-Strategy-on-Countering-Corruption.pdf.

extorting citizens in exchange for basic services and requesting and/or accepting payment to violate regulations.

State capture: when private entities corruptly influence a country's decision-making process for their own benefit.

Kleptocracy: a government that is controlled by officials who use their political power to appropriate the wealth of their nation. This may include state capture.

Strategic corruption: when a government intentionally uses corrupt practices as a part of its foreign policy. State-directed cross border investments can be an example of this. The U.S. Government considers this "weaponization of corruption" to be an emerging threat.[41] The U.S. government has stated that it will continue to study this form of corruption to understand its use and impacts on the United States and other countries and to understand how to thwart and build resistance against this threat.[42]

Bribery and corruption of course often go hand-in-hand, but we will focus mainly on bribery.

(d) Application

The global AB&C policy must state the persons and entities to whom it applies. Those writing the policy need to carefully consider how to draft the

---

41 *Id.* at 7.

42 *Id.*

scope of the policy so that legal requirements are satisfied, and so that the policy can be implemented from a practical perspective. At a minimum, the policy should apply to the organization's employees, as that term is understood and defined by the organization's Legal and Human Resources departments.

An organization must also consider how and to what extent it will seek to apply its policy (or the principles of its policy) to third parties with whom it does business—e.g., vendors, consultants, intermediaries, etc. The policy may include a general section to this effect. For example: "As Organization X deems appropriate, this policy may, in whole or in part, also be applied to third parties with whom Organization X does business." *See* Chapter 6 for a further discussion of third-party practices with respect to AB&C policies.

An organization must also consider whether and how its AB&C policy applies to entities in which it has an ownership interest and/or over which it exercises some degree of control. Organization X's policy may state, for example, that:

> This policy applies to all Organization X wholly and majority-owned legal entities and to those entities over which Organization X may otherwise exert significant control, including their respective subsidiaries, and all of the officers, directors, employees, representatives, and agents of same.

Note that this sample application statement includes entities over which the organization may exert "significant control". The concept of "significant control" would need to be separately defined. Certain of the organization's joint ventures may then, for example, become subject to the policy. Would it be desirable or realistic to require such joint ventures to be subject to Organization X's AB&C policy? Possibly yes, possibly no. This example illustrates the potential downstream effects of the "application" section and, correspondingly, the care that should be taken in drafting it.

(e) Responsibility

The global AB&C policy should be clear that every employee (i.e., every person to whom the policy applies) is responsible for complying with and upholding the policy. To wit, every employee is responsible for preventing, detecting, and reporting potential bribery and corruption.

Recalling our discussion of Conduct at the Top, the global policy may also refer to the responsibilities of senior management in promoting the policy and creating a culture of compliance. For example, a policy may state:

> "Organization X senior management is responsible for promoting this policy and is responsible for ensuring that a culture of ethics and integrity—a culture in which bribery and corruption is unacceptable—is developed, encouraged and maintained by Organization X's

employees and within Organization X's global operations."

(f) General AB&C Principles/Scope of Prohibited Conduct

The global policy may contain some overall AB&C principles. It should also define the general scope of prohibited conduct. For example, the FCPA only prohibits the active bribery of foreign officials. It does not prohibit passive bribery or commercial bribery. A threshold question is whether an organization is subject to laws, like the UKBA, that prohibit a wider range of conduct than the FCPA. However, even if the FCPA were the only law to which an organization was subject, the best practice (from both ethical and business perspectives) is to prohibit passive bribery and commercial bribery as well as active bribery of foreign officials. For example, a policy may state that:

- "All activity must be:
  - for a legitimate business purpose
  - reasonable and transparent
  - appropriately documented, including a business rationale
  - authorized at an appropriate level of seniority"

and that

- "No employee shall, (whether directly or indirectly) offer, promise, give, authorize, solicit, accept, or agree to receive Anything of Value:

- o that would breach applicable laws, regulations, this policy, or any of [Organization X's] policies;
- o that would create a conflict of interest between the interests of (any combination of) the employee, the offeror, the recipient, and Organization X;
- o that is intended to obtain or retain preferential treatment, business, or a business advantage;
- o that is intended to improperly influence a specific business decision;
- o that is intended as gratitude for the recipient having previously made a decision or acted in a way that directly or indirectly benefited Organization X; or
- o that could be viewed by a third party as lavish, disproportional to the business relationship, excessive, not work-related or lacking in a legitimate business purpose."

In addition, drawing from the FCPA's accounting provisions, the global policy may also include general principles relating to the creation and maintenance of accurate books and records and an adequate accounting system. For example:

- "Keeping accurate and detailed records is a core component of Organization X's anti-bribery and corruption controls. Organization X is required to:

- o create and maintain books, records, and accounts which, in reasonable detail, accurately and fairly reflect its transactions and disposition of assets;
- o create a system of internal accounting controls that will provide reasonable assurances that transactions are properly authorized; and
- o accurately record all amounts, regardless of value, in Organization X's books and records.

- To that end, Organization X clarifies the following prohibitions:
  - o false or misleading statements must never be made in Organization X's books and records for any reason;
  - o no undocumented accounts should be maintained for or on behalf of Organization X for any reason;
  - o no undocumented payments for or on behalf of Organization X may ever be made for any reason; and
  - o neither Organization X resources nor non-Organization X resources may ever be used to make payments prohibited by this policy or other applicable Organization X policies or procedures."

(g) Implementation Requirements

The global AB&C policy is, by its very essence, high level and largely principles based. Those principles then need to be operationalized. The global policy must set some expectations about how to do so. For example, an organization's global policy may state that all entities to which the policy applies must implement written procedures and related internal controls to ensure compliance with the standards set forth in the global policy within a prescribed period of time.

(h) Guidance on Specific Areas of Bribery and Corruption Risk

The global AB&C policy should explain and provide guidance regarding the organization's specific areas of bribery and corruption risk. For example, the global policy may provide a general explanation on the organization's approach to areas like facilitation payments, dealing with public officials, gifts and entertainment, charitable contributions, hiring practices, etc. We'll address the substance of these and other such areas in Chapter 6.

(i) Reference to Other Related Policies and Sub-Policies

Many global AB&C policies will state that readers should check other applicable policies for stricter requirements and the strictest requirement that applies to that employee will be the one that governs. As you can imagine, depending on how policies are organized and how well information is communicated, this can be confusing for employees. Where possible, AB&C Compliance should include cross references to other applicable policies so employees understand when they need to look at another document for guidance. Cross references to other AB&C policies should be included as well as cross references to policies that may be "owned" by other groups but that bear on the areas discussed in the global AB&C policy, such as hiring practices. A well-organized and well-publicized intranet site with the relevant policy links can also be very helpful in this regard.

(j) Statement on Conflicting Laws or Policy Standards

Relating to the previous section, the global policy should state that, to the extent that Organization X policies contain conflicting laws or rules, readers should assume that the strictest standard applies and should contact AB&C Compliance with any questions.

(k) Guidance

The global policy may include a brief section containing practical guidance to assist employees with complying with the policy. For example:

- "The following guidance may help employees comply with this Policy. Employees must never:

- do anything that would breach applicable laws, regulations, or Organization X policies;
- offer or authorize an improper payment to a current or prospective client, employee, or third party to attempt to persuade that current or prospective client, employee, or third party to do something illegal;
- offer or accept Anything of Value for the purpose of obtaining or retaining business or as a reward for business that was previously obtained or retained;
- do anything to facilitate or otherwise support the breach of this Policy by another person; or
- threaten or retaliate against another employee who has raised concerns under this Policy."

(l) Reporting of Potential Breaches and Anti-Retaliation

The global policy should state that those to whom it applies must comply with it and that a breach of the policy may be grounds for disciplinary action up to and including termination. However, such a statement should be carefully crafted and potentially balanced with a statement encouraging employees to raise good faith questions and concerns. It can be helpful to reiterate that preventing bribery and corruption is the responsibility of every employee—not just senior management.

The global policy should specify the person or group to which a suspected breach can and should be escalated. If desired by the employee, the first point of contact could be that employee's supervisor. The policy should also list a specific AB&C Compliance emailbox and/or phone number to which reports or questions could be directed, as well as provide the information for a reporting mechanism through which employees may anonymously report potential breaches.

The global policy should include a clear statement that an organization will not retaliate, and will not allow retaliation, against any individual for submitting a good faith report of a potential policy breach or for participating in an investigation involving any such report.

(m) Training

The global policy should provide a brief statement about the organization's training program. For example:

> Organization X will provide training to effectively implement and maintain this Policy and to educate employees about applicable anti-bribery and corruption laws and how those laws translate into this Policy's requirements. Employees are required, at a minimum, to take the annual anti-bribery and corruption electronic training. Depending on an employee's role(s) and responsibilities, additional training may also be required or recommended. For educational purposes, Intranet site X also

provides additional information and materials on anti-bribery and corruption.

(n) Monitoring, Testing, and Review

The global policy should provide a high-level explanation of the organization's framework for monitoring, testing and review. For example:

> "Organization X will monitor and test compliance with this Policy through relevant reviews, audits and inspections, as well as through its other anti-financial crime controls."

The policy may also include a brief explanation of the "three lines of defense" compliance model and how each line of defense contributes to risk mitigation.

(o) Effective Date and Dispensations

The global policy should have a clear effective date by which all persons, groups, and entities subject to the policy are expected to comply. This is important because policy requirements may sometimes necessitate the creation of new processes, documentation, etc. and it's important that people understand when they will officially be held to the policy's requirements.

The global policy should state that where a group or entity within the policy's scope is unable to comply with one or more requirements by the effective date, that group or entity must request a dispensation in writing from the global AB&C Compliance function. This may happen, for example, if the policy requires submitting requests through a certain system and that system is not yet available to a particular business unit. This should not be a common occurrence, but an organization should still have a process for it.

The global policy should set out clear requirements for submitting a dispensation request. For example, the dispensation request must explain why the group or entity is unable (not unwilling) to meet one or more policy requirements, its plan to achieve compliance, and the interim steps that it is taking to mitigate any bribery or corruption risks.

The reasons for granting or rejecting the dispensation should be detailed in writing. The dispensation should also be for a set period of time—not indefinitely—and an action plan should be put in place to bring the requester into compliance with the policy. For example, if the system referenced in the previous example was not yet available then possibly the affected business unit would resolve requests via an email box while it waited for the system to be implemented.

(p) Review Dates

The global policy should also list its review dates—i.e., the last time it was reviewed and updated and the next time it is due for review. At a minimum, the policy should be reviewed and updated on an annual basis. It should also be updated off-cycle as necessary to reflect any legal, regulatory, or industry practice developments.

(q) Contact Persons

A person, persons, or a group must be listed to contact in connection with questions about the global policy. However, no matter the organization, employees come and go. The best practice is to list a group email box for policy questions (e.g., ABC@OrganizationX.com) and have the appropriate AB&C Compliance group continually monitor that email box and respond to questions. Depending on resourcing, an organization can also add a phone number if that's practicable.

A common mistake that organizations make is to only include a generic statement like "contact Legal or Compliance with any questions about this policy." A sentence like that might be sufficient if the organization is small and there is a single Chief Compliance Officer/General Counsel with a limited staff. However, as an organization gets larger, a sentence like that becomes less practical and much less helpful. Consider, for example, a large multinational organization with 50,000-plus employees. There will likely be large Legal and Compliance departments compromised of multiple specialty subgroups so a direction to "contact Legal or Compliance" is hardly the level of detail that employees need.

Remember that an organization should want employees to ask any questions that they have about the policy. Questions show that people are reading the policy, trying to understand it, and are therefore more likely to try to comply with it. And the easier it is to ask questions, the more employees are likely to do so. A compliance mantra—keep it simple!

d. Country/Regional AB&C Policies and Procedures

Certain countries or regions may have stricter AB&C laws and regulations than others. If this is the case, then there may be country or regional addenda to the global policy or separate country or regional policies. However, operating on the assumption that the global policy sets the minimum required standards, these country and regional policies must be stricter than the global policy—they cannot be less restrictive. Generally, the same person(s) or group(s) that wrote and approved the global policy should also review and approve any country and regional policies. This helps to maintain consistency across AB&C policies and avoid coverage gaps or errors.

e. Business Unit or Population-Specific AB&C Policies

Sometimes a specific business unit will have its own AB&C policy or an AB&C section in another compliance-related policy or procedure. That business unit may have a specific product or service that has unique bribery and corruption risks that need to be addressed. There may also be policies or procedures relating to specific employee populations who may be subject to stricter rules and reporting requirements, possibly due to holding certain professional licenses.

f. AB&C Compliance Desktop Manual

The AB&C Compliance Desktop Manual is a set of operating guidelines for AB&C Compliance. Its purpose is to help members of AB&C Compliance—whether in one region or across regions—provide appropriate and consistent guidance so that the organization may effectively govern, manage, and control the bribery and corruption risks associated with its employees, customers and third parties, and comply with all applicable laws and regulations. The desktop manual should include sections such as:

- Purpose and Scope
- Objectives
- Definitions
- Systems and Tools in Use
- Roles and Responsibilities
- AB&C Governance Framework: This should explain the structure at the organization that the governs the AB&C function itself, including but not limited to the Board of Directors and any committee structure beneath it.
- AB&C Advisory Focus Areas
- AB&C Review/Workflow Process(es) for AB&C Advisory Focus Areas: This can include the mechanics of how requests come to AB&C Compliance for advice and then how those requests should be reviewed and decisioned.

- Process for Determining and Issuing Violations

AB&C Compliance functions may also keep a log of the guidance they have provided, possibly in a searchable database. Keeping track of advice provided by AB&C Compliance officers has a number of potential benefits.

First, it helps to ensure that AB&C Compliance officers are providing consistent advice to similar queries. To the extent that differences in advice are identified, AB&C Compliance officers can discuss and resolve the reasons for these differences.

Second, tracking of advice also helps identify (1) the substantive areas in which the most questions arise (e.g., how to identify a public official); and (2) the regions, individuals, or groups from whom the most questions come. This information is helpful because it can show areas—both substantive and organizational—where confusion may lie. Policies and procedures can then be clarified to better address these points and training materials can be updated to better address these questions. In addition, targeted trainings can be implemented to assist persons or groups who may be having more difficulty understanding policy requirements.

Finally, an advice log can help demonstrate some of the value that AB&C Compliance officers provide. In a world where organizational resources can be increasingly scarce, being able to concretely demonstrate a compliance function's contribution to an organization can be very helpful.

g. Additional Practice Tips for Effective AB&C Policies and Procedures

The sections below provide some additional practice tips to maximize the utility of AB&C policies and procedures.

i. Use Clear and Consistent Terminology

Use clear and consistent terminology to indicate actions that are required versus actions that are recommended—"must" versus "should". As a practical note, "shoulds" should be minimal. If something is necessary, then it should be required. Also use clear and consistent terminology for actions that are prohibited. For example, do not use the phrase "should not" with respect to prohibited actions; instead, use the phrase "must not". Explain these uses of terminology at the beginning of the policy.

ii. Emphasize the Online Policy Version

It's important that those subject to the policy have access to the most updated version. As a matter of habit and practice, some people will print out a hard copy and keep it for reference. The downside of that is that people will then sometimes end up reviewing an outdated version. There's no absolute way to prevent this. However, it's helpful to add a header or footer to the document to state that printed material should not be considered as the most current version and that only the online version (at a specifically designated intranet site) should be considered current and valid.

iii. Address the Use of Personal Devices and Third-Party Applications

The DOJ has stated that, "[a]s a general rule, all corporations with robust compliance programs should have effective policies governing the use of personal devices and third-party messaging platforms for corporate communications, should provide clear training to employees about such policies, and should enforce such policies when violations are identified."[43] As the DOJ has noted, "[h]ow companies address the use of personal devices and third-party messaging platforms can impact a prosecutor's evaluation of the effectiveness of a corporation's compliance program, as well as the assessment of a corporation's cooperation during a criminal investigation."[44] *See* Chapter 3 for a discussion of how this factor may play into cooperation credit.

4. COMMUNICATION AND TRAINING

An organization needs to tell employees about its AB&C policies and procedures and train employees on what those policies and procedures mean for them. When effective, communication and training can help to deter employees from engaging in improper conduct by enhancing their awareness of the organization's zero tolerance approach to bribery and corruption and the organization's related policies and procedures. Communication and training can help provide employees with the necessary knowledge and

---

[43] September 2022 Memo, *supra* Chapter 3, n.225, at 11.

[44] *Id.*

tools to apply the AB&C policies and procedures and more ably deal with questions and issues that may arise.

Regular, ongoing communication is a form of training and education that reiterates an organization's commitment to anti-bribery and corruption and can prevent employee misconduct. It should be incorporated into an organization's existing systems—e.g., a column of frequently asked questions in the organization's in-house newsletter, posters on bulletin boards, articles on organization intranets, email updates, etc. Efficient channels for communication must be in place and effective when changes or additions to policy or procedures occur. An organization should maintain records of its AB&C training communications.

In addition to regular communication, an organization should also have a formal AB&C training plan in place. Depending on the size and industry of the organization, this plan may be more or less detailed. The content, method and frequency of training should be risk-based. Large organizations often have an annual computer-based training with an exam that all employees need to pass. This is probably sufficient for the majority of an organization's employees. However, if an organization has individuals in high-risk roles from a bribery and corruption perspective, then it may consider supplemental or in-person training. Such higher-risk roles may, for example, deal regularly with public officials, actively entertain current and prospective clients and third parties, or be responsible for relationships with higher risk third parties.

a. Key AB&C Concepts for Generalized Training

Some key concepts to include in the general AB&C training are:

Definitions of Key Terms: The training should explain the meaning of key AB&C policy terms, including but not limited to "bribery," "corruption," and "anything of value".

Organization's Approach to Bribery and Corruption: The training should explain that the organization has a zero-tolerance approach to bribery and corruption. If an employee engages in prohibited conduct, there are a range of potential consequences, up to and including termination.

AB&C Policy and Compliance Framework: The training should explain the AB&C Compliance function and how it fits within the organization. It should list the policies that are applicable to the training audience—the Code of Conduct, the global AB&C Policy, and any additional policies. The training should explain how people can access the policies.

Key AB&C-Related Risk Areas: The training should explain key areas of AB&C risk—e.g., gifts and entertainment, third-party relationships, etc.

Intentions: As discussed in connection with the FCPA, a person's intent when taking certain actions is very important. It is this intent which can potentially trigger liability. If, for example, an employee improperly offers a benefit to a foreign official, that offer can result in liability *even if* the foreign official doesn't accept it. The training should explain that this is why the organization requires that certain conduct be pre-approved—so AB&C Compliance and/or Legal can review the proposed offer before it is made (and therefore before there is potential liability).

Trainings should give participants examples of questions that they can ask themselves to help objectively evaluate their own intent. For example, "By doing this, am I trying to influence the receiving person to take a specific action?" Or, "By offering them this benefit, am I trying to get them to do something for me in return?" If the answer to either of these questions is Yes, then the employee should consult AB&C Compliance before proceeding.

Business Rationale: The training should explain that conduct should always have a legitimate business rationale. Employees need to be able to articulate and document their reason(s) for offering a benefit to a current or prospective client or third party or for accepting such a benefit. For example, an appropriate rationale for inviting a client to a business dinner could be to discuss one of the organization's new services that may be suitable for that client.

The Appearance of Impropriety: The training should explain that employees should always try to think about how a situation might look from the outside to an objective observer. Consider the "New York Times Test": Would you (and your organization) be comfortable if your offer (or acceptance of someone else's offer), including all the attendant circumstances, were published on the front page of the New York Times?

Questions: The training should explain who to call or email if participants have questions about the training, any of its principles, or any of the related policies. An email mailbox that is monitored by the AB&C Compliance group is usually the best choice. As previously emphasized, avoid vague generalities like "contact Compliance or Legal with questions."

Reporting: The training should explain who the participant should contact if they believe that someone may have violated the applicable AB&C policy. It should lay out each of the options: line reporting (to the person's manager), to Legal or AB&C Compliance (again, providing specific phone numbers, emails, etc.) and the information for the anonymous reporting mechanism.

i. *Practice Tip: Develop and Deliver Training from a "Need to Know" Perspective*

If you are developing or delivering an AB&C training, think about the audience and what that audience actually needs to know. Do the participants need to know the ins and outs of DOJ guidance and recent FCPA resolutions or do they need to know key points from the AB&C policy or procedure that may be applicable to their day-to-day work—e.g., when an employee needs to ask AB&C Compliance for pre-approval to attend an event? AB&C trainings for general organization populations should not include components like statutory interpretation of the FCPA and its legislative history, etc. While interesting, that's not something that most employees need to know. AB&C trainings should not be geared toward turning all employees into AB&C Compliance officers.

Most employees need to have four take-aways from AB&C trainings:

- their organization is committed to complying with applicable AB&C laws and maintaining an ethical culture
- the policies and rules that apply to them
- how to identify potential bribery or corruption issues ("issue spotting")
- where to go with questions or to report a problem

An organization can always make additional educational resources available for employees who are interested and want to know more about preventing and detecting bribery and corruption. But the trainings themselves should be concise and on-point so that key messages don't get lost in the sea of training that employees are often required to navigate.

b. Tailored Training

Relating to the previous Practice Tip, tailored or role-based AB&C training can be very effective. In particular, it's helpful to provide specialized training for those who may be in high-risk roles from a bribery and corruption perspective, and for members of the Board.

i. High-Risk Role Training

Consider a specific AB&C training for individuals in the organization who may have particular exposure points to bribery and corruption risk. For example:

- Individuals who regularly interact with U.S. and foreign officials.
- Individuals whose roles involve sales or otherwise obtaining or retaining business—what might be called front-facing or client-facing roles.
- Individuals who have a high level of seniority because of their corporate title, because they are responsible for supervising staff, and/or because they manage the organization's strategic relationships.
- Individuals who manage high-risk third-party relationships.
- Individuals who are in higher-risk jurisdictions.

ii. Board Training

Where possible, an organization's Board of Directors should receive tailored AB&C training. Regulatory expectations about board knowledge and responsibility have increased over recent years. Board members are expected to be knowledgeable on compliance matters, especially with respect to areas that pose legal and regulatory risks to the organization. It's important for anti-bribery and corruption matters to be a part of the board's education.

As with any type of tailored training, the board training should be crafted with its audience in mind—very senior people with a very limited amount of time. The messaging must be precise and should focus specifically on any bribery and corruption risks to the organization and any significant related projects or initiatives. If time permits, giving the board a hypothetical fact pattern and talking it through with the members can also be effective. It may help keep the board engaged, will allow members to issue spot and ask questions, and will possibly highlight areas where more education or information is necessary.

c. The Benefits of Being Able to Demonstrate Employee Training: The Morgan Stanley Declination

It's important for an organization to be able to concretely demonstrate that it has delivered appropriate training. Training of course will hopefully help prevent employees from engaging in prohibited conduct. However, even when employees do act improperly, having proof that appropriate training was provided can help protect the organization itself. In the 2012 Morgan Stanley example, a Managing Director of its real estate investment and fund advisory business in China named Garth Peterson bribed a Chinese government official for his own personal gain. As the SEC explained it[45]:

> From at least 2004 to 2007, Defendant Garth Peterson, while employed at Morgan Stanley & Co., Inc.'s ("Morgan Stanley") real estate investment and fund advisory business, secretly acquired millions of dollars worth of real estate investments from Morgan Stanley's funds for himself, the former Chairman of Yongye Enterprise (Group) Co. ("Yongye")—a Chinese state-owned entity with influence over the success of Morgan Stanley's real estate business in Shanghai—and others. Peterson also arranged to have paid to himself and the former Chairman of Yongye ("the Chinese Official") at least 1.8 million in what he misrepresented were finder's fees Morgan Stanley's funds owed to third parties. In exchange for offers and payments from Peterson, the Chinese Official helped Peterson and Morgan Stanley obtain business while personally benefiting from some of these same investments. This self-dealing and misappropriation by Peterson breached the fiduciary duties he and Morgan Stanley owed to their clients.

---

45 *SEC v. Peterson*, Complaint, at 1 (Apr. 25, 2012) [hereinafter Peterson Complaint], https://www.sec.gov/litigation/complaints/2012/comp-pr2012-78.pdf.

Peterson ultimately pled guilty to a one-count criminal information charging him with conspiring to violate the FCPA's internal accounting controls provisions. He also agreed to settle civil FCPA charges from the SEC[46] by paying a fine, disgorging a portion of his profits and forfeiting certain real estate, and was permanently banned from the securities industry. The big news here was that both the DOJ and SEC declined to charge Morgan Stanley itself and publicly based much of the reasoning for that decision on their determination that Morgan Stanley had an effective AB&C Compliance program. A significant part of that determination focused on Morgan Stanley's training efforts.

The Information described Morgan Stanley's AB&C training program as follows: "Morgan Stanley's FCPA compliance program included live training presentations, web-based training, and additional FCPA reminders. Between 2000 and 2008, Morgan Stanley held at least 54 trainings for various groups of Asia-based employees on anti-corruption policies, including the FCPA."[47] The Information

---

46 *Id.* at 2. ("By engaging in the conduct described in this Complaint, Peterson violated the anti-bribery and internal controls provisions of the Foreign Corrupt Practices Act of 1977 ("FCPA")—namely Sections 13(b)(5) and 30A of the Securities Exchange Act of 1934 ("Exchange Act") [15 U.S.C. §§ 78m(b)(5) and 78dd–1]—and aided and abetted violations of the anti-fraud provisions of the Investment Advisers Act of 1940 ("Advisers Act")—namely Sections 206(1) and 206(2) [15 U.S.C. §§ 80b–6(1) and 80b–6(2)].")

47 *U.S. v. Peterson*, Cr. No. 12-224, Information, at 7 [hereinafter Peterson Information], https://www.justice.gov/sites/default/files/criminal-fraud/legacy/2012/04/26/petersong-information.pdf.

went on to recite the training-related information that Morgan Stanley had retained relating to Peterson:

- "Between 2002 [and] 2008, Morgan Stanley trained PETERSON on his duties under the FCPA at least seven times, including providing live and web-based training and a teleconference training session conducted by Morgan Stanley's Global Head of Litigation and Global Head of Morgan Stanley's Anti-Corruption Group. Among other things, Morgan Stanley specifically trained PETERSON that employees of Chinese state-owned entities could be government officials under the FCPA."[48]
- "Morgan Stanley also provided PETERSON at least 35 FCPA compliance reminders. These reminders included FCPA-specific distributions, such as written training materials that PETERSON kept in his office; circulations and reminders of Morgan Stanley's Code of Conduct, which included policies that directly addressed the FCPA; various reminders concerning Morgan Stanley's policies on gift-giving and entertainment; the circulation of Morgan Stanley's Global Anti-Bribery Policy; guidance on the engagement of consultants;

---

[48] *Id.*

and policies addressing specific high-risk events, including the Beijing Olympics."[49]

- "Morgan Stanley required PETERSON in multiple occasions to certify his compliance with the FCPA and kept those written certifications in PETERSON's permanent employee record."[50]

The DOJ used the *Peterson* case to herald a "sea change in corporate compliance efforts."[51] Assistant Attorney General Lanny Breuer explained that Peterson pled guilty (and was sentenced to prison time) for violating Morgan Stanley's internal FCPA controls but that the DOJ was declining to prosecute Morgan Stanley "[b]ecause Morgan Stanley voluntarily disclosed Peterson's misconduct, fully cooperated with our investigation, and showed us that it maintained a rigorous compliance program, including extensive training of bank employees on the FCPA and other anti-corruption measures .... That is smart, and responsible, enforcement."[52]

Was the lauding of Morgan Stanley's existing AB&C Compliance program an actual reason for the declination, a narrative spin by the DOJ, or does it even matter? Critics argued that it was a red herring

---

[49] *Id.*

[50] *Id.* at 8.

[51] *Assistant Attorney General Lanny A. Breuer Speaks at the New York City Bar Association*, U.S. DOJ, OFF. OF PUB. AFFAIRS (Sept. 13, 2012), https://www.justice.gov/opa/speech/assistant-attorney-general-lanny-breuer-speaks-new-york-city-bar-association.

[52] *Id.*

because the DOJ could not in fact have charged Morgan Stanley, pointing out that Peterson deliberately evaded Morgan Stanley's internal controls and that Morgan Stanley itself did not benefit from Peterson's conduct.

There are a couple of potential flaws in that critique. First, Morgan Stanley may have benefited, at least to a limited extent, from Peterson's wrongful conduct. Note the language in paragraph 1 of the SEC Complaint stating that "[i]n exchange for offers and payments from Peterson, the Chinese Official helped Peterson *and Morgan Stanley* obtain business while personally benefitting from some of these same investments."[53] Morgan Stanley obtained business in connection with Peterson's wrongful conduct and presumably had at least some profit from that business. The fact that Peterson personally profited from the transactions does not mean that Morgan Stanley did not.

Second, the DOJ chose to accept Peterson's plea that he intentionally circumvented Morgan Stanley's internal controls and leave it at that. It's possible that Peterson could have deliberately circumvented those controls *and* that those controls were ineffective or insufficient. The DOJ could potentially have found both of those things to be true. As a practical matter, whether internal controls are effective or sufficient is fact-specific and leaves room for a great deal of subjectivity. If the DOJ had wanted to find that Morgan Stanley's internal controls were

---

[53] Peterson Complaint, *supra* n.45, at 1 (emphasis supplied).

ineffective or insufficient—despite the many positive attributes of its AB&C Compliance program—then it likely would have done so. Instead, the DOJ chose to send a message about the importance of effective AB&C Compliance programs and the very real benefits that organizations can reap from having such programs. So why not take that message? It's not necessarily of any moment that the Morgan Stanley case may have been a convenient opportunity for the DOJ to announce it.

d. External Training and Communication

When we talk about training and communication, we are often thinking of those concepts with respect to employees. However, it's also advantageous to deploy these tools externally. For example, many organizations share their Code of Conduct publicly and some also share a statement on their approach to bribery and corruption or their global AB&C policies. Some organizations may also share information on their web site about bribery and corruption generally and provide links for additional information. Taking actions like these can help shape the public's perception of an organization as one that has a strong culture of compliance and that abides by laws and regulations. In turn, this can positively affect the types of employees who apply to work at the organization and the third parties who seek to do business with it.

5. REPORTING MECHANISM

An organization needs to have reporting pathways in place to learn about potential bribery and corruption issues. Aside from being a recognized component of an effective compliance program, it's in an organization's best interests to have the first chance to investigate a potential issue and remediate and/or self-disclose it if appropriate.

The first type of reporting that compliance programs want to encourage is line reporting. The best reporting system is an open door, so to speak. The ideal situation is to develop an organizational culture where employees feel comfortable talking with their supervisors (or a specifically designated Compliance or Legal contact) about any concerns. However, to the extent employees aren't comfortable speaking out (or if the concern involves a person to whom they might otherwise report) it's important to have a mechanism where employees can raise concerns—anonymously if they wish—without fear of retaliation. Thereby comes the need for a reporting mechanism.

Initial decisions about how to structure a reporting mechanism include (1) whether the reporting mechanism should be available only to employees or should also be available to third parties and/or the general public; and (2) whether the reporting mechanism should be maintained in-house at the organization or whether it should be outsourced to a third party. We'll address each of these in turn.

An organization needs to decide whether its reporting mechanism will be available only to employees or will be more broadly accessible. The benefit of opening access to the reporting mechanism is that the organization may receive reporting from third parties who work with the organization but who don't want to directly raise concerns for fear of harming their business relationship. A downside is that the report number may increase and people outside the organization may call to complain about organization employees for reasons that are not business related. However, best practices suggest opening the reporting mechanism beyond employees. Remember that the goal is to learn about potential bribery and corruption and that it's not just employees who may have reportable information. Third parties working with the organization may also be in a position to report misconduct in connection with the organization's business.

Regarding whether to maintain the reporting mechanism in-house or outsource it, the size and setting of the organization should inform this decision. A large organization that has a telephone reporting option may need 24-hour coverage.[54] For smaller organizations, 24-hour coverage may not be necessary, or may only be feasible through outsourcing, which can be costly. Also, the cost and resources needed for training internal staff on how to

---

[54] Some organizations may choose to eliminate a telephone reporting option. It's possible to set up a reporting system using email, where the email address of the sender can be hidden to maintain anonymity.

collect and manage reports must be weighed against the costs of retaining a professional outside service.

Key components of an effective reporting mechanism include compliance and anti-retaliation policies, a detailed procedure for how reports are collected and managed, and a documented information process flow to AB&C Compliance. We'll take each of these in turn.

a. Confidentiality and Anti-Retaliation Policies

Policies and procedures should assure that, to the extent possible, confidentiality and anonymity (where requested) are available in connection with the reporting mechanism. An organization must also have an anti-retaliation policy in connection with reports of potential misconduct. Employees need to be able to raise good faith concerns without fear of reprisal. If employees suspect there could be retaliation, then they will not come forward, creating fertile ground for whistleblowers, and exposing the organization to unchecked risk. Remember, however, that a limitation should be included in the anti-retaliation policy for "good faith" complaints or reports. Employees that concoct or report misinformation in bad faith should not benefit from an anti-retaliation policy.

Confidentiality and anti-retaliation often go hand-in-hand. For example, the decision-making process regarding a promotion can be tainted if the supervisor has been informed of an employee's report of a problem. Policies and procedures need to offer assurances to the employee but also must note that resolution of a problem, which could include legal action, may in certain circumstances require disclosure of identity. Legal counsel should be involved in the review of both the confidentiality and non-retaliation policies to make sure that they are sufficiently detailed and to ensure that unrealistic promises are not made.

b. Procedure for How Reports Are Collected, Reviewed, and Decisioned

Once a report of potential misconduct is received, how is it handled? Who reviews it and what are the criteria for that review? How is it determined which reports require further investigation? How is the decisioning of whether and how to proceed with reports maintained? There must be a detailed and documented process in place for how reports of potential misconduct are collected, reviewed, and decisioned.

c. Documented Process Flow to AB&C Compliance

Depending on the organization, the reporting mechanism may not be housed within the AB&C Compliance function. If it's not, then AB&C Compliance needs to make sure that it receives the information relating to bribery and corruption issues within an agreed-upon scope.

d. Practice Question

How does an organization know that its reporting mechanism is working?

For example, does a high number of reports indicate an effective reporting mechanism? Not necessarily. The number of reports alone is not an indicator of effectiveness. If, hypothetically, an organization has been able to create an environment where issues are raised through appropriate channels and the staff trusts they can report problems without fear of retaliation, then the reporting mechanism may not receive a high volume of reports. With that said, if an organization operates in high-risk jurisdictions, consider the overall reporting from those jurisdictions—confidential mechanism plus regular escalation. If there are not many reports coming in from high-risk jurisdictions, that in-and-of-itself is a red flag. The reporting mechanism may not be working properly, or people may be afraid to report for some reason.

In short, there's no single dispositive way to know if a reporting mechanism is effective. However, collecting and analyzing the appropriate data can help paint an overall picture. The DOJ's Evaluation of Corporate Compliance Programs guidance poses several helpful questions in this regard[55]:

---

[55] Corporate Compliance Programs, *supra* Chapter 3, n.293, at 6.

- "How has the company collected, tracked, analyzed, and used information from its reporting mechanisms?"
- "Does the company periodically analyze the reports or investigation findings for patterns of misconduct or other red flags for compliance weaknesses?"
- "Does the company periodically test the effectiveness of the [mechanism], for example by tracking a report from start to finish?"

An organization should make sure that it can answer these questions in the affirmative and that it is reviewing the information generated and taking any appropriate actions.

6. INVESTIGATION AND REMEDIATION

An organization must have a documented process in place for who conducts investigations involving potential bribery or corruption and how they are conducted. An important initial question is whether the suspected misconduct is a breach of the AB&C policy or a breach of the AB&C policy *and* a potential legal violation. Where a potential violation of law or regulation is even suspected, a good first step is a meeting between AB&C Compliance and legal counsel. An appropriate action plan, including an investigation, can then be developed.

An investigation should be conducted any time a potential violation of law or regulation is identified. This investigation may be conducted by internal and/or external staff and counsel. When deciding who will conduct the investigation, serious consideration needs to be given to preserving attorney-client and work product privileges and all reasonable steps should be taken to do so. An organization may later decide to waive privilege, in whole or in part, pursuant to discussions or negotiations with regulators or law enforcement. However, that possibility should not affect an organization's ongoing best practice of preserving attorney-client and work product privileges.

a. Scope of the Investigation

Before an investigation begins, careful thought should be given to its scope and its parameters—locations under review, personnel to be interviewed, sources of information to be reviewed, etc. The investigation needs to be scoped such that it can provide senior management with the necessary information within a reasonable time frame.

Senior management will need a rough outline of what may have gone wrong, who was involved, and how widespread the conduct may be or may have been. This will help inform the organization's decision about whether to voluntarily self-disclose the conduct to the SEC and/or DOJ. As previously explained, voluntary self-disclosure (as part of overall cooperation credit) can have a significant effect on how a potential enforcement action is resolved. While there's no specific time frame for voluntary self-disclosure, the DOJ has indicated that it will only consider self-disclosure to be voluntary if it's within a reasonably prompt time after the organization discovers the issue. After the organization's initial inquiry, the organization may need to proceed with a lengthier investigation.

b. Documentation of the Investigation

Detailed documentation of an investigation is critical if there is a government investigation or a civil matter arising out of the misconduct. Such documentation includes:

- A description of the potential misconduct and how it was discovered.
- A description of the investigative process that was undertaken.
- A list of all documents that were reviewed.
- A list of all employees and third parties who were interviewed.
- All interview materials, including but not limited to interview questions, documents that were shown to interviewees, and interviewer notes.
- A root cause analysis.
- Documentation of any actions that the organization took as a result of its investigation and root cause analysis (e.g., changes to policies and procedures, discipline of employees, senior management changes, termination of third-party relationships, etc.)
- The final investigation report.

The final report and any included documentation are sensitive materials—potentially privileged—and should be shared only on a very limited basis.

c. Role of AB&C Compliance in Internal Investigations

What is the ideal role of AB&C Compliance in internal investigations relating to bribery and corruption? Its actual role will of course differ depending on the organization and its infrastructure. AB&C Compliance should certainly play an integral role. However, ideally, that role should be a behind-the-scenes one. For example, AB&C Compliance should provide subject matter expertise on bribery and corruption to those conducting the investigation and advise on whether certain conduct violated the organization's AB&C policies and procedures.

Conversely, AB&C Compliance ideally should not conduct interviews of employees in connection with bribery and corruption internal investigations. The main reason for this is that the desired role of AB&C Compliance (and Compliance generally) is one of a trusted advisor. If a compliance function is viewed by employees as adversarial then then any trust attributed to that function can deteriorate and the function will then be less effective.

7. ENFORCEMENT, DISCIPLINE, AND INCENTIVES

When considering how to best encourage employees to be responsible, ethical corporate citizens and comply with applicable AB&C policies, there are a number of potential tools. We'll explore the use of discipline and incentives, particularly focusing on compensation.

a. Enforcement Generally

An organization's AB&C Compliance program should be promoted and enforced through both appropriate incentives to perform in accordance with the policy and procedures and appropriate disciplinary measures for engaging in improper conduct. Note that when we explore incentives and discipline, we are doing so in situations of breaches of policy and procedure. These are important and need to be properly addressed. However, they also need to be distinguished from conduct which (of course breaches policy) but may also amount to a violation of applicable law or regulation.

Assuming that AB&C Compliance owns the AB&C policy, it is AB&C Compliance who should be responsible for determining whether there has been a breach of that policy that constitutes a policy violation. However, the consequences of a policy violation will likely not be in AB&C Compliance's sole discretion. Depending on the size and nature of the organization, Human Resources or a similar function may be significantly involved in helping to determine and/or administer any consequences for violations of the AB&C policy.

b. Discipline: A Delicate Balance Between Education and Punitive Measures

An organization's disciplinary procedures and potential disciplinary measures should be spelled out in the appropriate policy. Employees should understand the potential consequences of breaching the AB&C policy. However, appropriately applying discipline can be a delicate balance between education and punitive measures. The AB&C policy needs to be enforced, but not to the extent that it discourages employees from voluntarily coming forward with questions or concerns. The method of providing discipline (especially for minor policy breaches) needs to be carefully calibrated to both deter employees from breaching the policy and to let them feel comfortable raising questions and potential issues. In this vein, additional training and education can be an effective way to deal with minor policy breaches. It's also a more efficient use of AB&C Compliance resources than spending a disproportionate amount of time dealing with minor policy infractions.

c. Discipline: The Importance of Consistency

Discipline must always be applied consistently across an organization based on the conduct at issue and regardless of employee seniority or other factors. Like conduct should have like consequences.

d. Compensation Structures That Promote Compliance

In its September 2022 Memo, the DOJ announced some additional metrics that would be relevant to prosecutors' evaluation of a corporation's compliance program and culture. One such metric was referred to as "Compensation Structures that Promote Compliance."[56] The DOJ stated that "corporations can promote an ethical culture by rewarding those executives and employees who promote compliance within the organization."[57] It's basically a carrot and stick approach—"[c]orporations can help deter criminal activity if they reward compliant behavior and penalize individuals who engage in misconduct."[58]

The DOJ explained that "[c]ompensation systems that clearly and effectively impose financial penalties for misconduct can incentivize compliant conduct, deter risky behavior, and instill a corporate culture in which employees follow the law and avoid 'gray areas' "[59] This makes sense—it's basic human nature. People often inherently link their behavior with its financial consequences. Steven Cutler, a former Director of the SEC's Enforcement Division spoke about this idea at a roundtable in 2004 and the SEC and the DOJ cited his remarks approvingly in

---

[56] September 2022 Memo, *supra* Chapter 3, n.225, at 9.

[57] *Id.* at 10.

[58] *Id.* at 9.

[59] *Id.*

the FCPA Resource Guide. Director Cutler advised organizations to[60]:

> [M]ake integrity, ethics and compliance part of the promotion, compensation and evaluation processes as well. For at the end of the day, the most effective way to communicate that 'doing the right thing' is a priority, is to reward it. Conversely, if employees are led to believe that, when it comes to compensation and career advancement, all that counts is short-term profitability, and that cutting ethical corners is an acceptable way of getting there, they'll perform to that measure.

Cutler also provided the following helpful example from "a different walk of life" to illustrate the difference between words and conduct and how conduct is what's most important: "[A] college football coach can be told that the graduation rates of his players are what matters, but he'll know differently if the sole focus of his contract extension talks or the decision to for him is his win-loss record."[61] In more corporate parlance, an organization must make sure that its incentives are aligned with its objectives. For example, whether an employee meets certain compliance objectives could

---

60 FCPA Resource Guide, *supra* Chapter 1, n.1, at 61 *quoting* Stephen M. Cutler, Director, Division of Enforcement U.S. Securities and Exchange Commission, *Speech by SEC Staff: Second Annual General Counsel Roundtable: Tone at the Top: Getting it Right*, U.S. SEC (Dec. 3, 2004), https://www.sec.gov/news/speech/spch120304smc.htm.

61 *Id.*

be included as part of the bonus compensation calculus.

In its September 2022 Memo, the DOJ laid out several questions that it will consider when determining whether a corporation has implemented a compensation structure that promotes compliance. Specifically, the DOJ has instructed prosecutors to consider:

- Whether the corporation's compensation arrangements "enable penalties to be levied against current or former employees, executives, or directors whose direct or supervisory actions or omissions contributed to criminal conduct."[62] The DOJ explained that "prosecutors should examine whether compensation systems are crafted in a way that allows for retroactive discipline, including through the use of clawback[63] measures, partial escrowing of compensation, or equivalent arrangements."[64] The rationale behind this "retroactive" aspect is that

---

[62] September 2022 Memo, *supra* Chapter 3, n.225, at 10.

[63] As Investopedia explains, a clawback is a contractual provision whereby money already paid to an employee must be returned to an employer or benefactor, sometimes with a penalty. Many companies use clawback policies in employee contracts for incentive-based pay like bonuses. They are most often used in the financial industry. Most clawback provisions are non-negotiable. Clawbacks are typically used in response to misconduct, scandals, poor performance, or a drop in company profits. Will Kenton, *Clawback: Definition, Meaning, How It Works, and Example*, Investopedia (May 13, 2021), https://www.investopedia.com/terms/c/clawback.asp.

[64] September 2022 Memo, *supra* Chapter 3, n.225, at 10.

misconduct is often discovered after compensation has already been awarded.[65]

- If the corporation has, at least as a matter of policy, compensation structures that promote compliance, has the corporation actually utilized those structures where appropriate? For example, "[i]f a corporation has included clawback provisions in its compensation agreements, prosecutors should consider whether, following the corporation's discovery of misconduct, a corporation has, to the extent possible, taken affirmative steps to execute on such agreements and clawback compensation previously paid to current or former executives whose actions or omissions resulted in, or contributed to, the criminal conduct at issue."[66]

- "[W]hether a corporation uses or has used non-disclosure or non-disparagement provisions in compensation agreements, severance agreements, or other financial arrangements so as to inhibit the public disclosure of criminal misconduct by the corporation or its employees."[67]

- "[W]hether a corporation's compensation systems provide affirmative incentives for compliance-promoting behavior."[68] The DOJ

---

65 *Id.*

66 *Id.*

67 *Id.*

68 *Id.*

> explained that "[w]hen effectively implemented, such provisions incentivize executives and employees to engage in and promote compliant behavior and emphasize the corporation's commitment to its compliance programs and its culture."[69] The DOJ provided the following examples of affirmative incentives: "the use of compliance metrics and benchmarks in compensation calculations and the use of performance reviews that measure and reward compliance-promoting behavior, both as to the employee and any subordinates whom they supervise."[70]

The DOJ emphasized its view that "[t]he use of financial incentives to align the interests of the C-suite with the interests of the compliance department can greatly amplify a corporation's overall level of compliance."[71] Correspondingly, the DOJ stated that additional guidance would be forthcoming "on how to reward corporations that develop and apply compensation clawback policies, including how to shift the burden of corporate financial penalties away from shareholders—who in many cases do not have a role in misconduct—onto those more directly responsible."[72]

---

69 *Id.*

70 September 2022 Memo, *supra* Chapter 3, n.225, at 10.

71 *Id.*

72 *Id.*

i. Practice Example

I once worked with an organization in which senior executives were given a "score sheet" in connection with their year-end bonus compensation. The score sheet had two sides. One side contained revenue-related metrics. The other side contained compliance-related metrics, such as whether the person's group had outstanding audit issues, the severity of the rating of those audit issues, whether that person's group had compliance policy violations, etc. Both sides of the score sheet were weighted equally for purposes of calculating bonus compensation. The result was a group of senior executives who were actively engaged in compliance issues—whether for the moral good, their personal compensation, or perhaps a combination of both.

8. ONGOING PROGRAM IMPROVEMENT

An organization's business can evolve and change over time—e.g., expanding into new markets, working with new third parties, developing new products, etc. The laws, regulations, and industry standards that apply to an organization can also change over time. Reflecting these realities, an AB&C Compliance program must also be dynamic—AB&C Compliance and Legal officers need to keep abreast of changes affecting their organization and make sure that the AB&C Compliance program sufficiently addresses new and changing risks as well as meeting its existing objectives.[73]

As the SEC and DOJ have acknowledged, it's in an organization's best interests to proactively review and improve its AB&C Compliance program. The "DOJ and SEC will give meaningful credit to thoughtful efforts to create a sustainable compliance program if a problem is later discovered. Similarly, undertaking proactive evaluations before a problem strikes can lower the applicable penalty range under the U.S. Sentencing Guidelines."[74]

On a practical level, many organizational factors can affect an AB&C Compliance officer's ability to make improvements and changes to an organization's AB&C Compliance program. One is the level of commitment by senior management to the AB&C Compliance program and another is available budget. Obviously, the former affects the latter. Because of that it's very important for the AB&C Compliance officer to be an ambassador for their program and to make sure that other employees, including those in senior management, understand what the AB&C Compliance program does and why it's important.

So, with all of this said, how do AB&C Compliance programs ensure that they are both meeting their stated objectives and sufficiently addressing new and/or changing risks? Some ways are through risk

---

[73] *See, e.g.*, FCPA Resource Guide, *supra* Chapter 1, n.1, at 66.

[74] *Id.* (internal citation omitted).

assessment, monitoring, and testing. Let's take each of these in turn.

a. Risk Assessment

As with many topics in this book, risk assessment could certainly be a volume by itself. Here we'll cover it at a high level, focusing on terminology, key considerations, and how risk assessments fit into an AB&C Compliance program.

i. A Brief Introduction to Risk and Controls

Before discussing risk assessments in the AB&C context, it's helpful to level-set with some common vocabulary:

> **Internal Control:** any action taken by a party or parties within the organization (e.g., management, the board, compliance, etc.) to manage risk and to achieve specific goals in connection with risk prevention and risk mitigation (e.g., gift and entertainment spending limitations and payment monitoring).
>
> **External Control:** any action or influence from a source outside of the organization that affects the organization's governance (e.g., laws prohibiting bribery and corruption).
>
> **Inherent Risk:** the risk that an activity would pose if there were no controls or other mitigating factors in place.
>
> **Residual Risk:** the risk that remains after the associated controls have been applied.

Risk Appetite: the level of risk at which an organization is comfortable operating.

Risk Appetite Statement: a statement that lays out the parameters for the organization's approach to risk and the level of risk at which an organization is comfortable operating. It is often set, and updated annually, by the organization's board of directors. It is operationalized through the organization's policies, procedures, and internal controls.

ii. Types of Bribery and Corruption Risk

Bribery and corruption can manifest themselves in multiple ways. Both external and internal risk factors should be considered. Risk categories, from an anti-bribery and corruption perspective, include but are not limited to[75]:

Country Risk: The overall bribery and corruption risk of countries varies. Some countries have a potentially higher likelihood for instances of bribery and corruption to occur. Such countries, for example, may have no AB&C legislation or have AB&C legislation that has not been effectively implemented and/or is not properly enforced. The international non-profit Transparency International publishes a Corruption Perceptions Index each year that ranks approximately 180 countries and territories around the world based on how corrupt their public sectors

---

[75] The risks here are written from a specific anti-bribery and corruption perspective. They can of course be written to apply more broadly. The list does not include risks of general application, such as risk of financial loss.

are perceived to be by experts and business executives. The results are provided on a scale of 0 to 100, with 0 being highly corrupt and 100 being very clean.

Sectoral Risk: Bribery and corruption are more common in some industries than in others. Such higher risk industries include the construction, extractive, and pharmaceutical industries.

Transaction Risk: Some types of transactions are higher risk from a bribery and corruption perspective. These include transactions involving licenses and permits, public procurement, charitable contributions, political contributions, cash or cash equivalents, and generally any transactions involving interaction with public officials.

Opportunity Risk: Opportunity risk refers to the bribery and corruption risk that is inherent in business opportunities. Opportunities that may have a higher bribery and corruption risk include those that are of very high value, do not appear to be at market prices, or those which do not have a clear business objective.

Third-Party Risk: Transactions that involve the use of third-party agents or intermediaries are inherently higher risk from a bribery and corruption perspective. These third parties may act improperly and their improper actions may then be imputed to the principal organization. The highest risk third-party relationships are those in which the third party is acting on the principal organization's behalf to obtain or retain business or an advantage in business and may interact with public officials in the course of that work. *See* Chapter 6 discussing relationships with third parties and related risks and controls.

Business Association Risk: From time to time organizations may enter into relationships with other entities over whom they do not have complete control. These relationships may be structured as consortia, joint ventures, or other arrangements. It's possible that the resulting entity may engage in improper conduct and then that improper conduct could be imputed to individual participating organizations. The bribery and corruption risks in this situation are similar to those that exist when dealing with third-party relationships. *See* Chapter 6 for a discussion of business relationship risks.

Strategic Risk: This is the risk that the organization's choice of business strategies and prioritizations jeopardize its goals of complying with all applicable AB&C laws, regulations, and policies.

Legal Risk: This is the risk that the organization does not comply with all applicable anti-bribery and corruption laws and regulations.

Operational Risk: This is the risk that the organization's people (including employees and agents), processes, or systems impede the organization's ability to comply with applicable AB&C laws and regulations and the organization's related policies and procedures

Culture Risk: This is the risk that an organization's culture may not reflect a zero-tolerance approach to bribery and corruption.

Reasons for this may be an aggressive sales culture and/or insufficient messaging from senior management that goals should not be accomplished through improper means.

Employee Risk: This is the risk that an employee will engage in bribery or corruption in the course of working for their organization. The employee may do this solely for their own benefit, for the benefit of the employing organization, or both.

Compliance Infrastructure Risk: This is the risk that an organization's Compliance program, including but not limited to AB&C Compliance, is not sufficiently robust. For example, Compliance may not be adequately staffed or resourced and the policies and procedures may not be clear about the standard of behavior that is expected from employees, including the parameters for permissible conduct and prohibited conduct. Employee training may also be insufficient.

Incentive Risk: This is the risk that employees may feel encouraged or incentivized to engage in risky, and potentially improper, conduct. Compensation structures have very real effects on behavior. If an organization's compensation structure includes, for example, bonuses that reward aggressive risk taking, the practical effect could be that improper behavior is incentivized.

Reputational Risk: This is the risk that the organization will be negatively perceived internally and/or externally. This risk can at times appear vague or esoteric. However, reputational risk has real potential consequences for an organization. For example, loss of reputation can mean loss of employee morale and confidence in the organization, which results in lost productivity, employee departures, and hiring difficulties.

An organization's strategic decisions need to be aligned with its bribery and corruption risk appetite. The two are inherently inter-related. Understanding the above risks in the context of your specific organization is very important.

iii. AB&C Risk Assessments

Risk assessments are a critical tool to identify whether and where in an organization particular risks exist or may be more likely to arise. As the DOJ and SEC state specifically in their FCPA Resource Guide, "[a]ssessment of risk is fundamental to developing a strong compliance program, and is another factor DOJ and SEC evaluate when assessing a company's compliance program."[76] A risk assessment exercise is often undertaken at the inception of an AB&C Compliance program to help inform how best to structure the program. The risk assessment helps to identify any potential concerns, policy or training needs, and helps inform how best to allocate resources.

In addition to being used as a diagnostic tool at the start of an AB&C Compliance program, risk assessments should be conducted at regular

---

[76] FCPA Resource Guide, *supra* Chapter 1, n.1, at 60 (internal citation omitted).

intervals—often annually or every two years. It's helpful to keep a core of key questions in the recurring risk assessments so you can see where any information has changed—e.g., perhaps a division that previously did not deal with public officials now does. It can illustrate how risk is changing in an organization.

The UK Bribery Act Guidance notes that successful risk assessments (i.e., those that accurately identify and prioritize an organization's bribery and corruption risks) generally share the following characteristics[77]:

- Oversight of the risk assessment by top level management.
- Appropriate resourcing—this should reflect the scale of the organisation's business and the need to identify and prioritise all relevant risks.
- Identification of the internal and external information sources that will enable risk to be assessed and reviewed.
- Due diligence enquiries (internal reference omitted).
- Accurate and appropriate documentation of the risk assessment and its conclusions.

---

[77] UKBA Guidance, *supra* Chapter 1, n.2, at 25.

(a) Practice Points

Risk assessments are most effective when they are based on real-time organizational data rather than data collected as a snapshot in time. However, the ability to integrate data real-time into a risk assessment will of course depend on an organization's resourcing and technological capabilities.

Risk assessments are generally electronically administered and often take the form of a questionnaire to be completed by representatives of different sectors and functions of an organization (sometimes referred to as "assessment units"). The questions should be objective and factual in nature to help identify information. For example, a question could be: Does your division interact with public officials? To help avoid confusion, the question should also include the organization's definition of public official. If the answer is yes, then there would be a set of follow-up questions on what controls (if any) exist and a request to either provide documentation of such controls or indicate their location in the organization.

The results of the risk assessment can be compiled to create what's called a risk map and can give AB&C Compliance and senior management a holistic picture of what bribery and corruption risk looks like across an organization. It can help identify potential gaps in policy, procedures, and controls. Where gaps or problems are identified, they must be remediated. Action plans with completion dates need to implemented, and the successful closure of the action plans needs to be documented. There is generally also a written report that summarizes the risk assessment's findings.

Many large organizations use what's called an Enterprise-Wide Risk Assessment. This is a risk assessment that addresses numerous potential risks in one assessment questionnaire, which is more efficient for the organization and for the individuals responding to the questions. In that case, the AB&C Compliance officer should weigh in on the AB&C-portion of the risk assessment—the questions, assessment units, review of responses, gaps and corresponding action plans, and ultimate report and risk map.

Risk assessments can either be developed by an organization's internal staff or by outside consultants. However, if an outside consultant develops the risk assessment, AB&C Compliance should be closely involved to make sure that the risk assessment questions and assessment units reflect the realities of the organization and are not too generic.

After the results of the risk assessment are collected and analyzed, it's important to use that information, as necessary, to improve the AB&C Compliance program. AB&C Compliance needs to act on the information that it has at its disposal. It should be able to point to examples from its risk assessments and concrete changes that it has made to the AB&C Compliance program—e.g., changes to policies, procedures, or controls—as a result of the risk assessment. For example, as the DOJ has recognized in its Evaluation of Corporate Compliance Programs guidance, there must be a logical linkage between an organization's identified bribery and corruption risks and the resources that the organization has allocated to address those risks.

b. Auditing and Monitoring

Another way that AB&C Compliance programs identify gaps or potential areas for program enhancement are recommendations from internal monitoring and auditing functions. Depending on the size of the organization there may be separate functions for monitoring and auditing. If the organization is large and follows the three lines of defense model then there may be a monitoring group which, like AB&C Compliance, is a second line function. In that case the monitoring group may be a collaborative function that does periodic testing of AB&C systems and processes to make sure they are effective and then provides the results to AB&C Compliance and other stakeholders on an informational basis.

Internal audit is usually a third line of defense function, and its review process can be somewhat formal. Audit will generally provide a document setting out the scope of the audit (often called the Terms of Reference) at the beginning of a review. Audit will subsequently interview employees, review documents, and test systems. Audit will then prepare a list of issues with associated severity ratings that will need to be remediated by the appropriate personnel. Terminology varies by organization, but

Audit will ask for MAPs—management action plans with completion dates—describing how the issue owner (the individual who is responsible for the control with the gap) plans to remediate the issue. Audit will prepare a formal report that will be circulated to a group of stakeholders and the issues will be tracked to make sure the MAPs are completed by the agreed-upon dates and that the issues are closed.

i. Practice Note

Audit is a very important stakeholder for AB&C Compliance and the two groups should have a functional and constructive relationship. Contact should not be limited only to audits. For example, as an AB&C Compliance head I scheduled monthly meetings with Audit to provide updates on positive program developments as well as challenges. I was candid about areas of success and areas for possible improvement. I made it clear that the continuing enhancement of the program was my priority and that I welcomed additional views. To that end, I also occasionally raised (or recommended that other functions or business units raise) what are sometimes referred to as "MSIIs"—management self-identified issues. Whether an AB&C Compliance group can do this may depend in part on the culture of the particular organization—some organizations do not believe in affirmatively raising issues to Audit. However, transparency is important. Also, raising MSIIs conveys that AB&C Compliance is actively reviewing and working to improve the program and generally contributes positively to the management grade portion of an audit result.

It's also helpful for AB&C Compliance to provide training on different topics to the Audit group. Every organization's Audit group will have a different level of fluency on bribery and corruption issues—you may have an auditor who was an AB&C officer previously and is very tuned into the issues or you may have an auditor that is looking at bribery and corruption risk for the first time. Either way, if you work well with Audit then an audit can be a positive and useful experience. AB&C Compliance needs to ensure that Audit identifies the right issues, frames them correctly, and prepares an appropriate management action plan with correct issue owners and a reasonable time frame for issue closure.

Rather than being bad news for an AB&C Compliance program, an MSII or audit finding can actually be helpful. Consider the possibility that there's a gap in an organization's AB&C Compliance program that the AB&C Compliance officer is aware of and wants to remedy but doesn't have the requisite senior management support and funding. An MSII or Audit finding can force a solution. The AB&C Compliance function will likely receive the support necessary to close the issue.

c. Lessons Learned: Internal and External

Consider both the internal and external lessons that the AB&C Compliance program can and should learn over time. Examine these lessons. Think of them as teachable moments and use them to improve your organization's AB&C Compliance program.

Internally, each time there is a bribery or corruption issue—and there will be no matter how well-run the organization or how solid its AB&C Compliance program—learn from it. Take the time to unpack what happened, why it happened, and why the controls that the organization had in place did not prevent it from happening. Do a full "root cause analysis" after each incident. Keep drilling down until you find the fault or gap that allowed the problem to occur or created the opportunity for it to occur. Then remediate that condition. Document the root cause analysis and remediation process and retain that documentation.

AB&C Compliance and Legal officers can also learn from incidents that have occurred at other organizations. Consensual government resolutions, like deferred prosecution agreements, are a good source of information. Review such resolution documents, especially those of companies in your organization's industry. Read the facts and consider whether it might be possible for a similar problem to occur in your own organization or whether you believe that the risk has been appropriately mitigated. If it may be possible for a similar problem to occur at your organization, take steps to review the relevant controls, analyze any gaps, and put together a remediation plan. Having regular communications with those in a similar role at other organizations can also be greatly beneficial. Off-the-record discussions about bribery and corruption-related challenges that other similar institutions may be having can also help you evaluate and improve the program at your own organization.

CHAPTER 6

ANTI-BRIBERY AND CORRUPTION COMPLIANCE SUBJECT AREAS

The sections below address the advisory subject-matter areas that are often part of AB&C Compliance programs. These include public officials, gifts and entertainment, charitable giving, hiring practices, third party practices, business transactions, and AB&C representations and warranties. In addition, we'll also touch on political contributions and reputational risk, two areas that are related to AB&C and often have at least some overlap with an organization's AB&C Compliance program.

A. PUBLIC OFFICIALS

In our exploration of bribery and corruption, why do we specifically single out public officials? Public officials are a focus of many AB&C laws and instruments because they are in a unique position to influence the use of government (i.e., public) funds. If public officials are improperly influenced (via bribery) regarding how to direct or allocate these funds, then the public can be directly harmed. This makes preventing the bribery of public officials a matter of concern for society as a whole.

It's important for AB&C Compliance programs to address both foreign and domestic public officials. AB&C Compliance programs need to create their own terms for domestic and foreign public officials, and then define those terms based on applicable law and available guidance. It's helpful to consider definitions from the FCPA, the UNCAC, the OECD Convention, and the UKBA. Organizations are not bound by the OECD and UNCAC definitions because those instruments apply to state actors. Organizations, depending on the geography of their business, may also not be legally bound to comply with the FCPA or the UKBA. However, all of these sources are informative and can be used to help develop an organization's own tailored definition(s) of domestic and foreign public officials. As you read through the respective definitions, you'll notice a common core. First, we'll address foreign officials.

1. FOREIGN OFFICIALS

Recall that the FCPA defines "foreign official" as "any officer or employee of a foreign government or any department, agency, or instrumentality thereof, or of a public international organization, or any person acting in an official capacity for or on behalf of any such government or department, agency or instrumentality, or for or on behalf of any such public international organization."[1]

The UNCAC defines "public official," "foreign public official," and "official of a public international organization," essentially including parts of the FCPA definition of foreign official as well as creating a framework for a definition of domestic public officials.

---

1 FCPA Resource Guide, *supra* Chapter 1, n.1, at 19, 108 n.112.

The UNCAC defines "public official" as:[2]

> (i) any person holding a legislative, executive, administrative or judicial office of a State Party, whether appointed or elected, whether permanent or temporary, whether paid or unpaid, irrespective of that person's seniority; (ii) any other person who performs a public function, including for a public agency or public enterprise, or provides a public service, as defined in the domestic law of the State Party and as applied in the pertinent area of law of that State Party; (iii) any other person defined as a 'public official' in the domestic law of a State Party.

For the purposes of some specific UNCAC provisions, "public official" may also mean "any person who performs a public function or provides a public service as defined in the domestic law of the State Party and as applied in the pertinent area of law of that State Party[.]"[3]

The UNCAC defines "foreign public official" as "any person holding a legislative, executive, administrative or judicial office of a foreign country, whether appointed or elected; and any person exercising a public function for a foreign country, including for a public agency or public enterprise[.]"[4]

---

2 UNCAC, *supra* Chapter 2, n.42, Art. 2(a).

3 *Id.*

4 *Id.* at Art. 2(b).

The UNCAC defines "official of a public international organization" as "an international civil servant or any person who is authorized by such an organization to act on behalf of that organization[.]"[5]

As explained in the UKBA Guidance, the UKBA defines "foreign public official" as[6]

> includ[ing] officials, whether elected or appointed, who hold a legislative, administrative or judicial position of any kind of a country or territory outside the UK. It also includes any person who performs public functions in any branch of the national, local or municipal government of such a country or territory or who exercises a public function for any public agency or public enterprise of such a country or territory, such as professionals working for public health agencies and officers exercising public functions in state-owned enterprises. Foreign public officials can also be an official or agent of a public international organisation, such as the UN or the World Bank.

An organization needs to draft its own definition(s) for one or more types of public official(s) based on the laws and regulations to which it is subject. Organizations that do business in the U.S. or are otherwise subject to the FCPA may create definitions for "Foreign Official" and "U.S. Official" and may have different internal rules for dealing with each. The FCPA does not address the bribery of U.S. public

---

[5] *Id.* at Art. 2(c).

[6] UKBA Guidance, *supra* Chapter 1, n.2, at 11.

officials. Nevertheless, it is wise for an organization that does business with or in the U.S. to have an AB&C Compliance program that also addresses the bribery and corruption risks of dealing with U.S. government officials.

For illustrative purposes, an organization subject to the FCPA might define Foreign Official as:

> Any person (regardless of rank, seniority, title, and regardless of whether elected, appointed or hired) who is employed by or who is acting in an official capacity on behalf of:
>
> (1) any national, regional, local, or municipal government
>
> (2) any state-owned or controlled entity
>
> (3) any public international organization
>
> For example, legislators, ministers, judges, regulators, clerks, members of the military and law enforcement, and members of a royal family and candidates for political office outside of the U.S. should all be considered Foreign Officials.
>
> Regarding (2) 'any state owned or controlled entity' means any entity in which a government has a 30%[7] or greater ownership interest or, which otherwise has substantial indicia of

[7] There is no prescribed percentage of government ownership that is determinative of government ownership and control. AB&C Compliance and Legal must make a risk-based decision to set the percentage.

government control based on the existence of various factors, including but not limited to:

- whether, and to what extent, the government provides financial support to the entity;
- whether the government has designated board seats and/or government officials otherwise sit on the board;
- whether the government has the ability to directly or indirectly appoint or dismiss board members or members of senior management;
- whether the government has any special voting rights;
- whether government officials serve in executive positions at the entity; and
- whether the entity provides services that are traditionally associated with a government function (e.g., security or defense services).

Whether an entity should be considered state-owned or controlled such that its employees and those acting for or on its behalf should be considered Foreign Officials is in the sole and final discretion of AB&C Compliance.

a. Practice Question

How should an organization determine whether an entity that it is interacting with is an instrumentality of a foreign government such that its officers, employees, and representatives should be considered foreign officials for purposes of the FCPA's anti-bribery provisions?

Answer

Through conducting an analysis of both ownership and control as laid out below.

- Ownership: Is the entity ___% (as defined by the organization) or more owned by a foreign government?
  - If YES, then the entity is deemed to be government-owned, and its employees and representatives should be considered foreign officials.
  - If NO, then are some or all of the *Esquenazi* factors present?
    - If NO, the analysis ends—the entity is not state owned or controlled and its employees are not foreign officials.
    - If YES, then AB&C Compliance/Legal must make a determination.

A Cautionary Note: Even if, after appropriate analysis, an organization determines that the entity that it's dealing with is *not* an instrumentality of a foreign government, the FCPA-related risk doesn't end there. As the SEC and DOJ have noted, "[c]ompanies and individuals should also remember that, whether an entity is an instrumentality of a foreign government or a private entity, commercial (i.e., private-to-private) bribery may still violate the FCPA's accounting provisions, the Travel Act, anti-money laundering laws, and other federal or foreign laws. Any type of corrupt payment thus carries a risk of prosecution."[8]

As part of the training and resources that are made available to employees, it's helpful to provide a non-exhaustive list of the types of entities of which employees and representatives will be classified as foreign officials, as that term is defined by the organization. This means that any person who works for any of these entities (regardless of seniority) should be considered a foreign official. This clarification should always be reiterated because it's a common point of confusion for employees. Even if an employee recognizes that an entity is state-owned or controlled, they may not consider the person at the entity they are dealing with to be a foreign official because they don't think the person has enough seniority.

Examples of types of entities whose employees, or those acting for or on their behalf, that may be classified as foreign officials include:

- government agencies and ministries (e.g., Ministry of Justice)
- sovereign wealth funds
- central banks
- political parties
- development banks

---

[8] FCPA Resource Guide, *supra* Chapter 1, n.1, at 21.

- state universities
- regulators
- public international organizations (e.g., the United Nations, the World Bank)
- royal families

Whether or not someone is a domestic or foreign public official, as defined by the organization, is an objective matter. It is not situational. For example, a person does not cease to be a public official by purporting to act in a personal or private capacity or by providing services without compensation.

2. U.S. OFFICIALS

For illustrative purposes, an organization could define a U.S. Official as "any elected or appointed official or any employee of the legislative, executive, or judicial branches of the U.S. federal government or of a state, city, municipal or local government. Examples of U.S. Officials include not just employees of government departments and agencies, but even employees of state universities and employees of public pension funds."

3. PRACTICAL TIPS FOR ORGANIZATIONS DEALING WITH PUBLIC OFFICIALS

For many organizations, dealing with public officials is a part of ordinary and ongoing business. This doesn't have to be a problem so long as the associated bribery and corruption risks are appropriately managed. As an initial matter, it's helpful to reduce the number of situations where a public official could potentially solicit a bribe. There are a few ways to do this:

Use Electronic Government Services: To the extent possible, conduct necessary business through electronic government portals and channels.

Minimize 1:1 Meetings with Public Officials: Where possible, have more than one person from an organization present in any meetings with a public official. Having several people present in a meeting could have a chilling effect on a potential bribe offer or request.

Mandate Documentation: Require that public officials' requests (whether monetary or non-monetary) be made in writing. Employees should be taught to cite organizational policy or refer them to AB&C Compliance or Legal if public officials push back on this documentation requirement.

Incentivize Good Compliance: Make sure that employees and third-party representatives understand that the organization does not want them to engage in bribery, even that means losing a significant business deal.

Educate Employees About Detection Controls: Employees who do not comply with AB&C policies should know that there is a good chance that they will be caught. Emphasize the systems that the organization has in place to detect improper conduct.

B. GIFTS AND ENTERTAINMENT

There's nothing per se wrong with offering or accepting gifts and entertainment. As the SEC and DOJ recognize in their FCPA Resource Guide, offering or accepting hospitality is a common part of building and maintaining business relationships, promoting an organization's products and services, and enhancing an organization's brand.[9] The UKBA Guidance similarly acknowledges that "[b]ona fide hospitality and promotional, or other business expenditure which seeks to improve the image of a commercial organisation, better to present products and services, or establish cordial relations, is recognised as an established and important part of doing business and it is not the intention of the [UKBA] to criminalise such behaviour."[10]

The FCPA itself recognizes the legitimacy of appropriate gifting and entertainment with its reasonable and bona fide business expenditure affirmative defense, previously addressed, which states generally that the offer, payment, or provision of anything of value was a reasonable and bona fide expense—such as for travel and lodging—in connection with[11]:

- The promotion, demonstration, or explanation of products or services;

---

[9] FCPA Resource Guide, *supra* Chapter 1, n.1, at 14–15.

[10] UKBA Guidance, *supra* Chapter 1, n.2, at 12.

[11] FCPA Resource Guide, *supra* Chapter 1, n.1, at 24, 110 n.149 *citing* 15 U.S.C. §§ 78dd–1(c)(2), 78dd–2(c)(2), 78dd–3(c)(2).

or

- The execution or performance of a contract with a foreign government or its agency.

It is this provision which is inherently relied upon by AB&C Compliance programs as a justification for reasonable business hospitality, entertainment, and gift giving. However, like anything of value, G&E can of course be used for improper purposes. As the UKBA Guidance notes, it is "clear that hospitality and promotional or other similar business expenditure can be employed as bribes."[12]

The terms "gift" and "entertainment" are not defined in the FCPA or the UKBA. But they of course fall within the concept of "anything of value." Organizations generally develop their own working definitions of these terms and include them in the relevant policies and procedures. For example:

- "Gift" could be defined as "anything of value—whether monetary or non-monetary—given to the recipient, excluding entertainment where the offeror is present. Examples include but are not limited to gift baskets, bottles of wine, tickets to shows where the offeror is not present, etc."

- "Entertainment" could be defined as "anything of value—whether monetary or non-monetary—given to the recipient, including but not limited to meals, conferences, sporting events, concerts, and

---

[12] UKBA Guidance, *supra* Chapter 1, n.2, at 12.

any related travel or accommodation so long as the offeror is present."

What do you notice about the difference between Gifts and Entertainment in these proposed definitions? In theory, the same thing could be a Gift or Entertainment, *but it depends on whether the offeror is present*. This is a common distinction that AB&C Compliance programs make. Why? Generally, the rationale is that if the person who is offering the benefit is going with the recipient to an event, meal, etc., then a relationship building element is present. Perhaps the offeror is discussing the organization's products and services and how those products and services could be useful to the recipient. In other words, there's a legitimate business purpose to the entertainment. Is this relationship building aspect different with a Gift? Potentially. With a Gift, there isn't the element of the offeror and the recipient spending time together. As a result, the legitimate business connection is a little more of a reach. For this reason, organizations generally have stricter rules around Gift giving than Entertainment.

Some hallmarks of appropriate gift giving (from the FCPA Resource Guide and practice) are that the gift is[13]:

- Given openly and transparently

If something is non-confidentially offered to a wide audience, then it's more likely to be considered transparent. However, if the person offering the

13 FCPA Resource Guide, *supra* Chapter 1, n.1, at 14.

benefit or the person receiving it have concerns about it becoming known, it's probably not reasonable to offer the benefit.

- provided only to reflect esteem or gratitude
- properly recorded in the giver's books and records
- permitted under local law
- not lavish or disproportionate to the business relationship

Gifts and Entertainment must not be lavish or disproportionate to the business relationship. Why are we interested in the concept of lavishness? Whether a Gift or Entertainment is lavish is a potential proxy for our ultimate question of whether the offeror is intending to improperly influence the recipient. As the UKBA Guidance aptly phrases it[14]:

> [T]he more lavish the hospitality or the higher the expenditure in relation to travel, accommodation or other similar business expenditure provided to a foreign public official, then, generally, the greater the inference that it is intended to influence the official to grant business or a business advantage in return.

What is lavish or disproportionate to a particular business relationship are of course subjective questions. Some of the factors that should be considered are:

---

14 UKBA Guidance, *supra* Chapter 1, n.2, at 13.

- the complete G&E picture over a period of time—e.g., what is the value of the G&E that the offeror has given the recipient and the recipient's organization over the past 12 months?

- the recipient's seniority and personal means. For example, if the recipient is extremely wealthy then it's unlikely that they will be improperly influenced by an expensive dinner. If, however, the value of the Gift or Entertainment offered is beyond the recipient's ordinary means then it is more likely to improperly influence the recipient.

- any contracts that may be in place that specify particular benefits (e.g., paying travel expenses in connection with an annual training).

- industry norms or standards that may apply.

In addition to specific rules, AB&C policies may include some general principles on G&E to help guide employees and relevant third parties. For example:

All G&E (whether offered or received) must:

- be for a legitimate and documented business purpose;

- be offered or received in compliance with all applicable Organization X policies and procedures and all applicable laws and regulations;

- be reasonable in value and proportional to the business relationship;
- be appropriate considering all of the surrounding circumstances (e.g., frequency, timing given potential and recently completed business, etc.);
- be properly recorded in Organization X's books and records; and
- be transparently offered/accepted and suitable to be openly discussed—i.e., if the instance of G&E was reported to the media, it would not reasonably be expected to cause embarrassment to the offeror, the recipient, or Organization X.

1. THE SCOPE OF G&E PROGRAMS

As a reminder, the FCPA's anti-bribery provisions prohibit the corrupt payment of money or anything of value to a foreign official (whether directly or indirectly) in order to obtain or retain business. When we think of "anything of value," G&E is a common topic and key part of most AB&C Compliance programs. If we consider G&E in the FCPA context we would be concerned only with the (potentially improper) offering or providing of G&E to a foreign official. However, as a practical matter, AB&C Compliance programs should address G&E beyond that limited scope. There are a number of reasons for this.

First, depending on where an organization does business, an organization may be subject to other

AB&C laws that are broader than the FCPA. Take, for example, the UK Bribery Act. The UKBA is broader than the FCPA in several ways. For example, it prohibits commercial bribery (bribery of private persons) in addition to bribery of public officials. It also prohibits passive bribery (meaning the acceptance of bribes) as well as offering bribes. The UKBA also includes a corporate offense of failing to prevent bribery.

So, if an organization is subject to an AB&C law like the UKBA, what would that mean for how that organization would need to design its G&E program? In short, the program would need to address both the giving and receiving of G&E by the organization's employees to and from both public officials (foreign and domestic) and private individuals.

But what if the organization is not subject to an AB&C law broader than the FCPA? Should it still address both the giving and receiving of G&E to and from both public and private individuals? In short, yes. From a governance and regulatory perspective, an organization should work to have a culture of ethics and compliance. It should not have an atmosphere where benefits and incentives are exchanged for business advantages even if it's technically legal. Moreover, having an ethical and compliant culture is beneficial from a pure business standpoint. Consider the situation where an organization has an employee responsible for choosing its software vendors. These contracts are very lucrative, and several vendors are competing for the privilege to serve the organization. The vendors are "wining and dining" the employee, as the saying goes, and perhaps providing the employee with monetary or non-monetary incentives to choose their software company over the others. This creates the potential that the employee will choose the vendor that provides them with the most personal benefit as opposed to the vendor that may be best for the organization. Whether as a Legal or AB&C Compliance officer, or as a businessperson, wouldn't you want to have line of sight over that type of risk?

2. REVIEWING A G&E REQUEST: PROCESS POINTS

AB&C Compliance generally will not review and approve all G&E requests. An organization's AB&C policy will define the parameters of the requests that require AB&C Compliance review. Organizations need to use a risk-based approach to devise their own effective method for recording and reviewing G&E that is offered to third parties and received from third parties. In some cases, the method or process is wholly owned by AB&C Compliance. But more commonly, it's likely a hybrid—AB&C Compliance requires and maintains certain documentation and the organization's Accounting or Finance Department also requires and maintains certain documentation.

There are often several different components to a G&E review and approval process: recording, pre-approval, post-review, and post-approval. We'll take each of these in turn.

a. Recording

Recording is what it sounds like—it's keeping a record of G&E given and received. Generally, this is done in an electronic system. Depending on an organization's G&E policy, some G&E will need to be recorded within a certain time frame even if it does not need AB&C Compliance pre-approval. Why might this be the case? There are several possible reasons. First, it's important to maintain accurate books and records and accounting controls from a pure business perspective as well as to comply with the FCPA.

Second, it allows G&E to be aggregated over a period of time. Then AB&C Compliance will still have line of sight over G&E spend even if it's below the thresholds that trigger AB&C Compliance pre-approval. The accurate recording of G&E means that AB&C Compliance will be able to generate useful metrics—e.g., which division is giving and receiving the most entertainment, which employees are providing the highest priced entertainment, what third parties are being entertained most frequently, etc. It's important to be able to have the methods and tools in place to generate comprehensive reporting. Finally, depending on the organization's industry, recording of all G&E given and received may be necessary for employees who are subject to specific licensing or regulatory requirements.

b. AB&C Compliance Pre-Approval

Pre-approval refers to when AB&C Compliance reviews a request for a gift or entertainment prior to an employee offering or accepting that gift or entertainment. Pre-approval is an important concept that is rooted in the FCPA. Think about the FCPA language—corrupt *offer* of anything of value. *Offer* is the key word. Liability can arise at the time an offer is made, regardless of whether or not the offer is ultimately accepted. Pre-approval is a chance for AB&C Compliance to review proposed conduct before liability potentially arises.[15]

What types of G&E requests might be reviewed by AB&C Compliance? This of course depends on the particular organization and its policies. Many organizations have a table with monetary thresholds for gifts and entertainment, which are usually treated as distinct for this purpose. AB&C Compliance will review requests over the designated monetary threshold amounts.

There is generally a lower pre-approval threshold for gifts than for entertainment. There is also generally a lower pre-approval threshold for G&E involving public officials, whether foreign officials or U.S. officials. Other factors, besides cost, may also trigger AB&C Compliance review. For example, if the proposed entertainment would involve inviting a guest's spouse or children or if there is pending or

---

15 Although the FCPA only addresses the "supply" side bribery of foreign officials, as defined in that statute, AB&C Compliance pre-approval of G&E that is offered to an organization's recipients is important for various reasons, including but not limited to the applicability of broader AB&C laws such as the UKBA and U.S. domestic bribery laws.

recently completed business with the proposed invitee or their organization.

c. AB&C Compliance Post-Review

Some AB&C Compliance programs also have the concept of a post-review. Generally, this is a review of documentation that has been submitted after a pre-approved gift or entertainment occurred. Depending on an organization's resources and risk appetite, a post-review may be conducted for every transaction that was subject to pre-approval. Alternatively, it may only be done for a sampling of such transactions. Finally, there may be no "post-review" category per se. Instead, this may be part of ongoing monitoring by AB&C Compliance and/or another internal monitoring function.

If AB&C Compliance has already pre-approved a gift or entertainment, then why would it be necessary for AB&C Compliance to conduct a post-review of the documentation of that gift or entertainment after it has been given or experienced? In short, to make sure that the actual gift or entertainment was substantially the same as presented to AB&C Compliance and pre-approved in terms of costs, specific attendees, etc. It's also a way of keeping track of amounts of the actual money spent—remember the importance of maintaining accurate books and records! If the pre-approved amount was exceeded, AB&C Compliance then becomes aware and can follow up as necessary. For example, AB&C Compliance may provide the employee at issue with additional AB&C training or escalate the matter to the employee's manager or the organization's Human Resources Department for consideration.

Finally, AB&C Compliance post-review is a way to ensure that any pre-approval conditions that may have been imposed by AB&C Compliance were met. For example, perhaps for a higher-priced event AB&C Compliance imposed a pre-approval limitation that no foreign officials could be invited. Then, what if foreign officials were actually invited and/or attended? AB&C Compliance would want to know this information so it could record it and take any appropriate action.

d. AB&C Compliance Post-Approval

Some AB&C Compliance programs also include a post-approval component. This is where AB&C Compliance reviews a gift or event that would have required pre-approval, but only after the gift or entertainment has already taken place. This is an exceptional process component that is intended only for the situation where something occurs unexpectedly such that it was not possible to obtain AB&C Compliance pre-approval beforehand.

This exceptional process reflects a business reality. For example, an employee attends a conference and starts talking with a prospective client at a break. They then decide to go out for drinks and dinner after the conference. Given the unexpected nature of the meeting and the impromptu timing it would not have been possible to obtain AB&C Compliance pre-approval before the event. Note—not possible means *not possible*. It does not mean *inconvenient*.

Some AB&C Compliance programs use post-approval when necessary but may or may not address post-approval in the main AB&C and G&E policies. Including the concept of post-approval in the applicable policy may encourage employees to seek post-approval for gifts or entertainment even where it *was* possible to seek approval beforehand. This can be true even if the policy explains that post-approval is *only* available in very limited circumstances. Such employee conduct is of course not ideal. However, AB&C Compliance maintains line-of-sight over G&E and can provide supplemental training to the employees who submitted technically incorrect post-approval requests.

A downside of not including an explanation of post-approval in the main AB&C or G&E policy is that it may result in employees not disclosing certain gifts and entertainment. Employees may think that they will be disciplined for not submitting a required pre-approval request and so will try to avoid scrutiny. As always, determining the right approach for a particular organization will involve balancing the need to encourage employees to comply with policy and the goal of making employees comfortable enough that they will raise questions or concerns, or offer information, to AB&C Compliance.

e. G&E Systems

Ideally an organization will have a single system where employees can record G&E, submit it for pre-approval, and request reimbursement. This is better for employees because the information is centralized, and they don't have to enter it into multiple systems. This is also more efficient for AB&C Compliance because the relevant information is in one place. This makes it easier for AB&C Compliance to review requests and to generate Management Information, or "MI" for short.

Keeping accurate books and records is of course important. It's also important for an organization to be able to be able to organize and analyze information in a way that can inform the organization about its bribery and corruption risk. Bare numbers are not enough. For example, knowing that an organization's Department C submitted 100 entertainment requests last quarter totaling $250,000 doesn't indicate much about the bribery and corruption risk relating to Department C or the overall organization. More is needed. For example:

- Who were the individuals who requested the most entertainment by percentage? By cost per person?
- Who were the individuals who received the most entertainment by percentage? By cost per person?
- Who were the entities, whether current or potential clients or third parties, who were entertained the most?
- Who were the entities, whether current or potential clients or third parties, who entertained the most Organization X employees?

- For any of the above, was there any pending or recently completed business at or around the time the G&E was requested or occurred?

Answers to questions like the ones above can help take the basic G&E numbers beyond just a counting exercise to identifying potential bribery and corruption red flags.

More sophisticated G&E systems can also route items to AB&C Compliance for review based on programmed "triggers" like price threshold or public official status of offerors or invitees. Some systems have a live feed that identifies public officials based on the organization's own definitional parameters. The larger and more well-funded the organization, the more sophisticated that regulators will expect its systems to be.

To the extent possible, AB&C Compliance and employees submitting requests should work within the requisite G&E system. For example, if a request that has been submitted does not have sufficient information, the request should be returned to the submitting employee through the system with the explanation that additional information is required. This helps preserve the audit trail of requests and demonstrates that an organization has a working process.

3. REVIEWING A G&E REQUEST: DATA POINTS

As previously discussed, AB&C Compliance will generally not review every G&E request. The triggers for review will generally be spelled out in the policies or procedures. Below is a list of informational points that AB&C Compliance may review when considering a request.

a. Date of Request

The Date of Request is the date that the request is submitted to AB&C Compliance to review a gift or entertainment. This data point has at least two practical ramifications. First, the relevant policy will generally require that a request be submitted a certain amount of time prior to the actual event/ purchase of the gift for review and approval. (Of course, things do come up at the last minute and AB&C Compliance also needs to have an effective way to deal with last-minute requests. *See* the above explanation of post-approval.

Second, the relevant AB&C policy or procedure may also have a general "turn-around" time guideline or requirement for AB&C Compliance to review and opine on a request. This type of guideline/ requirement has both benefits and down-sides. It can be helpful because it sets employees' expectations about when they will receive a response. However, it can also cause difficulties when employees submit requests that they believe are complete but, in fact, are not. For example, employees sometimes submit requests that facially appear complete but involve one or more higher risk components (not necessarily recognized by the employee) that require follow-up. These requests naturally take more time (and their resolution is also partially dependent on the employee providing additional information) which can also cause delays.

b. Name and Position of Requestor and Managerial Approver

It's of course basic information to know the name and position of the employee who is making the G&E request. In addition, even if a request doesn't require AB&C Compliance approval, it may require managerial approval. Such managerial approval is usually done by an employee's direct supervisor, but this may vary by organization.

The managerial approval is generally given from a cost or budgetary perspective. However, the managerial approver should also be taking into account any facts he or she may be aware of that may affect the approval decision from a bribery and corruption perspective. For example, perhaps there is a significant transaction pending with a client and inviting that client to an expensive outing would not be appropriate at that time. Remember, if an organization has a three lines of defense compliance model, it is the first line that ultimately bears the bribery and corruption risk. This should be made clear in the applicable policies and trainings. *See* Chapter 5 for a further discussion of the three lines of defense model and potential concerns with the first line assuming bribery and corruption risk.

i. Practice Note

It's important to make sure that the identity and corporate title of the managerial approver is appropriate for the requesting employee. The organization's internal policies and procedures should explain the reporting structure and the requisite titles and levels for different types of approvals. In some cases, approver names will be automatically populated by a system. However, in the case of systems where employees can select or change their own approvers in the system, AB&C Compliance should be aware of the potential for misuse. For example, an employee might change an approver's name to that of a friend who has the requisite title seniority rather than choose an approver in that employee's direct reporting line. This can be a way to hide inappropriate expenditures.

Second the managerial approver should effectively be a level of quality control to make sure the request is complete and includes all necessary information for review by AB&C Compliance. AB&C Compliance is generally an advisory function with finite resources. Having to review incomplete requests wastes time and money.

c. Date of Event

The date of a proposed event is of course basic information. However, it's also important from a timing perspective. As previously referenced, some organizations will have policies that require employees to submit requests a certain number of calendar or business days prior to a proposed event to allow AB&C Compliance sufficient time to review the request.

d. Location and Cost of Event

Like the date of a proposed event, an event's location and cost is basic record keeping. However, it also goes beyond that. It's information that AB&C Compliance can use to determine whether the proposed event is appropriate to the business relationship or whether it might be considered inappropriate or lavish. It raises the discussion of price paid versus value being offered and how these two concepts should be used to review entertainment requests.

i. Hidden Value and Unique Venues

AB&C Compliance should "sense check" the stated cost of an event as compared to the details of the event itself, even if that stated cost is within the organization's accepted entertainment parameters. For example, what if an organization hosts a cocktail party in a private room at a venue like the New York Public Library for a stated cost of $150 per person? Depending on the invitees, purpose, etc. that price may seem reasonable from a pure cost perspective. However, it may also seem low considering the nature of the venue. What if the organization is a member of the New York Public Library, at a cost of $50,000 per year, and it is that membership that allows the organization access to book events at the Library? Should AB&C Compliance factor this membership fee into the per person cost of a specific event or consider it a sunk cost of the organization? And, if AB&C Compliance does consider it a sunk cost of the organization, then is the per person price being recorded truly reflecting the value that the organization is providing to an invitee? An organization must consider these questions and determine an approach.

The concept of hidden value should also be considered with respect to unique venues or unique opportunities. What if an event is at a unique venue that the invitee might not otherwise have access to? When evaluating requests, AB&C Compliance should be considering whether the invitee may be improperly influenced by receiving a certain benefit. It's more likely that a person will be improperly influenced when they are being offered something that they could not have otherwise independently obtained. AB&C Compliance should consider whether events have an intrinsic value beyond the specific per head price that the organization may pay.

e. Valuation Date for an Event

As of what date should the value of an event be calculated? Is it at the time the invitation would be extended to the invitee, at the time that the invitee accepts the invitation, or at the time the event occurs? Consider the example of the US Open tennis tournament. An employee purchases tickets to the US Open finals one month before the US Open is set to begin. The employee pays $500 per ticket at that time. What should AB&C Compliance consider to be the value of each ticket when reviewing the employee's eventual request to invite certain clients? Should it be $500 per ticket? Would it make a difference if the employee purchased the $500 per ticket from a direct retailer or from a ticket broker on the secondary market?

Should the value of the ticket be the price the employee paid for the ticket, or should it be the ticket's market value? If it should be market value, then market value as of what date? Continuing the US Open example, what if it subsequently turns out that the world's first-ranked tennis player will play in the final match and has announced that it will be her last tournament appearance? The value of a ticket to the final match obviously goes up as it becomes a unique opportunity to view a tennis great's final match. How could/should an AB&C Compliance officer consider the per ticket value in light of this information?

Part of an AB&C Compliance officer's role is to instill consistency and measurability in a program. Also, think about the FCPA and its "offer" language—an offer made with a corrupt intent is when FCPA liability can potentially arise. So, for valuation purposes, the important time is when the offer is made. Based on that, it's helpful to use the price paid (as long as there was no special purchasing advantage), assuming that the purchase was close in time to the offer or invitation. If there was a special purchasing advantage, then consider using the market value at the time of purchase.

Some AB&C Compliance programs recommend using market value for valuing entertainment. But that creates practical difficulties that those programs then need to manage. Market value is somewhat subjective and, if this option is being utilized, then the AB&C Compliance program would need to have a specific method and documented procedures for determining market value. As we just addressed, what would be the date of the relevant market value determination? What if, as with the US Open ticket example, the value significantly increased after purchase? Would you use the higher value or the original purchase price? And how do people go about getting the market data? The AB&C Compliance program would need to have a process in place so that consistent and reliable determinations could be made. For these and other reasons a simple approach is best—value an entertainment using the cost at the time of the purchase.

f. Type of Event/Business Rationale of Event

What is the business rationale for the event being held? Employees should be asked to supply a business rationale when submitting a G&E request to AB&C Compliance for review. The chart below highlights some "good" and "bad" examples of business rationales.

"Good" Examples	"Bad" Examples
Transportation and lodging, pursuant to contract, to view factory construction	VIP client
Business meal to discuss new product that may be appropriate for client	Client likes fancy dinners
Discuss current market developments applicable to client's business	Received $250K in fees from client last year [if VP is not invited to Kentucky Derby, then he is likely to move his company's business]

Notice that the "good" examples specifically reference contracts, business opportunities, and the organization's products and services. Conversely, the "bad" examples refer to the client's important status, entertainment preferences, and fees generated from the client. The last "bad" example is the most concerning. When the bracketed language is added in, there's the appearance of a quid pro quo—offering the client's employee a benefit in exchange for retaining the client's business.

The employee submitting the request should identify the type of event and the business rationale for the event. Different types of events often have varying levels of bribery and corruption risk. For this reason, concerts, business meetings, and conferences may all be treated differently in terms of policy and process.

Consider the difference between inviting someone to a U2 concert and to a conference on widgets. Although there might be some business-related discussion at the concert's intermission, the two events would appear to have drastically different levels of business content. If the organization sells widgets and invites a prospective customer to its conference on widgets, then it's much easier to assume that the invitation is related to a legitimate demonstration of the company's products and services and therefore lower risk from a bribery and corruption perspective. The business rationale for the concert may be general relationship building with a potential client, which is not necessarily inappropriate. However, because of the limited business content and the potentially higher price tag for the concert, the concert is likely higher risk from a bribery and corruption perspective.

Because of a perceived difference in the bribery and corruption risk of pure entertainment events versus conferences, organizations sometimes have different monetary thresholds for their AB&C Compliance review and approval. However, if an organization decides to make this distinction, then it should define the term "conference". Generally, that definition will include a required amount of business content. AB&C Compliance should also require a conference agenda for its review as a condition for pre-approving a conference to ensure that there is sufficient business content and that any related entertainment events are within acceptable parameters. For example, if the conference is held in Aspen and involves two 30-minute optional breakfast presentations and the rest is skiing and social events, is it really a "conference"? Probably not. This doesn't mean the event can't happen or that there's necessarily anything wrong with it. However, in that case AB&C Compliance should review it as if was pure entertainment and speak to the requestor about the proper categorization of events and conferences.

There can be legitimate business rationales for concerts, conferences, and other types of events. The important thing is that they are properly documented, reviewed, and approved.

g. Names and Entity Affiliations of Invitees

The names and entity affiliations for all proposed event invitees should be provided to AB&C Compliance. This should also include guests of potential invitees if guests are permitted. Whether an invitee can bring a guest to an event should separately be considered by AB&C Compliance. It will not be appropriate for every event. Some things to consider are whether it's the type of event to which it would be reasonable to bring a guest—e.g., a charity dinner where the participants from the host organization are also bringing partners or an afternoon sporting activity to which people might commonly bring children.

Note that if an invitee brings a guest, then that will also increase the value that the organization is providing to the invitee. For example, if event tickets are $200 and an invitee is permitted to bring a guest then it should be recorded that entertainment of a $400 value was provided to the invitee.

The entity affiliation of invitees is useful because it helps identify public officials. It also helps inform AB&C Compliance whether a significant number of people are being invited from a specific entity. AB&C Compliance can then consider whether invitations are appropriate given the totality of the circumstances.

h. Public Official Status of Invitees

The name and entity affiliation of an invitee help AB&C Compliance to determine or confirm whether an invitee is a public official. Depending on an organization's particular policy, it may be the responsibility of the employee submitting the entertainment request to identify whether a proposed invitee is a public official. However, even if this is the case, in practice employees often make incorrect determinations regarding public official status. This is particularly true when dealing with invitees from non-U.S. state-owned or controlled entities because employees often have difficulty with this aspect of the FCPA's foreign official definition. At a minimum, AB&C Compliance should sample check whether employees are correctly identifying public officials in their G&E submissions.

i. Pending or Recently Completed Business with an Invitee/Invitee Entity

When considering a G&E request it's important for AB&C Compliance to be aware of whether there is pending or recently completed business with the invitee and/or the invitee's entity. Recall the FCPA's language of corruptly offering anything of value *in connection with obtaining or retaining business*. The timing of when a benefit is offered is key when analyzing bribery and corruption risk.

If it could appear that a benefit is being given close in time to a decision-making event, like whether the receiving individual/entity enters into a contract or extends an existing contract, then that timing can be problematic. That is also the case if a benefit is being given close in time *after* a receiving individual/entity decides to enter into or extend an existing contract. Even though the benefit is being provided after a decision was made, it could be viewed as being given in return for the decision to obtain or retain business. Beware the appearance that the benefit is a quid pro quo. Remember that regulators will look at the timing of these transactions and with the 20/20 vision of hindsight. AB&C Compliance should consider denying a request where timing creates even the appearance of impropriety.

j. History of G&E with an Invitee/Invitee Entity

When reviewing a G&E request, AB&C Compliance should consider that request within the totality of the relationship with the invitee and the invitee's entity, taking into account the recent G&E history. For example, has there been a significant amount of entertainment (or a limited amount of high value entertainment) in the last 12 months? If so, perhaps the particular request (even if modest in nature) should be declined. AB&C Compliance needs to have a method of aggregating G&E data per individual and per entity so this information is readily available for review and consideration.

4. DECISIONING A G&E REQUEST

What happens when AB&C Compliance reviews a request? There are several possible outcomes. First, AB&C Compliance can of course approve the request outright. Second, AB&C Compliance can approve the request with conditions. Third, AB&C Compliance can request more information if additional details would be helpful. Finally, AB&C Compliance can decline the request or advise against it. Whatever the decision and advice, it needs to be appropriately documented.

a. AB&C Approval with Conditions

AB&C Compliance may approve a G&E request subject to certain conditions. However, if AB&C Compliance imposes one or more conditions on its approval, then it needs to have a way to monitor or confirm that all such conditions are met. If AB&C Compliance has no way of confirming this information, then the condition is meaningless.

i. Practice Question

If AB&C Compliance determines that an event is higher risk from a bribery and corruption perspective, what are some conditions or controls that AB&C Compliance could implement?

Answer

Some examples (to the extent relevant) are:

- Attendees pay their own airfare
- Lower priced hotel accommodations
- Lower priced tickets
- No public officials
- No gifts
- Attendees cannot bring guests
- This is the only event that the attendees (and possibly anyone from their organization) can come to during the next 12 months.
- Transparency letter

b. Transparency Letter

A transparency letter is a letter from the inviting organization to the invitee's organization that identifies the invitee and states the details and cost of the event. It further states that the invitation is not being made in return for any expectation of future business. It also requests that, in responding to the invitation, the organization or invitee note any limitations on the invitee's acceptance of the offer—

e.g., if the invitee organization will pay for its attendee's own meals or accommodations.

There are a number of considerations for AB&C Compliance to weigh when considering whether and how to utilize a transparency letter. For example:

- Who will send the transparency letter? For example, should it come from Legal or AB&C Compliance at the offeror's organization or directly from the person who is extending the invitation? If the letter is sent by Legal or AB&C Compliance, make sure that the person who is actually extending the invitation is aware of the letter's contents and that it's being sent out. Note that regardless of who sends the letter, the text of it should be written by Legal or AB&C Compliance.

- Who will AB&C Compliance send the transparency letter to? Some options are the invitee's manager or their organization's Legal, or Compliance Department(s).

- Will the inviting organization require a countersignature from the invitee's organization acknowledging the contents of the letter? Before putting this requirement into use, consider all the possible ways that this scenario may play out and how each of those possible scenarios could be effectively handled. For example, picture the scenario where the inviting organization requires a counter-signed letter, doesn't receive it, and the invitee attends the event anyway. Now the

> inviting organization is in a worse position than had it not sent the letter at all. If the inviting organization sends a transparency letter and requires it to be acknowledged and returned, then it must set a firm date significantly in advance of the event by which the letter is required and, if it is not submitted by that date, the invitation must be rescinded in writing.

Transparency letters can be a helpful risk mitigation tool. However, as indicated by the potentially problematic scenario above, they must be used with careful forethought. It's also worth mentioning that there can be cultural or other pushback on sending these letters. People extending and receiving invitations may consider these letters insulting because these letters spell out the price of hospitality that is being offered—something that under normal circumstances would probably be considered rude. Invitees may feel self-conscious that a letter is being sent either to their superior or to Legal or Compliance at their organization. However, in these times of heightened compliance awareness, many organizations appreciate receiving transparency letters and will respond that their employees will attend but that they will pay for their employees' travel or meals to keep the event in compliance with their own internal policies.

Finally, as a reminder, for any conditions that AB&C Compliance imposes, it must have the controls in place to confirm that they have been satisfied. For example, how would AB&C Compliance be able to confirm if an attendee at a high value event was or was not invited to another event within the next twelve months? If AB&C Compliance has no way of confirming that a condition has been satisfied, then AB&C should not impose that condition.

5. COMMON G&E ISSUES AND QUESTIONS

There are many common topics that AB&C Compliance officers need to regularly address both through drafting policy requirements and answering employee questions. The sections below explore a number of these topics.

a. High-Value Entertainment

Some organizations include a definition of "high-value entertainment" in their policies. Based on the organization's risk tolerance, the organization would define those events by a particular monetary amount—e.g., $1,000 per person. The policy would then limit the number of such events that could be attended by particular invitees and/or invitee entities within a certain period of time. This of course helps mitigate the risk of providing excessive or lavish entertainment.

b. G&E Received

At many organizations the heavy focus is on G&E that the organization's employees are offering or providing to current or prospective clients, employees, and third parties. While this is of course important, it's also important not to lose sight of G&E

that is offered to the organization's own employees or accepted by them.

There are also practical business reasons to place governance around G&E offered to or received by an organization's employees. For example, consider an organization that is looking to retain a third party to provide it with telecommunication services. What if potential third-party vendors provided incentives to the person or persons at the organization responsible for choosing the organization's telecommunications provider? It's possible that the organization's decision-maker(s) could be improperly influenced to choose a provider based on the personal incentives they received rather than based on what was best for the organization. This would obviously not be a desirable outcome from an organization's business perspective.

i. G&E Received: Infrastructure Functions

An organization's G&E policies should apply to all employees (as properly defined) and potentially some third parties. However, even where this is the case, G&E programs often largely focus on the individuals in the first line of defense—i.e., the "business," those individuals that are client-facing. That's a somewhat natural tendency as it's these are the individuals who are likely interacting the most with current and prospective clients and *offering* the most G&E. However, it's employees in infrastructure functions who are *being offered* and *potentially accepting* the most G&E.

Recall our previous example regarding one or more infrastructure function employees who are responsible for choosing their organization's telecommunications vendor. Infrastructure employees are commonly responsible for selecting vendors and other third parties to provide services to their organizations. These are often high value contracts, increasing the incentive and the potential for bribery. As with all bribery, this potential is a combination of incentive and opportunity. It exists even in the Legal Department, where in-house attorneys may be entertained by current and potential outside counsel.

c. Promotional Items

An organization's promotional items will often be exempted from its AB&C and G&E policies, meaning that they are not subject to recording or approval requirements. The rationale for this is that promotional items are inherently unlikely to improperly influence the recipient.

The term "promotional item" should be specifically defined in an organization's AB&C or G&E policy. That definition should include two requirements. First, the item must contain the organization's logo. Second, the item must be of nominal value. "Nominal value" may or may not be defined by a specific dollar amount. Common examples of promotional items that would likely satisfy these two criteria are items like pens, eyeglass wipes, mugs, and possibly baseball caps. Note that both requirements must be satisfied for an item to qualify as a promotional item and be exempt from the policy requirements. Otherwise, in theory, an iPad with an organization's logo on it could be passed off as a promotional item and given or received without regard to policy requirements.

d. Travel and Accommodation

In recent years it has become less common for organizations to pay for the travel and accommodation of individuals whom it invites to meetings, conferences, etc. There are many reasons for this. One is simply budgetary. Another is the appearance of offering something lavish. To address this issue, an inviting organization and an invitee's organization may essentially share the cost. For example, the inviting organization may pay for the invitee's stay in the hotel in which its conference is held, and the invitee's organization may pay for the travel to attend the conference. This is a practical compromise from a budgetary standpoint, and it also helps mitigate the risk from a bribery and corruption perspective. If both the inviting and invitee organizations are committing resources to attend an event like a conference, it bolsters the assumption that the conference is for the legitimate business benefit of both parties and that the invitee is not being inappropriately incentivized.

When travel and/or accommodation may be offered, those requests are generally pre-approved by AB&C Compliance. If an organization does pay for an invitee's travel or accommodation, then the organization should directly pay vendors like hotels and airlines. In addition, invitees should not be given a travel allowance or a per diem.

e. Cash and Gift Cards

AB&C policies should prohibit the giving of cash and gift cards as gifts. Cash can be defined as currency made up of physical notes or coins which are legal tender or cryptocurrency. Many organizations will also include gift cards in this definition and prohibition because, in many circumstances, gift cards can be considered convertible to cash. For example, a policy might state that the "giving or receiving of cash, cryptocurrency, and cash equivalents (e.g., gift cards, gift certificates, checks, vouchers, gold or silver coins) to or from third parties is prohibited."

The policy may or may not provide for a potential exception upon written approval from Legal or AB&C Compliance. If the organization does business in countries with certain customs, then the organization may provide exceptions in limited situations. For example, in China it is customary at the Lunar New Year to present friends and family with a red envelope containing money. This red envelope symbolizes good wishes for luck and prosperity in the year ahead. Organizations dealing with Chinese companies or individuals may make a policy exception and allow employees to give red envelopes containing a small (and specifically prescribed) amount of money to respectfully observe the Lunar New Year tradition.

f. Employees' Use of Personal Funds

An organization's policy should state that employees cannot use personal funds to provide gifts, entertainment, or charitable contributions to the organization's current or prospective clients or third parties. Some might ask why this is an issue and why employees would ever use their personal funds in this way. However, as a practical matter, employees may engage in this conduct to avoid the scrutiny of AB&C Compliance and the attendant record-keeping. This is particularly true when there is a potential transaction and the employee may receive significant incentive compensation if the transaction comes to fruition.

How can this scenario be prevented, detected, and deterred? It's of course very difficult to know, and generally not the business of an organization, how its employees spend their personal funds. The best way to prevent this situation from occurring is to have a robust culture of compliance and an effective AB&C training program. In addition, monitoring can be a useful detection tool. For example, the organization can monitor employees' work emails for references to gifts and events and then confirm whether the referenced gifts or events were recorded and/or submitted to AB&C Compliance for review. This is, of course, not a comprehensive check. An organization would also need to weigh whether, given its technology and resources, it would be an effective tool to utilize.

g. Life Events

Many AB&C policies also specifically address "life events" like weddings, births, and funerals. The policies may allow gifts for these types of occasions and provide specific review and approval threshold amounts for them that are different from other types of gifts.

h. Speakers

Many organizations, from time to time, may engage speakers, possibly individuals who are experts on certain topics. These speakers may be paid or unpaid. The organization may utilize them, for example, in connection with in-house events or in connection with conferences for current and prospective clients. The applicable policy should provide specific requirements in connection with the engagement of speakers and experts. As with other areas, like G&E, AB&C Compliance will likely not opine on every speaker engagement. However, the policy should provide escalation criteria (e.g., if the proposed speaker is a current or former public official) that will trigger AB&C Compliance review.

When reviewing a request to engage a speaker, AB&C Compliance should collect due diligence information about the proposed speaker, including but not limited to the following:

- Name of the individual
- Corporate or organizational affiliation of the individual

- Whether the individual is a public official. (Note: If the individual is a public official, consider whether other individuals within your organization—e.g., a government affairs function—may also need to opine on the propriety of engaging the individual as a speaker and may want to review the proposed contents of the speaker's remarks)
- Whether the individual will be compensated via a speaker fee or honorarium and, if so, in what amount. If the speaker will be compensated:
    - o Does the fee amount seem appropriate based on the totality of the circumstances (including but not limited to the individual's experience, the importance of the event, market comparisons, etc.)?
    - o Is the payment being made directly to the speaker or to the entity to which they are affiliated? (Most organizations prefer to pay other organizations rather than individuals. This may be at least in part because of the implicit assumption that an organization will have some form of a compliance program. But know the role of the entity that's being paid. Is the speaker a principal in that entity or is the entity just a middleman?)
- Whether, separate and apart from any speaker fee, the organization will provide travel, accommodations, meals, etc. and the

proposed cost of each of those. With respect to any such hospitality:

- o Could it be considered lavish?
- o Has the speaker made any specific requests regarding hospitality? If yes, would such hospitality comply with the organization's AB&C policy requirements and guidelines?
- o Has the speaker requested that the organization make a charitable contribution on their behalf?

- Name, date and purpose of the event that the speaker will attend
- Reason for engaging the particular proposed speaker (e.g., acknowledged expert in the field of X, etc.)
- How the proposed speaker came to the organization's attention (e.g., referral from client, etc.)
- Whether the speaker and/or their affiliated entity is a current or prospective client or otherwise has a current or contemplated business relationship with the organization
- Whether there is any negative news concerning the speaker and/or their affiliated entity
- Whether the engagement could give rise to an actual or potential conflict of interest

After due consideration AB&C Compliance can then advise whether it recommends proceeding, whether it needs additional information to review the request, whether it advises to proceed with certain conditions, or whether it recommends against engaging the speaker. Note that there should always be a signed engagement letter or a contract between the organization and the speaker, regardless of whether the speaker will be compensated.

i. Employee-to-Employee Giving

Gifts and entertainment between employees—e.g., taking a co-worker out to lunch for their birthday—are generally outside the scope of AB&C and G&E policies. This, of course, assumes that the employee is not also a client or third party and being gifted or entertained in that regard.

j. Personal Friend or "Acting in a Personal Capacity"

Most AB&C and G&E policies are written so that the giving or receiving G&E in a personal capacity is outside the scope of the policy. However, what does it really mean for an employee to give or receive a benefit in a personal capacity such that it is separate from any business goals or efforts of the organization? This is a common question in AB&C Compliance practice because there will be situations where (1) an employee of the organization and a current or prospective client or third party were friends prior to the business relationship; and (2) where these same people may become personal friends over time through the ongoing business relationship. In short, it's a very fact-specific question.

i. Practice Example

An attorney in the Legal Department receives an invitation to a wine tasting event from an attorney at a law firm that is regularly used by her organization and is on its approved counsel list. There is ongoing business between the organization and the law firm but no specific potential or recently completed engagements. The invitee from Legal is not a decision-maker regarding law firm choice or retention. The inviting outside attorney and the organization's Legal Department invitee were law school friends and the inviting attorney was paying for the event personally and not seeking reimbursement from her law firm. Given these facts, it would be reasonable to consider that the invitation was being made and considered in a personal capacity and, as such, was outside the scope of the applicable AB&C or G&E policy.

k. Reviewing G&E of Senior Personnel

We previously addressed the concepts of managerial approval of G&E and AB&C Compliance pre-approval of G&E. Often, managerial approval of G&E will be required even where AB&C Compliance pre-approval is not. However, what about personnel in the organization who don't have a "manager" per se? This category could include very senior personnel such as the CEO, CFO, board members, etc. Even though these personnel are very senior (and, arguably, perhaps *especially because* they are very senior) they must still have appropriate oversight from an AB&C Compliance perspective. In such cases, organizations can devise their own tailored process that makes sense with their particular organizational structure. For example, the CEO's G&E requests might be routed to the Legal Department and/or head of AB&C Compliance for tracking and approval where necessary.

1. Roadshows (Specific to Financial Institutions)

Roadshows can take many forms but can generally be defined as a series of group and/or individual meetings, presentations, and/or site visits by a potential client or investor with investors, analysts, fund managers or corporates, which is arranged and managed by one or more financial institutions.

Roadshows can be broken up into at least three broad categories—"Deal Roadshows," "Non-Deal Roadshows," and "Custom Roadshows." A Deal Roadshow is a roadshow that is conducted in connection with a specific transaction under consideration. Its purpose is to either market the potential transaction or to evaluate market interest in the potential transaction.

Conversely, with a Non-Deal Roadshow, there is no specific transaction under consideration. Its purpose is to update investors and shareholders on the financial implications of an entity's corporate or management changes, future strategy, or other topics.

Custom Roadshows can include what might be termed "Reverse Roadshows" and "Industry Expert Roadshows." Reverse Roadshows are roadshows where a financial institution takes one or more investors to meet a range of corporates. An Industry Expert Roadshow is where an expert updates potential investors on a specific market or topic.

Each of these types of roadshows may involve more than one location and may involve a series of events that take place over a number of days. Roadshows often involve travel, meals, entertainment, and other types of hospitality so roadshows should be subject to the financial institution's AB&C and G&E policies.

From an AB&C Compliance perspective, it's important to consider a roadshow as an overall event with various components as opposed to separate and unrelated instances of G&E. To help with this, a roadshow should be understood as a series of events that take place consecutively over a defined period of time. That period of time can be one week, two weeks, etc., but it has to have a specified beginning and end that AB&C Compliance can understand (and may define) as the "Roadshow Period." It's also helpful to have a set of definitions specific to roadshows to make sure that both the business and AB&C Compliance are on the same page. These definitions should be included in the applicable policy or policy section regarding roadshows. Common issues around roadshows include the involvement of public officials, cost considerations, whether and how the cost of the roadshow is being shared between one or more financial institutions, and whether the financial institution(s) will be reimbursed for the cost of the roadshow.

m. Gifts: Special Considerations

The information being collected, and the rationale for its collection, are similar between gifts and entertainment events. However, there are some additional specific considerations that should be noted with respect to gifts, including how to properly calculate the value of a gift and how to handle received gifts that are valued above the permissible policy limit.

i. Calculating the Value of a Gift

The method for valuing a gift should be similar to the method for valuing entertainment. The gift should be valued at its cost at the time of purchase, assuming that there is no special purchasing power and that the gift is given close in time to its purchase (i.e., not enough time has passed where the value of the gift may have significantly changed). Special purchasing power refers to an advantage that the purchaser may have with respect to buying an item that is not generally available or not available without a separate cost. For example, a purchaser may receive a 20% discount on an item. However, the purchaser may only receive that discount because they are a member of a club for which they paid a separate annual fee.

Consider this example about special purchasing power with respect to gifts. After a deal closed, each member of a deal team at a financial institution received a pair of sneakers from the client sneaker company as a thank-you. The sneaker company sent a letter to the financial institution's AB&C Compliance function that the sneakers cost about $10 per pair. However, the online cost of the sneakers was about $150 per pair. Which valuation should AB&C Compliance use when considering the propriety of the gift and recording its value? AB&C Compliance should use the $150 per pair because that was the actual value of the sneakers. The sneakers cost only $10 per pair for the sneaker company because the sneaker company had special purchasing power by virtue of having made the sneakers.

ii. Receipt of Gifts Above Policy Limits

There will be times when an organization's employee receives a gift from a current or prospective client or third party that is valued above the permissible gift limit in the applicable policy. There are a few different ways to handle this scenario. First, the employee can of course return the gift with the explanation that, while the employee is appreciative, the gift is not permitted by policy. However, returning a gift can be awkward and potentially create tension in a business relationship. If the gift is returned, it should be noted in the relevant record that the gift was received and then returned.

If the gift is of the type that can be divided—e.g., a gift basket—then several people could share the gift. That would effectively reduce the per-person value of the gift. Finally, the gift item or its value could be donated to a charity.

n. G&E Hypotheticals

The hypotheticals in the proceeding sections illustrate some of the G&E concepts that we have addressed.

i. Hypothetical 1

During a site visit to a client, the client gives the Organization X relationship manager a bottle of wine worth approximately $800. The client states that he is gifting the wine as a token of his gratitude for the ongoing and productive relationship with Organization X. The relationship manager thanks the client but says that it's not necessary. The relationship manager recalls that Organization X's G&E policy does not allow him to accept gifts from clients or third parties worth over $100. As something of an oenophile, he suspects this bottle is worth more. However, the client seems offended by the idea that the relationship manager will not accept the gift, so the relationship manager thanks the client again and accepts the wine.

Possible actions and outcomes:

1. Assuming the hypothetical ends as written, it's possible that the relationship manager may keep the wine without reporting it to

Legal or AB&C Compliance. This would be a clear policy breach that Legal and AB&C Compliance may or may not detect. However, if they did, then consequences for the relationship manager would likely be more severe than if he had initially reported that he accepted the wine.

2. In an alternative ending to this hypothetical, the relationship manager could have continued to decline the wine. He could have done so with or without explanation. The client seemed offended by the relationship manager's initial declination. However, he may not have been offended (or may have been less so) if the relationship manager thanked him profusely but explained that Organization X has a strict compliance program that would not allow him to accept the wine.

3. Assuming that the hypothetical ends as written, it's possible that the relationship manager accepts the wine and promptly contacts AB&C Compliance after the meeting. The relationship manager determines that the bottle of wine is worth approximately $800 and shares this information with AB&C Compliance. AB&C Compliance then advises the relationship manager to give the bottle to Organization X's Corporate Sustainability group. Corporate Sustainability will then donate the bottle to a charity auction.

4. Again, assuming that the hypothetical ends as written, it's possible that the relationship manager accepts the wine and promptly contacts AB&C Compliance after the meeting. The relationship manager determines that the bottle of wine is worth approximately $800 and shares this information with AB&C Compliance. Through discussions between AB&C Compliance and the relationship manager, it becomes known that the relationship manager's team has an upcoming quarterly meeting. The relationship manager suggests sharing the bottle of wine with the team after the quarterly meeting and highlighting the client's gratitude for the team's good work.

Commentary: Both the second and third options are acceptable outcomes. Ideally, the relationship manager would not have accepted the wine. However, offending a client who is trying to make a gesture of good will is a realistic commercial concern and one that AB&C Compliance as well as the business must appreciate. If, alternatively, we tweaked this hypothetical and the client expressed a different intent with giving the wine—e.g., "to cement our understanding that my company will be given a role in syndicate deal XYZ"—then the third option likely would not have been permissible. The relationship manager could not have accepted the wine with the understanding that it was being offered in exchange for a business opportunity.

To play devil's advocate, how could the third option be appropriate because, whatever the reasoning, Organization X still kept the expensive wine? There are a few points here. First, the relationship manager did not keep the wine—he turned it over to Organization X. So, there was no benefit to the relationship manager himself. Organization X's Corporate Sustainability group then planned to donate the wine to a charity auction. However, wouldn't this still be a benefit to Organization X because it might get credit for donating the bottle to the auction—possibly both in terms of being named at an event as a donor and the charitable donation tax credit? In short, yes. One way to ameliorate this is for Organization X to donate the bottle anonymously to the charity auction and to speak with a tax professional about how to manage any tax benefit to Organization X that might be attendant to the donation.

There are of course related concerns with the fourth option. In this case, the bottle of wine is kept by the relationship manager, but he shares the bottle with other team members. In practice, this is a common way that organizations deal with holiday baskets and similar items that might be above the applicable policy's per-person limit for received gifts but which, for various reasons, are not practical to return. However, since the bottle of wine is so high-priced, does sharing it solve the problem? Sharing the wine among a group of people would still likely amount to a per head cost of more than $100, the policy limit for gifts that can be received. However, remember that policy exceptions can be made so long as those exceptions are proper pursuant to the policy and are appropriately documented. As long as none of the employees sharing in the gift were subject to legal or regulatory requirements limiting their acceptance of gifts, then a policy exception could be made (and documented) if deemed appropriate.

As the hypothetical and its commentary demonstrates, there is often more than one correct way to handle any given situation. Many factors need to be considered in situations like these, including but not limited to the nature of the business relationship, the reason why the benefit is being offered, and how the situation can be practically dealt with both to effectively use compliance resources and to minimize bribery and corruption risk. Dealing with the situation transparently and documenting it will go a long way toward accomplishing both of those goals.

ii. Hypothetical 2

An Organization X staff member is attending a neighbor's party and begins talking with another attendee. This attendee mentions that she works for a local regulator and the Organization X staff member comments that Organization X is currently being examined by that regulator. The conversation turns to sports and the regulator staff member begins talking about the US Open tennis tournament and how she has enjoyed attending in the past. She remarks that she would like to attend this year's US Open but has not yet been able to secure tickets. The Organization X staff member knows that

Organization X has a block of tickets to the US Open and considers offering the regulator staff member a pair of those tickets.

Possible action 1:

- The Organization X staff member offers the regulator staff member the pair of tickets and she accepts.

Commentary: This is far from ideal. The tickets belong to Organization X and have now been offered to a staff member of a regulator during an ongoing exam with that regulator. Organization X's applicable AB&C policy likely prohibits providing G&E to regulators without AB&C Compliance or Legal pre-approval and the employee's conduct has likely violated the policy.

Based on the fact pattern we don't know if the regulator staff member has any association with the Organization X exam or is in any position to influence the exam. However, we must take the most cautious inference here and assume that the staff member has some involvement in the exam or some ability to influence its outcome. Even if neither turns out to be the case, the offer of the tickets has the appearance of impropriety and should not have been made.

However, the offer has now been made and accepted. Assuming that the Organization X employee properly logs the tickets so Legal and AB&C Compliance become aware, Organization X's Legal department will need to advise the regulator of the offer and acceptance of the tickets and discuss the next steps. Note that most regulators have their own internal policies about G&E that their employees are permitted to accept, and acceptance of these tickets may have violated the regulator's own policy as well.

Possible action (and outcome) 2:

- The Organization X employee is not sure whether she can properly offer the tickets to a regulator staff member. She decides to hold off on offering the tickets, to check the policy, and to contact AB&C Compliance the next day to ask. AB&C Compliance advises the employee that the policy prohibits offering G&E to regulator employees, with the exception of limited food and beverages during meetings. AB&C Compliance explains that if the employee offers the tickets, it could be viewed as if they were trying to improperly influence that regulator in the course of conducting its exam. The employee did not offer the tickets and AB&C Compliance documented the employee's question and the advice that it provided.

Commentary: As we've emphasized, liability can arise at the time that an offer is made. This is why it's so important for employees to first check with AB&C Compliance if they are unsure about whether they can offer a certain benefit or advantage to a third party. We've also emphasized that documentation is important. In the second action, AB&C Compliance properly documented the question and the advice. The fact that this question came to AB&C Compliance and that AB&C Compliance provided and recorded advice according to the policy helps demonstrate that the AB&C Compliance program is working.

C. CHARITABLE GIVING

A charitable contribution is a thing of value that can be improperly provided in return for obtaining or retaining business or a business advantage. Like gifts, entertainment, and business hospitality, there's nothing per se wrong with charitable giving. Legitimate charitable giving doesn't violate the FCPA or other AB&C laws and charitable giving is often an established part of an organization's culture and community outreach. *However*, (as the SEC and DOJ point out in their FCPA Resource Guide) beware of charitable giving that is being used as a vehicle to conceal payments made to corruptly influence foreign officials or other individuals. Improper charitable giving is sometimes part of a larger pattern of an organization's offering of improper inducements. However, two enforcement actions have focused solely on improper charitable contributions—*Schering-Plough* and *Nu Skin*.

1. *SCHERING-PLOUGH*

In the *Schering-Plough* enforcement action, the SEC alleged that the pharma company violated the FCPA's books and records and internal controls provisions when its subsidiary in Poland made improper payments of about $76,000 to a charitable organization called the Chudow Castle Foundation. The head of the Chudow Castle Foundation was the Director of the Silesian Health Fund, a Polish governmental body that "among other things, provided money for the purchase of pharmaceutical products and influenced the purchase of those products by other entities, such as hospitals, through the allocation of health fund resources."[16]

The SEC alleged that none of the payments that Schering-Plough Poland made to the Chudow Castle Foundation were accurately reflected in its books and records.[17] The SEC also alleged that "the company's system of internal accounting controls was inadequate to prevent or detect the improper payments."[18] Schering-Plough, without admitting or denying the allegations, consented to pay the SEC a civil penalty of $500,000.[19]

2. *NU SKIN*

Nu Skin Enterprises, Inc.'s ("Nu Skin US") alleged FCPA violations arose from an approximately $154,000 payment that Nu Skin US' China subsidiary made to a charity in return for a high-ranking Chinese Communist party official to intervene in an on-going provincial agency investigation. The party official had set up the charity. Two days after a donation ceremony, Nu Skin China received notice from the province that the company wouldn't be charged or fined.

---

[16] *SEC v. Schering-Plough Corporation,* No. 1:04CV00945, at 2 (D. DC. 2004), https://www.sec.gov/litigation/litreleases/lr18740.htm.

[17] *Id.*

[18] *Id.*

[19] *Id.*

The SEC alleged that Nu Skin US violated the FCPA's books and records provision because "in its wholly-owned subsidiary's expenditure authorization form, the purpose of the payment to the charity was inaccurately and/or unfairly described as a donation rather than an improper payment to obtain the Party Official's influence."[20] The SEC also alleged that Nu Skin US violated the FCPA's internal controls provision because "it did not devise and maintain a reasonable system of internal accounting controls over operations in China to ensure that transactions were recorded as necessary to maintain accountability for assets and/or [that] access to assets is permitted only in accordance with management's general or specific authorization, particularly with regard to due diligence and controls surrounding foreign charitable donations."[21]

Nu Skin US consensually resolved the matter with the SEC without admitting or denying the SEC's allegations. The company disgorged $431,088 and paid prejudgment interest of $34,600, and a civil penalty of $300,000.[22]

---

[20] *In the Matter of Nu Skin Enterprises,* Inc, No. 3-17556, at 5 (Sept. 20, 2016), https://www.sec.gov/litigation/admin/2016/34-78884.pdf.

[21] *Id.* at 4 ("Specifically, given the well-known corruption risks in China, Nu Skin US did not ensure that adequate due diligence was conducted by Nu Skin China with respect to charitable donations to identify links to government or political party officials and to prevent payments intended to improperly influence such persons in violation of the company's anti-corruption policy and the FCPA.")

[22] *Id.*

3. TYPES OF CHARITABLE GIVING

It's important to know where charitable giving may originate within an organization and the approval and payment pathways for those contributions. As with G&E, charitable contributions that an employee makes *purely* in his or her personal capacity are generally outside the scope of an organization's AB&C policy.

When thinking about charitable giving it's important to divide it into two buckets—the type of charitable giving and the source of the charitable giving. Many organizations develop their own definitions for different types of charitable giving based on their own activities. This can be very helpful from a risk management perspective.

Large organizations may have a corporate sustainability or similar function. This is generally an infrastructure function that is separate and apart from the organization's business units. Broadly speaking, corporate sustainability refers to an approach to business that includes a focus on ethical, social, environmental, and cultural aspects as well as a focus on economic success. A corporate sustainability function generally handles charitable contributions that are made by the organization as an entity according to set priorities that are often updated on an annual basis. For example, an organization may designate child literacy and access to clean water as two priorities. A corporate sustainability function may then direct corporate funds to charities that support those goals. Because it operates as an independent infrastructure function, its charitable contributions are sometimes outside the scope of AB&C Compliance review. The reason for this is that those contributions are presumed to be made as part of a separate sustainability agenda and (at least not directly) connected to attempts to obtain or retain business. Whether this presumption is in fact the case will of course depend on each particular organization and AB&C Compliance should determine whether there is a need to be involved in the review process for such contributions.

The source of the main types of charitable contributions that are reviewed by AB&C Compliance are from business units/the first line. These come under AB&C Compliance scrutiny because such contributions are often requested by current or prospective clients or third parties. Or, alternatively, they are made by the first line without a specific request but while knowing that a current or prospective client or third party is closely connected with a particular charitable organization (e.g., a member of the charity's board).

Sample definitions highlighting potential different types of charitable activities within an organization, assuming the existence of a corporate sustainability function, are:

> Charitable Giving: an over-arching term that refers to all types of charitable activity, whether monetary or non-monetary (e.g., volunteer activities), and whether made through Corporate Sustainability or otherwise. Charitable Giving includes Charitable

Donations, Charitable Contributions, and Fundraising, as those terms are separately defined.

Charitable Donation: any giving, whether monetary or non-monetary, made to a charitable organization by Corporate Sustainability. This includes giving where there is no expectation of a specific return benefit to the organization as well as giving where there *is* an expectation of a return benefit (e.g., branding on event t-shirts, etc.) Volunteer activities and projects may be Charitable Donations.

Fundraising: the organization's collection of funds from employees and third parties for charitable purposes.

Charitable Contribution: any giving, whether monetary or non-monetary, made to a charitable organization other than through Corporate Sustainability. This includes giving where there is no expectation of a specific return benefit to the organization as well as giving where there *is* an expectation of a return benefit (e.g., branding on event t-shirts, etc.) Volunteer activities and projects may be Charitable Contributions.

Charitable Contributions, as we've defined them, are intentionally quite broad. It's important to understand all the types of activities that go on in an organization that may fall within this category. For example, there may be events or corporate sponsorships that occur in connection with charities. These types of activities may be handled by functions like Marketing and so may not immediately come to the attention of AB&C Compliance. However, it's important that AB&C Compliance maintains a line of sight over these activities and reviews and opines on them as specified in the organization's applicable policy. The proceeding section explores due diligence and controls for Charitable Contributions.

4. DUE DILIGENCE AND CONTROLS FOR CHARITABLE CONTRIBUTIONS

Developing and implementing appropriate controls, including conducting due diligence, are key to managing the bribery and corruption risks of Charitable Contributions (as previously defined). Varying levels of due diligence can be conducted depending on the assessed bribery and corruption risk of the Charitable Contribution and the organization's overall risk appetite. As the SEC and DOJ have noted, "[p]roper due diligence and controls are critical for charitable giving. In general, the adequacy of measures taken to prevent misuse of charitable donations will depend on a risk-based analysis and the specific facts at hand."[23] There must

---

[23] FCPA Resource Guide, *supra* Chapter 1, n.1, at 18. Note that this book's exploration of charitable giving is written from the perspective of an organization that is offering charitable giving. However, like gifts and entertainment, charitable giving can also be "received" by an organization's employees. This may be dealt with through conflicts of interest policies pursuant to which employees must disclose their outside business interests including, for example, their membership on the boards of charitable organizations. An employee would then be required to disclose when a current or prospective client or third party of the organization donated to a charity connected with that employee.

be a clear process for determining the due diligence requirements and controls to apply, and for determining who is responsible for collecting the specific information that AB&C Compliance will review.

The FCPA Resource Guide addresses charitable giving and, referring to prior opinion releases, explains that the DOJ has previously approved proposed grants or donations based on due diligence and controls such as:[24]

- certifications by the recipient regarding compliance with the FCPA;
- due diligence to confirm that none of the recipient's officers was affiliated with the foreign government at issue;
- a requirement that the recipient provide audited financial statements;
- a written agreement with the recipient restricting the use of funds;
- steps to ensure that the funds were transferred to a valid bank account;
- confirmation that the charity's commitments were met before the funds were disbursed; and
- ongoing monitoring of the efficacy of the program.

---

[24] *Id.* at 19 (internal citations omitted).

Due diligence information regarding proposed Charitable Contributions that should be collected and retained by the contributing organization include:

Requesting Employee

- Name and title/position of the employee requesting to make the Charitable Contribution; and
- If there is a managerial approval requirement, the name and title/position of employee approving the Charitable Contribution. Note that, as part of this requirement, the approving employee may be asked to attest in writing that he or she has ensured that all of the required due diligence has been completed.

Charity

- Charity name;
- Registered address of the charity;
- Physical address of the charity's principal place of business (if different than the registered address);
- Charity web site address;
- How long the charity has been in existence;
- Any applicable charity registration numbers;
- If a U.S. charity, whether it is a 501(c)(3). If a non-U.S. charity, other indicia of

reliability such as inclusion in an official governmental charitable register, etc.;

- Names of the control persons of the charity, including any advisory board members;
- Public official status (whether foreign or domestic) of any charity control persons
    - If a control person is a public official, does that control person/public official have decision-making authority regarding the contributing organization's business with their government?
    - Is there pending or recently completed business between the organization and the charity control person/public official's government?
- Connection(s) between any charity control persons and the contributing organization
    - For example, is one or more of the charity's control persons a current or potential client or third party (a "Connected Control Person") of the contributing organization? If yes, was the Charitable Contribution requested by the Connected Control Person? Is there is any pending or recently completed business between the organization and the Connected Control Person or that Connected Control Person's charity?
- Connection(s) between the charity and the contributing organization

- For example, is the charity a current or potential client or third party of the organization? If yes, was the Charitable Contribution requested by the charity? Is there any pending or recently completed business between the contributing organization and the charity?

Reason(s) for the Charitable Contribution

- What is the business rationale, if any?
- What is the charitable rationale? Is the proposed Charitable Contribution consistent with the organization's internal guidelines on charitable giving?
- Does the organization have a history of contributing to this charity? For how long, how frequently, and in what amount(s)?
- Whether the proposed Charitable Contribution is conditioned (explicitly or implicitly) upon receiving business or other benefits (or could be viewed as such in hindsight).

Payment of the Charitable Contribution

- The Charitable Contribution should be paid directly from the contributing organization to a bank account in the charity's name. It should not be paid to or from an individual.

Background Search

- Whether there is any negative information about the charity or its control persons, including but not limited to allegations involving financial crime.

Conflict of Interest or Appearance of Impropriety

- Whether the proposed Charitable Contribution could cause an actual or apparent conflict of interest or could cause the appearance of impropriety.

As with G&E, AB&C Compliance will not likely review and opine on all instances of charitable giving. An organization's policies and procedures should set the parameters for how and when requests for charitable giving will be escalated to AB&C Compliance for review and advice. This means that the onus is on employees outside of AB&C Compliance to collect the data referred to in the points above and to correctly identify when escalation to AB&C Compliance is necessary. This also means that how to do this needs to be part of AB&C training.

Examples of situations where proposed Charitable Contributions may be escalated to AB&C Compliance include:

- if the charity is a current or prospective client or third party of the organization;
- if the Charitable Contribution was requested by a current or prospective client or third party of the organization;
- if one or more of the charity's control persons is a U.S. or foreign official;

- if the Charitable Contribution was requested by a U.S. or foreign official;
- if there is pending or recently completed business with an individual or entity who is closely connected with the charity; and
- if there is negative news about the charity relating to any type of financial crime.

Upon escalation, AB&C Compliance would then need to opine whether to approve the Charitable Contribution, to request additional information, to approve the Charitable Contribution conditioned upon the implementation of certain conditions, or to advise against proceeding with the Charitable Contribution.

5. G&E AND CHARITABLE CONTRIBUTION CROSSOVER

Organizations will sometimes make Charitable Contributions or Charitable Donations in connection with a specific event and in return for which the organization may receive brand recognition. For example, an organization may make a $10,000 donation to a charity and, in return, receive a table for ten people at the charity's gala dinner and a listing of its name in the charity's gala program.

These types of hybrid events raise some practical issues. For example, what if the organization then invites current or prospective clients or third parties to the gala as its guests? There is then an overlap between the Charitable Donation and G&E. And, if this is the case, how will the benefit that the organization is providing to its invitees be calculated? (i.e., face value of ticket, non-tax deductible portion of ticket, etc.)?

6. PRACTICE POINTS

Other common issues relating to charitable giving include volunteering and soliciting charitable contributions from employees and third parties. We'll address each of those in the following sections.

a. Volunteering

How should an organization deal with volunteering? Recall that our working definitions of Charitable Donations and Charitable Contributions both potentially included volunteer activities and projects. There are always organizational costs associated with volunteering. At a minimum, if employees are volunteering on the organization's time, then the organization is paying those employees while they volunteer. Essentially, then, the organization is contributing the service of paid employees to a charity for the duration of the project. There are of course other costs that can be associated with volunteering, e.g., the cost of transporting employees to and from the volunteer site. Some charities also require a volunteering organization to pay for some or all of the costs associated with the specific project, such as building materials.

There is no single correct way to handle volunteer activities. The important thing is to have a documented and consistent policy and approach. Some organizations may, for example, choose to carve out volunteering from the definitions of Charitable Donations and Charitable Contributions on the theory that paying for employee time is a sunk cost. However, if an organization does take that approach, AB&C Compliance should still review the situations where employees are volunteering *and* there is a specific related cost to the volunteering—e.g., paying for the building supplies associated with a project—if the criteria for AB&C Compliance review are otherwise met. There should not simply be a presumption that volunteer projects are outside the scope of AB&C Compliance review.

b. Soliciting Charitable Giving from Employees and Third Parties

Many organizations have blanket policies that prohibit employees from soliciting Charitable Giving, as previously defined, from other employees and from third parties associated with the organization. For example, an employee would not be able to ask colleagues to participate in their child's school fundraiser. One reason for such policies is so that employees aren't made to feel pressured or uncomfortable in the workplace. Another reason is of course to avoid situations that create the potential for bribery and corruption.

7. HYPOTHETICAL

Your organization has a potential transaction with a client company where the client company is deciding whether to hire your organization. The president of the client company sends a letter asking your organization to sponsor a fundraising bike-a-thon for a charity that supports local food pantries and of which he is a board member.

- Can your organization sponsor the bike-a-thon?

Possibly.

- What factors should you consider?

Aside from due diligence about the charity itself, there is a pending transaction with an organization whose decision-maker (the president) has asked your organization for a charitable contribution. Based on these facts, the proposed sponsorship would be high risk from a bribery and corruption perspective.

- What if the president sends a follow-up email asking the organization for confirmation of whether or not it will sponsor the event, noting that "we like to do business with companies who share our values."

This comment further raises the bribery and corruption risk of the potential sponsorship. AB&C Compliance and Legal should confer regarding an appropriate response to the request.

- Does it affect your view if your organization has sponsored this bike-a-thon for the last three years before the potential transaction with this client?

This is a mitigating factor and the organization will have to make a decision based on its own risk appetite. However, aside from actual bribery and corruption risk of the situation, there could still be the appearance of impropriety. The timing of the request for the sponsorship while there was pending business between the two organizations, coupled with the president's follow-up email expressing a near quid pro quo, does not give a positive impression. Remember, decisions like these will be viewed in hindsight by regulators and law enforcement.

D. HIRING PRACTICES

Recent enforcement actions have made clear that employment opportunities are a thing of value, including when offered to a third party to favorably influence a public official. To effectively address the bribery and corruption risks attendant to hiring, an AB&C Compliance officer needs to understand the different categories of employees that its organization hires and the different hiring pathways that may exist.

In large organizations, there are often many potential avenues for different types of staff to be hired. AB&C Compliance programs commonly put controls around what is often the main pathway—hiring through official Human Resources channels. However, AB&C Compliance sometimes does not fully address other employment inroads that may exist, especially those for temporary hiring. For example, sometimes the hiring of temporary employees and consultants is either outsourced from the organization or managed through an internal function that is separate from Human Resources. If the AB&C Compliance officer is not aware of this, then a potential gap in controls can exist.

1. "CONNECTED CANDIDATES"

When should AB&C Compliance become involved in the hiring process? In short, where there is a "Connected Candidate." A Connected Candidate can be defined as:

> a candidate who is a close contact of a current or prospective client, current or prospective third party, or a public official, such that offering an opportunity to that candidate could influence the current or prospective client, current or prospective third party, or public official to maintain ongoing business or engage in new business with the hiring organization or to otherwise use their influence in favor of the hiring organization.

a. Practice Questions

How do you find out whether a candidate is a Connected Candidate? The answer to this question will depend on the organization's hiring process. Some organizations use a triple review check to ascertain this information. This would include:

- forms completed by referring employee (if any) that include the question of whether the candidate is connected to any current or prospective client, current or prospective third party, or public official;

- forms completed by candidate that include the question of whether the candidate is connected to any current or prospective client, current or prospective third party, or public official; and
- a background check.

***Can* Connected Candidates be hired?** Yes. ***Should* Connected Candidates be hired?** It depends. The answer to this question will be based on the facts of each particular case and the organization's risk appetite. AB&C Compliance should consider the answers to the following questions when determining its advice:

- Is there any pending or recently completed business between the hiring organization and the connection or the connection's organization or government entity?
- If the Connected Candidate was referred, was that referral in any way tied (whether implicitly or explicitly) to current or future business with the hiring organization?
- Was there an existing role or is a role being created for the Connected Candidate?
- Is the Connected Candidate qualified for the role?
  - This question should generally be the province of Human Resources. However, AB&C Compliance should have an understating of the role and the candidate pool so that it can identify potential red

flags. For example, if the grade cut-off for interviews is generally a 3.4 GPA and the Connected Candidate has a 2.9 GPA, then other factors may be at play.

- Did the Connected Candidate go through the standard interviewing and vetting process? If so, do the results of that process support hiring the candidate?

- Would the Connected Candidate's compensation be in line with that of others in similar roles?

The bottom line is that an organization must have a standard, merits-based hiring process from which it does not deviate.

If you, as the AB&C Compliance officer, do not oppose hiring a particular Connected Candidate, what are some of the controls that you could implement?

- Requiring that the referring employee (if any) is not the sole decision-maker in the hiring process.

- Requiring that the Connected Candidate, upon hiring, be walled off from any business involving that candidate's connection(s).

2. HIRING PRACTICES ENFORCEMENT ACTIONS

There has been a spate of FCPA enforcement actions relating to hiring practices in the financial institution space, kicked off by the JPMorgan Chase

& Co. ("JPM") case. That investigation and resulting enforcement action involved the bank's "sons and daughters" program, pursuant to which children of Chinese government officials or executives at Chinese state-owned enterprises were allegedly hired so that the government officials/executives (foreign officials for FCPA purposes) would direct business or transaction mandates to JPM.

The Connected Candidates, as we've defined the term, allegedly had fewer interviews than others and were fast-tracked into roles even though, as graphically expressed in internal JPM emails, all may not have been ideal candidates. For example, in 2010 one Asia-Pacific region ("APAC") banker ("Banker A") emailed a banking colleague who assisted him with staffing that "[w]e picked up a new mandate in Taiwan today—all we have to do is get [referral candidate] a full time analyst job at JPM in NY. Mission impossible?"[25] The problem, the recipient APAC banker responded, was that the candidate's "napping habit will be an eye-opening experience for our NY colleagues if he gets a job."[26]

Other correspondence also highlighted the connection between hiring and obtaining business, going so far as to use the term quid pro quo. In one email entitled "client referral," Banker A emailed a group of U.S. investment bankers regarding the same potential mandate and potential hire. Banker A

---

[25] *In the Matter of JP Morgan Chase & Co.*, No. 3-17684, at 10 (Nov. 17, 2016), https://www.sec.gov/litigation/admin/2016/34-79335.pdf.

[26] *Id.*

stated that "[w]e have a very good [private sector] client in Taiwan who has asked that we find an IB analyst role for his son in NY .... We are being offered now a [mandate] and the quid pro quo, is an analyst IB job for his son... Can we in [an investment banking group in New York] adopt him, or can you recommend a safe place for him where he won't get too scarred." After the candidate was hired in New York, follow up correspondence stated that the son was a "happy young man! And his dad will also be very pleased."[27] Another APAC banker responded that "I am sure this will go a long way for us in terms of [referring client entity] and [the candidate's father, a senior executive of the entity.]"[28]

As Kara Brockmeyer, then-Chief of the SEC Enforcement Division's FCPA Unit stated, "[t]he misconduct was so blatant that JPMorgan investment bankers created 'Referral Hires vs Revenue' spreadsheets to track the money flow from clients whose referrals were rewarded with jobs. The firm's internal controls were so weak that not a single referral hire request was denied."[29] The SEC's Cease-and-Desist order found that JPM violated the FCPA's anti-bribery, books and records, and internal controls provisions.[30]

---

27 *Id.* at 10–11.

28 *Id.* at 11.

29 *JPMorgan Chase Paying $264 Million to Settle FCPA Charges*, Release No. 2016-241, Fed. Sec. L. Rep. (CCH) (Nov. 17, 2016), https://www.sec.gov/news/press-release/2016-241.

30 *Id.*

JPM did not voluntarily self-disclose its misconduct, but it did cooperate with authorities. It resolved the matter with DOJ (through an NPA) and SEC (through the referenced Cease-and-Desist Order and related settlement offer) for a combined amount of approximately $264 million. This resolution was made possible in part because JPM took decisive action against employees who were directly involved in the misconduct. However, JPM Legal and Compliance apparently did not do enough to prevent and detect the wrongful conduct[31]:

> For example, in 2006, a JPMorgan APAC paralegal tasked with organizing and submitting Referral Hire questionnaires for review informed a JPMorgan APAC attorney that she was told by an investment banker that JPMorgan APAC was "now pitching for a . . . project" from a referring client, and that the project "may potentially result from the hiring of [candidate] as a summer analyst. I don't feel quite comfortable about this and would like to have your views." The paralegal drafted a memorandum to members of the APAC legal and compliance staff, noting that "[w]e will be exposed to a risk of being alleged of bribing [the client] for the . . . project or any other . . . projects," especially considering that the candidate would not otherwise be hired on her own merits. The hire was nonetheless approved

---

[31] *In the Matter of JP Morgan Chase & Co.*, No. 3-17684, at 7–8 (Nov. 17, 2016), https://www.sec.gov/litigation/admin/2016/34-79335.pdf.

> after another JPMorgan APAC investment banker stated that the hire was not in exchange "for return of any business from [the client]."

As the SEC underlined its view of Legal and Compliance's failures[32]:

> JPMorgan APAC legal and compliance staff did not understand the actual nature and operation of the Client Referral Program, and did not take adequate steps to fully investigate the extent and purpose of the Program during the relevant time period. This was due in part to JPMorgan APAC investment bankers failing to share complete information about the Client Referral Program with legal and compliance personnel. It was also due to a fundamental misunderstanding of the Client Referral Program by JPMorgan APAC legal and compliance, and a failure to investigate potential issues when they arose.

The SEC's remonstration is an important reminder and cautionary note for AB&C Compliance and Legal officers. It's always important to understand the nature of hiring programs and their potential bribery and corruption risks to identify any red flags, and to investigate, remediate, and report misconduct.

3. HIRING OF PUBLIC OFFICIALS

Particular care should be taken when considering whether to provide any type of employment opportunity to a public official, who will of course be

---

[32] *Id.* at 6–7.

considered a Connected Candidate. Organizations may want to include a specific section on this in their applicable AB&C policy. For example:

> Any employment opportunity (whether paid or unpaid, temporary, or permanent), including but not limited to speaking engagements, of a Public Official, must be pre-approved by AB&C Compliance and/or Legal. AB&C Compliance and/or Legal must provide a written authorization before any employment offer to a Public Official may be made.

Whether potential employment offers to public officials are reviewed and opined on by AB&C Compliance or by Legal will depend on the particular organization and the applicable policy should reflect that decision.

a. Hiring Hypotheticals

Organization X is a technology company based in the U.S. and traded on the New York Stock Exchange. Consider the following hypotheticals involving Organization X and hiring practices.

i. Hypothetical 1

The CEO of one of Organization X's major clients asks her Organization X relationship manager if her college student daughter can intern at Organization X for the summer. The CEO states that it would mean a lot to her if her daughter could have that type of valuable work experience and that her daughter does not need to be paid. Could/should Organization

X extend an internship offer to the client CEO's daughter?

Commentary: Is the client's CEO a foreign official for FCPA purposes? Is Organization X subject to the UK Bribery Act? Hypothetical 1 does not give us enough information to answer these questions. However, even if the answer to both questions is No, we should still analyze the facts in the same manner as if the answer to both questions was affirmative. Why? Organization X is subject to U.S. domestic laws governing commercial bribery and may also be subject to bribery laws of other nations. Moreover, as we explored in Chapter 5, our goal as AB&C Compliance officers is to create and maintain an organizational culture where compliance and ethics are paramount and there is a zero-tolerance approach to bribery and corruption.

Ideally, the Organization X relationship manager should thank the CEO for her interest and explain that all internships are coordinated through Organization X's formal internship program, which has a competitive admissions process that is open to the public. The relationship manager can then direct the CEO to the appropriate internet site or other resource for applications.

In making her request, the CEO did not refer to any currently pending or recently completed business between her company and Organization X. However, the CEO's comment that the internship opportunity "would mean a lot to her" is a potential red flag. Is the CEO merely voicing a genuine sentiment that she appreciates opportunities for her child or is she implicitly linking the fulfilment of her request to her company's business relationship with Organization X? It's difficult to tell.

If the CEO's daughter subsequently applies to Organization X, the AB&C Compliance process in place should identify her as a Connected Candidate and the appropriate due diligence should be triggered, including learning whether there is any pending or recently completed business between the CEO's company and Organization X. Any such pending or recently completed business, coupled with the CEO's comment that the employment opportunity for her daughter "would mean a lot to her" is problematic. It could imply a linkage between Organization X offering the employment opportunity and Organization X obtaining or retaining business from the CEO's company that may amount to bribery. At a minimum, the appearance of impropriety may weigh against hiring the CEO's daughter.

The CEO said that her daughter did not need to be paid. Does this affect our analysis of the situation? In short, no. Providing the CEO's daughter with any type of employment would still be a benefit to the CEO so that is not a mitigating fact.

ii. Hypothetical 2

A local government official in São Paulo, Brazil is reviewing Organization X's application for utility permits in connection with Organization X's new office building. The official tells Organization X that there are some delays with processing the paperwork and further documentation may be required. However, the official notes that if his son could be employed at Organization X's new office, he might be able to "push it through" anyway. As a factual matter, Organization X is short staffed, and the official's son appears to be qualified for at least one open position. Could/should Organization X extend an internship offer to the foreign official's son?

Commentary: This hypothetical describes interaction between Organization X, a U.S. issuer, and a local Brazilian government official (a foreign official) who is soliciting a benefit from Organization X in return for "pushing through" Organization X's utility paperwork. We are squarely in FCPA territory.

Should it make any difference in AB&C Compliance's analysis that the foreign official's son might have been hired anyway because he was qualified and because Organization X was short staffed? No. What matters is the *intent* with which Organization X's employment offer could be made—i.e., it could be made because Organization X wanted to influence the foreign official to "push through" its paperwork. The offer could certainly be viewed that way in hindsight by a regulator. After the foreign official offered to "push through" Organization X's paperwork in return for his son's employment, it became nearly impossible to extend an offer to the foreign official's son. At best, the employment offer would have the appearance of impropriety. At worst, it would be a bribe.

Alternatively, consider a variation on the situation where the foreign official did not solicit employment for his son. Rather, the foreign official's son applied for employment at Organization X through proper channels and was qualified for the role. If the hiring portion of Organization X's AB&C Compliance program was effectively designed and implemented, then AB&C Compliance should learn in the ordinary course that the son is a Connected Candidate. It's possible to hire Connected Candidates as long as the appropriate controls are in place. However, this situation has the additional factor that the Connected Candidate's foreign official parent is in the current position of making decisions involving Organization X. Given this situation, AB&C Compliance may still advise that the official's son should not be hired because of the appearance of impropriety.

E. THIRD PARTY PRACTICES

Using third parties is a reality for companies operating both domestically and internationally. However, using third parties isn't without risk. Third parties have commonly been used to conceal the payment of bribes. Recognizing this, the FCPA's anti-bribery provisions prohibit corrupt payments made to "any person, while knowing that all or a portion of such money or thing of value will be offered, given, or promised, directly or indirectly," to a foreign official.[33] The majority of FCPA enforcement actions involve corrupt payments made to foreign officials

---

[33] 15 U.S.C. §§ 78dd–1(a)(3), 78dd–2(a)(3), 78dd–3(a)(3).

through third parties. An organization can (and will) be held liable for the actions of a third party who acts on its behalf—including for bribery. As a result, how to manage third-party risk has become a key component of compliance programs and specifically AB&C Compliance programs.

As a threshold matter, an AB&C Compliance officer needs to understand the types of third parties with whom their organization interacts. Third parties can be broadly defined as "any persons or entities outside of the organization who provide services to the organization, or who act on behalf of the organization, or with whom the organization otherwise has an ongoing relationship."

There are many different types of relationships that an organization can have with a third party and they are not created equal from a bribery and corruption risk perspective. It's important to understand and categorize these relationships and then risk rate them accordingly. The risk rating, which should be based on a number of factors, can then determine the level of required ongoing due diligence and monitoring, etc. It's helpful to think about two types of third-party relationships that are at opposite ends of the risk spectrum to illustrate varying levels of bribery and corruption risk. (Of course, many organizations have relationships that fall somewhere in the middle).

First, consider a vendor relationship. A vendor can generally be defined as "a person or entity that provides goods or services to an organization in return for compensation." A vendor may provide a customer organization with copy paper, bottled water, etc. Absent other factors, vendors are generally considered low risk from a bribery and corruption perspective.

Second, at the opposite pole, consider introducer relationships. An introducer can be broadly defined as "a person or entity that acts on an organization's behalf, for the purposes of helping the organization maintain or develop business relationships and opportunities, in return for compensation." Unlike a vendor, an introducer is acting on the organization's behalf. In addition (and, again, as contrasted with a vendor), the introducer's *very purpose* is to help its retaining organization maintain or develop business. Both of these factors increase the bribery and corruption risk of the organization's relationship with the introducer. Introducers may also interact with public officials in the course of their work, further increasing the bribery and corruption risk of their relationship with the retaining organization. Generally speaking, an organization's highest risk third parties will be those third parties acting on its behalf, and in doing so interacting with public officials, for the purpose of obtaining or retaining business or a business advantage for their employing organization.

Because an organization is potentially liable for the conduct of a third party acting on its behalf, it's important to conduct the appropriate level of due diligence on that third party. The organization should have a policy or procedure detailing the methodology for risk rating its third parties and the corresponding required due diligence based on the assigned risk ratings.

The purpose of due diligence is to ensure that the organization has considered relevant, available information about the third party so that it can effectively determine and mitigate the level of bribery and corruption risk that the relationship may pose to the organization. Indeed, it serves two purposes—it helps to both assess and mitigate risk. For example, knowing negative information about a third party will both affect the risk assessment of entering into a relationship with that third party and will allow the organization to mitigate its risk by putting appropriate limitations or controls around that relationship.

1. DUE DILIGENCE

The following sections explain various types of due diligence as well as some of the underlying mechanics of how to conduct that due diligence.

a. Initial Due Diligence and Risk Assessment

A third party's assigned level of bribery and corruption risk should be a result of the onboarding due diligence and an initial risk assessment based on that due diligence. Generally, the onboarding due diligence on a third party that's required by an organization's policies and procedures should be completed prior to beginning the legal relationship or engagement with the third party. That requirement should be stated in the appropriate policy and procedures as should the criteria and authority for granting any exceptions to that requirement.

A key threshold (or "onboarding") question is why an organization is retaining a third party. This is of course even more of a focus with higher risk third parties, but it is also relevant to low risk vendor relationships. It's important for an organization (1) to have a legitimate business purpose/need for engaging *a* third party; and, once that is established (2) to have a legitimate business reason for engaging a *particular* third party.

Why is this second prong important? Consider, for example, a scenario in which your organization needs to purchase ten copy machines and this need is undisputed. However, there are several potential vendors from which to purchase the copiers. How is the decision of which vendor to select made and who is responsible for making it? Without adequate controls in the procurement process, there could be a situation where an employee of your organization is receiving a bribe or kickback to direct the business to a certain vendor—perhaps one whose contract terms are not the most advantageous to the organization. This is one reason why large organizations, in particular, have rigorous processes for vendor selection and management. As in all areas involving anti-bribery and corruption compliance, a standard, transparent, and documented process is key!

b. Types of Due Diligence: Initial, Periodic, and Trigger

As explained in the previous section, initial due diligence should be conducted as part of the onboarding process. That due diligence should be completed prior to commencing the relationship with the third party. However, conducting due diligence on a third party should not be a one-time event. Rather, due diligence (and the corresponding risk assessment) should be refreshed at set intervals of time based on the assigned risk of each third party. For example, the highest risk third parties may be reviewed on an annual basis and the lowest risk third parties every three years. This is generally referred to as periodic due diligence.

In addition to initial and periodic due diligence, due diligence should be conducted as necessary based on "trigger events". A trigger event refers to a change of circumstance that warrants confirmation of existing due diligence information and/or collection of new and updated information. Trigger events, for example, may include discovery of negative information about the third party or a change in the nature of the services provided by the third party.

A trigger event may occur if significant negative information about a third party becomes known. Such negative information may, for example, be an investigation or regulatory action against that third party for potential bribery or corruption or other financial crimes. An organization needs to have a process in place for conducting negative news screening—possibly of just the name of the third party but also (depending on the assigned risk) possibly for the third party's control persons as well.

A change in the services provided by the third party, including a change in the location of the services being provided or the nature of the services being provided, should also be considered a trigger event. It's important to review third party relationships on an engagement-by-engagement basis. Practitioners should not rely on their general understanding of the third party's business or even on the nature of the organization's past relationship with that third party. The nature of the specific engagement, as reflected in the contract, can change the nature of the bribery and corruption risk of the relationship.

i. Practice Example

A multinational corporation that is headquartered in the U.S. and trades on the New York Stock Exchange has an enterprise-wide engagement with a large telecom company. For several years, the telecom company provided the corporation with desk phones for its offices and limited technology support. Accordingly, the telecom company was onboarded and maintained as a low risk vendor. About ten years into the relationship, the corporation and the telecom company negotiated a new contract. The new contract reflected that the telecom company would provide expanded services to the corporation. These services would include installing phone lines and internet service in various non-U.S. jurisdictions. As part of this work, the telecom company would be authorized to negotiate on the corporation's behalf with local governments in those jurisdictions regarding the necessary permits.

AB&C Compliance conducted a trigger review of the telecom company and changed the risk rating of the telecom company from low to high. What had changed? *The difference was in the nature of the services being provided*. Instead of simply delivering phones, pursuant to the new engagement, the telecom company would now be responsible for installing phone lines in higher risk jurisdictions and, most importantly, negotiating on the corporation's behalf with local governments for the necessary permits, etc. to install those phone lines. Instead of simply being a vendor, the telecom company would be empowered to act on the corporation's behalf in dealing with foreign officials. This doesn't mean that there's anything wrong with the relationship or with the arrangement, but it *does* mean that there is heightened bribery risk and that additional steps should be taken to mitigate that risk.

c. The Mechanics of Due Diligence

The following sections address some of the "nuts and bolts" concepts of conducting and applying due diligence, including identifying potential source material, creating, and maintaining due diligence documentation, and standard and enhanced due diligence.

i. Source Material

Whether conducting due diligence on a current or prospective employee, customer, or third party, there are many different sources to keep in mind. The initial source is often the due diligence target itself. Assuming it's an entity, the target may provide basic information such as documentation regarding its legal entity status, ownership, and control person(s).

As we think about risk-based AB&C Compliance programs, the extent of due diligence that we conduct and the source(s) of due diligence that we use will depend in part on the significance of the potential relationship, in part on our perceived bribery and corruption risk of that relationship based on the applicable risk assessment, and in part on cost considerations. Use of premium research services and/or consultants increases due diligence costs. Organizations can of course search for information using open sources. Many organizations search public records, such as those related to criminal records and bankruptcy filings. Organizations also look at credit scores, available financial data, politically exposed person status, and adverse news. A rising trend is to review the social media entries relating to prospective employees, customers, and third parties.[34] Social media may provide information that other sources would not, including social and political views and political connections. Note that

---

[34] *2021 Anti-Bribery and Corruption Benchmarking Report*, KROLL, at 18, https://www.kroll.com/en/insights/publications/compliance-risk/anti-bribery-and-corruption-benchmarking-report-2021.

organizations should also always screen potential employees, clients, and third parties using sanctions and restricted party lists.

ii. Due Diligence and Documentation

As with so many aspects of an AB&C Compliance program, documentation is critical. It's important to have an organized and systematic way of (1) conducting third party due diligence; (2) maintaining the results of that due diligence; and (3) maintaining a record of any decisions made based on that due diligence.

For example, if you, as an AB&C Compliance officer found an irregularity in the payments made to a third party, what did you do? How did you handle this "red flag"? Your actions, and rationale for those actions, must be documented. Or, if your organization exits a relationship with a third party based on bribery and corruption concerns, that exit and its rationale must be documented. The names of the third party, and potentially its owners and control persons, should also be added to the appropriate list or database to prevent potential re-onboarding without due deliberation.

All organizations of course do not have the same level of resources. The important thing is that due diligence is systematically conducted, acted upon where appropriate, and that associated documentation and decisions are recorded.

iii. Standard Due Diligence

Examples of standard due diligence that can be collected/conducted (and that could potentially affect the third party's risk rating) include those listed below. These examples as written generally assume that the third party is an entity, but the same concepts can be applied to third parties who are individuals:

- Name of the third party
- Geographic location(s) of the third party (e.g., main headquarters, legal domicile, jurisdictions in which it operates)
  - How the third party's geographic location correlates with its bribery and corruption risk (e.g., whether it is in a high-risk jurisdiction)
- If an individual, whether he or she is a public official or a politically exposed person. Note that the terms "public official" and "politically exposed person" must be defined in the relevant policies and procedures.
- Type of legal entity (e.g., corporation)
- Whether the third party is a government, government agency, royal family, political party, sovereign wealth fund, state-owned or controlled entity, or in a joint venture with a state-owned or controlled entity
- Ownership structure of the third party

- Name(s) of the third party's owner(s) and control person(s)
    - Whether any of those persons had a previous employment relationship with the organization or have any personal contacts at the organization
    - Whether any of those persons are public officials or politically exposed persons
- How long the third party has been in business and its industry reputation
- The third party's industry sector and how that sector correlates with bribery and corruption risk. High risk sectors for bribery and corruption have generally been identified as oil and gas, construction, money service businesses, pharmaceutical, and any cash intensive businesses.
- Proposed fees and compensation structure
    - How the third party's proposed fees compare to industry or sector standards
    - Whether the compensation structure includes an incentive component
- Whether the third party will act on behalf of the organization
    - Whether the third party will interact with public officials on behalf of the organization

- Documentation of the legitimate business purpose for engaging the particular third party
- Whether there is any negative news about the third party (and if an individual, about the entity (if any) with which the third party is affiliated.) Negative news generally means negative information that may indicate increased bribery and corruption risk (e.g., news relating to any type of financial crime). It may come from various sources, such as open source data (e.g., internet searches), information regarding past legal actions or settlements, or even first-hand dealings with the third party itself.

iv. Enhanced Due Diligence

For relationships that present a certain higher level of bribery and corruption risk, as defined in an organization's applicable policies and procedures, enhanced due diligence is warranted. Some triggers for enhanced due diligence may include red flags that arise during the standard due diligence process—for example, that the third party operates in a high-risk jurisdiction, that the third party has connections with public officials, or that the third party has an unclear or unverifiable ownership structure.

Pursuant to the applicable policy, AB&C Compliance should prepare an initial risk assessment questionnaire to be completed as part of the onboarding process for all third-party relationships. The questionnaire, where possible, should have answer fields to choose from and a built-in scoring mechanism. Based on the initial scoring and the score ranges (as also determined by AB&C Compliance), third parties can be assigned different bribery and corruption risk levels. Based on those levels, as should be spelled out in the applicable policy, certain due diligence requirements will apply. In short—the higher the risk, the more extensive the required diligence.

2. ADDITIONAL CONTROLS

Additional controls besides due diligence should also be implemented to mitigate the bribery and corruption risk of third-party relationships. These controls include a written contract, a relationship owner, and relationship monitoring.

a. Written Contract

Every third-party relationship should be conducted pursuant to a written contract. As with nearly everything else with respect to third-party relationships, the form and provisions of each contract should depend on the assessed bribery and corruption risk of the relationship. For example, a one-off transaction with a low-risk vendor may be subject to little more than a detailed invoice. Conversely, ongoing and/or higher risk third-party relationships should be subject to more extensive and detailed contracts. In addition to basic contractual provisions like termination, compliance with applicable law, etc., every contract should contain a detailed description of the services to be provided, the fees to be paid for those services, the method of payment, intervals of payment, and an explanation of any incentive payment structure.

Contracts may also contain:

- AB&C representations and warranties

Contracts may include appropriate anti-bribery and corruption representations and warranties. Whether this is deemed necessary will likely depend on the risk rating of the third party and the type(s) of services that the third party is providing.

- Subcontractor provision

Where a third party may potentially subcontract with a fourth party to provide services under the direct contract with the organization, there should be a subcontracting provision in the contract. This provision may explain how the third party will manage bribery and corruption risk in its relationship with the fourth party.

- Provision regarding discretionary use of funds

The contract may contain a provision regarding whether, and pursuant to what conditions and controls, a third party may spend money on behalf of the organization or in connection with its engagement with the organization. If the third party is acting as an agent or intermediary for the organization, particularly if it is interacting with public officials on the organization's behalf, it would be wise to detail spending parameters in the contract.

- Audit rights clause

An audit right generally means a right to access and review the books and accounts of a third party for the purpose of ensuring that the third party is complying with the terms of the contract. If an organization has the practice of including audit rights clauses in its contracts, it should be prepared to exercise those rights at certain intervals (at least for a sample of its third-party relationships). The organization also must decide whether any such audits will be performed by its own staff or be outsourced to a reputable third-party auditor.

A third party should not begin doing work for an organization unless and until an appropriate contract has been fully executed. Any exception to this requirement should require the written approval of Legal. In addition, a third party should not perform services outside the scope of the written contract. If it does so, then that situation should be escalated to Legal for advice.

b. Payment Monitoring

Payment monitoring includes setting up a systematic process for reviewing the amounts paid to the third party, confirming whether those amounts are consistent with the contract terms, and confirming that the third party actually performed the services for which it has been paid. Payments should also only be made to an account in the same name as that of the contracting party. Payment monitoring is an example of how good compliance walks hand-in-hand with good business. Aside from mitigating bribery and corruption risk, an organization should want to know that it's getting what it's paying for and that it's in a third-party relationship that makes commercial sense.

i. Practice Example

As part of a bribery and corruption risk mitigation strategy, I once led an organization's efforts to review its relationships with a large section of its third parties—including conducting and reviewing much of the due diligence that we have referenced here: contract terms, services provided, payment reconciliation, checking whether payment arrangements were commensurate with the value of the services provided, etc.

The organization's business lines were not initially in favor of the project but were ultimately pleased with its results. From the business perspective, the organization was able to streamline its list of third parties to a more manageable number and save a significant amount of money by eliminating duplicative service providers and terminating contracts where the services were no longer required or the contract terms were not sufficiently advantageous. The project was also a success from the AB&C Compliance perspective because a number of high-risk relationships were wound down and additional controls were implemented to manage the bribery and corruption risks of the organization's third-party relationships.

c. Relationship Owner

It's helpful to assign a specific individual to be responsible for each third-party relationship. This relationship owner has primary responsibility for the management of the third-party relationship from its inception through its renewal and/or termination, including:

- Collecting all necessary due diligence
- Reviewing the due diligence and assigning a preliminary risk rating to the third party (which may later be reviewed and confirmed by AB&C Compliance and/or a third-party relationship management function)
- Obtaining all necessary internal (and external if applicable) approvals for engaging the third party
- Ensuring that an appropriate written contract is in place
- Overseeing the third party's conduct
- Overseeing the payments made to the third party
- Updating due diligence as necessary
- Otherwise ensuring compliance with all of the organization's requirements for maintaining a third-party relationship

The relationship owner is responsible for making sure all of the organization's requirements for onboarding and maintaining the relationship with the third party, such as due diligence, are satisfied. The relationship owner should be made aware that any questions about the relationship will be directed to them. Often the relationship owner is the individual who signed the contract on behalf of the organization, but it can be someone else as well. Ideally, the higher the potential bribery and corruption risk of the third-party relationship, the more senior the relationship owner.

The relationship owner may delegate administrative tasks relating to the third-party relationship. However, the relationship owner retains ultimate responsibility for the relationship. This makes practical sense from an administrative perspective and, perhaps more importantly, accountability is a powerful compliance tool. If an individual knows that he or she will be held responsible for a third-party relationship, then that individual will likely be more thoughtful in assessing the risks of that relationship and more careful in their decision-making.

In a large organization, it is possible that some third parties may have different contracts with different parts of the organization. In this case, the best practice from both compliance and efficiency standpoints is to have one "global" relationship manager for that third party. This will avoid potentially duplicative due diligence efforts as well as support a holistic view of the organization's relationship with the third party and the possible bribery and corruption risks of that relationship. This may pose internal coordination and technology challenges (e.g., if different business units or regions use different systems) but the benefits of making it work can be significant.

On a practical process note, an organization needs to have a systematic way to become aware of when a relationship owner is leaving an organization so that another relationship owner can be assigned, and a third party relationship is not left unattended.

3. RED FLAGS

Now that we've addressed due diligence and controls regarding third-party relationships, we'll consider the potential red flags that may arise, some of which we'll have touched on already in our discussion about due diligence and controls. Red flags could fall into several possible categories, including reputational concerns, organizational structure, relevant capability and expertise, position on AB&C representations and warranties in the contract, fees and payments, connections with public officials, and conflicts of interest. We'll explore each of these potential red flag categories in the following sections.

a. Reputational Concerns and Third Party Structure

Red flags relating to the third party's reputation and structure include the following:

- There are allegations relating to bribery, corruption, or other financial crimes involving the third party in media reports or online. Other negative information may also be relevant, but these types are the most directly related to a third party's potential bribery and corruption risk.

- References provided by the third party cannot be reached or have been reached but do not seem forthcoming.
- The third party may have an undisclosed beneficial owner.
- The third party is an individual.
- The third party is located or does business in high-risk jurisdictions.
- The third party uses shell companies or entities registered in known tax havens.
- The third party's business address is a mail drop location, PO box, or virtual office.

b. Third Party's Relevant Capability

Red flags relating to the third party's relevant capability include the following:

- The third party has not been in business very long or has only recently been incorporated or otherwise legally formed.
- The third party does not have a track record of providing the services for which the organization may retain it.
- The third party has poor financial statements or poor credit.

- The third party does not have adequate offices, facilities, or staff to perform the work for which it may be retained.
- The third party's plan for performing the work is vague and/or suggests a reliance on contacts or relationships.

c. Third Party's Contractual Position re: AB&C Representations and Warranties

It's a red flag when a third party will not agree to the retaining organization's proposed contractual anti-bribery and corruption representations and warranties. However, with that said, the situation of the specific entities involved always must be considered. For example, if the third party is a large and sophisticated entity it may not want to agree to the retaining organization's proposed representations and warranties simply because it has its own standard language that it prefers to use. Or, regardless of its size and sophistication, if the third party does business only in one jurisdiction (or is subject to the anti-bribery laws of only one jurisdiction), then it may not want to contractually agree to comply with the requirements of other anti-bribery laws. A couple of practice points: (1) the retaining organization can be flexible on its desired legal language so long as the resulting contractual language provides the organization with the desired level of protection; and (2) the retaining organization should make sure that the third party contracts to comply with the anti-bribery and corruption laws applicable to the retaining organization. For example, if the third party is not subject to the UK Bribery Act but the retaining organization is, the retaining organization should ensure that the third party contractually agrees to comply with the UK Bribery Act's requirements in connection with all of its work for the retaining organization.

d. Fees, Invoices, and Payments

Red flags relating to fees, invoices, and payments include the following:

- The third party will not provide detailed or itemized invoices.
- The third party's fees are higher than those that are typical in the relevant industry.
- The third party requests that payments for its services be made to a company or a person that is not clearly linked to the third party.
- The third party requests that payments be made to an account in a country where the third party is not located.
- The third party offers gifts or entertainment to the individuals at the retaining organization who are responsible for managing the relationship with the third party.
- The third party's invoices show large amounts for gifts and entertainment or "miscellaneous" expenses.

- The third party's invoices reflect that it has made cash payments.
- The third party is in a high-risk sector such as oil and gas, construction, pharmaceuticals, etc.
- The third party requests that the retaining organization make a donation to a charity.
- The third party requests a sudden and/or large increase in its compensation.

e. Connections with Public Officials

Red flags relating to a third party's connections with public officials include the following:

- The third party has known business dealings or associations with public officials.
- The third party has owners or control persons who are public officials.
- The third party or one of its owners or control persons is a politically exposed person.
- The third party or one of its owners or control persons was previously a public official or worked in a government agency relevant to the work that the third party will be performing for the retaining organization.
- The third party makes large or frequent political contributions.

f. Conflicts of Interest

In the context of third-party relationships, the phrase "conflicts of interest" refers to the possibility that there are one or more connections between the third party and the retaining organization that could put the third party and/or an employee of the retaining organization in the position of having competing interests. For example, it is a potential conflict of interest if one or more of the third party's owners or control persons is a family member of someone who works at the retaining organization.

g. What Happens if There Are Red Flags?

Now that we've identified a number of potential red flags that can arise in third-party relationships, what happens if one or more actually do arise? The question then becomes how serious the red flags are and the extent to which their risks can be sufficiently mitigated by appropriate controls. Additional due diligence will sometimes be part of the answer. Consider the situation where an organization is contemplating doing business with a third party that is or was under investigation for bribery and corruption. Potential mitigating factors may include if the matter has been resolved and if the third party cooperated with authorities in voluntarily disclosing and remediating the problem. If the matter has been resolved, much or all of this information will be publicly available. If the investigation is still underway, the retaining organization may explore its concerns directly with the third party's General Counsel and/or Chief Compliance Officer.

Who in a retaining organization considers information regarding potential red flags and decides how to proceed? Organizations need to have a process in place for evaluating negative developments in third-party relationships, such as those previously referenced, and how to act on the available information. In large organizations, this process may include a committee with representatives from business units, Legal, AB&C Compliance and other stakeholders. Depending on the severity of the circumstances, additional controls may be imposed on the relationship, or the relationship may even be exited. If the decision is made to exit the relationship, that decision needs to be carefully documented. Steps must be taken to ensure that decision is recorded in appropriate systems so that the third party (and any control persons, if relevant) cannot be re-onboarded without full consideration of the reasons for the exit (and the attendant determination that the concerns that drove that exit have since been ameliorated).

i. Practice Question

Should an organization provide AB&C training to its third parties?

A number of considerations go into answering the question of whether an organization should provide AB&C training to some or all of its third parties. An organization of course wants to ensure that its third parties comply with the organization's AB&C policy. However, just how far could or should an organization go to ensure this? We have explored a number of anti-bribery and corruption controls for third-party relationships in this chapter, such as a detailed written contract, a relationship owner, various types of due diligence, and payment monitoring. Is there a need to go further? Returning to a favorite term, that decision should be "risk based". Some questions to keep in mind when deliberating:

- Why is the organization considering providing training?

Is it simply to provide basic information about the organization's AB&C policy and guidelines for third parties? If that is the case, then the organization's front-facing policy may be sufficient and training may not be required. Conversely, if the third party is high risk from a bribery and corruption perspective, then in-person training may be appropriate.

- Has a particular third party requested training?

If so, it's important to understand the reason for that request. While a third party's candor in asking for assistance could be a positive, it may also be a red flag. For example, is the third party a small organization with a limited Compliance or Legal staff and an insufficient knowledge and technology infrastructure to provide its own training? If this is the case, then retaining that third party may not be desirable.

- Related to the previous questions, what type(s) of training might the organization provide?

Will it be in-person training provided by one of the organization's Legal or AB&C Compliance officers?

There are always cost and resource aspects to consider. As we addressed in Chapter 5, communication and training can and should take various forms based on the bribery and corruption risk of the relationship. In this vein, training options for third parties may include: email reminders, in-person on-site training, live virtual training, recorded online or web-based training, the third party's acknowledgement of the organization's front-facing AB&C policy, or a certification included in contract materials.

4. THIRD PARTY PRACTICES HYPOTHETICALS

a. Hypothetical 1

A law firm that represents Organization X occasionally refers its own clients to Organization X as client prospects. This is outside the scope of the law firm's legal representation of Organization X and is not a formally documented relationship. It is subsequently discovered that one of Organization X's senior staff members has been giving one of the partners at the law firm various gifts as a "thank-you" for the referrals.

Commentary: This matter should be raised to AB&C Compliance as soon as it's discovered. Although ad hoc, there is certainly a referral relationship between the law firm and Organization X. This relationship, even if it results in only an occasional referral, should be documented in writing. Any compensation arrangement between the law firm and Organization X for the referrals must also be documented in writing. Gifts to a partner at the law firm in return for referrals is not appropriate. Any compensation for referrals should be pursuant to a written agreement and paid directly to the law firm (not to an individual partner). Otherwise, there could be the potential inference of commercial bribery—Organization X giving a law firm partner personal gifts in return for client referrals.

This scenario tees up several issues that AB&C Compliance and Legal officers should watch out for—informal referral arrangements, ad hoc/sporadic referrals, and referrals from law firms.

b. Hypothetical 2

Organization X is based in the United States but is in the process of opening a local office in Brazil. Organization X has hired a local consultant to assist with the logistics of opening the office. Organization X receives an invoice that includes a line item stating "miscellaneous—sub-contractor payment" for $50,000.

Commentary: The Organization X employee reviewing this invoice should contact AB&C Compliance. A "miscellaneous" line item, especially in a large amount, should always be considered a red flag. Organization X's contract with the third-party should include requirements for detailed invoicing and anything labeled "miscellaneous" should be presumed to have insufficient detail. The miscellaneous line item refers to a subcontractor payment. The contract should be reviewed to determine whether the use of subcontractors is in fact permitted. Organization X should contact the consultant in writing and request specific details about the purpose of the payment. Depending on the consultant's response, Organization X may have to conduct a trigger-based review of the consultant and its relationship with the consultant and consider whether it may be necessary to terminate the relationship.

F. TYING IT TOGETHER: THIRD PARTIES AND THE ACCOUNTING PROVISIONS

We addressed the FCPA's accounting provisions in Chapter 3 and explored third-party relationships in Chapter 6 as part of our coverage of AB&C Compliance subject areas. To better understand the real-world implications of these topics, it's helpful to look at enforcement actions where both the accounting provisions and issues with third parties came into play. We'll contemplate one of the United Nations Oil For Food Program enforcement actions as well as an enforcement action against Deutsche Bank to highlight points on both topics.

1. EXAMPLE 1: UN OIL FOR FOOD PROGRAM ACTIONS

According to the allegations in the UN Oil For Food Program actions, beginning in 2000, the Iraqi government demanded that the suppliers of humanitarian goods make a payment, usually valued at 10% of the contract price, to the Iraqi government in order to be awarded a contract.[35]

Some suppliers recorded these payments as "After-Sales Service Fee[s]" ("ASSFs") even though these payments did not represent any actual service being performed by the suppliers.[36] Other suppliers disguised the payments by inserting fictitious line items into contracts, and still others inflated their contract prices by 10% to account for the 10% they would pay to the Iraqi government. The alleged conduct did not breach the FCPA's anti-bribery provisions because the payments went to the Iraqi government itself rather than to individual foreign

---

[35] *See e.g., SEC v. AGCO Corp.*, Civil Action No. 1:09-CV-0186, at 5 (D.D.C. 2009) [hereinafter AGCO Complaint], https://www.sec.gov/files/litigation/complaints/2009/comp21229.pdf. As background, "[t]he Oil for Food Program provided humanitarian relief to the Iraqi population during the time that Iraq was subject to international trade sanctions. The program required that Iraq could purchase necessary humanitarian goods and related services through a UN escrow account." *Id.* at 2. The SEC alleged that

> [s]tarting in the middle of 2000, the Iraqi government made a concerted effort to subvert the [Oil for Food] Program by demanding secret kickbacks from its humanitarian goods suppliers. Although contracts entered into pursuant to the Program were subject to UN review and approval, the Program gave Iraq discretion to select the companies from which it purchased goods. After the Iraqi ministry would accept the bid, the ministry would inform the supplier of the requirement that the supplier make a secret payment in the form of an "After-Sales Service Fee ("ASSF") to Iraq in order to win the contract. The Iraqi ministry would also inform the supplier that the ASSF would have to be paid prior to the goods entering into the country, or the goods would be stopped at the border until the ASSF payment was paid.

Id. at 5.

[36] *See e.g., id.*

officials. Numerous companies—e.g., Chevron, Volvo, General Electric, Fiat, Ingersoll-Rand—resolved enforcement actions alleging violations of the FCPA's books and records and internal controls violations.

The AGCO Corp. ("AGCO") matter is an example of one of these actions. AGCO, headquartered in the United States, is a manufacturer and supplier of agricultural machinery.[37] During the Oil for Food Program, AGCO Ltd., an AGCO UK subsidiary, "marketed and negotiated the sales of equipment and spare parts to Iraq through AGCO S.A., located in France, and AGCO Danmark A/S, located in Denmark."[38]

The SEC alleged that AGCO paid approximately $6 million in kickbacks to Iraq through a Jordanian agent.[39] According to the SEC, the payments were disguised or improperly recorded in subsidiary books and records. "AGCO's subsidiaries authorized and paid kickbacks to Iraq in the form of 'after-sales service fees' on sales of its product to Iraq. AGCO knew or was reckless in not knowing that kickbacks were paid in connection with subsidiaries' transactions."[40] The SEC alleged very specific books

---

37 *Id.* at 3.

38 *Id.*

39 *Id.* at 1, 6.

40 *Id.* at 1. AGCO was ordered to pay more than $20 million in fines, penalties, and disgorgement in connection with cases brought by the SEC, the DOJ, and the Danish State Prosecutor's office. *AGCO Corp. to Pay $1.6 Million in Connection with Payments to the Former Iraqi Government Under the U.N. Oil-for-Food Program*, U.S. DOJ, OFF. OF PUB. AFFAIRS (Sept. 30, 2009) at https://www.justice.gov/opa/pr/agco-corp-pay-16-million-

and records and internal controls deficiencies of the kind we've addressed in this book. Just a few such examples are:

- Due Diligence
  - AGCO did not conduct any due diligence on the Jordanian agent or require that he undergo FCPA training.[41]
- Accounts
  - The account in which the kickbacks were recorded was created by AGCO's Marketing staff with almost no supervision from the Finance department, which caused accounts to be created and payments to be made without proper documentation.[42]
  - No one at AGCO questioned why there were dual accounts or why one account contained approximately 10% of the contract value even though there was no contract requirement that 10% be paid to the Iraqi government or anyone else.[43]

---

connection-payments-former-iraqi-government-under-un-oil-food#:~:text=The%20program%20mandated%20that%20the,and%20other%20necessary%20infrastructure%20items.

41 AGCO Complaint, *supra* n.35, at 11.

42 *Id.* at 10.

43 *Id.* at 9.

- Contracts
  - Sales and Marketing personnel were able to enter into contracts without supervision or approval of the Legal Department.[44]
  - The agent's contract did not accurately explain the agent's services and payments and did not contain any AB&C language.[45]

2. EXAMPLE 2: DEUTSCHE BANK ENFORCEMENT ACTION

The Deutsche Bank ("DB") enforcement action also involved payments through third parties and violations of the FCPA's books and records and internal controls provisions. It resulted in a three-year deferred prosecution agreement with the DOJ, a nearly $80 million criminal penalty, and $43 million in disgorgement and pre-judgment interest that was paid to the SEC via the coordinated resolution.[46] Three separate FCPA-related factual scenarios were explained in the deferred prosecution agreement. We'll focus on one.

DB entered into a contract with a special purpose vehicle ("SPV"). That SPV was beneficially owned by the wife (the "Business development consultant" or

---

[44] *Id.* at 10.

[45] *Id.* at 11.

[46] *Deutsche Bank Agrees to Pay Over $130 Million to Resolve Foreign Corrupt Practices Act and Fraud Case*, U.S. DOJ, OFF. OF PUB. AFFAIRS (Jan. 8, 2021), https://www.justice.gov/opa/pr/deutsche-bank-agrees-pay-over-130-million-resolve-foreign-corrupt-practices-act-and-fraud; DB DPA, *supra* Chapter 5, n.36, at 7–8.

"(BDC") of an individual who was responsible for managing the family office and the personal investments (the "Family Office") of a Saudi official (the "Family Office Manager").[47] Under the terms of the contract, the SPV would be paid fees that were falsely recorded in DB's books as "referral fees".[48] Their true purpose was for DB to make corrupt payments to the Family Office Manager so he would not move the Saudi official's business to another bank[49].

In addition:

- "To facilitate corrupt payments to the Family Officer Manager through the [] BDC," DB helped the BDC to establish a shell company in the British Virgin Islands and opened a bank account for that company into which DB made payments to the BDC.[50]
- A DB director falsely represented the BDC as the source of business with the Family Office in documentation given to the bank's headquarters.[51] Other senior employees also knew it wasn't true.[52]
- The relationship with the Family Office had been brought over from another bank by the relationship manager when he joined DB. The

[47] DB DPA, *supra* Chapter 5, n.36, at 8.

[48] *Id.*

[49] *Id.* at 8–9.

[50] *Id.* at 9.

[51] *Id.* at 9–10.

[52] *Id.*

relationship at the prior bank also involved false finder's fees and DB senior management was aware that the same would be expected at DB.[53]

- Multiple senior executives approved the relationship despite knowing it was corrupt—one cited the "high value of the client" as a justification for paying the BDC.[54]
- DB did have a contract with the BDC. However, DB made payments not authorized by the contract. DB also falsely recorded the payments—e.g., one as a "goodwill payment," one as an "exceptional payment," etc.[55]
- DB loaned the Family Office Manager money to buy a home in France.[56]

As per the Statement of Facts incorporated in the DPA, DB agreed that it violated the FCPA's books and records provision and that it conspired to violate and violated the FCPA's internal controls provision. DB admitted that it "knowingly and willfully conspired and agreed with others to maintain false books, records, and accounts that did not accurately and fairly reflect the transactions and dispositions of [DB's] assets . . . ."[57] DB also admitted that it "knowingly and willfully failed to implement and maintain a system of internal accounting controls

[53] DB DPA, *supra* Chapter 5, n.36, at 9–10.

[54] *Id.* at 10.

[55] *Id.* at 10–12.

[56] *Id.* at 12.

[57] *Id.* at 2.

sufficient to provide reasonable assurances regarding the reliability of financial reporting and the execution of transactions in accordance with management's authorization, and which would have helped detect and stop [DB] from continuing to make corrupt payments to and through BDCs."[58]

G. BUSINESS TRANSACTIONS

Organizations are of course different in the types of business transactions that they conduct. An AB&C Compliance officer should always be familiar with the types of transactions in which its organization engages, the bribery and corruption risks attendant to those transactions, and the process for due diligence and documentation of those transactions (e.g., loans, real estate transactions, purchase and sale agreements, etc.).

Areas that AB&C Compliance may look at in connection with business transactions include:

- Any negative information regarding the transactional counterpart and its control persons;
- Whether the transactional counterpart has an AB&C Compliance program and the quality of that program; and
- Whether to include AB&C representations and warranties in the contract and, if so, the appropriate language.

---

[58] *Id.* at 3. DB also admitted that it conspired to violate the internal accounting controls provision. *Id.*

1. MERGERS AND ACQUISITIONS

Mergers and acquisitions ("M&A") are classic transactional examples in which bribery and corruption risk may arise. Successor liability, a core concept in corporate law, is especially relevant here. Among other things, successor liability prevents a company from avoiding liability by reorganizing itself. An acquiring company can be held liable for the wrongful conduct of the company that it acquires—*even conduct that took place before the acquisition*. When one company acquires another company, the acquiring company essentially inherits all of the other company's problems, including those involving bribery or corruption. The acquiring company can then become liable for the target company's bribery and corruption issues post-acquisition. Both *pre*-acquisition due diligence and *post*-acquisition due diligence are important in mitigating the bribery and corruption risks inherent in mergers and acquisitions. We'll take each in turn.

a. Pre-Acquisition Due Diligence

As explained in the FCPA Resource Guide, an organization that doesn't perform adequate pre-acquisition due diligence exposes itself to both legal and business risks. This general proposition makes both legal and common sense (i.e., caveat emptor—let the buyer beware). Nevertheless, there have been a number of enforcement actions where the failure to conduct sufficient pre-acquisition due diligence was at issue.

Pre-acquisition due diligence has several important purposes. For example, it:[59]

- "helps an acquiring company to accurately value the target company."
- "identif[ies] business and regional risks and can also lay the foundation for a swift and successful post-acquisition integration into the acquiring company's corporate control and compliance environment."
- allows "the consequences of potential violations uncovered through due diligence [to] be handled by the parties in an orderly and efficient manner through negotiation of the costs and responsibilities for the investigation and remediation."
- "[d]emonstrates a genuine commitment to uncovering and preventing FCPA violations."

But what does pre-acquisition due diligence really mean in practice? The bottom line is that an organization should try to get enough information so it can effectively analyze the transaction risk and decide whether to proceed with the transaction, to proceed with altered terms, or to withdraw. Some basic pre-acquisition due diligence questions are:

- In which countries does the target company do business?

---

[59] FCPA Resource Guide, *supra* Chapter 1, n.1, at 29.

- Who/what are target company's current and prospective customers?
- What types of third parties does the target company use and for what purposes?
- What touchpoints (if any) does the target company have with public officials in the course of its business operations?
- What does the target company's existing AB&C Compliance program look like? Is it adequate to cover its risks? Is there a record of policy breaches and compliance issues?

b. Post-Acquisition Due Diligence

As a practical matter, an acquiring company may not be able to conduct all of the pre-acquisition due diligence that it would ideally want. This may be because of timing limitations with respect to when the transaction needs to close, because there are foreign legal impediments in the target company's country, or simply because there is greater access to the target company's relevant documents and personnel after the transaction closes. If, after completing the pre-acquisition due diligence, the acquiring company decides to continue with the acquisition, it should also conduct post-acquisition due diligence. Post-acquisition due diligence includes integrating the acquired/newly merged entity's AB&C Compliance program in as timely a manner as possible. The SEC and the DOJ have indicated that where sufficient pre-acquisition due diligence wasn't possible, they will look to the adequacy of the acquiring company's post-acquisition due diligence and compliance integration efforts in determining whether to pursue an FCPA enforcement action.

As part of the post-acquisition due diligence/ integration phase, the acquiring company should:

- Conduct a review, gap analysis, and revision and consolidation of the Code of Conduct/Code of Ethics and any AB&C policies and procedures of all merged or acquired entities.
- Roll out the updated Code and AB&C policies to the complete organizational population.
- Train the directors, officers, employees, and potentially the high risk third parties, of the newly acquired/merged entity on the updated Code and AB&C policies and procedures.
- Conduct a bribery and corruption specific audit of the newly acquired/merged entity.

If there is a bribery or corruption issue in the newly acquired/merged entity, it's best for that entity to investigate it, remediate it, and consider voluntarily disclosing it. The DOJ specifically discusses mergers and acquisitions in its FCPA Corporate Enforcement Policy, the CEVS Policy's predecessor, and highlights the possibility of a declination to prosecute even in cases where there are aggravating circumstances with respect to the acquired entity. As the CEP states[60]:

---

[60] JM, *supra* Chapter 3, n.100, § 9–47.120. Note 3 to that section further states that "In appropriate cases, an acquiring

> The Department recognizes the potential benefits of corporate mergers and acquisitions, particularly when the acquiring entity has a robust compliance program in place and implements that program as quickly as practicable at the merged or acquired entity. Accordingly, where a company undertakes a merger or acquisition, uncovers misconduct through thorough and timely due diligence or, in appropriate instances, through post-acquisition audits or compliance integration efforts, and voluntarily self-discloses the misconduct and otherwise takes action consistent with this Policy (including, among other requirements, the timely implementation of an effective compliance program at the merged or acquired entity), there will be a presumption of a declination in accordance with and subject to the other requirements of this Policy.

The CEVS Policy does not specifically address mergers and acquisitions. However, it's reasonable to believe that the DOJ's approach under the CEVS Policy would be similar to its approach as expressed in the CEP.

2. JOINT VENTURES

Joint ventures ("JV"s) can take many forms. In general, joint ventures may operate through a contractual arrangement between existing entities

---

company that discloses misconduct may be eligible for a declination, even if aggravating circumstances existed as to the acquired entity." *Id.*

(where a separate legal entity is not formed) or through a separately formed legal entity. JVs can be challenging because they represent some combination of third-party risk and parent/ subsidiary-like risk. As a result, compliance principles from both areas may apply.

If the JV is a contractual arrangement between existing entities, and a new entity is not created, then the due diligence and other controls should be similar to those that we explored with respect to third-party risk. This is also true if an organization is joining or investing in an already-existing JV that is a separate legal entity. However, in that case, there would need to be due diligence on both the JV entity itself as well as on the other persons or entities who are participating in the JV.

Initial due diligence points would include verifying ownership, reviewing the JV's formation and governance documents, reviewing the JV control persons' backgrounds (including confirming that they have sufficient compliance expertise), assessing any connections between the JV (and its control persons) and public officials, reviewing the JV's qualifications for its proposed purpose, reviewing the JV's professional reputation (including whether there is any negative information about the JV or its control persons relating to financial crime), and reviewing the JV's existing AB&C Compliance program. Initial due diligence may also include reviewing the JV's relationships with its existing agents (if any).

The organization entering into the relationship with the JV entity should also draft, or review and revise, the JV's internal policies and procedures and ensure that they:

- Clearly delineate the compliance infrastructure, including oversight responsibilities; and
- Where appropriate, require higher or independent level(s) of approval for transactions and relationships that present a higher level of bribery and corruption risk, such as those involving public officials or those in high-risk markets.

The JV agreement itself can and should contain various compliance-related provisions. For example, depending on the potential bribery and corruption risk of the JV relationship and the organization's risk appetite, JV agreements may include:

- representations by the JV partners, and the JV itself, that they will not engage in bribery or corruption (as defined in the JV agreement) and that they will comply with applicable AB&C laws (as defined in the JV agreement);
- representations that the JV will maintain accurate books and records and maintain a system of effective accounting controls;
- a clause giving the JV partners the right to terminate the JV agreement in the event of a potential (as defined in the JV agreement)

breach of the applicable (as defined in the JV agreement) AB&C laws;

- a clause giving the JV partners the right to (periodically or under specified circumstances) audit the JV's books and records; and

- a clause granting a specified JV partner or partners the right to appoint JV positions particularly relevant to AB&C, such as the Chief Compliance Officer or General Counsel.

3. NEW AND UPDATED PRODUCTS AND SERVICES

AB&C Compliance may have a defined role in reviewing and helping to vet an organization's new product and service initiatives or significant modifications to existing products and services. Organizations should have a standard due diligence process and checklist for evaluating risks concerning new and updated products and services. AB&C Compliance review, based on certain triggers, should be a built-in part of this process. Regarding evaluation of new and updated products and services, AB&C Compliance may consider:

- Whether and how third parties are being used in connection with the development and distribution of the product or service;

- Whether the product or service will be offered in one or more high risk jurisdictions;

- Whether the product or service will be offered to public officials (with the understanding that if the product will be offered to the general public, and only to public officials to the extent they are part of the general public, then that does not result in heightened bribery and corruption risk); and
- If the first line (i.e., those directly involved in the sales and distribution of the new product or service) will be permitted to give or receive gifts, entertainment, or anything of value in connection with selling and distributing that product or service.

H. REPRESENTATIONS AND WARRANTIES

One of the controls that we explored with respect to third-party relationships was the inclusion of AB&C representations and warranties in the applicable contract. Where an organization regularly enters into a certain type of transaction, that organization may have a standard form contract with AB&C language that it prefers to use. Whether the language is agreeable or sufficient of course depends in part on the role and position of the counterparties. For example, a contract may be drafted such that all parties are agreeing to certain AB&C representations and warranties or drafted such that only one of the parties is doing so. To that point, the bargaining power between the parties is also relevant. If the parties' bargaining power is roughly equal then there may be a certain amount of back-and-forth over the contract terms. Conversely, if the potential relationship is lop-sided, then the contract and its language may be almost a "take it or leave it" proposition.

When considering the use of bribery and corruption representations and warranties, it's helpful to review a hypothetical fact pattern and draft language.

1. HYPOTHETICAL

Corporation B is a software company that is publicly traded on the New York Stock Exchange. It has offices in the U.S. and the UK. Developer A is a commercial contracting company that is based in India. Developer A and Corporation B enter into a contractual arrangement (the "Contract"), whereby Corporation B is paying Developer A to build an office complex in India. The "Contract Term" is specifically defined in the Contract and generally runs from the date of the Contract's execution to when the office complex has been completed and has successfully passed the inspections required by local law. Corporation B has requested that Developer A agree to certain AB&C representations and warranties as part of the contract. Developer A has also provided its own proposed language.

As a matter of practice and risk mitigation, Corporation B will want the most expansive representations and warranties that it can negotiate, and Developer A will want to keep them as narrow as possible. Below are some draft representations and warranties for discussion purposes.

Language Proposed by Corporation B:

Developer A, for itself and its directors, officers, and employees, and on behalf of all subcontractors, and each of their respective officers, managers, employees, independent contractors, representatives and agents, represents and covenants that (i) it will use funds relating to the Contract for lawful purposes, (ii) it has not violated and will not violate applicable anti-corruption laws, including without limitation, the Foreign Corrupt Practices Act ("FCPA"), the United Kingdom Bribery Act of 2010 ("UK Bribery Act") and the OECD Convention on Combating Bribery of Foreign Public Officials in International Business Transactions ("OECD Convention"), (iii) it has not and will not, directly or indirectly, give or offer anything of value, including, but not limited to, cash, contributions, gifts, or entertainment, to foreign or domestic government officials or to any private commercial person or entity for the purpose of gaining an improper business advantage in violation of any such applicable anti-corruption laws and (iv) it has established and will continue to implement sufficient internal controls and procedures to ensure substantial compliance with applicable anti-corruption laws, including, but not limited to, the FCPA, the UK Bribery Act and the OECD Convention.

Commentary:

- Developer A would be making these AB&C representations and warranties on behalf of several categories of individuals and/or entities. From Developer's A's perspective, it would need to make sure that it had sufficient oversight over these groups. This is particularly a concern with respect to subcontractors and those potentially acting on behalf of those subcontractors—individuals and entities over whom Developer A may not ordinarily have full (or any) AB&C oversight. Ideally, Developer A would only make representations on behalf of itself and its own officers and directors.

- The first subclause states that Developer A will use funds "*relating to the Contract*" (emphasis added) for lawful purposes. From Developer A's perspective, it's positive that this language is limited specifically to funds relating to the Contract. However, as a practical matter, money is of course fungible so arguably this provision provides little protection for Developer A.

- In the second subclause, Developer A represents that it "*has not* violated and will not violate" the applicable AB&C laws and in the third subclause Developer A represents that it "*has not* and will not" engage in certain prohibited conduct (emphasis added). Both of these representations describe prohibited conduct broadly in scope—as written, prohibited conduct could have taken place before the Contract became effective and/or in the course of work wholly unrelated to the Contract. Developer A would want to limit these representations only to prospective conduct that is undertaken in furtherance of the Contract. Two best practice points: (1) Do not make representations as to past conduct. An organization rarely has perfect institutional knowledge about what it has done in the past and making representations as to its past conduct can only be unhelpful; (2) Do not make representations that are linked to conduct that is unrelated to the Contract. Such represetations are overly broad and create unnecessary risk.

- The third subclause is superfluous. It's basically an amalgam of the active bribery provisions of the FCPA and UKBA. Developer A has already agreed to comply with those laws, so this clause is unnecessary.

- The fourth subclause is a variation of the "we have a compliance program" representation. Rather than make specific representations about past and ongoing conduct, Developer A might seek to include a representation that it has an AB&C Compliance program in place. That's a common and effective approach for organizations that are in Developer A's position. However, the phrase "ensure substantial compliance with applicable anti-corruption laws" is problematic in two ways. First, no internal controls and procedures will *ensure* compliance with applicable AB&C laws. A program can, however, be "reasonably designed and implemented to effect compliance with applicable AB&C laws." Developer A should seek to edit the language along these lines. Second, the phrase "substantial compliance" is meaningless. For example, an organization either complies with the FCPA or it doesn't—there's no such thing as "substantial" compliance.

- The OECD is included as an "applicable anti-corruption law." Though a somewhat common practice, this is technically incorrect because the OECD applies only to state parties. However, if Developer A is actively negotiating its edits with Corporation B and seeking to minimize its redlining, there's really no harm in leaving it in.

- Regarding "applicable anti-corruption laws," it's helpful to include additional language clarifying the party or parties to which that term is referring. Separate and apart from the Contract, the parties may be subject to different AB&C laws based on the jurisdictions in which they operate. However, they may contractually obligate themselves to comply with laws to which they would not otherwise be subject. In this case, Corporation B will want Developer A to agree to comply with all of the AB&C laws to which Corporation B is subject even if Developer A would not otherwise be subject to them. This will be especially important if Developer A will be acting on behalf of Corporation B in any capacity. One way to clarify the applicability issue is to add a specific representation in the Contract that

"Developer A will comply with all of the AB&C laws that are applicable to itself and those that are applicable to Corporation B." Another way is to state that one or both parties will comply with a specific list of laws and then define those laws as "applicable AB&C laws."

Language Proposed by Developer A:

For the Contract Term, Developer A shall not knowingly make any payment to any Person in violation of the U.S. Foreign Corrupt Practices Act, as amended from time to time, (the "FCPA"). Developer A represents and warrants to Corporation B, as of the date hereof, that the employees of Developer A are subject to a written compliance policy with respect to giving gifts and entertainment that is reasonably designed to seek to avoid any violation of the FCPA or of any other applicable ethics or anti-corruption laws of the United States or any other jurisdiction to which Developer A is subject.

Commentary:

- This clause is much more limited in scope, and therefore much more advantageous to Developer A, than that of the first sample proposed by Corporation B. For example, it's limited to the "Contract Term." There are no representations as to past conduct.

- This clause includes an AB&C program representation that's extremely bare bones. Actually, it's not even a program representation—it's a policy representation. Literally, as of the date of the Contract (which makes one wonder whether any such policy previously existed), Developer A's employees are subject to a policy on gifts and entertainment that addresses the *giving* (so presumably not the receipt) of gifts and entertainment. G&E is of course only one subject area of many of an AB&C Compliance program. Finally, that policy is "reasonably designed to seek to avoid" violating the FCPA or other applicable laws. "Reasonably designed to seek to avoid" a violation of applicable law is a far cry from "ensuring" compliance with applicable law as in the first sample.

- The policy representation referenced above ends with some surprisingly broad language considering the very limited nature of the initial portion of the provision. It refers to "any violation of the FCPA or of any other applicable ethics or anti-corruption laws of the United States or any other jurisdiction to which Developer A is subject." Including "applicable ethics . . . laws" is unnecessarily broad.

- Both of the previous language samples refer to applicable laws. That's the correct approach. Such clauses sometimes reference applicable rules, regulations, standards, etc. However, such references are too vague and too broad. If there is a specific standard or rule with which one or more parties is expected to comply then the specific standard or rule should be referenced by name.

Language Proposed by Corporation B:

Developer A: (i) will fully comply with all applicable anti-corruption laws, including without limitation, the Foreign Corrupt Practices Act ("FCPA"); and (ii) has not and will not directly or indirectly, give or offer anything of value, including, but not limited to, cash, contributions, gifts, or entertainment, to foreign or domestic government officials or to any private commercial Person for the purpose of gaining an improper business advantage in violation of such applicable anti-corruption laws.

Commentary:

- Many of the points made with respect to the previous two language samples also apply here. In addition, Developer A represents that it will "fully comply" with applicable AB&C laws. As we discussed with respect to "substantial," there is either compliance or non-compliance. "Fully" is an unnecessary and redundant addition. One might say that leaving it in is not harmful. However, there may be other "compliance with applicable law" clauses in the contract. If those clauses do not include the "fully" descriptor then hypothetically (though somewhat nonsensically) it could be later argued that less than full compliance with those laws was contemplated.

Note that we're discussing these AB&C clauses in isolation. However, they will of course be part of a larger contract. Legal should consider how these clauses interact with other contractual provisions—e.g., whether breach of these clauses would trigger any termination provisions or indemnity provisions.

2. PRACTICE NOTE

An organization's attorney or legal department may be very knowledgeable regarding AB&C representations and warranties or not very familiar with them. This is certainly an area where Legal and AB&C Compliance can and should collaborate. AB&C Compliance can work with Legal to develop a set of AB&C representations and warranties to use in different types of contracts and/or based on the bribery and corruption risk of counterparties. They can also work together to develop an approach to negotiating these representations and warranties with counterparties—e.g., when and where there can and cannot be compromises on proposed language. For example, an organization may want to use more extensive and rigorous language in contracts with higher risk third parties.

I. AB&C-ADJACENT AREAS

As explained, every organization should scope and design its AB&C Compliance program with respect to its nature and its particular bribery and corruption risks. We previously addressed several areas that are typically included in AB&C Compliance programs. However, depending on how an organization's compliance program is structured, other topic areas may also fall under the AB&C Compliance remit. We'll very briefly address a couple of these—political contributions and reputational risk—as "AB&C-adjacent" areas.

1. U.S. POLITICAL CONTRIBUTIONS

Broadly speaking, political contributions should be considered anything of value that is given or loaned in furtherance of influencing a campaign or election taking place in the United States. The area of political contributions is sometimes included in an organization's AB&C Compliance program. This makes some intuitive sense because when we think about bribery and corruption, improper payments to government officials often come to mind. However, organizations should always remember that political contributions is a very specific area involving federal, state, and local law. As a result, even large, sophisticated organizations often rely heavily on outside counsel for support in this area.

To side-step at least some of the complexity surrounding political contributions, and avoid their attendant risks, an organization may prohibit political contributions unless approved in writing by the General Counsel with two possible carve-outs—contributions made through the organization's Political Action Committee (if applicable) or its employees in their own personal capacities. An organization's AB&C policy may state, for example:

> No political contribution, as defined in this policy, should be made whether directly or

indirectly (other than through the Political Action Committee), with the organization's funds or assets even if the contributions are legal under the laws of the jurisdiction in which they are made. An exception to this rule is if the proposed contribution is approved in writing by the General Counsel and the record of that approval is maintained by the General Counsel's office. Organization X recognizes that employees may participate in national or local political processes in their own personal capacities—i.e., not in the capacity of Organization X employees or representatives. Any such participation in an individual capacity must be on an employee's own time, using their own resources, and in accordance with applicable laws, rules, regulations, and any related Organization X policies.

2. REPUTATIONAL RISK

Reputational risk is the risk that an organization will be negatively perceived due to certain actions or inaction. This risk sometimes arises in the context of situations that involve bribery and corruption. Reputational risk can be difficult to quantify. Its downstream effects can include a decline in stock price, loss of consumer confidence, decline in employee morale (which can lead to employee attrition and difficulty recruiting new employees), and damage to relationships with third parties.

Organizations may have a specific policy and process in a place for evaluating potential reputational risk associated with contemplated transactions or decisions. For example, a committee with designated members may meet to discuss and decision any matters involving reputational risk. If this is the case, such a committee should only consider transactions or decisions where the sole remaining impediment to proceeding is the potential reputational risk. If, for example, there is also legal or regulatory risk, then those risks should have been signed-off on prior to the matter proceeding to the reputational risk committee.

CHAPTER 7

EMERGING DEVELOPMENTS

In recent years, the truth that corruption is a threat to our collective existence is finally taking hold. As Drago Kos, Chair of the OECD Working Group on Bribery said, "Corruption permeates—and facilitates—some of the most important global threats of our time, such as terrorism, climate change and the refugee crisis. It is vital that we ramp up our fight to eradicate corruption."[1] In line with that sentiment, in 2021 the United States established the fight against corruption as a core national security interest. In the following sections we'll consider the U.S. Strategy on Countering Corruption and some of the actions that have been taken thus far in support of that strategy.

A. THE U.S. STRATEGY ON COUNTERING CORRUPTION

On June 3, 2021, U.S. President Joseph Biden announced that the fight against corruption is a core national security interest. In doing so, he stated that "[c]orruption threatens United States national security, economic equity, global anti-poverty and development efforts, and democracy itself. But by effectively preventing and countering corruption and demonstrating the advantages of transparent and accountable governance, we can secure a critical

---

[1] Fighting the Crime of Foreign Bribery, *supra* Chapter 2, n.11, at 6.

advantage for the United States and other democracies."[2]

On December 6, 2021, the White House published the first U.S. Strategy on Countering Corruption (the "Strategy"), pursuant to the National Security Study Memorandum on Establishing the Fight Against Corruption as a Core United States National Security Interest ("NSSM-1").[3] The Strategy noted that federal departments and agencies had conducted an inter-agency review as required by NSSM-1 to evaluate existing U.S. government efforts and to identify and try to correct continuing gaps in the fight against corruption. At the same time, the departments and agencies also began to accelerate and expand their efforts to "prevent and combat corruption at home and abroad; bring transparency to the United States' and international financial systems; and make it increasingly difficult for corrupt actors to shield their activities."[4]

The Strategy highlights the link between corruption and money laundering. It "places special emphasis on the transnational dimensions of the

---

[2] *Fact Sheet: U.S. Strategy on Countering Corruption*, THE WHITE HOUSE (Dec. 6, 2021), https://www.whitehouse.gov/briefing-room/statements-releases/2021/12/06/fact-sheet-u-s-strategy-on-countering-corruption.

[3] *United States Strategy on Countering Corruption, Pursuant to the National Security Study Memorandum on Establishing the Fight Against Corruption as a Core United States National Security Interest*, THE WHITE HOUSE (Dec. 2021), https://www.whitehouse.gov/wp-content/uploads/2021/12/United-States-Strategy-on-Countering-Corruption.pdf.

[4] *Id.* at 4.

challenges posed by corruption, including by recognizing the ways in which corrupt actors have used the U.S. financial system and other rule-of-law based systems to launder their ill-gotten gains."[5]

The Strategy states that the government will organize its efforts around five "mutually reinforcing pillars of work."[6] Each of these pillars is supported by strategic objectives. On March 29, 2023, the White House published a Fact Sheet entitled Implementing the United States Strategy on Countering Corruption: Accomplishments and Renewed Commitment in the Year of Action (the "Fact Sheet"). This Fact Sheet reiterated the five pillars, listed steps taken thus far as well as a provided "look ahead" for each pillar that previews anticipated efforts.

The pillars are listed below, along with a summary of the accomplished and anticipated U.S. actions in support of those pillars and their objectives:

Pillar 1: Modernizing, Coordinating, and Resourcing U.S. Government Efforts to Better Fight Corruption

Strategic Objectives:

- Enhance corruption related research, data collection, and analysis
- Improve information sharing both domestically and internationally

---

[5] *Id.*

[6] *Id.* at 5.

- Increase focus on the transnational dimensions of corruption
- Organize and resource the fight against corruption both domestically and internationally
- Integrate anti-corruption considerations into regional, thematic, and sectoral priorities

In support of these objectives, efforts have included the following:

- Various federal departments and agencies have taken steps to enhance their anti-corruption efforts both internally and externally, including by appointing new senior staff dedicated to those efforts. For example, "the Department of State appointed its first Coordinator on Global Anti-Corruption and created a senior-level Anti-Corruption Policy Board to mainstream and prioritize anti-corruption in foreign policy."[7]

---

[7] *Fact Sheet: Implementing the United States Strategy on Countering Corruption: Accomplishments and Renewed Commitment in the Year of Action*, THE WHITE HOUSE (Mar. 29, 2023) [hereinafter *Fact Sheet: Implementing the US Strategy on Countering Corruption*], https://www.whitehouse.gov/briefing-room/statements-releases/2023/03/29/fact-sheet-implementing-the-united-states-strategy-on-countering-corruption-accomplishments-and-renewed-commitment-in-the-year-of-action/.

- USAID published its first ever anti-corruption policy.[8] The policy[9]:

  articulates a new definition of corruption as a system in which the powerful subvert the public good in service of their own personal, economic, and political interests and that of their allies and family members. And, consistent with the U.S. Strategy on Countering Corruption, this Policy solidifies USAID's focus on transnational corruption, grand corruption, and kleptocracy. These forms of corruption normalize and institutionalize the abuse of power, creating a vicious cycle in which officials at all levels act with impunity, and inflict the most damage on development and democratic governance. This shift in focus will allow us to address the underlying causes—not just the visible symptoms—of endemic corruption.

- USAID also published a Dekleptification Guide, a Guide to Countering Corruption Across Sectors, and a handbook on countering corruption in the global health sector.

- Various departments and agencies increased their AB&C training efforts, increased the number of staff in AB&C-dedicated roles, and

---

[8] *Id.*; *Anti-Corruption Policy*, USAID (Dec. 2022) [hereinafter USAID Anti-Corruption Policy], https://www.usaid.gov/sites/default/files/2022-12/USAID-Anti-Corruption-Policy.pdf.

[9] USAID Anti-Corruption Policy, *supra* n.8, at 4.

established inter-agency efforts directed at tackling corruption.

- The DOJ prioritized the fight against corruption in its 2022–2026 Strategic Plan. "Because transnational corruption can empower corrupt regimes and destabilize foreign governments—potentially resulting in significant threats to our national security—the Department will redouble its efforts to investigate and prosecute foreign corruption and to build the capacity of our foreign partners to combat corruption before those threats reach our shores."[10] Objective 4.2 in the Strategic Plan, entitled Combat Corruption, Financial Crime, and Fraud, includes three strategies: (1) to deter and prosecute corporate crime, (2) to combat public corruption, and (3) to combat corporate corruption and advance international anti-corruption efforts.[11] The Strategic Plan also includes the following key performance indicators by which its success will be measured[12]:

    - Percent of corporate criminal cases in which individual responsibility was evaluated

    - Percent of corporate criminal resolutions containing compliance reporting

---

[10] *FY 2022–2026 Strategic Plan*, U.S. DOJ, at 53, https://www.justice.gov/doj/book/file/1516901/download.

[11] *Id.*

[12] *Id.* at 54.

obligations that are evaluated by DOJ at least annually

- o Number of criminal disruptions or dismantlements in public corruption and fraud against the government
- o Percent of new contacts by the FBI with foreign anti-corruption agencies that progress to mutual sharing of information or assistance or result in a new international corruption case

Looking ahead, USAID plans to create a Bureau for Democracy, Human Rights, and Governance, with a dedicated Anti-Corruption Center.[13]

Pillar 2: Curbing Illicit Finance

Strategic Objectives:

- Address deficiencies in the US AML framework
- Work with partners and allies to address governance weaknesses, tighten global AML frameworks, increase information sharing and law enforcement cooperation, and close existing safe havens while preventing the establishment of new safe havens

In support of these objectives, efforts have included the following:

---

[13] *Fact Sheet: Implementing the US Strategy on Countering Corruption, supra* n.7.

- FinCEN has included corruption as one of its anti-money laundering enforcement priorities. In 2022, referring to the establishment of anti-corruption as a core national security interest, FinCEN issued an advisory on kleptocracy and foreign public corruption. The advisory, with specific reference to Russia's occupation of Ukraine, provides financial institutions with information about typologies and potential indicators associated with kleptocracy and foreign bribery and corruption.[14] FinCEN's goal was to help U.S. financial institutions to more effectively identify and report possible corruption-related transactions.

- The Treasury Department increased its efforts to implement the Corporate Transparency Act ("CTA").[15] FinCEN issued a final rule requiring most corporations, limited liability companies, and other entities created in or registered in the United States to report information about their beneficial ownership to FinCEN.[16] The rule went into effect on

---

[14] Advisory on Kleptocracy and Foreign Public Corruption, FinCEN, April 14, 2022, https://www.fincen.gov/sites/default/files/advisory/2022-04-14/FinCEN%20Advisory%20Corruption%20FINAL%20508.pdf.

[15] *Fact Sheet: Implementing the US Strategy on Countering Corruption*, *supra* n.7.

[16] *Id.*; *FinCEN Issues Final Rule for Beneficial Ownership Reporting to Support Law Enforcement Efforts, Counter Illicit Finance, and Increase Transparency*, FinCEN (Sept. 29, 2022), https://www.fincen.gov/news/news-releases/fincen-issues-final-rule-beneficial-ownership-reporting-support-law-enforcement.

January 1, 2024, and it will increase transparency of corporate ownership and control information. The goal is to reduce the opportunities for criminals to hide the proceeds of crime behind opaque corporate structures. Following this final rule, FinCEN also issued a proposed rule for comment. The proposed rule sets out the circumstances under which the collected beneficial ownership information could be disclosed to federal agencies, state, local, tribal, and foreign governments, and how it must be protected.[17]

- The U.S. has reinforced various cross-border partnerships, including through the U.N. Global Operational Network of Anti-Corruption Law Enforcement Authorities. ("GlobE")[18] GlobE was launched in 2021 and is open to specialized law enforcement bodies from all UN member states and UNCAC parties. One of GlobE's goals is to improve direct communication and cooperation between anti-corruption law enforcement

---

17 *Fact Sheet: Implementing the US Strategy on Countering Corruption*, *supra* n.7; *FinCEN Issues Notice of Proposed Rulemaking Regarding Access to Beneficial Ownership Information and Related Safeguards*, FinCEN (Dec. 15, 2022), https://www.fincen.gov/news/news-releases/fincen-issues-notice-proposed-rulemaking-regarding-access-beneficial-ownership; *Fact Sheet: Beneficial Ownership Information Access and Safeguards Notice of Proposed Rulemaking (NPRM)*, FinCEN (Dec. 15, 2022), https://www.fincen.gov/nprm-fact-sheet.

18 *Fact Sheet: Implementing the US Strategy on Countering Corruption*, *supra* n.7.

authorities in different countries, one of the UNCAC's key commitments.[19]

Looking ahead, curbing illicit finance will remain a priority and the Treasury Department will continue its efforts to implement the CTA. In addition, part of the plan is to "assess the illicit finance risks associated with key financial gatekeepers, such as investment advisors, lawyers, and accountants."[20]

Pillar 3: Holding Corrupt Actors Accountable

Strategic Objectives:

- Enhance existing enforcement efforts
- Update the tools available to hold corrupt actors accountable both domestically and internationally
- Work with partner nations to bolster anti-corruption enforcement
- Strengthen the ability of foreign partner nations to justly and equitably pursue accountability
- Further support the ability of civil society, media, and the private sector to prevent corruption and to encourage accountability

---

[19] *Global Operational Network of Anti-Corruption Law Enforcement Authorities*, UN, https://globenetwork.unodc.org/#:~:text=The%20Global%20Operational%20Network%20of,Convention%20against%20Corruption%20.

[20] *Fact Sheet: Implementing the US Strategy on Countering Corruption*, *supra* n.7.

In support of these objectives, efforts have included:

- Enforcement actions by the DOJ, the SEC, the CFTC, and federal law enforcement involving international bribery and resulting in guilty pleas, other convictions, penalties and forfeitures of over $1 billion, and the DOJ's return to Nigeria of $20 million of forfeited corruption funds.[21]

- The U.S. Department of the Treasury started a Kleptocracy Asset Recovery Rewards Program[22], though that program lapsed on January 1, 2024.

- The DOJ and federal law enforcement launched KleptoCapture, an inter-agency task force that investigates violations of sanctions regulations, export restrictions, and economic countermeasures that were imposed in response to Russia's war on Ukraine. "Working with international partners, the Task Force has seized over $500 million in assets, including investment accounts, real estate, and yachts."[23]

- The United States, in cooperation with other nations, launched the Russian Elites, Proxies, and Oligarchs ("REPO") Task Force to target individuals responsible for and benefiting

---

[21] *Id.*

[22] *Id.*

[23] *Fact Sheet: US Strategy on Countering Corruption*, *supra* n.7.

from Russia's war on Ukraine.[24] As reported, more than $30 billion of assets beneficially owned by sanctioned Russian parties has since been frozen.[25]

Looking ahead, the United States plans to use a number of tools at its disposal, including financial sanctions, visa restrictions, and civil, criminal and administrative enforcement actions to fight corruption. In addition, the U.S. will work to strengthen its coordination with international partners and civil society to counter kleptocracy, state capture, and strategic corruption.[26]

Pillar 4: Preserving and Strengthening the Multilateral Anti-Corruption Architecture

Strategic Objectives:

- Strengthen existing anti-corruption frameworks and institutions
- Continue anti-corruption efforts in a range of international fora

In support of these objectives, efforts have included:

- The United States participating in and/or taking the lead with respect to multilateral events targeting corruption. For example, the U.S. hosted the 10th Conference of States Parties in 2023, continued to participate as a

---

24 *Id.*

25 *Id.*

26 *Id.*

member state of the Group of European States Against Corruption ("GRECO"), increased collaboration with the North Atlantic Treaty Organization ("NATO") Building Integrity Program, and launched its 5th National Action Plan in the Open Government Partnership ("OGP") and was elected to the OGP Steering Committee.

- The U.S., along with its partner nations in the Financial Action Task Force ("FATF") included commitments to fight corruption in the 2022 FATF Ministerial Declaration and FATF agreed to take on projects to promote the UNCAC's implementation.

Looking ahead, among other actions, the U.S. will continue to participate in multi-lateral alliances against corruption.

<u>Pillar 5</u>: Improving Diplomatic Engagement and Leveraging Foreign Assistance Resources to Advance Policy Goals

<u>Strategic Objectives</u>:

- Elevate and expand the scale of diplomatic engagement and foreign assistance that address corruption
- Protect anti-corruption actors
- Leverage innovation in anti-corruption efforts
- Improve coordination and risk analysis across foreign assistance

- Improve security assistance and integrate corruption considerations into military planning, analysis, and operations

In support of these objectives, efforts have included the following:

- The State and Treasury Departments developed an Anti-Corruption Solutions through Emerging Technologies initiative ("ASET") which was launched via the Global Anti-Corruption Day TechSprint in June 2022. The TechSprint brought together participants from government, law enforcement, financial institutions, civil society, and academia to consider how to utilize technology to fight corruption. TechSprint included a set of "problem statements" that participants were asked to consider—e.g., "How can we leverage technology to analyze the data and identify patterns to detect suspected corrupt activity?"[27]
- The State Department developed the Global Initiative to Galvanize the Private Sector as Partners in Combating Corruption ("GPS") to advance the dialogue between the public and private sectors.
- USAID's Anti-Corruption Response Fund piloted new assistance approaches in the

---

[27] *TechSprint Problem Statements*, ASET, https://www.anticorruptiontechsprint.org/home/#problemstosolve.

Dominican Republic and the Democratic Republic of the Congo.

- USAID launched the Countering Transnational Corruption ("CTC") Grand Challenge for Development. The Grand Challenge seeks to leverage the knowledge of a diverse set of stakeholders to develop ways to prevent corruption. "The CTC Grand Challenge solutions will detect and disrupt illicit finance and trafficking in commodities; strengthen transparency and accountability in global supply chains; promote standards, practices, and norms that enhance integrity in the public and private sectors; and address other significant dynamics of transnational corruption."[28]

Looking ahead, among other actions, the U.S. will work with other nations to advance the Blue Dot Network, "to increase transparency, reduce corruption, and mobilize private capital for infrastructure investment in emerging economies."[29] The Blue Dot Network was initiated by the United States, Australia, and Japan with the support of the OECD and its member nations. Its goal is to identify

[28] *Countering Transnational Corruption Grand Challenge*, USAID, https://www.usaid.gov/anti-corruption/countering-transnational-corruption-grand-challenge.

[29] *Fact Sheet: US Strategy on Countering Corruption*, *supra* n.7.

and encourage "market-driven, transparent and sustainable infrastructure projects.[30]

Across all five of these pillars, the U.S. Government will do the following three things[31]:

- "Consult and Coordinate": The U.S. Government will consult and coordinate with various individuals and entities from the domestic and international public and private sectors.
- "Elevate and Engage": In line with NSSM-1, the U.S. Government will prioritize efforts to reduce corruption as a national security concern within all relevant policy-making processes and elevate and encourage anti-corruption as a priority in both international diplomatic interactions with U.S. state and local jurisdictions.
- "Continually Assess and Refine our Approach": The U.S. Government will take an agile approach to fighting corruption that takes manages risks, assesses impact, learns

---

[30] *The Blue Dot Network, A Proposal for a Global Certification Framework for Quality Infrastructure*, OECD, at 3 (2022) https://web-archive.oecd.org/2022-03-30/627058-blue-dot-network-proposal-certification.pdf.

[31] *United States Strategy on Countering Corruption, Pursuant to the National Security Study Memorandum on Establishing the Fight Against Corruption as a Core United States National Security Interest*, THE WHITE HOUSE, at 9 (Dec. 2021), https://www.whitehouse.gov/wp-content/uploads/2021/12/United-States-Strategy-on-Countering-Corruption.pdf.

from setbacks and that can adjust to new challenges and opportunities.

In reading these Pillars, their Strategic Objectives, accomplishments achieved thus far, and plans for the future, a number of themes emerge. For example, we notice an emphasis on international cooperation in investigations and enforcement as well an emphasis on the efforts of non-governmental actors. We also see the recognition of the linkages between different types of financial crime—particularly between bribery and corruption and money laundering.

B. ANTI-CORRUPTION AS AN AML PRIORITY

The Anti-Money Laundering Act of 2020 required the Secretary of the Treasury to establish public priorities for AML and counter-terrorism policy.[32] Correspondingly, on June 30, 2021 FinCEN issued the first government-wide priorities for AML and counter-terrorism.[33] FinCEN called out corruption as one of its eight AML priorities (the "AML Priorities").[34] In naming corruption as a priority, FinCEN referred to the NSSM-1's language that

---

[32] *Interagency Statement on the Issuance of Anti-Money Laundering/Countering the Financing of Terrorism National Priorities* at 1, FinCEN (June 30, 2021) (internal citations omitted), https://www.fdic.gov/news/financial-institution-letters/2021/fil21046a.pdf.

[33] *FinCen Issues First National AML/CFT Priorities and Accompanying Statements*, FinCEN (June 30, 2021), https://www.fincen.gov/news/news-releases/fincen-issues-first-national-amlcft-priorities-and-accompanying-statements.

[34] *Id.*

corruption fuels instability and conflict and undermines economic growth.[35]

The AML Priorities identify and describe "the most significant AML [and counter-terrorism] threats currently facing the United States."[36] Each of these threats are predicate crimes for money laundering.[37] FinCEN believes that addressing the money laundering risks associated with corruption will, in turn, strengthen efforts to counter corruption.[38]

---

35 FinCEN 2021 Priorities, *supra* Chapter 1, n.3, at 3.

36 *FinCen Issues First National AML/CFT Priorities and Accompanying Statements*, FinCEN (June 30, 2021), https://www.fincen.gov/news/news-releases/fincen-issues-first-national-amlcft-priorities-and-accompanying-statements. In addition to corruption, the other priorities are cybercrime, domestic and international terrorist financing, fraud, transnational criminal organizations, drug trafficking organizations, human trafficking and human smuggling, and proliferation financing. *Id.*

37 FinCEN 2021 Priorities, *supra* Chapter 1, n.3, at 2.

38 *Id.*

INDEX

References are to Pages